MALIGNED GENERAL

MALIGNED GENERAL

The Biography
of
Thomas Sidney Jesup

CHESTER L. KIEFFER

PRESIDIO PRESS
San Rafael, California & London, England

Published by Presidio Press of San Rafael,
California, and London, England,
with editorial offices at
1114 Irwin Street,
San Rafael, California 94901

Library of Congress Cataloging in Publication Data

Kieffer, Chester L
  Maligned General: the biography of Thomas Sidney
Jesup.
  Bibliography: p.
  Includes index.
  1. Jesup, Thomas Sidney, 1788–1860. 2. Generals—
United States—Biography. 3. United States. Quarter-
master's Dept.—Biography. 4. United States. Army—
History—19th century. I. Title.
U53.J47K53   355.3'31'0924 [B]   78-24028
ISBN 0-89141-027-9

Portrait photos courtesy of Library of Congress.
Locust Grove Restoration photo courtesy of
Historic Homes Foundation.

Book design by Hal Lockwood

Jacket design by Kathleen A. Jaeger

Printed in the United States of America

To my wife

Contents

Illustrations

Preface

In the era between the War of 1812 and the Civil War, when so many noted men held the spotlight of public attention, Thomas Sidney Jesup is considered a secondary figure. Although his name appears frequently in military and congressional documents and in the newspapers of that era, no biography of him has yet been published. History-minded Major General Nathanael Greene summed up the reasons when he wrote: "No body ever heard of a quarter Master in History." In military history, supply officers never receive credit in victory, only blame in defeat.

As a young second lieutenant, disillusioned and disgusted with conditions he found when he entered the service in 1808, Thomas Sidney Jesup could hardly have foreseen that one day he would be called upon to reform the army supply system. Yet in 1818, when Secretary of War John C. Calhoun directed a thorough reorganization of the army and the War Department, Jesup was appointed quartermaster general, with full authority to reestablish the Quartermaster's Department and place it on a businesslike basis. Although he was only twenty-nine, ten years' service in the field and his dedicated study and firm determination to become a complete master of his profession had made him an authority on military affairs. He was the first quartermaster general to be permanently stationed in Washington, D.C. During the forty-two years he retained the post, Jesup served under eleven presidents and performed a conspicuous role in the development of the army in the period preceding the Civil War. He won widespread recognition for his abounding energy and zeal, administrative ability, intellectual capacity, sterling integrity, intense patriotism, and steadfast insistence upon placing "the public good" above his own personal interests. His loyalty to his many friends was constant, and his personal life was beyond reproach.

Yet upon occasion during his long public service, his motives and actions were misunderstood, misrepresented, or deliberately distorted. Few men have been more cruelly and unfairly assailed in Congress and in public print than was Jesup during the Creek War and the Second Seminole War in the 1830s when he was in command of troops in the Florida wilderness. The Indian conflicts occurred during a bitter political campaign as the new Whig party waged a determined fight to gain the White House by discrediting Andrew Jackson and defeating his hand-picked successor, Martin Van Buren. Although Jesup never took part in partisan politics and was the most successful of the generals in command during the seven-year war, he became, as President Jackson's commanding general in the field, the favorite target of Whigs in Congress and of the Whig press. For five years he was made a football of politics in Congress, severely denounced on one hand by the Whigs and strongly defended on the other by supporters of the Democratic administration.

Unfortunately, General Jesup is remembered today principally for an alleged violation of a white flag in ordering the capture of Osceola rather than for his long and honorable public career and his valuable contributions to the military service. Many writers who have recorded the history of the period knew little, if anything, of Jesup's personal life and his sterling qualities. Thus they have tended to fasten upon him a character quite foreign to his own. One misconception relates to his policy towards the Indians. Research shows conclusively that he demonstrated more sympathy and compassion for the Indians than did those who condemned him for his alleged mistreatment of the red man. Clearly, those who knew him intimately never took seriously the charge that he had tarnished his own or his country's honor.

His career covered more than a half-century of the formative years of the United States Army; for most of that time he served as quartermaster general, the principal logistics officer of the service, as it was then organized. He introduced many innovations to the supply organization, including a system of strict accountability for public money and property. Jesup was one of the foremost advocates of a policy of training military leaders in time of peace to serve as a nucleus for the expansion of the armed forces in time of war. At that time, few members of Congress saw a need for a standing army; to meet the demands of national security, most favored dependence upon state militia and volunteers. So far-sighted were some of Jesup's recommendations that they were not adopted until a half-century or more after his death. One of his proposals was the establishment and training of permanent supply units to provide more efficient support for combat troops.

Considering his lengthy public career, his intimate acquaintance and association with leading public figures of his time, his first-hand knowledge of many historical events and his active participation in some of them, it is unfortunate that Jesup never found time to write his memoirs. He did, however, take special care to preserve his own papers, the bulk of which are now in the Manuscript Division of the Library of Congress; the remainder may be found in other depositories scattered across the country. His official War Department records are in the National Archives in Washington.

I believe this book to be the first study to make use of the Jesup Papers. My intent is to correct some misconceptions and distortions concerning the character and conduct of a man who has been much maligned, particularly with regard to his role in the Creek and Seminole Wars, and to discuss his role in the development of the army.

I received excellent assistance from the staffs of both the Manuscript Division, Library of Congress, and the National Archives. I am also appreciative of the kindness and helpfulness extended to me by the staffs of The Filson Club of Louisville, The William L. Clements Library, The Cincinnati Historical Society, The Henry E. Huntington Library, and The Historical Society of Pennsylvania.

I wish specially to acknowledge the contributions of Dr. Samuel W. Thomas, Director of Archives and Records Service, Jefferson County, Kentucky. While serving as Research Director and Curator for the restoration of Locust Grove at Louisville, Kentucky, he made much data available to me, particularly that pertaining to the Croghan family and to Locust Grove. I am also deeply indebted to my wife Erna for reading my manuscript and making many valuable suggestions.

Washington, D.C.   CHESTER L. KIEFFER
August 1977

CHAPTER 1

A RESOLUTE
YOUNG SOLDIER

THOMAS SIDNEY JESUP was born on 16 December 1788, as the new American nation was experiencing its own birth pains. Of English and Irish ancestry, he was a descendant of Edward Jessup (the family later shortened the spelling to one "s"), who emigrated to the colonies from England in the mid-seventeenth century.

Thomas's father was James Edward Jesup, a native of Connecticut, whose military service in the Revolutionary War ended when a severe saber wound left him with a crooked arm—one of the few things that Thomas remembered about his father. After leaving the service, James Jesup migrated to Virginia to settle in Berkeley County, which later became part of West Virginia. There he married Ann O'Neill, who had come to America from Ireland with her parents while she was quite young. Thomas Sidney, the couple's first son, was born in Berkeley County. When the boy was barely four, the family moved to Mason County, Kentucky, in pursuit of a better livelihood. James built a cabin and cultivated a small tract of land rented from Col. John Pickett. The family grew with the births of two more sons and a daughter. Older people of the community later remembered the Jesups as "proud, intelligent, and self-respecting" but possessing a "very limited abundance of worldly goods."[1] Only four years after moving to Kentucky, James Jesup died at the age of thirty-one, leaving a widow and four small children in the rugged frontier country.

1

Left fatherless at the age of eight on the Kentucky frontier, Thomas Jesup was scarcely a likely prospect to become a distinguished military officer. Given his limited background, only a youth of exceptional talents could have attained success. Little is known of his childhood but that it was not easy. Jesup later said that he never had a boyhood; after his father's early death, he felt himself to be the man in the family, obliged to take care of his mother and younger brothers and sister. This sense of obligation became so ingrained that later in life it was only natural for him to assume the burden of supporting the children of his youngest brother after William's death.[2]

Thomas was a studious youth, "working when others idled, and reading when others slept."[3] Even with little opportunity for formal education, he developed into a well-read and cultured man. The slender but seemingly sturdy, brown-haired, brown-eyed lad of medium height grew into a personable young man. A painting of him as a young army officer shows a smooth-shaven, pleasant face, a firm mouth, and expressive, intelligent eyes.[4] His first employment was as a clerk in a store in Maysville, Kentucky, where he displayed a "happy faculty for administration." But his "sensitive conscience exacted too high a standard of morality for the purposes of his employer; and so, after a decisive difference of opinion . . . they parted company."[5]

Jesup may have been influenced to apply for an appointment in the army when his spirit of patriotism was stirred by the *Chesapeake–Leopard* incident, which followed British insistence upon the right to search American vessels during the war with France and to seize any alleged deserters from the Royal Navy. The practice sometimes led to the impressment of American citizens. Growing American resentment climaxed in June of 1807, when the British frigate *Leopard* fired upon the American frigate *Chesapeake* off Hampton Roads, Virginia. Three Chesapeake crewmen were killed, twenty others wounded, and four seamen, three of them American citizens, were impressed. Another war with the British loomed as a possibility. In April 1808, Congress passed a law "to raise for a limited time an additional military force,"[6] doubling the size of the regular army and enabling young men so inclined to join. Jesup took advantage of the opportunity, as did Winfield Scott, Zachary Taylor, and others who were to achieve distinction in the service of their country.

Thomas Sidney Jesup, the young officer.

Jesup had left Maysville to go to Cincinnati, Ohio. Among the influential and lasting friends he made there was James Findlay, a prominent lawyer who held several federal posts, was twice mayor of the town and later served four terms in Congress. In Cincinnati Jesup received a letter from Secretary of War Henry Dearborn stating that he had been commissioned a second lieutenant in the 7th Infantry as of May 1808. The message did not reach him until a month later.[7] He was nineteen years old. Although he had had no military experience, he had doubtless read and absorbed everything he could find on the subject of military service.

Almost from the day Jesup entered the army, he recognized many of its shortcomings. The military service was in its infancy. Not only did the service lack proper organization, training, and discipline, but it displayed other serious deficiencies. Political consideration rather than merit was often the basis for the appointment and promotion of officers. The contract system of supplying troops was inefficient and haphazard, primarily because contractors were not subject to military control. The Quartermaster's Department, the principal supply agency of the army, was in a state of confusion and disorganization. Operations were conducted in a wasteful, slipshod manner; no effective methods existed for the accounting of public money and property.

The young lieutenant served first at Newport, Kentucky; he was assigned as brigade quartermaster under Brig. Gen. James Wilkinson, then commander of the army on the Mississippi. Jesup, eager to advance rapidly in rank, soon discovered that political support was virtually a necessity to gain recognition, yet he did not want advancement unless his own character, qualifications, and conduct warranted it. Not until 1 December 1809, about twenty-two months after he entered the service, was he promoted to first lieutenant.

A brush with the unscrupulous Wilkinson was almost inevitable for the young soldier with the sensitive conscience. In the summer of 1811, while stationed at Cantonment Baton Rouge, Louisiana, Jesup obtained permission from Secretary of War William Eustis to go to Washington to settle his quartermaster accounts. He did not arrive in Washington until the following January, when a War Department accountant informed him that his account was to be debited for an item which rightly should have been charged to General Wilkinson. Jesup became incensed. The accountant explained the charge must be made because the general's account had "accumulated to an enormous amount." Declaring this practice unfair and improper, Jesup referred the matter directly to the secretary of war.

Eustis must have been impressed with the character, integrity, and mettle of the young officer who had the audacity to appeal to him twice to settle an account of seventy-nine dollars. Jesup was adamant in his appeal: "There would be as much propriety in holding the soldier accountable for the mistakes and improper conduct of his superior on the field of battle, as in holding me accountable for the orders of General Wilkinson on the subject of fuel, transportation, or anything else." If he were made responsible for Wilkinson's account, he must consider it a direct charge that he had failed to do his duty as a military officer and had violated the laws of his country. If Wilkinson were not entitled to the allowance, Jesup wrote, ". . . there must have been a failure of duty and a violation of the law somewhere, and the punishment being inflicted on me, shows that I am considered, by the department, as the guilty person." He added that he hoped Eustis would not think him presumptuous in his appeal.[8]

The secretary of war apparently was swayed by the logic and tenacity of the young officer, for by 20 February the accounts had been settled to Jesup's satisfaction. But the young soldier had become discontented with conditions he found in the army and disillusioned concerning his prospects for advancement and recognition. He wrote to a friend, "The American service has become extremely irksome to me. It presents a very contracted field for enterprise, and such influence has the genius of leaden headed ignorance obtained in the military department that nothing but the most powerful political friends can bring an officer into notice. A knowledge of military science is no recommendation to him." If a young man were so "unfortunate as to give a correct opinion on a point of duty and thereby expose the ignorance of a Superior," only a miracle would keep him from being persecuted out of the service. The war, Jesup thought, was still as far distant as it had been three years before, adding, "We must experience greater outrages from the European powers before we can be prevailed on to commit our destinies to the decision of the sword."[9]

Young Jesup wrote his friend of his determination to become a military expert and of his eagerness to court danger and win distinction—if not in his own country, then in another. He expected to remain in the army two or three years more and to direct all of the energies of his mind to his profession. "I am determined to become a compleat master of every branch of it, and then, should my country not think proper to give me promotion, I shall seek it in a distant land. . . . When I reflect that I have attained my twenty-fourth year without having performed a single action to distinguish me . . . I can scarcely avoid regretting that I have lived." If he had not considered it cowardly to leave his country during the crisis, he thought he might "abandon all . . . prospects [in America] and court danger and distinction in the patriot ranks in South America."[10]

The views reflect the young, restless, ambitious, and immature Jesup. Years later, after a large dose of armed combat, he had a complete change of heart concerning war. "As ardent as I once wished for war, I now think it would be the greatest calamity that could befall our country. It is true the injuries & insults which we have recd. demand an appeal to arms but that appeal, under existing circumstances, would be to expose us to disaster and disgrace."[11]

After Jesup settled his accounts in Washington, he was ordered to Ohio to engage in recruiting. He spent considerable time in the Cincinnati area, where his circle of influential friends continued to grow. On 13 May 1812 he was initiated into the Masonic Lodge. The second war with England proved not nearly so distant as the young lieutenant had earlier feared. Within only a few months, he found himself in the midst of it.

The generals who led the American troops at the start of the War of 1812 constituted "an array of incompetence scarcely equalled in the world's history, certainly never surpassed."[12] Among them was William Hull, who had as a young man conducted himself valiantly throughout the Revolutionary War and attained the rank of lieutenant colonel in 1779. In 1812, he was a gray-haired man of fifty-nine serving as governor of the Michigan Territory, a post to which he had been appointed in 1805 by President Thomas Jefferson in recognition of his service in the War of Independence.

Jesup had been in Washington when Hull arrived in February of 1812 to request that President James Madison provide a protective force for the northwestern frontier. In response to Hull's plea,

Madison called upon Ohio Governor Return Jonathan Meigs to raise a militia force of fifteen hundred. He also ordered the 4th Infantry, stationed at Vincennes under the command of Lt. Col. James Miller, to join the militia at Urbana, Ohio, for the march to Detroit. Hull at first declined Madison's offer but finally agreed reluctantly to accept command of the troops. In the event of war, he was to invade Upper Canada.

Jesup, then on recruiting duty at Lebanon, Ohio, saw in the Detroit expedition an opportunity to achieve the recognition he had been seeking. He eagerly volunteered, and when General Hull selected his personal staff, he chose the twenty-three-year-old Jesup as his brigade major and acting adjutant general.[13] The volunteers were organized into three regiments commanded by Cols. Duncan McArthur, James Findlay, and Lewis Cass.

Hull assumed command at Dayton on 25 May. By early June the militia and regulars had joined forces thirty miles east of Urbana. The easiest part of the expedition had been completed, but Detroit still lay two hundred miles ahead. Between the troops and their destination was an almost unbroken wilderness whose treacherous morasses terminated in the Black Swamp.[14] The men of the three regiments performed the laborious task of cutting a road adequate for the hauling of supplies and heavy equipment, each regiment taking its turn. At the site of the present city of Findlay, Hull received his first dispatch from the War Department. Though it was dated 18 June, Eustis made no mention that war had been declared that day; he merely urged Hull to hasten to Detroit to await further orders.

When the weary troops reached the Maumee River, which flows into Lake Erie, they welcomed the sight of the schooner *Cuyahoga* riding at anchor—the boat presented an easy means of transporting much of the heavy baggage and equipment that had impeded their progress. If these materials were sent by boat, their march to Detroit would be hastened. Hull succumbed to what he did not realize was a dangerous temptation. His trunk, containing the muster rolls showing the size and makeup of his army and his official orders outlining the plans for the campaign, was placed aboard by mistake. The *Cuyahoga* sailed on 1 July with its precious cargo. The following day, the British captured the schooner. Only then did a courier arrive with a second dispatch to Hull from Eustis announcing belatedly that hostilities had begun.[15]

On 5 July, Hull's army arrived at Spring Wells, high on the bank of the Detroit River, four miles below the Detroit settlement of some 800 residents. The troops eagerly awaited action, but Hull's order to invade Canada did not come until 9 July. Three days later Hull led his troops into Canada, but instead of attacking Malden he established himself in a fortified camp near Sandwich (now the city of Windsor) across the river from Detroit. Malden lay eighteen miles to the south. Hull's failure to launch an immediate attack on Fort Malden, the only British post on the Ontario Peninsula, was but the prelude to one of the strangest exhibitions of generalship in the military annals of the United States.

The general's timidity bred distrust and contempt for his leadership among his men. The British were equally bewildered by Hull's strange behavior, but they seized the opportunity to strengthen their post and obtain reinforcements. Hull was worried, almost obsessed, about his supply situation and the need to keep open his line of communications with Ohio.[16] He assembled almost daily councils of war at which the question of attacking Malden was frequently discussed. The general himself steadfastly opposed the attack on the grounds that his heavy artillery was not mounted on field carriages. One such meeting, held on 1 August, was described in considerable detail by Brigade Major Jesup in a confidential letter in which he divulged his opinion of Hull: "Our commander is a man of talents and a highly accomplished gentleman. . . . But I some times doubt whether he possesses personal courage. I have not ventured to hint my doubts even to my most intimate friends here."

Hull, Jesup related, cited the fall of Mackinac, the failure of those on the Niagara frontier to cooperate with him, the neglect of the government to send reinforcements to keep open the line of communications with Ohio, and the hostility of the Indian nations of the Northwest as his reasons for seeking his officers' advice. The general proposed that his command recross the river and attempt to open communications with Ohio by establishing posts at Brownstown and the River Raisin. He suggested that a garrison be left at a small stockade between the army's position and the town of Sandwich.

Most of the officers expressed great disappointment over Hull's proposed measures. They urged an immediate attack on Malden as the surer means not only of opening the communications with

Ohio but of checking the hostile movements of the Indians. Jesup wrote, "The General was evidently hurt and provoked at finding his propositions canvassed so freely, and opposed so firmly; and perceiving that not more than two or three of those present favored his views, he petulantly remarked: 'Well gentlemen, if you are determined to go to Malden I will lead you.' A majority decided in favor of immediate attack." By a narrow margin, the council approved a three-day delay so that the heavy artillery, needed for taking Malden, could be made ready.

Jesup was convinced that Hull had no intention of making an attack. When he called at the general's headquarters the following morning for the orders of the day, Hull reiterated that, with communications with Ohio closed, neither supplies nor reinforcements could reach them. A force must be sent to open communications. Jesup suggested that a movement on Malden would be preferable, even if the Americans were compelled to take a position beyond the range of enemy guns and wait for their own artillery. The enemy troops would at least be compelled to remain close in their quarters, which would prevent them from supplying the Indians who had interrupted the communications. Hull's reactions to Jesup's suggestion might have been anticipated.

> [Hull] dwelt upon the hazard of such a measure, and of the many opportunities that would be afforded to the enemy to annoy us by sorties, but he did not seem to reflect that we were stronger than the enemy and that it was desirable that he should meet us in the open field. But that which was suspicion is ripening into conviction. He is a coward and will not risque his person; and if he could conquer his pride (for he is proud of his Revolutionary Character) so far as to allow this Army to march without him all would be well. Malden would be taken . . .[17]

In the meantime, Capt. Henry Brush and a company of volunteers from Ohio had reached the River Raisin, thirty miles from Detroit, with seventy packhorses, each carrying two hundred pounds of flour, and a drove of about three hundred beef cattle, along with other provisions and mail. In response to his request for an escort into Detroit, Hull on 4 August detached Maj. Thomas B. Van Horne with two hundred men for that purpose. Upon receiving the order to detail the command, Jesup, fearing for the detachment's safety, suggested that either Van Horne's command be strengthened or the troops be moved immediately close enough to Malden so that they could hold the garrison in check and prevent an enemy force from attacking Van Horne. Hull insisted the detachment was in no danger. Later, in a terse account, Jesup explained: "The detachment moved out and, as every one except the Genl. anticipated, was attacked by a superior force and defeated with the loss of nearly half the officers."[18] The detachment was ambushed near Brownstown, and Van Horne lost Hull's dispatches to the War Department as well as soldiers' letters containing information valuable to the enemy.

On 7 August when the heavy artillery was ready, the general called another council, which decided to begin the march immediately. The near-mutinous spirit which had been aroused among the troops by their commander's bizarre conduct gave way to cheerfulness and high hopes. At last, they believed, the moment for the long-delayed assault had arrived. But once more Hull changed his mind, bitterly disappointing his eager troops, and did not lead the promised march on Malden. Instead, without consulting anyone, he abruptly ordered the army to recross the river and take refuge in Detroit. That night and the next morning, the sullen and humiliated army abandoned Canada. Thus ended Hull's invasion.

Back on American soil, the general once more turned his attention to the task of rescuing Captain Brush and his supplies. But Hull's overcautious orders kept the supplies and reinforcements out of his army's reach. While Hull pursued his cautious and unrewarding course, Gen. Issac Brock arrived to take command of the British forces, which began erecting at strategic points opposite Detroit batteries from which they could shell both the town and the fort. The American troops watched these preparations with fury, but Hull seemed unwilling to do anything that might irritate the foe.[19]

Jesup, however, was not content to remain idle in the face of the British preparations. On the night of 15 August, when he rode along the river to observe the enemy's situation, he discovered no more than twenty-five men at the British batteries. The remainder of Brock's forces was concentrated about four miles below, preparing to cross to the American shore. Hurrying back to the fort, Jesup urged the general's permission to lead a force of from 100 to 150 across the river in the darkness to destroy the enemy's batteries and spike their guns. His efforts were in vain. Hull rejected the proposal, saying that if these guns were destroyed, they would be replaced by others from the ships.

Even if Hull had been correct in his conjecture, Jesup commented later, "he would have gained from one to two days by the destruction of the batteries, which would have enabled him to strengthen his position and to call in the detachment under Colonel [Duncan] McArthur." The colonel had been sent to aid Captain Brush. The British force had landed near the Huron River—"a deep and miry stream." He maintained that the enemy could have been checked at that point had the American forces been properly distributed; Brock and his men would have found themselves in a cul-de-sac formed by the Huron and Detroit rivers and could have been cut to pieces if they did not surrender.[20]

On 15 August, Brock demanded the unconditional surrender of Hull's army, and Hull boldly rejected the demand. The following day the enemy's bombardment resumed, and Brock and his troops marched toward Fort Detroit. He was accompanied by about six hundred Indians under Tecumseh, chief of the Shawnees, who was aiding the British effort. Hull immediately capitulated. In less than two months, the general had not only failed in his mission to invade Canada and capture Malden but had, without offering any defense, turned over to the enemy his army, Fort Detroit and the Detroit settlement, and all of Michigan Territory.

Execution of the inglorious details of the surrender fell to Jesup. Once the terms had been agreed upon, Hull, who had been greatly agitated, appeared tranquil and perfectly composed. As Jesup testified:

> He said that he was sorry I had disapproved of his conduct, as he had always respected me; that no man felt more on the occasion than he did; and made some observations that conveyed the idea that he considered the government had abandoned him; and he hoped I would continue to act until the troops were marched out of the fort; to which I replied, that I would do my duty. I then received . . . a copy of the articles of capitulation, which I was directed to read to the troops, who were marched out by battalions about 12 o'clock, and formed in a hollow square below the fort, had the articles of capitulation read to them, and stacked their arms.[21]

Jesup, who had joined Hull's expedition in the hope of gaining military distinction, now found himself in the humiliating position of being a prisoner of war. Although Brock placed the American volunteers and militiamen on parole and permitted them to return to their homes, he held Hull and the army regulars as prisoners, eventually taking them to Montreal. On 18 August, while still at Detroit, Jesup appealed formally to Brock to grant him a parole. Inasmuch as Jesup was a regular, Brock promptly rejected his plea.[22]

The prisoners were taken to Malden and loaded on the *Queen Charlotte*, the *Hunter*, and other British vessels which carried them as far as Fort Erie, opposite Buffalo. From Fort Erie they were required to march to Fort George, where they were again placed on ships and taken to Kingston. They were then marched past curious and jeering spectators to Montreal, a galling experience for Jesup and the other prisoners. En route, Hull wrote to the secretary of war recapitulating his reasons for the surrender. He added that he could not consent to the useless sacrifice of his brave men when he knew that his situation was impossible to sustain. He paid tribute to his "respectable associates in command" and expressed his obligation to Brigade Major Jesup "for the correct and punctual manner in which he discharged his duties."[23]

On 10 September, Hull and eight of his officers were paroled. Jesup was undoubtedly among the parolees, for on 4 October he wrote to inform Eustis of his arrival in Cincinnati. He refreshed the secretary's memory, if it needed refreshing: "I was unfortunately attached to the Army which was sacrificed at Detroit, and have been permitted, by the British Commander-in-Chief, to return to this State as a prisoner of war."[24] The secretary apparently had already known that Jesup was on his way to Cincinnati. On 9 October, Eustis had directed Adj. Gen. Thomas H. Cushing to order Jesup to come to Washington at his earliest convenience. Cushing, a friend of Jesup's, added, "[the secretary of war] has something in view which I apprehend may be to your advantage, and I hope it may serve to keep up your spirits until we are able to set you at liberty."[25] Cushing's letter reached Jesup on 1 November at the headquarters of Gen. William Henry Harrison near Cincinnati where, although as a parolee he was not permitted to bear arms, he was serving as a messenger. He promptly arranged to leave for Washington, arriving at the capital on 14 December, two days before his twenty-fourth birthday.

William Henry Harrison, under whom Jesup served in the War of 1812. Harrison was elected president of the United States in 1841.

The next night he wrote to Thomas Sloo, Jr., a friend in Cincinnati, that he had been ill and was still "much indisposed" but had spent the greater part of the day at the War Office. Although Eustis had resigned, he was continuing the duties of secretary of war until a successor was appointed. "I have not met a person either in his office, or that of the Adjt. Genl. who is able to inform me why I have been ordered here," Jesup wrote. Moreover, having examined the *Army Register*, he expressed dismay at his prospects for promotion. Thirteen of the officers who had served under him now outranked him. Among them was a man from Cincinnati who had been promoted to captain, causing Jesup to exclaim: "Good God, Sloo, how partial is Fortune in the distribution of her favors!" Hull, he discovered, had many advocates in Washington; many influential members of Congress supported the general and attributed his expeditions's failure to the conduct of the volunteer officers. "Indeed, my friend," Jesup added, "altho' an eye witness to the cowardice and perfidy of the General, I begin to doubt the result of a trial."[26]

Two weeks later Jesup still had not the slightest inkling as to why he had been summoned to Washington, and he was indignant. James Monroe, who still retained his post as secretary of state, had taken temporary charge of the War Department, but so long as Eustis remained in Washington, Jesup thought it "indelicate" to ask Monroe the reason for his summons. Unfortunately, after Eustis departed, Monroe was too busy to see him. Jesup was exasperated: "What in the name of heaven could induce Mr. Eustis to put me to the expense and inconvenience of a journey of six hundred miles, barely to inquire [as to] the effective force at Detroit on the day of surrender," when he could have obtained that information by letter? He was tired of "such a service." Considering his prospects for promotion "distant and uncertain," he felt more than ever inclined "to exchange Ney for Blackstone." At the bar his advance would depend in a great measure on his own exertions. "But in the Army," he wrote, "the strictest attention to duty, the most unwearied application to professional studies, and the most scrupulous attention to character and honor, will give me no other advantage than that derived from self approbation." If he continued in the service of his country, he would have to be content "to glide down the stream of military enterprise, undistinguished from the crowd of ignorance & stupidity with which [the] Army abounds."[27]

But Jesup's prospects for promotion were less "distant and uncertain" than he had supposed. On 20 January 1813, while still a prisoner of war on parole, he was advanced to the rank of captain —the first of four promotions he would receive within an eighteen-month period. Suddenly, he found himself actively occupied. Under Monroe's orders, he was to assist in preparations for Hull's court-martial, which was scheduled to begin on 25 February in Philadelphia. On 4 January Jesup submitted to Monroe the list of prospective witnesses he had been requested to prepare. The following day he sent to Adjutant General Cushing a "statement of facts" concerning the events at Detroit and Hull's conduct during the campaign.[28]

One month before the trial was to begin, General Cushing instructed Jesup to proceed to Philadelphia as soon as possible to attend the trial as a witness. Cushing directed the young officer to give Alexander J. Dallas, who had been selected as judge advocate of the court-martial, such information as might be in his power to furnish, and to afford Dallas every assistance in his power, compatible with his situation as a witness and a prisoner of war.[29]

Jesup carried a letter from Cushing to Dallas, instructing him to consult with Jesup and to "make out and arrange each specification." Of Jesup, Cushing wrote, "He possesses talent, integrity, and honor, and is respected & esteemed by all who know him."[30] The court-martial convened on 25 February, with Gen. Wade Hampton presiding, but the trial was not held. President Madison, without giving any reason, abruptly ordered the court dissolved. Hull returned to his farm, where he waited nearly a year before being summoned to appear before another court-martial. Jesup, still wondering why Eustis had ordered him to the nation's capital, was no doubt puzzled further by the strange actions of the administration as he made his way back to Washington.

Before his return, Gen. John Armstrong, ex-senator and former minister to France, had become secretary of war on 13 January 1813, succeeding Acting Secretary Monroe. Jesup was pleased by this development: "[Armstrong's] talents and exertions will repair the blunders of the last campaign. How unfortunate for our country that he was not called twelve months ago, to his present station."[31] Early in March, Jesup learned to his surprise and gratification that his faith in Armstrong was reciprocated.

The new secretary of war informed him that he was being detailed with the temporary rank of deputy quartermaster general to supervise the construction at Cleveland of boats to be used for transporting the troops of General Harrison's army on Lake Erie. These vessels were to be known as Schenectady boats—sharp at the head and flat-bottomed, each capable of carrying from forty to fifty men with their baggage, arms, accoutrements, and provisions for the voyage. If workmen and materials could not be found in Cleveland or elsewhere along the lake, Jesup was to have them sent on without delay from Pittsburgh. Funds for this purpose would be put under his control, and he was to make weekly progress reports.[32]

The young army captain set out promptly on his mission, faced with a formidable and highly responsible task. From Pittsburgh on 27 March Jesup wrote Armstrong that he had contracted there for the first of the boats to be delivered at Cleveland. He intended to leave immediately for that town where he planned to construct the other boats. Since Cleveland was "an extreme frontier" town, he indicated that a guard would probably be required to protect the boats and material. The population was so small that the enemy could easily land and destroy the transports before a militia force large enough to repel an attack could be collected. By May Jesup had established three boatyards busily engaged in turning out the transports.

Before Jesup left Washington, he had been assured by Armstrong and Secretary of State Monroe that his name was on the list of prisoners exchanged, and that he was thus free to act in any military capacity. But the young officer with the sensitive conscience could not be content until he had written notification releasing him from the oath he had given his British captors not to take up arms until officially exchanged. He brought up the subject in a letter to Armstrong. Dilatory official action and a misdirection of mail delayed until 8 May Jesup's receipt of the formal certification of his exchange.[33]

On 6 April, Jesup was promoted from captain in the 7th Infantry to major in the 19th, and placed in command at Cleveland, one of the outposts of Harrison's northwestern army. For a time, he wore two hats, for he was still acting deputy quartermaster general in charge of the boat-building program. Until that program was completed, he would be unable to join his new regiment. In the interim, his command consisted of about 230 regulars and militia sent to Cleveland by General Harrison and Governor Meigs to guard the boats.

On 30 April he wrote to a friend: "[I am] now employed preparing transports for about four thousand men, destined for the invasion of Upper Canada. I hope to be exchanged before they are ready to march. . . . It is thought by some we will have peace with England shortly. I am not of the number who believe so." He expressed his wish to resume correspondence with his friend. His concluding sentence revealed that in the back of his mind remained the idea of courting danger and winning distinction in a revolution elsewhere, should the war with England end before he had gained recognition in his own country: "Write me immediately on receipt of this and give me all the news you have—particularly with respect to the revolution in Mexico."[34]

The winter campaign, designed to recapture Detroit and undertaken at the urging of then-Secretary Eustis against Harrison's better judgment, had not only failed miserably but had brought more disasters to American land forces. The British, having driven the Americans out of Canada, still held a firm grip on Lake Erie; they became bolder and launched an invasion of their own. As the enemy descended into Ohio, alarm spread throughout the region. On 4 May information reached Major Jesup that Fort Meigs at the rapids of the Miami River had been under siege by a large force of British and Indians under Col. Henry Proctor and Tecumseh; the incessant firing of cannon could be heard in Cleveland. Jesup became concerned for the safety of Harrison and his army. From the messenger who brought the news, he learned that important mail had fallen into the hands of the enemy. Fearing that the captured mail contained valuable information concerning movements planned by American troops under Maj. Gen. Morgan Lewis on the Niagara frontier, Jesup dispatched a courier on 7 May to warn Lewis. He then turned his attention to preparing a defense of Cleveland and the boats he was building. Fewer than two hundred stacks of arms were available in the town and nearby counties; learning that Huron had a supply of public muskets, Jesup sent for five hundred more.

General Lewis not only sent Jesup a letter of thanks but exhibited his gratitude by offering him a position on his staff. Jesup responded that to join Lewis would afford him satisfaction but that a War Department regulation provided that no officer above the rank of a subaltern could be employed as an aide-de-camp. "Tho I cannot join you as an aid I should have no objection to join you in any other department of the staff that of Q.Master excepted."[35] This was not the first nor the last time that the young officer expressed his distaste for quartermaster duties.

The enemy's invasion of Ohio and the disturbing fact that British ships still patrolled Lake Erie at will compelled Jesup to keep his small command of troops on almost constant alert against the danger that the British, hostile Indians, or both might try to seize or destroy the shipyards and the boats. Should they capture Fort Meigs or other American strongholds, Cleveland would be in dire peril. On the morning of 13 June, two British ships appeared on the lake a few miles off the Cleveland shore. Jesup was prepared to give them a "warm reception," but a severe thunderstorm frustrated the enemy's plans. Two weeks later, General Harrison warned Jesup that an assault was expected immediately somewhere along the lake shore; again the attack did not materialize. On 5 July Harrison paid a visit to Jesup to have a look at the boats, remaining until the fifteenth. By then sixty-nine of the boats had been inspected and accepted, and seven more were nearing completion. The general set out for Lower Sandusky, where he ordered the boats to be sent.[36]

On 24 July Jesup learned that Fort Meigs was again under enemy attack and sent boats to aid General Harrison. Two days later he wrote to Secretary Armstrong of his action, sounding a grave warning: "Unless we obtain the command of the Lake, immediately, nothing can be accomplished by this Army. I have provided boats—transportation sufficient for the three thousand men, but it will be impossible to put them in motion unless we have armed vessels to protect them."[37]

The second attempt by the British and their Indian allies to destroy Fort Meigs failed as completely as the first. Although Proctor and Tecumseh were annoyed and frustrated by their failures, they were still not ready to admit defeat. They did not risk another assault on Fort Meigs; instead, they selected as their next target Fort Stephenson, located on the Sandusky River at the site of the present city of Fremont, Ohio. The fort was commanded by

Young George Croghan, the hero who defended Fort Stephenson against the British, and later became Thomas Jesup's brother-in-law.

twenty-one-year-old Maj. George Croghan, a nephew of George Rogers Clark, from Locust Grove, now part of Louisville, Kentucky. His small garrison consisted of about 160 regulars, and his only artillery piece was a six-pounder.

Harrison considered the fort entirely too weak to withstand the artillery fire of the enemy, and directed Croghan to abandon it if attacked. But the young major decided that to attempt escape through the enemy lines was much riskier than to stay put and defend the fort. He sent word to Harrison that he was determined to remain at his post and was convinced that he could hold the fort. Angered by the arrogant young officer's disobedience, Harrison promptly relieved him of the command, ordering him to appear immediately at the headquarters at Fort Seneca to explain his conduct. When Croghan appeared, Harrison was so impressed by his earnestness and his justification for his decision that he restored the officer's command and permitted him to return to Fort Stephenson.

The rest of the story is recorded indelibly in history. Croghan and his small band so skillfully defended the fort on 1 August against repeated attacks of some five hundred British and seven or eight hundred Indians that the enemy not only gave up the fight but also abandoned the invasion plans and returned to Malden. Croghan became a national hero.[38] Although the two were strangers at the time, Croghan was later to become Jesup's brother-in-law.

When the last of the boats had been completed, Jesup left his Cleveland post to join Harrison's army. His service as acting deputy quartermaster general was at an end, and he was free to become part of a fighting unit as he had long been waiting to do. Early in September he was assigned to the temporary command at Fort Stephenson, relieving young Croghan, who had so recently become a celebrity.[39]

While Jesup was at the fort, he and the country at large were cheered by the news that Commodore Oliver Hazard Perry had decisively defeated and captured the British fleet on Lake Erie. For the first time, Lake Erie was in American hands. The way had finally been cleared for Harrison's army to cross the lake in the boats constructed by Jesup, invade Upper Canada, and try to recapture Detroit. On 20 September 1813, under the protection of

Perry's fleet, the army embarked from Put-in-Bay in open boats, landing at Middle Sister Island. A week later, when Harrison was satisfied that everything was in readiness, his army crossed the last stretch of water, came ashore in Canada at Hartley's Point, and marched inland to Amherstburg, which it found in ruins.

Major Jesup, bent on retaliation for the humiliation he had suffered when Hull surrendered his army more than a year before, was among the first to set foot on Canadian soil. Some opposition had been expected from the enemy, and battle lines were quickly formed, but the preparation proved unnecessary. The British and their Indian allies had fled. Jesup, serving under Col. James Ball, made the dispositions to cover the landing of the army and commanded the advance. When the enemy was discovered to have fled, Harrison moved the army to Malden.[40] The loss of the British fleet was a severe blow to Proctor, who, after evacuating and burning all the public buildings in Malden, retreated to Sandwich, opposite Detroit. From there, he could gain access to the Thames River, on which he could transport his supplies and equipment.

On 29 September the Americans reoccupied Detroit, much to the elation of Jesup and others who had suffered the ignominy of having been surrendered there to the British the previous year. Harrison was determined to pursue the retreating British and Indians. Lacking horses, he had to await the arrival of a regiment of some one thousand mounted riflemen under the command of Col. Richard M. Johnson, a congressman from Kentucky, who had volunteered his services. Because horses could not be taken across Lake Erie in the boats which transported the troops, Johnson and his riders followed the land route to Detroit. They arrived at the settlement on 30 September and on 2 October led the advance in pursuit of Proctor and his army.

The American force overtook the British commander on 5 October near Moravian Town on the Thames. Proctor had selected a good spot for his defense, but his troops were no match for the fierce onslaughts of Johnson's mounted riflemen. The Battle of the Thames ended quickly with a complete American victory. The British army was destroyed; the greater number of the enemy were captured. Tecumseh was killed, and Proctor, when he foresaw defeat, deserted his army and fled the scene of battle. The Americans were jubilant over their decisive victory, which they believed had vindicated the nation's honor. Glory on the battlefield still eluded Jesup; he and his command were held in reserve and did not actively participate.[41]

Following the battle, Major Jesup joined Gen. Lewis Cass, newly appointed military and civil governor of Michigan Territory, at Fort Shelby, as the fort at Detroit had been renamed. On 8 November Jesup was granted a three-week leave of absence to visit friends in Cincinnati. Upon his return, he was transferred as commander of the 19th Infantry to Fort Niagara, New York, where, on 2 December, he received orders from the War Department to report at Albany to serve as a witness at Hull's rescheduled trial.[42]

The second court-martial assembled for the trial of sixty-one-year-old General Hull convened on 3 January 1814 in the New York State Capitol at Albany. Presiding was Maj. Gen. Henry Dearborn, who at the outset of the war had been stationed on the Niagara front. The strategy had called for him to hold the enemy in check there to prevent reinforcements from being sent to Detroit. Instead, Dearborn had entered into an armistice with the British which excluded Hull's army and the British forces in the Northwest. President Madison had rebuked him for the unauthorized armistice and had ordered it ended, but his orders had come too late to help Hull. Now Dearborn was to be president of the court sitting in judgment of Hull. The only other general officer on the court was Brig. Gen. Joseph Bloomfield; the other members were colonels or lieutenant colonels. Lt. Col. James G. Forbes, a supernumerary member, recorded the proceedings, and Martin Van Buren served as special judge advocate. Hull offered no objections to the makeup of the court at the outset, but after its verdict he became highly critical of it. The official charges against him were treason, cowardice, neglect of duty, and conduct unbecoming an officer. To all charges, Hull entered a plea of not guilty. Since only Jesup and three other witnesses were so far present, the court adjourned to await the arrival of the others. The actual taking of testimony began about two weeks later.

Among those preceding Jesup on the witness stand were Gen. Duncan McArthur, Maj. Thomas B. Van Horne, Maj. Josiah Snelling, and Capt. Samuel McCormick—all of whom were highly critical of the conduct of their former commander. Also introduced into evidence was a letter written by Lewis Cass soon after his release by the British; it had been widely printed in newspapers and had done much to prejudice public opinion against Hull.

Jesup waited in Albany about five weeks before he was finally called to the stand on 9 February, and his testimony and questioning continued into the following day. The bulk of his testimony described his own activities and the conduct and reactions of General Hull in the twenty-four-hour period leading up to the surrender of Detroit.

Sometime on 15 August, Jesup testified, he had met the general after Hull had rejected Brock's summons to capitulate. In response to Jesup's inquiry, Hull had indicated the troop disposition but the general had been apprehensive that the Indians would burn the town. He had rejected Jesup's suggestion to cut down a cornfield that might have sheltered the Indians. When Jesup discovered that certain detachments of McArthur's and Cass's regiments would be greatly exposed if the enemy attacked, he had proposed joining them either to the regiment of Col. James Findlay or that of Lt. Col. James Miller. Hull had at first ordered them joined to Findlay's regiment; then, changing his mind, he had stated that he would communicate the disposition orders. However, when Jesup had later visited the lines with Hull, the detachments were still in place, "exposed to the enemy's fire." At that time Hull appeared "pale and very much confused."

On the morning of 16 August firing had begun again, and at Hull's orders Jesup had placed troops about a quarter of a mile below the fort. He had then reconnoitered the enemy and reported to Hull that the British troops, marching in a column through a lane, could be taken in the flank by the dragoons. Hull had directed Jesup to assume command of the dragoons, permitting him to take out some pieces of artillery, but by the time Jesup met with some dragoon officers, the American line was breaking up, and a white flag was flying over the fort.

As he concluded his testimony, Jesup was questioned first by the court and then by Hull. To the court's inquiry, Jesup responded that the brigade orderly's book had been turned over to the British under the terms of the capitulation. As to the conduct and spirit of the troops when the articles of capitulation were read to them, he stated, "They evinced the greatest dissatisfaction and indignation." Had the troops been posted so as to enable them to make a defense in the event that General Brock insisted upon degrading terms? No, Jesup testified, the men had been crowded into the fort in the utmost disorder. "The enemy's troops were permitted to approach so near the fort as to be able to take possession of the batteries."

Jesup's earlier testimony held that, according to estimates from the adjutants of the various corps, the total number of men fit for action at the time of the surrender was one thousand—not including the detachments absent from the fort with Cols. Cass and McArthur. Hull's cross-examination sought to bring out that, according to a paper prepared by Jesup on the evening of 15 August, the effective aggregate of the three regiments was about seven hundred. This figure, Jesup pointed out, included the whole of Colonel Findlay's regiment and only what remained of the regiments of Cols. Cass and McArthur but did not include the 4th Regiment, as he had explained at the time.[43]

By 1 March the government had completed its case, and the court adjourned temporarily to give Hull and his lawyers time to prepare his defense. When the trial resumed Hull justified his actions primarily upon certain basic arguments. His army was inferior in numbers to General Brock's. His provisions were almost exhausted and could not be replenished. His communications, through which additional supplies might have been forwarded, were cut off; all his efforts to open them had proved unsuccessful. Lake Erie was completely under the control of the British; even if Hull had fought and held off the army in front of him, the enemy's ships and swarms of hostile Indians from the Northwest could have overwhelmed him. His situation was hopeless. To fight would have been a useless expenditure of lives—not only those of his brave soldiers but also those of the women and children in the fort—and would have exposed the inhabitants in the Michigan Territory to Indian massacres and cruelties. He had not created the situation his army found itself in; the government shared the blame for not sending aid, as did the American army on the Niagara front for its failure to engage in diversionary tactics which could have prevented the enemy in that sector from sending reinforcements to Malden.

Hull closed his defense on 18 March. A week later the court reached its verdict, which was not made public. Instead, the papers were sealed and sent to Washington. On 25 April, a month later, the War Department announced the findings. The court acquitted Hull of the charge of treason but found him guilty of the other charges and ordered him shot. But in consideration of his Revolutionary services and his advanced age, the court recommended that the president extend him mercy. Madison approved the verdict and followed the court's recommendation in remitting the death sentence, but he directed that Hull's name be removed from the army's rolls.

Although Jesup believed that Hull had been justly punished, he felt, as did many, that the convicted general should not alone have been held to blame for what happened at Detroit. He contended that while the general's conduct was "marked by weakness and indecision, . . . some of his superiors evinced the most criminal neglect, or the most childish imbecility."[44]

CHAPTER 2

GLORY ON

THE BATTLEFIELD

A WEEK BEFORE Hull's conviction was announced, Major Jesup was transferred from the 19th to the 25th Infantry and took command of his new regiment in April. Some important changes had been made in the command of the army as a result of its many earlier disasters. Relieved from duty in addition to Hull were such other aged officers of the Revolutionary War as Dearborn, Hampton, and Wilkinson. Jacob Brown, a Quaker, who was advanced to the rank of major general and appointed commander of the American forces on the Niagara frontier, proved an excellent choice. Assigned to his staff as his top-ranking officers were Winfield Scott and Eleazer W. Ripley, both of whom had only recently been promoted to brigadier general.

The available force in Brown's army, exclusive of Indians, was approximately thirty-five hundred. Two brigades of regulars—one headed by Scott, the other by Ripley—were supported by four companies of artillery under Maj. Jacob Hindman. A third brigade, commanded by Brig. Gen. Peter Buell Porter, former quartermaster of the New York militia, was comprised of some three hundred militia volunteers from Pennsylvania and about four hundred friendly Seneca Indians. General Scott's brigade consisted of four regiments—the 9th, 11th, 22nd, and Jesup's 25th Infantry. Col. Hugh Brady was assigned to command the 22nd but was late in arriving, so Maj. Henry Leavenworth was originally in charge of his own 9th as well as Brady's 22nd. Maj. John McNeil commanded the 11th. General Ripley's brigade consisted of two regiments—the 21st, under Col. James Miller, and the 23rd, under Maj. Daniel McFarland. No regiment had more than half of its complement. Although classed as regulars, most of the men were recruits from Massachusetts, New York, Pennsylvania, Vermont, and Connecticut, as in the case of Jesup's 25th.

General Brown was not a professional soldier. Before his commission on 19 July 1813, his only military experience had been as a brigadier general in the New York volunteers. Possessed of great zeal, courage, sound judgment, and initiative, he quickly won the confidence of his fellow officers and was able to establish strict discipline among his troops and imbue them with a fighting spirit. Recognizing the importance of troop training, he directed General Scott to organize a school of military instruction at Buffalo. Scott formed the officers into squads, which he personally instructed; the officers, in turn, drilled the men in their own commands. Major Jesup, a zealous student of the military tactics employed by the British and French armies, was well qualified as an instructor. He kept his command under arms from seven to ten hours a day. "The consequence," he later wrote, "was that when we took the field in July, every corps maneuvered in action, and under the Enemy's Artillery, with the accuracy of parade."[1] Brown's army was doubtless the best-drilled and most efficient American force yet to face the British.

The American situation was critical. Efforts by Wilkinson and Hampton late in 1813 to invade Canada and attack Montreal had ended in another dismal failure. On the Niagara front the Americans held only Buffalo, which had been burned and virtually destroyed by the British on 18 December in retaliation for the earlier burning of Newark in Canada by an American force. Before burning Buffalo and a number of other New York villages, the British and Canadians had taken possession of Fort George on the Canadian side of the Niagara near its mouth, crossed the river at night to Fort Niagara on the opposite bank, captured it, and slaughtered most of its garrison. Directly across from Buffalo, on the Niagara where it flowed into Lake Erie, was Fort Erie, also in British hands. Thus, of the four principal fortifications on the Niagara front, three were held by the enemy. Moreover, Great Britain's long struggle with Napoleon's French forces was drawing to a close; soon, she would be able to send strong reinforcements of veteran soldiers to her army in America.

General Brown, then, was charged with staving off further catastrophe. His first objective was to force the surrender of Fort Erie. The strategy, formulated by Secretary of War Armstrong, then called for Brown to move up along the Canadian side of the Niagara—provided he had the cooperation of the American fleet, commanded by Isaac Chauncey—to seize Fort George, headquarters of Gen. Phineas Riall. He was then to recross the river to recapture Fort Niagara. On the morning of 2 July, Brown informed his staff that the army would embark in boats that night and would attack Fort Erie at dawn. Scott's brigade and a corps of artillery, commanded by Major Hindman, were to embark from Buffalo and land about a mile below Fort Erie. Ripley's brigade was to embark at the same time from Black Rock, a few miles above Buffalo, and go ashore about a mile above the fort. After landing the invading forces, the boats were to return immediately to the American side to transport the rest of the army and the baggage and supplies.

Scott's force, closely followed by Brown and his aides, crossed the river in small boats in the darkness and landed without incident on the Niagara shore. Scott ordered Jesup's 25th Infantry to reconnoiter closer to the fort. Jesup soon discovered that Ripley's brigade had not taken its assigned position. Fearful that the enemy might attempt escape in that direction, he sent his adjutant, Lt. Stanton Sholes, to report the situation to Brown. When the general learned that the initial movement of Jesup's regiment had driven back into the fort an enemy detachment sent out to offer resistance, he considered the situation so favorable that he decided to invest the fort without waiting for Ripley. Although Ripley had not arrived, a portion of his brigade had landed below the fort instead of above it. Brown directed his adjutant, Col. Charles K. Gardner, to form those men into a corps, proceed above the fort, and extend his left flank to link up with Jesup's command, thus completing the fort's encirclement.

Meanwhile, Lieutenant Sholes had returned to Jesup's position, accompanied by the engineers, Majs. William McRee and Eleazer D. Wood, to inform him of Brown's decision. Acting under his new instructions, Jesup ordered his regiment to advance. Brown, after earlier consulting with the engineers, was engaged in directing the movement of batteries to sites selected for use in shelling the fort. Before retiring to the rear, he asked Scott to name an officer to carry a flag of truce to the fort with a demand for its surrender. Scott designated Jesup for the honor.[2]

When Jesup reached the fort, he was met by the garrison commander. After explaining the hopelessness of the enemy's situation, Jesup gave the British officer two hours to consider the demand for his capitulation. He decided quickly, and shortly after their meeting sent a white flag to Jesup. The terms of surrender were quickly arranged; the commander, along with his garrison of nearly two hundred, marched out and stacked their arms. General Brown had attained the first objective of his campaign. Likely his prompt action alone had made success possible, for British reinforcements were already en route to the fort.[3] The youthful Jesup undoubtedly took some pride in the knowledge that he was beginning to achieve, at least in small measure, the recognition he had long sought.

Irked by the intrusion of the Americans into Canada and by the loss of Fort Erie, General Riall was determined to launch an immediate attack on Brown's army but was persuaded to delay until reinforcements could arrive. On the morning of the Fourth of July, General Brown learned from his patrols that Riall's light troops were in the neighborhood. He promptly ordered Scott's brigade to move toward Chippewa to confront the enemy. The British slowly retreated, with Scott in close pursuit. According to Jesup, the sixteen-mile march "was a continual skirmish and on the plains between Street's Creek and Chippewa [the American] light troops were constantly vigorously attacked but maintained their ground most gallantly."

When Scott discovered that the enemy was strongly posted behind Chippewa Creek, he called in his light troops and took a position in the rear of Street's Creek, where he encamped his brigade. Brown and his staff arrived about midnight, accompanied by Ripley's brigade and Hindman's artillery. The opposing armies spent that hot Fourth of July night about a mile apart, facing each other across the two small streams. To the east was the nearby Niagara River, into which the two creeks flowed. Parallel to the river near its bank, a road crossed each stream over narrow bridges. Less than a mile to the west was a dense woods.

At dawn on 5 July the British began attacking the pickets of

Scott's brigade and kept up a desultory fire for several hours. Scott was reinforced during the forenoon by the arrival of General Porter with three to four hundred Indian warriors and about three hundred Pennsylvania volunteers. Observing enemy troops in the woods, Brown ordered Porter to advance and disperse them. Porter was successful but in his pursuit soon found himself confronting the main British army advancing in battle order. Porter's forces rapidly withdrew. Brown, receiving the news, rode to the rear to set Ripley's brigade in motion. Passing Scott, he shouted, "You will have a battle," supposing that Scott was aware of the approach of the entire British army and was going out to meet it. Actually Scott had served a belated anniversary dinner to his brigade to commemorate the Fourth of July and, as part of his disciplinary action, had followed it with an order for "a parade of grand evolutions."[4] Not until the first of his columns had started across the Street's Creek bridge did he know that Riall's entire force was rapidly advancing upon him. What had begun as parade maneuvers suddenly turned into a full-scale battle.

As Scott's surprised troops began crossing the bridge, they were met by a murderous fire at almost point-blank range. After the brigade had crossed, covered by Capt. Nathan Towson's artillery, Jesup was ordered to go to the extreme left and "be governed by circumstances." Perceiving that the enemy greatly outnumbered the Americans, Jesup moved his regiment in column until he attained a position within 120 paces of that occupied by the Marquis of Tweedale, in an attempt to deceive him as to the size of the regiment. The marquis commanded the right of Riall's line of battle. Jesup's troops were subjected to a destructive fire from the grenadiers and light infantry in front and from the Indians and militia in the thick woods on the left flank.

Finding his position untenable, Jesup had either to retreat or advance. Ripley's brigade was not yet on the field; to have fallen back would have uncovered Scott's left flank and enabled the marquis to attack it. Coupled with the pressure exerted by a superior force in front, this exposure would have caused Scott's defeat. To gain time to enable the second brigade to come to the relief of the first, Jesup ordered a bayonet charge, relying on the discipline of his troops. Tweedale's forces fled in confusion, despite their strong position. Jesup detached Capt. Daniel Ketchum with one of the light companies of the 25th to harass and prevent the enemy from rallying. He then formed the remainder of his regiment across the flank of the British line that was engaged with Scott and assailed it in front by an oblique fire. Support of the enemy line gave way but rallied immediately behind a fence. While Jesup was rearranging his troops to drive the enemy from his position, Brown rode up to assure him of immediate support.

About the same time, Maj. Henry Leavenworth, commanding the 9th and 22d Regiments, and Maj. John McNeil, commanding the 11th, were operating in the center of Scott's line of battle, along the whole of which the fighting raged. The operations of the 25th Regiment under Jesup relieved the pressure on McNeil. Sweeping forward under Scott's orders, Jesup and Leavenworth led a charge which broke the enemy's resistance. The whole British line gave way, and the enemy fled rapidly behind the Chippewa.[5]

The victory was decisive for the Americans, who jubilantly pursued the hastily retreating British troops back to the safety of their strong entrenchments. While the chase was in progress, a late afternoon thunderstorm broke over the plains, drenching the troops of both armies, and the Americans returned to their own camp. Despite the defeat inflicted on them by Brown's army, the opposing forces that night occupied the same relative positions they had held before the battle.

The great bulk of the 335 American casualties—61 killed, 255 wounded, and 19 missing—from the earlier skirmishes and the battle itself occurred among the troops of Scott's brigade, which had borne the brunt of the fighting. The British losses were much greater—236 killed, 322 wounded, and 46 missing. During the battle, Towson's artillery silenced the enemy's most effective battery by blowing up an ammunition wagon; that explosion may have accounted for some of the missing.[6]

After the battle of Chippewa, Scott had high praise, especially for four of what he termed his "excellent officers," one of whom was Jesup. Five months shy of his twenty-sixth birthday, he was brevetted with the rank of lieutenant colonel for "distinguished and meritorious service." Similar brevets were bestowed on Leavenworth and McNeil, and Towson was brevetted with the rank of major. In his official report of the battle, Scott stated that these officers deserved "everything which conspicuous skill and gallantry can win from a grateful country." He also noted that Jesup's horse "was shot under him" during the fighting.[7]

The number of troops involved in the battle of Chippewa was relatively small. The fact that the smaller American force had emerged triumphant was a tribute to the strict discipline instilled in Brown's army by Scott, Jesup, and other officers through the training program at Buffalo. The men had demonstrated that they could attain on the field the same excellence achieved by American seamen on the water. As historian Henry Adams wrote, "Never again after that combat was an American army of regulars beaten by British troops. Small as the affair was, and unimportant in military results, it gave the United States Army a character and pride it had never before possessed."[8]

The battle was significant for other reasons. The American Indian allies, who had remained faithful to the English cause after Tecumseh's death, became disenchanted and deserted the British. In his *Memoirs,* published fifty years later, Scott summed up the situation:

> Few men now alive are old enough to recall the deep gloom, approaching despair, which about this time oppressed the whole American people. . . . History had recorded many victories on a much larger scale than that of Chippewa; but only a few have wrought a greater change in the feelings of the nation. Everywhere bonfires blazed; bells rang out peals of joy; the big guns responded, and the pulse of Americans recovered a healthy beat.[9]

Brown's army devoted 6 July, the day after the battle, to treating and removing the wounded, burying the dead, and reconnoitering the countryside. Reconnaissance revealed a deserted timber road that ended only a short distance from Riall's camp. On the basis of a report made by Brevet Lieutenant Colonel Jesup, Major Wood, and Captain Ketchum, the engineers promptly restored the road to usable condition. With Scott's brigade and part of the artillery holding the enemy in check in the front, Brown ordered Ripley's brigade, Porter's forces, and two companies of artillery to move rapidly over the road, build a temporary bridge across the Chippewa, and attack Riall's right flank.

Riall was so alarmed at the movements of Brown's army that instead of making a stand in defense of his position, he destroyed his heavy artillery, wrecked the permanent Chippewa bridge, abandoned his fortifications, and retreated some seven miles to Queenston. That night Scott's and Ripley's brigades crossed the Chippewa by boat in pursuit. The following morning they pressed forward to Queenston, only to discover that the British had departed. While Brown was establishing his camp on Queenston Heights, Riall detached part of his force to Fort George; with the remainder, he took a position in the open country about a dozen miles from the fort. Brown's army remained at Queenston until 20 July. During that period, the general sent out several detachments to reconnoiter in the vicinity of Fort George near Lake Ontario.

From the beginning of his campaign, Brown had relied on Commodore Isaac Chauncey's fleet for assistance in capturing Fort George. When Chauncey and his fleet failed to appear, Brown called a council of his officers. He had two choices: he could either attempt to destroy Riall's army in the field or attack Fort George without Chauncey's aid. Most of his officers, including Jesup, favored battle with Riall, but Scott, second in command, stubbornly insisted that the fort be attacked. Brown finally agreed. Accordingly, on 20 July 1814, he moved the army from Queenston to the vicinity of Fort George. Two companies of Jesup's 25th Infantry drove back the enemy's pickets outside the fort. Jesup, who was officer of the day, advanced with the two companies, reconnoitering the ground and observing the enemy until the time came to post guards for the night. Brown apparently decided upon reflection that to attack the fort at this time was not wise after all, for on 22 July he ordered the army to move back to Queenston.

Jesup always had great admiration for Jacob Brown, but he believed the general had made a serious error in agreeing to attack Fort George. Brown's army did not have the heavy artillery necessary to destroy the fort, and the force was insufficient to carry the place by storm, particularly when Riall was within striking distance: "It is an axiom in military science that where the alternative is presented of a fort to be attacked, or an army in the field to be fought, the army should be fought first, because, even with a numerical superiority the assailant might be so crippled in the attack on the fort as to fall an easy prey to the army in the field." Jesup was convinced that if Riall had been attacked, his whole force could have been captured or destroyed before

Gen. Gordon Drummond arrived with British reinforcements. "But the favorable moment was allowed to pass, and we were consequently during the remainder of this campaign, thrown upon the defensive."

Early on 23 July, Brig. Gen. Edmund P. Gaines, commander at Sackett's Harbor, informed Brown that Chauncey was seriously ill, that his fleet was bottled up by British ships, and that to attempt to send any reinforcements would be too perilous. Brown was thus forced to abandon any hope of gaining the fleet's co-operation or obtaining additional troops. When he learned the following morning that General Drummond was on his way to Queenston with strong reinforcements, he ordered his army to retreat behind the Chippewa. He hoped by this retrograde movement to induce Riall's army to return to the same general area where the Americans had defeated the British nearly three weeks earlier.[10]

About 2 P.M. on 25 July, a day which had dawned bright and clear, Jesup crossed the Chippewa bridge to confer with Leavenworth, officer of the day, who told Jesup that he had seen a detachment of the enemy at Niagara Falls, near Table Rock. Brown was convinced that the enemy's objective was not to attack him but rather to assault Fort Schlosser, on the American side of the Niagara, where Brown had stored supplies and kept his sick and wounded. His assumption was based on information (later proved false) that the British had thrown what was thought to be a large force across the river to Lewiston from where it could march down to Fort Schlosser. He believed that General Drummond had pushed forward a few light troops to conceal his real purpose. Lacking boats to transport troops across the river to defend the fort, Brown reasoned that the most effective way to counteract the British movement would be to make a feint toward Fort George. He therefore ordered Scott with his brigade, Towson's artillery, and all available cavalry and mounted men to move immediately to Queenston, directly opposite Lewiston.

At about 5 P.M. Scott led his brigade out of camp, crossed the Chippewa bridge, and proceeded along the Niagara toward Queenston. His entire force slightly exceeded 1,200. Jesup's 25th Regiment numbered about 350. The other regimental commanders were Leavenworth, McNeil, and Brady. As the troops advanced, they began to hear in the distance the faint roar of

Niagara Falls. Not much daylight remained; in about forty minutes the sun would set. Scott had doubts about his assignment; like Brown, he was certain that the main British force was on the other side of the river. But he was in for a big surprise. Within minutes, he was embroiled in the most savage conflict of the war—the battle of Lundy's Lane (sometimes called the battle of Niagara, or Bridgewater). As his brigade rounded a bend in the road into an open space, it suddenly faced a much larger British force than the one Brown's army had beaten at Chippewa.

Jesup described the battle in his account of the Niagara campaign. Riall was in command of the enemy force; only a woods, no more than a half-mile in width, separated the British and American armies. Scott called in the 9th Regiment, which had been detached to the left, dispatched an officer to inform Brown of the position and probable size of the enemy force, and then informed the officers in command that he would attack immediately. He directed Jesup and his 25th Regiment to the right, with instructions to pass through the woods and be governed by circumstances. When the enemy fired on the American advance commanded by Capt. John Pentland, the 9th, 11th, and 22d Regiments passed the woods and formed within four hundred paces of the enemy's line. The savage conflict lasted about an hour. "On our side both officers and men evinced a most heroic courage, but the enemy was so superior in force and his battery so destructive, that no impression could be made upon him," Jesup wrote.

In moving to the right, Jesup discovered a narrow road through the woods that the enemy had either not observed or had neglected to occupy and decided to avail himself of its advantages. Leaving Lt. Thomas Seymour with one light company to occupy in extended order the whole front which the regiment would have covered in line and advancing rapidly on the road, Jesup was soon on the enemy's flank. He routed several British detachments, taking numerous prisoners. While making dispositions to attack the enemy battery in the rear, Jesup learned from a prisoner that Drummond was close behind with a large reserve force.

Jesup realized that to carry out his planned attack upon the enemy's rear would be folly under the circumstances. The safety of the army depended upon keeping Drummond out of action until Brown could arrive with Ripley's and Porter's brigades. Consequently, he seized the Niagara road, took a position to attack any force that might advance, and detached Captain Ketchum with his company to make prisoners of all who attempted to pass to the front or rear. Riall and ten or fifteen other officers, among them one of Drummond's aides, were captured along with several hundred of their men. All were disarmed and sent to the rear of the American line. Night had fallen, and in the darkness and confusion, some of the officers and nearly all of the soldiers managed to escape, though Riall remained a prisoner.

With darkness, the firing slackened. Soon after Riall was taken to the rear, a rumor spread among the American troops that Scott had been defeated and driven from the field. The report proved false. Jesup, who was moving his command to the rear, learned that Brown, who had arrived on the scene shortly after 9 P.M. with his entire force, was about to renew the action. In the faint light of a waning moon, friend and foe were difficult to distinguish.

Not knowing where to find Brown or Scott or where to apply for orders, Jesup decided to resume his former position in the rear. He had nearly reached it when he encountered an advancing force of the enemy, which he attacked and routed "with great slaughter." At about that time, Brown rode up to inform him that Colonel Miller and his men had carried the Heights by bayonet and had captured the enemy's artillery. Brown ordered Jesup to fall back and join General Ripley on the heights; Ripley posted Jesup and his command on the right of the American line which was then forming.

Despite the loss of their heavy cannon and the top of the hill, the British continued their relentless attack. Supported by strong reserves, the enemy left was almost in contact with the 25th Regiment before the firing began. Jesup's men took deliberate aim. Their fire "was so terrible" that in a few minutes the British line recoiled, then broke and fled from the field. Jesup's surviving men adjusted their line and replenished their cartridges from the boxes of their dead and wounded comrades.

The enemy regrouped, approaching again in great force and in good order in about half an hour. After another savage exchange of firing which lasted fifteen or twenty minutes, the British once more fled from the field. Jesup, who had been wounded earlier when a ball passed through his right shoulder, was hit two more times during the encounter. He suffered a slight wound in the neck, and a shot which shattered the hilt of his sword drove fragments of it through his right hand, permanently disfiguring it.

Disheartened by repeated repulses, the British were on the point of yielding the contest when they received reinforcements from Fort George. An hour later, they returned to the desperate struggle.[11] Jesup's regiment had lost so many men that he was obliged to form those remaining in a single rank to preserve his front. The fighting was now more obstinate than in any of the previous attacks by the enemy, and it was destined to take a surprising toll of American officers, as well as heavy casualties on both sides. For half an hour "the blaze from the muskets of the two lines mingled," but the American fire was so well directed and destructive that the enemy was again compelled to retire from the field. During this fighting, Scott came over to talk with Jesup; as the two conversed, Scott suffered such a severe wound in the left shoulder joint that he was compelled to leave the field. Moments later, Brown, himself badly wounded, also had to retire, leaving General Ripley as senior officer in command. Soon thereafter, Jesup was struck violently in the chest either by a piece of shell or by the stock of a rocket which knocked him to the ground. In spite of this fourth wound, he was able to rise and resume his command in a few moments.[12]

The bloody battle of Lundy's Lane had lasted more than five hours, and the officers and troops were completely exhausted. They were also suffering from thirst, with no drinking water nearer than the Chippewa. When it became evident that no more fighting would occur that night, General Ripley informed Jesup that Brown had sent orders for him to conduct the troops back to camp. As soon as the wounded were removed, Jesup, though suffering severely from his own wounds, led the army slowly to their camp behind the Chippewa, reaching it about midnight.

The American army losses in killed and wounded were 76 officers, and 679 rank and file. Of these, the first brigade lost 38 officers and 468 men. Scott, commander of the brigade, as well as every regimental commander—Jesup, Leavenworth, McNeil, and Brady—was wounded, and both Scott and Jesup had two horses shot under them.[13] Both sides claimed victory, and although twice as many Americans were killed as British, the battle might more accurately be described as a draw, since the total casualites of each army were surprisingly close in number. Total American losses were 852—171 killed, 571 wounded, and 110 missing; British losses numbered 84 killed, 559 wounded, 193 missing, and the 42 prisoners captured by Jesup's regiment—a total of 878.[14] Considering the number of troops involved—about 4,500 British and 2,600 Americans—losses were extremely high.

The Americans claimed victory because their army had successfully repulsed every British attack during the five-hour battle and was in possession of the field when it left that night. The British claimed an ultimate victory because they returned to the field before daybreak the next morning and were so firmly in control that Ripley, who had replaced the injured Brown in command, dared not attempt, in view of his badly crippled army, to challenge the enemy. He not only left the scene but abandoned the camp at Chippewa and retreated fourteen miles to the ferry opposite Black Rock, a short distance below Fort Erie. Brown was indignant at Ripley's tardiness in obeying his instructions to return before dawn and maintain possession of the hard-fought ground. From his hospital bed in Buffalo, he ordered the army to encamp at Fort Erie.[15]

The morning after the battle, Jesup and the other wounded were taken by boat to Buffalo, arriving that evening. The boat transporting Scott, Jesup, and the other seriously wounded officers narrowly escaped plunging over Niagara Falls after leaving the mouth of the Chippewa, because the "towboat was large and unwieldy, and the soldiers (militia men) elected as oarsmen [were] feeble and inexperienced." [16]

Jesup was highly critical of Ripley's conduct after assuming the command. "Had General Drummond availed himself of this blunder, not a man of our Army could have escaped . . . but fortunately for his reputation, and that of the Country, Drummond outblundered him, and failed to avail himself of any of the advantages thus offered to him." Brown lost faith in Ripley and ordered General Gaines at Sackett's Harbor to go to Fort Erie and take over the command.[17]

Jesup was brevetted with the rank of colonel "for gallant conduct and distinguished skill" at the battle of Lundy's Lane. Brown, in his official report written from the hospital in Buffalo, paid special tribute to the "distinguished gallantry" of Generals Scott and Porter, Colonel Miller, and Major Jesup. Jesup, he reported, ". . . had succeeded in turning the enemy's left flank—had captured (by a detachment under Capt. Ketchum) Gen. Riall and sundry other officers, and showed himself again to his own army, in a blaze of fire, which defeated or destroyed a very superior force of the enemy."[18]

Jesup's wounds were slow to heal; he remained in Buffalo for more than six weeks. He and Riall, also badly wounded, recuperated in the same house, and the British general presented his sword to the young army major to replace the one broken in battle. Many years later, Capt. W. S. Ketchum, son of the late Capt. Daniel Ketchum, wrote to Quartermaster General Jesup to express his claim to the sword. He believed the weapon should have been given to his father for capturing Riall and then handed down to him. Jesup replied that after the battle he had directed the elder Ketchum to restore all captured swords to their British owners. Riall, unable to leave his room when the sword was returned to him, directed that it be presented to Jesup "as a small testimonial" of the young major's courtesy to him and his companions during their captivity. "I have always believed that he presented the sword to me, not so much as a personal compliment, as because his own command had broken my sword . . ." Jesup stated. "I retain the sword not as a trophy, but because it was presented to me by its owner."[19]

Still suffering from his wounds but no longer confined to bed, Jesup requested assignment to any duty he was physically capable of performing. During Jesup's convalescence, General Drummond had made an unsuccessful effort to regain Canada's Fort Erie. Brown, who had recuperated from his wounds, resumed command of the fort on 28 August, establishing headquarters at Buffalo on 2 September to facilitate recruitment and movement to Fort Erie of volunteers and militia from New York.[20] During talks with the general, Jesup learned that Brown was determined to attack the enemy in the trenches as soon as he could assemble a sufficient force. Although three of his wounds were still open and his right arm was in a sling, Jesup volunteered to join the garrison at Fort Erie, believing that his example of dedication might serve to inspire the troops. To enable him to do so, Brown dissolved the court-martial on which Jesup was then serving.[21]

With his right arm in a sling because of his crushed hand and injured shoulder, Jesup became ambidextrous. Using his left hand, he wrote from Buffalo to a friend, commenting on the shortcomings of the army and its imperfect organization: "If we avoid disgrace our country should consider us victorious." He was critical of the contract system of supplying the army: "Contractors have pecuniary responsibilities only, and should the Army be sacrificed by their neglect, the Nation can have no redress. . . . It is madness in the extreme to attempt to carry on war with such a system." Contractors, he felt, should be either dismissed or placed under military control.[22]

For the first time in forty-six days, Jesup left Buffalo, arriving to take command at Fort Erie on 9 September, despite his physical condition. A council of officers had just ended. Brown was obviously displeased with the council's result. He expressed himself in great warmth in regard to some of the officers. "We must keep our own counsel. The impression must be made that we are done with the affair: *but as sure as there is a God in heaven, the enemy shall be attacked in his works, and beaten too, so soon as all the volunteers have passed over* [from Buffalo]."

Drummond's forces, beaten back a month earlier, renewed their bombardment. For two days the British kept up a constant heavy cannonading. Shelling was intermittent during the next two days, but midmorning on 17 September, the firing once more became incessant. Brown summoned Jesup to inform him that he would be left with the 25th Infantry, about 150 strong, along with the artillery and invalids, to protect the fort and camp and to cover the retreat of the army should it be repulsed in its sortie. Brown and his troops moved out about 2 P.M., under cover of fog. The general attacked and carried the enemy's batteries and blockhouses, captured or destroyed one-third of the British force, and left the enemy without a single heavy gun or howitzer. His losses were 80 killed and 480 wounded, while British casualties were about 500 killed or wounded and 385 captured. Jesup wrote, "The sortie from Fort Erie was by far the most splendid achievement of the campaign, whether we consider the boldness of the conception, the excellence of the plan, or the ability with which it was executed. . . . To General Brown the whole credit is due."[23]

Drummond retreated behind the Chippewa after this defeat and took no further important part in the war. The Niagara campaign established Jacob Brown's reputation as a general; he later became commander-in-chief of the army. The Americans retained possession of Fort Erie until 5 November, when they blew it up, crossed back over the Niagara, and went into winter quarters. Jesup meanwhile made what was probably his last visit to his grandfather Blackleash Jesup, who died in March of 1816. Jesup continued his recuperation on his grandfather's farm in Wilton, Connecticut. On 18 November the young officer who had won distinction in the Niagara campaign, and who on 16 December would attain his twenty-sixth birthday, was back in Washington, where a surprise assignment awaited him.

CHAPTER 3

AN OFFICER OF REPUTE

WHEN BVT. COL. Thomas S. Jesup arrived in Washington in mid-November of 1814, the city was rife with rumors of peace, though definite word of the final settlement would not reach the nation's capital until mid-February of the following year. The administration was chiefly concerned with rumors emanating from New England. The Massachusetts legislature had invited the other New England states to send delegates to a convention to meet at Hartford, Connecticut, on 15 December.

New England grievances, both real and imaginary, had been accumulating since 1800, when the Republicans gained control of the government. With New England interests imperiled by the outbreak of war in 1812, opposition to administration policies was vigorously renewed. The Federalists attributed the poor showing of the military in the opening campaigns of the war to Republican mismanagement. At the same time, the Federalist-controlled New England states opposed taking an active part in the war and discouraged regular army enlistments. Massachusetts, Connecticut, and Rhode Island refused to fill federal government requisitions for militia. Difficulties in meeting army manpower needs continued throughout the war. In response to congressional request, Secretary of War James Monroe, who succeeded John Armstrong on 27 September 1814, proposed to raise a large force of men by conscription. His proposals brought a strong, unfavorable reaction from the Federalists. Their war opposition climaxed in 1814 when New England was invaded and the federal government failed to come to its defense.[1] President Madison was gravely concerned that the

James Monroe, secretary of war under James Madison and elected president of the United States in 1817.

Hartford meeting might lead the participating states to secede from the Union and form a Northern Confederacy.

Monroe had summoned Jesup to Washington to inform him that he was being ordered to Connecticut at the President's request. Ostensibly, as his orders indicated, Jesup was to recruit replacements for his 25th Infantry; in reality, he was to observe the convention proceedings and keep the administration informed of developments. Monroe verbally directed Jesup to make periodic confidential reports to him.[2]

Jesup was probably selected for the assignment in part because the 25th Regiment he had commanded at Chippewa and Lundy's Lane had been recruited largely from Connecticut. He was doubtless flattered by the confidence in him demonstrated by two top government executives. Further respect for the young officer was expressed by Army Adjutant and Inspector General Daniel Parker: "I have the honour to enclose to you the expressions of the favorable opinion entertained by the President and Sect. of War of your gallantry & Military character during the last campaign. . . . I hope you will do me the favor to accept assertions of my individual respect & regards."[3] Monroe's high opinion of Jesup never changed. Two years after completing his second term as president, he wrote to Quartermaster General Jesup that he retained the same feelings toward him that he had held in 1814: "In the late war our relation was always very friendly, & in some instances, particularly in your service at Hartford, during the session of the Convention, very confidential. I respected you also for your gallantry in the field, & have always entertained the same sentiments & feelings for you."[4]

During the two weeks Jesup spent in Washington before leaving for Hartford, he met frequently with Monroe. In their talks he divulged to Secretary Monroe that early in 1812, when war appeared inevitable, he had submitted to Secretary Eustis in a "confidential memoir" a bold plan for neutralizing the great superiority of the British navy in the event of hostilities. He had foreseen that the enemy would blockade the coast of the United States, and he knew that the British naval depot at Halifax, Nova Scotia, was the only place on the American side of the Atlantic where the enemy could recruit seamen and refit its vessels. Consequently, he had proposed sending a force at the outset of war to threaten Halifax. This move, he was convinced, would have compelled the British to concentrate their ships in the city's defense, leaving the seacoast free of blockade. Or, if the Americans had succeeded in capturing Halifax, the British would have been severely handicapped by having to recruit and refit in Europe. That necessity, he had predicted, would have made impossible British maintenance of an effective blockade.

Further, from his study of European maritime and military history, Jesup had concluded that great naval power depended less upon ships of war than upon seamen to man them. Many seamen in the coastal states earned their livelihoods from fisheries and commercial marine, he noted, and in each industry, the United States was second only to Great Britain. With strong government support, his plan could succeed in preventing a blockade, he had reasoned, allowing seamen to continue their work. The plan's success, he believed, would unify the country, dispelling the opposition to the war voiced in some states. The twenty-four-year-old Jesup had maintained that Britain's North American fisheries constituted "the principal pillar of British Naval power"; he believed that if the United States made the most of its opportunity, ". . . an entire revolution might be affected in the Naval and Commercial power of the globe; and . . . the Empire of the seas would pass from old to New England."

Eustis, Jesup related, "did not comprehend the subject and scarcely noticed it," other than to remark, "'Tis a very pretty plan, sir." But Monroe immediately perceived the plan's advantages and consulted President Madison, who approved it. Monroe then authorized Jesup to confer with leaders in New England on the subject, urging him ". . . at the same time to use the authority discreetly, and not commit the Administration without a reasonable prospect of support and cooperation on the part of the Northern people."[5]

At Hartford, Jesup discussed the subject confidentially with a convention delegate with whom he had considerable contact. His confidant advised him that if the administration were in earnest about taking the country on which the New England fisheries depended and were to assure that it would never be surrendered, New England would go along with the plan. He added, "We can take it as readily ourselves, as we took Louisburg in a former war [the Louisburg expedition of 1745]." Had the war continued,

Jesup believed, Halifax would have been a principal point in Monroe's plan of campaign for 1815, "as he often afterwards assured [Jesup]."[6]

Jesup's plan, drafted early in his career, indicates the extensive military knowledge he had acquired through studious habits as a youth. The plan revealed his talent, logic, and foresightedness—qualities which gained him the respect of high government officials more than twice his age.

Twenty-six Federalists attended the Hartford convention. Contrary to many dire predictions, the convention came under the control of conservatives. With few exceptions, its delegates were a distinguished group, including prominent judges, lawyers, and merchants. But their decision to conduct the proceedings in secret aroused suspicion and wide speculation. Wild rumors circulated that the delegates were planning such iniquitous schemes as conspiracy, nullification, secession, and treason.

Jesup arrived in Hartford as the excitement neared its highest pitch, after stopping in New York to confer with Governor Daniel D. Tompkins and sounding out sentiment in various sections of Connecticut. Before the convention, Jesup reported to Monroe that Tompkins thought the delegates would "complain, remonstrate, and probably address the people" but that the proceedings would result in neither an attempt to sever the Union nor a determination to resist the government's measures by force. From information obtained from his Connecticut friends, Jesup was inclined to the same view. Some men were willing to go all out to support the British, but though the leading Federalists, particularly in Boston, possessed wealth, they did not have the "influence attached to talents and character." They were well aware, he added, "that a single hour of revolution may deprive them of fortune and its consequent influence."[7]

When the convention convened on 15 December, Jesup was surprised at how little excitement it had aroused. While the majority of voters in Connecticut were Federalists, he reported, most of her fighting men favored the government. He suggested that brevets be given to Capts. George Howard, Thomas M. Read, and Edward White of his 25th Infantry, all of whom had "powerful connections" in Connecticut and should be able to provide valuable service to the government.[8]

Historian Henry Adams, in his account of the Hartford Convention, commented that Jesup, ". . . famous at Chippewa and Lundy's Lane . . . reported constantly to the President and War Department; but he could tell nothing of the convention that was not notorious. His letters were mere surmises or unmilitary comments on the treasonable intentions of the meeting."[9] This description of Jesup's reports may be fairly accurate, yet despite the lack of statesmanship displayed by Jesup as a raw recruit in the field of diplomacy, he established at least one valuable delegate contact and assured Madison and Monroe, based on his own soundings of public sentiment, that the people of New England would not support drastic Federalist action. He was correct in his early "surmises" regarding secession issues and the use of force. He observed "a degree of caution amounting almost to timidity" in the Federalists' opposition, "notwithstanding many of their acts have all the moral qualities of treason." The sole aim of the Federalists, he concluded, had been to intimidate the administration.[10] He had little opportunity to learn more of the convention's activities, since the meetings were conducted in strict secrecy.

After three weeks of secret sessions, the convention adjourned, made public its recommendations, and appointed a committee to present its demands—far less drastic than generally anticipated—to officials in Washington. The convention recommended seven amendments to the Constitution and proposed several ways of protecting New England interests. But all of their work came to naught, for while the committee was en route to Washington, its members learned on 12 February of Gen. Andrew Jackson's crushing defeat of the British troops at New Orleans. Two days later, officials in Washington confirmed rumors that the peace treaty had been signed at Ghent.

The adjournment of the Hartford Convention marked not the end but the beginning of vexing problems for Jesup during his Connecticut assignment. In October the state legislature had passed a law which, according to Jesup's predecessor in charge of recruiting, was designed to "lay the foundation for the exclusion of the U.S. recruiting parties in the future from incorporated cities within the State." He further maintained that the law was inexcusable because the recruiting officers had scrupulously respected the rights of citizens. No trouble had arisen between the soldiers and the citizens while he had been in charge of recruiting. "Martial music, to which a portion of this town are remarkably sensitive . . . , has not been permitted by me, nor by the officers under my command on the Sabath day, near religious meetings, courts of justice, or sick persons." [11]

On 5 January 1815, about two weeks after the convention was dissolved, the Common Council of Hartford, acting under the authority provided by the new state law, passed an ordinance intended to exclude federal troops from the city. Among other provisions, it banned troops from marching in certain areas, including the public square and principal streets of the city, and stipulated that a fine of ten dollars was to be imposed on every officer commanding any military corps "parading" in those streets and areas. [12]

Interpreting the law as an attempt by the city and state to usurp the powers of the federal government, Colonel Jesup met the challenge head-on. He informed the city officials that neither the state nor any city had the legal power to pass any laws governing United States Army troops and that he would resist attempts to enforce the ordinance. A committee from the council called at his office to assure him that his conduct and that of his command had been entirely satisfactory but that his predecessors had disregarded civilian rights. The ordinance was not intended, they told him, to correct any existing abuses but rather to prevent the recurrence of former abuses. Jesup replied that the city council had no right to make a law regulating his duties and contended that the legislature could not legally confer on any corporation an authority it had no right to exercise itself. Moreover, he told the committee, the legislature could not remove him or any recruiting officer from any point in the state. "I assured them that I would not be deter'd from the prosecution of my duty—that I conceived the passage of the law an act of usurpation, and that if an attempt was made to enforce it, it would become my duty . . . to resist it."

The next day when he called on the mayor to ascertain the city's plan of action, he was received politely. The mayor wished to make an arrangement satisfactory to both parties. Jesup felt that to enter into any definite arrangement would have been "an admission of [the mayor's] right to interfere." He did announce his willingness to make a disposition of the troops "as might conduce to the accommodation and convenience of the citizens." Jesup also gave the mayor distinctly to understand that he would "never acknowledge the right of any City or State authority to make rules & regulations for the government of Troops of the United States." Although the law had been sent to the printer for publication before Jesup's meeting with the mayor, the city officials seemingly had second thoughts; they withdrew the proposed ordinance from the printer. When Jesup left Connecticut in March of 1815, it was still unpublished.[13]

Civil authorities had taken other actions to harass recruiting officers and federal troops in general. "No regard is paid here to the laws or authority of the United States," Jesup wrote. One officer had recently been arrested for debt and was still confined to jail. Another had been fined; being without funds, he had been thrown into prison, where authorities insisted he remain until the fine was paid. In some areas, lawsuits had been brought against officers for debts of soldiers under their command, and recruiting officers were threatened daily with prosecution on charges of enlisting minors. If an attempt was made to seize the public stores, Jesup reported, "Whatever may be the consequences to myself, I will raise such a storm as this country has never witnessed, and which, in its course, shall overwhelm all those turbulent Demagogues who are labouring to overturn the Government." Despite all the difficulties, real and imaginary, he reported that recruiting was proceeding much better than anticipated.[14]

Late in January, the Connecticut legislature passed a law preventing army enlistment of minors. It declared that the law enacted by Congress to permit such enlistments was "repugnant to the Spirit of the Constitution of the United States, and an unauthorized interference with the laws and rights of this State." This Connecticut legislation originally provided for a fine of five hundred dollars or imprisonment for one year of anyone convicted of persuading a minor "to depart from this State, with intent to enlist him into the Army of the United States without the consent of his parents, Guardian & Master." Upon learning of this provision, Jesup instantly decided that if the measure passed as introduced, he would not submit to it; he had so advised several members of the legislature. To Monroe he wrote, "The Speaker of the House of Representatives and many other Gentlemen exerted themselves to have it amended, and it finally passed without the provision for imprisoning officers."[15]

Late in March 1815, Jesup was relieved of his assignment in

Connecticut and returned to Washington. With the war over, Congress, as was to become its general custom, wasted little time in whittling down the peacetime military establishment to its barest essentials. On 3 March, while Jesup was still at Hartford, it ordered the army reduced from its wartime peak of approximately sixty thousand to ten thousand—despite President Madison's warning against a hurried demobilization. The belief prevailed in Congress then and for many years thereafter that a large standing army was unnecessary; volunteers and militia could be depended upon to augment the small force of regulars in the event of Indian wars or other emergencies.

On 17 May, a board of officers was assembled to formulate plans for the reduction. The board agreed to separate the army into a Northern Division and a Southern Division, the dividing line to be the Ohio River, the southern boundaries of Maryland and Pennsylvania, and the western boundary of Indiana Territory. Maj. Gen. Jacob Brown was named commander of the Northern Division, and Maj. Gen. Andrew Jackson was to command the Southern Division. Both possessed identical status; each was supreme commander in his territory. In seeming contradiction to this arrangement, Brown was designated "Commander of the Army" on 15 June. One casualty of the reorganization was the Quartermaster's Department, which was abolished; its officers were discharged and replaced by four officers from the line to serve as brigade quartermasters. One important detail was overlooked: The Quartermaster's Department was still faced with such demobilization problems as settling claims and disposing of surplus property. Consequently, Quartermaster General Robert Swartwout and two of his deputies had to remain on duty until they could complete these tasks.[16]

Jesup was transferred to the 1st Infantry on 17 May 1815 and assigned to the Southern Division. Although brevetted a colonel nearly ten months earlier, his official rank and pay were still those of a major in the regular army, a brevet being only an honorary commission which the War Department could bestow in recognition of meritorious service without raising an officer's pay. During his recuperation from severe wounds and the busy months that followed, Jesup had neglected to settle his accounts as deputy quartermaster general supervising boat construction at Cleveland. Noting this oversight, Adjutant and Inspector General Parker ex-

Gen. Andrew Jackson, commander of the army's Southern Division in 1815, elected president of the United States in 1829.

empted Jesup from regimental duty until his accounts were settled. He directed him to notify General Jackson of his temporary change in status and to make monthly progress reports. In what was probably his first letter to General Jackson, Jesup passed the information along to the hero of New Orleans, adding that he would be in Chillicothe, Ohio. [17]

Jesup's chore of putting his papers in order was not simple. More than two years had passed since he had gone to Cleveland to construct the boats, and he had been on the move so much during the interim that his records were scattered. Moreover, the trunk containing his papers and vouchers had been on a boat that sank when he was crossing Lake Erie with Harrison's forces. He appears to have finished his disagreeable task by the end of July. Noting that Jesup had made no mention of his accounts in his monthly report of 31 August, Parker ordered him on 3 October to report to General Jackson for duty as soon as convenient. [18]

In New Orleans, Lt. Col. George Croghan was unhappy when he learned in mid-October that he was to be replaced as commander of the 8th Military Department by Brevet Colonel Jesup. Croghan immediately dispatched a letter to General Jackson requesting a furlough. He felt that Jesup was "a brave intelligent fellow," an officer to whom he was "fervantly much attached," but he was not pleased at being replaced by an officer much his junior. "In justice (excuse the expression) I should have been a Col. too." [19]

Jesup was delayed in arriving in New Orleans to take over command until 5 June 1816. Meanwhile, he too had been concerned about his status. Would his new assignment entitle him to his brevet rank of colonel and its perquisites? The question of how much weight a brevet rank carried was long a subject of controversy among officers and an embarrassment to the War Department. (Ironically, about seven years later Jesup himself would be called upon by Secretary of War John C. Calhoun to rule on the matter in a case involving the feuding Maj. Gens. Winfield Scott and Edmund P. Gaines.) Jackson held that Jesup would be entitled to only his rank in the line. The situation was somewhat complicated by the fact that the command of the department had been assigned to Bvt. Brig. Gen. Daniel Bissell. In his absence, Croghan, the next senior officer, had been placed in command of the regiment and department. Jesup was to replace Croghan. General Jackson, recognizing that "different opinions are entertained" regarding brevet rank, agreed to submit the matter to the secretary of war for clarification. Jesup won his point and the right to sign his dispatches as colonel while serving as commander of the 8th Department.[20]

Meanwhile, on 24 April, Congress had authorized further changes in the War Department. William H. Crawford, a Georgia lawyer and wealthy plantation owner who had served as a senator and as minister to France, had become secretary of war on 1 August 1815, succeeding Monroe. Crawford recommended that Congress establish a "stationary" army general staff, whose members would be permanently located in Washington in time of peace as well as war. The proposal was radical, since all staff officers, including the quartermaster general, had always been appointed only in wartime to serve with the principal army in the field. Congress failed to adopt the secretary's recommendation. Instead, it enacted legislation providing for one quartermaster general, with the rank of colonel, and a deputy for each of the two army divisions created a year earlier.[21]

Louisiana had been admitted to the Union only four years before Jesup arrived in New Orleans, and affairs in the Southwest were still in a state of turmoil. Both East and West Florida were owned by Spain, yet when Louisiana became the eighteenth state on 30 April 1812, it included a portion of West Florida claimed by Spain; the boundary question remained unsettled. American settlers, who had long been crowding into the Florida Territory, were demanding access to the Gulf of Mexico, barred to them by Spanish control of the coast. At the same time, Luis de Onís, the Spanish minister, was complaining to the United States about the activities of filibusters, charging that some had actually moved onto Spanish soil. The Spanish Empire was thought to be crumbling, yet reportedly the Spanish threatened to seize American territory. Because of the general uncertainty, the War Department instructed General Jackson to concentrate troops at New Orleans and Baton Rouge to meet any emergency.[22]

In the Southeast, Creek and Seminole Indians, who had retreated into Florida after their defeat by Jackson in the War of 1812, were again making border raids against settlers in Alabama and Georgia. British agents had led them to believe that the Ghent peace settlement provided for the restoration of the land they had ceded to the United States in the treaty of 9 August 1814. In the spring of 1816, Jackson, from his Southern Division headquarters at Nashville, sent General Gaines to guard the border. The general built Fort Scott near the mouth of the Flint River in Georgia, only a few miles from Spanish-held Florida.[23]

Fearing war with the Indians, Gaines had requested Croghan, then preparing to leave for New York, to send ammunition and other supplies to Fort Scott. One of Jesup's first responsibilities as the new commander of the 8th Department was to comply with this request. He decided to send more than had been requested and wrote to Jackson that he would forward to Gaines several pieces of artillery and a quantity of ordnance stores. The supplies could be spared; as they might be necessary "to insure success to the operations of the General," Jesup took upon himself the responsibility of furnishing them. Five companies of troops that Croghan had sent to Baton Rouge would be "held in readiness to march at a moment's notice." The next day Jesup arranged with Navy Commodore Daniel F. Patterson for a gunboat and the brig *Boxer* to provide a convoy for the transport.[24]

Jesup's prompt action in sending aid to Gaines met with Jackson's "highest approbation." Fortunately, Gaines had recently been advised of a more peaceable disposition on the part of the Indians. Aid from the 1st Infantry was no longer necessary, and the troops sent to Baton Rouge were to be "hutted" there. Jackson was much agitated about the "total deficiency of Quartermaster funds" in the 8th Department and had requested the War Department to remedy the situation.[25]

On 13 July, Jesup transferred his headquarters from New Orleans to Baton Rouge, 125 miles up the Mississippi River. About three weeks later, he received an ominous warning from Jackson to keep his troops on constant alert against possible attack by a Spanish force. He was admonished to exercise "the most cautious vigilance throughout [his] department, particularly . . . Mobile Point and Petite Coquille." The warning was based on Spanish accounts that the newly appointed governor of Cuba was reportedly on his way north with thirty-five hundred troops. Pointing out that negotiations with Spain were pending, the general warned that the presence of this strong force within a few days sailing time of Pensacola and that a portion of Florida claimed by the

Spanish monarchy "should awaken caution, if it does not excite suspicion of some hostile intention, or at least a disposition on the part of that Government to take advantage where opportunities offer."

Jackson assured Jesup that he was placing full reliance upon his "zeal, activity & military talents" and was depending upon him to forward the earliest intelligence of any hostile or suspicious movements of Spanish troops which might come to his knowledge. He wanted particularly to learn of attempts to reinforce or strengthen the defenses of Pensacola and urged Jesup to "use every exertion to acquire correct information."[26]

From the moment he read Jackson's letter, Jesup appears to have become obsessed with the conviction that war with Spain was a virtual certainty and began at once to make his plans accordingly. He hurried to New Orleans to arrange for strengthening the specified posts and to ascertain all he could about the activities of the potential enemy. He learned that the one hundred troops at Pensacola had been augmented by four hundred men. The small force was badly organized and of questionable loyalty to the Spanish government. The fortifications were in a state of disrepair, the guns were old and damaged with rust, the gun carriages were unfit for service, and the powder supplies were insufficient "to fire a salute."

Jesup found "outrageous in the extreme" the conduct of the men of Spanish-national vessels who were boarding American ships off the Louisiana coast and plundering some of them of their small stores. Two Spanish-national vessels were attached to Florida, he discovered, while seven other Spanish ships (four brigs and three schooners) were cruising between Pensacola and Havana. Jesup advised Jackson that if the Spanish made an attempt on Mobile or any other post of his department, and Commodore Daniel F. Patterson agreed to cooperate, he would take immediate possession of Cuba.

Jesup next sought the cooperation of Patterson and his naval force stationed at Bay St. Louis. He explained his intentions to the commodore, informing him that he could raise from three to four thousand men for this mission, which he believed, along with the naval force, would be ample: "Indeed, I would not wish to be embarrassed with a greater number of troops."[27]

Believing duty demanded he warn the administration of what he was convinced was a Spanish intrigue against the United States, Jesup addressed a confidential letter to Secretary of State Monroe suggesting his own plan for dealing with the crisis. He had "positive information" that the Spaniards were contemplating an attack on New Orleans. Reportedly, Spanish Minister Onís had agents in Louisiana who were trying to establish contact with individuals sympathetic to Spain and were using other means to organize a revolution. Jesup was not at liberty to reveal his source of information, but he assured the secretary it was reliable.

If Spanish forces attempted any hostile action, Jesup would strike directly at Havana, which he thought he could take and hold with three thousand men aided by a naval force—the same plan he had earlier outlined for Jackson. While his communication was not to be considered official, it might serve to put the government on its guard. "If I can ascertain that papers of a treasonable nature are in the hands of the Consul or any other Spaniard here, I shall not hesitate to seize them for the use of the Government."[28]

Jesup sent two more letters that day to Jackson. In the first, he reported the alleged Spanish plot and pointed out the woeful defense posture of nearly every post in his command. The weakest was Petite Coquille, which was "absolutely defenceless." Both Mobile and Fort Bowyer required considerable repairs, along with more heavy cannon. Gun carriages sent from Pittsburgh had proved to be entirely useless, and many more suitable ones were needed. The 8-inch howitzer shells procured from France did not fit the English-made 8-inch howitzers. Still, he expressed confidence in his ability to repulse any attack: "I feel no apprehension, however, for the safety of my department. My only fear is the Dons will not have the courage to attack me."[29]

In his second dispatch to Nashville, Jesup seems to have realized upon reflection that if an expedition were sent to Cuba, Jackson himself might want to lead it. Otherwise, Jesup thought himself entitled to the command: "It would afford me much pleasure to serve under you in such an enterprise but, as the plan is my own, I would not be willing to yield to another." The recent depredations committed by Spanish-national vessels on American merchantmen, he suggested, provided an excellent excuse for sending an officer to Havana. "Should you determine to send one

I hope you will employ me. It will afford me an opportunity of becoming acquainted with the country."[30]

New Orleans was filled with so many stories and rumors that to differentiate between fact and fiction was difficult. Jesup succeeded in becoming friends with a reputed confidant of the Spanish consul. When he obtained what he considered to be reliable information from this source, Jesup passed it along to Monroe:"A secret negotiation is said to be going on between the Courts of Madrid and London, for the purpose of transferring to Great Britain the Floridas and the Island of Cuba, for which it is understood she is to assist in reducing to subjection the revolted Colonies of Spain."

Jesup hurried off another confidential message to Monroe. The captain general of Cuba was allegedly acting in concert with Spanish Minister Onís in a scheme to "detach" New Orleans from the United States. "A paper purporting to be the translation of an extract from his last letter to his principal agent here has been shown me. He either has been, or is to be appointed Viceroy of Mexico, and is assembling an army with the ostensible object of putting down the insurrection there. He awaits large reinforcements from Spain." Those scheming to gain control of New Orleans were counting heavily upon the support of the Catholic population of Louisiana but would "find no countenance or support" there."[31]

On 8 September, in the fourth and last of his series of letters to Monroe on the subject, Jesup reiterated his determination to take over Cuba in response to a hostile Spanish movement. But he went much further: He urged the administration to order Cuba's seizure without waiting for further provocation. His eleven-page communication indicated the thorough study he had given the matter before reaching his conclusion that American seizure of Cuba might prevent future wars.

The United States had nothing to fear from Cuba so long as it was in "the feeble hands of Spain," he argued, but in the hands of Great Britain "it must become so formidable as to menace the independence of [America]." Because of Cuba's strategic location at the entrance to the Gulf of Mexico, he considered her the "key to all Western America"—militarily, commercially, and politically. A strong foreign maritime power, with the aid of a few battalions of troops, he pointed out, "could easily shut up the Gulf as England can the Baltic." That the United States keep its channels of commerce free from the control of foreign nations was of vital importance. "The military policy of the country should be to secure every assailable point," he emphasized.[32]

Jesup's plan to seize Cuba was not adopted. Great Britain did not purchase Florida, and war with Spain—an outgrowth of Cuban insurrection against Spanish rule—did not erupt until eighty-two years later. His correspondence in the summer of 1816, however, reflects both the tension between the United States and Spain and America's distrust of England.

On 11 September Jesup wrote Jackson from New Orleans that he had just received information that "a Spanish Royal Squadron, a few days since, attacked and captured the United States vessel *Firebrand*. . . ." This act, he was convinced, was but the prelude to further outrage.[33] He sent a similar letter to Secretary of War Crawford. The ship's capture proved to be an isolated incident; in the weeks that followed, no further attacks of this nature occured nor were any hostile movements on land reported. Threats of Spanish aggression appeared to be waning.

Calm prevailed throughout October. In Washington, Crawford had resigned his War Department post on 22 October to become secretary of the treasury. George Graham had been named acting secretary of war. Although Jesup still believed war with Spain to be inevitable, when by mid-November the situation at New Orleans still presented no immediate cause for concern, he decided he could safely leave the century-old city and return to his headquarters. He took passage on one of the early steamboats plying the Mississippi and headed upstream for Baton Rouge.

Coincidentally, he found awaiting him a letter from Col. Henry Leavenworth, who shared Jesup's indignation over a publication on the Niagara campaign attributed to Gen. E. W. Ripley. The general's account claimed that the entire American line had recoiled during the last British charge at Lundy's Lane and that the troops had been rallied only with difficulty. Leavenworth declared that the troops under his own and Jesup's commands had held their ground despite tremendous casualites, arguing that, had they not done so, the American army would have been annihilated.[34] Fate ordained that Jesup, after six months as commander of the 8th Military Department, would within a few days be serving under Ripley—the officer whose conduct had been the subject of his and Leavenworth's criticism.

Both Croghan and Jesup had headed the 8th Military Department when no general officer was available for the assignment. When finally one was available, it was, of all people, Bvt. Maj. Gen. Eleazer Wheelock Ripley. He took over the command on 5 December, announcing his first general order that he would establish his headquarters at New Orleans, rather than at Baton Rouge. Jesup's new assignment—Command of the 1st Infantry— remained the same, but he was given the additional title of commander at Baton Rouge. The ambitious Jesup must have been unhappy at this turn of the wheel of fortune, which represented a disappointing setback in a career hitherto marked by rapid advance. He pondered whether he should retain his new post at Baton Rouge.[35]

Despite earlier differences, relations between Ripley and Jesup appear to have been friendly, at least on the surface. Their correspondence was cordial. The general wrote that when the 8th Infantry arrived, he would collect the scattered companies of the 1st Infantry, concentrate them at New Orleans, and move them to Baton Rouge as soon as barracks could be provided.[36]

Jesup decided to retain his post at Baton Rouge and requested permission from General Jackson to visit the various recruiting stations. Ranks of the 1st Infantry were being depleted because the terms of many of the soldiers were expiring and because of a number of desertions. Such a trip, he believed, would enable him to help increase enlistments. From Jackson's headquarters came word that Jesup could make the tour as soon as the necessary arrangements could be made, but before the plans were completed, Ripley ordered Jesup to New Orleans to preside over a court of inquiry.[37]

After an absence of twenty-seven days, Jesup returned to Baton Rouge on 23 March 1817. His per-diem allowance for the New Orleans trip was one dollar. For transportation of his baggage, he was remunerated at the rate of two dollars per hundredweight per 100 miles traveled. Since the distance between New Orleans and Baton Rouge was calculated at 125 miles and he had 500 pounds of luggage, he was allowed $12.50 for a one-way passage. Upon his return to regular duty, he was finally able to make his long-delayed tour of recruiting stations. During the next two months he appears to have devoted the bulk of his time and efforts to speeding up enlistments. He signed his correspondence "Superintendent of Recruiting Service."[38]

Jesup's correspondence reveals that he made many friends in Louisiana—and a few enemies, intent on doing him harm, bodily or otherwise. Two of these—Maj. Reynold Marvin Kirby, assistant adjutant general, and Maj. William McDonald, assistant inspector general—were men he earlier would have little suspected of being unfriendly. Both were former comrades-in-arms who, like himself, had been brevetted for distinguished service in Brown's army on the Niagara. No precise reason has been found for their seemingly sudden animosity towards Jesup. Since both men were on Ripley's general staff, their antagonism may have stemmed from their close association with the general. They undoubtedly knew of the criticism Jesup had leveled at Ripley. Likely, out of a sense of loyalty to their commander, they took it upon themselves to defend him.

Kirby threatened Jesup with a physical attack or a challenge to a duel on the field of honor; McDonald appears to have adopted a less violent and more subtle course of action—a verbal assault in reports to the War Department. When Jesup learned of the reports, he wrote to Acting Secretary Graham that he considered it his duty to protest any credit being given to Major McDonald's reports which might be construed to censure him or his command. He had reason to believe the major was hostile to him, adding, ". . . as he understands neither the wants nor the duties of a common soldier, I, of course have but little confidence in his reports."[39]

Jesup wrote in a similar vein to the adjutant and inspector general: "From the conduct of General Ripley and his staff towards me, I have determined never again to serve under his command." McDonald, he added, "has been in the habit of calumniating me, by the most infamous falsehoods and as soon as I arrive at Washington City I shall prefer charges against him for lying." Whether Jesup took the threatened action is not clear, but three years later, on 17 October 1820, McDonald was dismissed from the service.[40]

Although Ripley continued to be cordial, Jesup had found cause to suspect him of duplicity. A widely circulated report (later proved true) said that Ripley had secretly offered Jesup's post as commander of the 1st Infantry to another officer. Jesup was so incensed at this affront that he seriously considered a resort to dueling pistols. He also determined that the duel, if it occurred, would be with the commander himself, not with one of his subordinates.[41] Though in this era duels were commonplace in America —a more or less accepted method of settling a point of honor— so far as records reveal, Jesup considered only this one during his career.

General Gaines was among the friends who sought to dissuade Jesup from doing anything rash. The veteran officer had heard of the matter at his headquarters far to the east. "I write to warn you of what I am sure your own sense of propriety will have suggested . . . Your reputation stands in no need of your permitting yourself to become a mark of intriguing demagogues, and the tool of demagogues to shoot at." After expressing his high personal regard for Jesup and his desire to have him serve under his command, Gaines added: "Let no petty combination of intriguers deprive the public of your service . . . believe me when I assure you, you are, in my estimation, above the reach of your enemies."[42]

Whether heeding the advice of Gaines or his own judgment, Jesup decided against challenging Ripley, though his suspicions concerning the general's duplicity were confirmed in a letter from Lt. Col. William A. Trimble in Natchitoches, Louisiana. In response to a communication from Jesup, Trimble admitted that Ripley had indeed offered him the command of the 1st Infantry five months earlier. He had been invited to the general's headquarters and offered his choice of the commands at Baton Rouge or Natchitoches. Trimble, who had informed the general that he preferred a small command, was later assigned to Natchitoches.[43]

About that time, Jesup received word that President Monroe, on 20 April, had promoted him to the full rank of lieutenant colonel in the 3d Regiment. He was ordered to Washington to settle his accounts. Ripley made the announcement on 13 June in a general order which noted that Jesup was "relieved in pursuance of his own request from the command of the 1st [Regiment] & of the Cantonment of Baton Rouge." No hint of animosity marred the warm tribute the general paid the departing officer. Ripley tendered his thanks to Jesup "for the faithful, assiduous & attentive manner" in which he had discharged his duties. He expressed his "sincere regret" of losing from his immediate command the services of so valuable an officer.[44]

Jesup left New Orleans on 5 August aboard the *Governor Griswold* for the long trip to Washington by way of the Mississippi, the Gulf of Mexico, and the Atlantic Ocean. Upon his arrival he found a letter from Lt. Trueman Cross of the 1st Infantry, giving him news from Baton Rouge, where the two men met and developed a lasting friendship. (When Jesup later became quartermaster general, Cross was among the first officers he selected for his department, and the two were intimately associated for nearly three decades until Cross's tragic death in 1846.) Cross wrote, "I did expect that you would scarcely have left [this] sod, before invectives would have been heaped upon you from different quarters, . . . and I was prepared to hear them—but I must say, I have been agreeably disappointed. I have rather heard you eulogized by those from whom the most inveteracy might have been apprehended." Cross had been told: "[General Gaines] has required of Genl R. a positive contradiction of some statements set forth in a pamphlet (perhaps) entitled his memoirs, and is anxiously waiting an answer. So it seems the clouds are . . . lowering and they must burst ere long to the Consternation of some of the parties concerned."[45]

Although he had been ordered to Washington to settle accounts, Jesup soon found himself sitting on another court-martial case, during which he received a letter from Maj. Gen. Jacob Brown, commander of the Northern Division. Brown offered him the post of adjutant general of his division, soon to be made vacant with the resignation of Col. Charles K. Gardner. The person who fills that office, Brown wrote, ". . . must not only be my official organ in most cases, but I desire also that he should be my confidential friend, and selected from that class of officers who were most distinguished during the late war." Brown had no doubt that the office would be as permanent as any in the army. "I certainly would not desire you to accept it," Brown added, "did I not believe that it would . . . have a tendency to elevate you to a higher station with as much certainty as any situation you can at present fill." President Monroe had agreed to approve Brown's nominee.[46]

Jesup was flattered by the general's offer, which would mean another advancement in rank and the chance to serve under a man who had demonstrated his friendship—a welcome relief after his experience with Ripley. Yet he had to delay his acceptance until he finished putting his accounts in order. Then, too, he was assigned to yet another court-martial, this time in New York, over which he presided from 24 December until 17 January 1818. Three days after the court adjourned, he was in Philadelphia, from where he enclosed to Adjutant and Inspector General Parker a copy of an order from General Brown assigning to him the duties of adjutant general of the Northern Division. Jesup finally arrived at Brownville on 27 March 1818 to assume officially his new role with the full rank of colonel.[47]

During the winter of 1817-1818, the first important step was taken toward a thorough overhauling of the army organization in an effort to correct the deficiencies which Jesup and others had long recognized. President Monroe appointed an astute secretary of war who made a study of the weaknesses in the military service and took meaningful measures to rectify them. The president, during his first seven months in office, had sought without success to find a man both capable and willing to tackle the job. He had approached Henry Clay and a number of lesser figures, but all had declined. Finally, on 8 October 1817, somewhat reluctantly, he offered the post to John C. Calhoun. Possibly Monroe was adverse to welcoming into his official family the influential and highly popular senator from South Carolina. The thirty-five-year-old Calhoun, aspiring to higher office, hesitated for many weeks before accepting the proffered post. He eventually took the oath of office on 8 December and turned his attention at once to reorganizing the War Department.

The heart of Calhoun's plan was the establishment in Washington of an army general staff directly responsible to the secretary of war. Heretofore such staff officers had served with the army in the field, usually only in wartime. As proposed, each would now head a permanent department in the nation's capital, thereby creating the first bureau system in the federal government. Its continued existence in peacetime was designed to provide greater

John Calhoun, secretary of war under James Monroe.

efficiency in the management of military operations in wartime. Calhoun's proposals were embodied in the legislation Congress enacted on 14 April 1818, providing the legal basis for the long-overdue War Department reorganization.[48] Members of the general staff included the quartermaster general, the adjutant and inspector general, the judge advocate general, the commissary general of subsistence, and the surgeon general.

The alert and ambitious Jesup followed the proceedings in Congress with keen interest. For two years the army had been divided into Northern and Southern Divisions, each with its own quartermaster general. If Congress approved, as seemed likely, Calhoun's recommendation that the army be reunited under a single commander, only one quartermaster general would serve. Never one to pass up even a remote opportunity for advancement, Jesup wrote to Sen. John J. Crittenden of Kentucky on 9 March requesting support of his candidacy for the office. That was more than a month before Congress enacted the legislation and eighteen days before he assumed his duties as adjutant general of the Northern Division, a position that would be abolished under the proposed reorganization. Crittenden's reply was most favorable and offered encouragement.[49]

On 30 April, Calhoun revealed his selection for the post of quartermaster general—not Colonel Jesup, but William Cumming of Georgia, a former colonel who had resigned from the army in March of 1815 after only two years of service. Three days before the order was published, Cumming wrote the secretary of war that he was "compelled reluctantly to decline" the offer, "as an acceptance would be altogether inconsistent with [his] present pursuits." He thanked Calhoun for this "mark of confidence & friendship," and added: "The new organization of the Q. M. Department will I trust remove many abuses."[50]

According to Calhoun, "No branch of the general staff is more important or difficult to be managed than the quartermaster's; none requires more eminently the control of a single responsible head."[51] Congress agreed. It provided that the department was to include, in addition to the two deputy quartermasters general and four assistant deputy quartermasters general already authorized, one quartermaster general and as many assistant deputy quartermasters general as the president deemed necessary but not to exceed twelve in number. The newly authorized permanent department was to consist of a total of nineteen officers. Since it could also use the services of eighteen regimental and battalion quartermasters, the personnel thereby totaled thirty-seven.[52]

CHAPTER 4

BIRTH OF
A SUPPLY BUREAU

"HEREWITH ENCLOSED YOU will receive the appointment of Quarter Master General and the Secretary of War directed me to require you forthwith to repair to this place as he wishes to adopt some arrangements for your Department before he leaves the City."[1] That brief message from Brig. Gen. Daniel Parker, the adjutant and inspector general of the army, was addressed on 8 May 1818 to Brig. Gen. Thomas S. Jesup at Brownville, New York, then serving as Gen. Jacob Brown's adjutant general. The 29-year-old Jesup who was being promoted the third time in slightly more than a year, was now entitled to the rank, pay (three thousand dollars a year), and the emoluments of a brigadier general. He thus became the first quartermaster general of the army to have permanent Washington headquarters.

When the letter finally reached him on 24 May, he expressed surprise: "One hour before receiving the appointment, I had as little expectation of it as taking a voyage to the moon. It places me in the second rank in the army; and presents a more extensive field than any other military situation in time of peace." He was concerned only about obtaining the necessary security. He need not have been troubled. Both James Findlay, his close friend at Cincinnati, and his former commander, Gen. William Henry Harrison, were more than willing to sign his bond.[2]

The trip to Washington took eight days. He arrived on 4

June—too late to see either Secretary Calhoun or President Monroe. Both were on a tour of the defenses in the Chesapeake Bay area until mid-June. Jesup took up residence at Mrs. Peyton's boardinghouse and devoted his full attention to the task of organizing the Quartermaster's Department under the provisions of the new legislation. In a letter to the secretary of war, he outlined his views concerning his department and the personnel to staff it: "I am well aware that some reputation is risqued in the attempt to give system to a Department, which has hitherto in our service, been in a state of confusion and disorganization." He was sure that with Calhoun's support he could make the department first in the army, as were similar departments in all European services. "I wish to give it that character, and those features, which will render it efficient in time of War, and which in both peace and war, will insure a strict responsibility in all of its branches," he added.

He proposed that the duties of his office be performed by a staff of young, intelligent subalterns who had seen active service in the field and were familiar with military procedures rather than by professional clerks with no service background or military knowledge. Thus his office could serve as a training ground for developing officers competent to perform the various functions of the department. "By employing young officers thus we shall have a corps compleately educated in time of peace, from which an efficient staff may be formed in time of war," he wrote to Calhoun.[3]

Jesup actively assumed his duties on 15 June. For ten years a student of the military affairs of the French, Prussian, and British services, he intensified his study in search of ideas that might assist him in organizing his department on an efficient, practical, businesslike basis. By examining the correspondence of earlier quartermasters general—Gens. Thomas Mifflin and Nathanael Greene and Col. Timothy Pickering, who had served in the Revolutionary War—he learned of past administrative policies in the American army. From his study of these sources, and his own experience in the staff and line, including several stints as a quartermaster, he evolved his concept of the nature and functions of the Quartermaster's Department and the rules and regulations which were to guide its officers for many years.

Within the framework of Calhoun's reorganization plan,

Jesup was given a free hand in formulating the rules and regulations of his department and in selecting the officers to perform its functions. His first appointees were drawn from all sections of the country. For the rank of captain he named Trueman Cross of Louisiana, Thomas F. Hunt of North Carolina, Hezekiah Johnston of Pennsylvania, J. S. Findlay of Missouri Territory, Thomas S. Rogers of Georgia, and his boyhood friend, James C. Pickett, who lived in the Alabama Territory. Selected for second lieutenants were Thomas Johnson of Maryland and Charles Burbridge of Connecticut. Jesup described his appointees as men of education, intelligence, and honor. The new quartermaster general established his office in Room 14 on the first floor of the War Department Building. He ordered Captain Cross at New Orleans to report without delay to serve as deputy quartermaster general in the Washington bureau. An officer who served as clerk completed his office staff. (Women were not employed as government clerks until long after Jesup's era.) Captain Hunt, designated as the other deputy quartermaster general, was stationed at New Orleans. Hezekiah Johnston was assigned to Pittsburgh, and the veteran William Linnard, who had been a military agent as early as 1802 and later a deputy quartermaster during the War of 1812, was retained at Philadelphia. The other assistant deputies were stationed at various posts through the country.[4]

In formulating his regulations, Jesup made certain that he retained control over the officers he appointed. Deputies or assistants assigned to the posts at Philadelphia, New York, Pittsburgh, Detroit, St. Louis, and New Orleans could not be removed from their stations except by the authority of the War Department. No quartermaster was to be detailed or employed on duties other than those of the department except by order of the secretary of war or a general commanding a division.[5]

Jesup also imposed a code of conduct—applicable to all personnel in the department, including himself—for the maintenance of the highest standards of integrity. A rule drawn from his study of Revolutionary War practices stated that no officer of his department was to be permitted to engage, either directly or indirectly, in trade or traffic of any description nor to accept any gift from anyone with whom his department might have business transactions. He never departed from this rule. Years later, in the midst of the Mexican War, when a New Orleans business firm presented him a "pic nic case" as a gift, Jesup promptly returned it.[6] By precept and example, he encouraged, from the beginning of his administration, the maintenance of high standards in the conduct of the department's business. When Boston newspapers criticized the quartermaster there for giving drafts to his own brother in the procurement of supplies, Jesup was satisfied the officer had done nothing illegal. However, he admonished him: "You have lived long enough in this world to know that it is necessary not only to act correctly, but to pursue such a course as to put it out of the power of malignity itself to misconstrue your motives." He advised the officer that when supplies were required he was "to create as much competition as possible either by giving public notice . . . or by written notes to the principal dealers in the articles which may be necessary."[7]

The nature of the Quartermaster's Department and its functions were described by Jesup in rules and regulations submitted to Calhoun on 17 July, which the secretary approved without change. As Jesup defined them, the objectives of his department were: "To ensure an ample and sufficient system of supply. To give the utmost facilities and effect to the movements and operations of the Army. And to enforce a strict accountability on the part of all officers and Agents charged with monies and supplies." As one writer noted, "A better conception of the duties of the department has never been put in so few words."[8]

Specifically, the Quartermaster's Department was responsible for transporting troops and supplies by land and by water. When movement was by land, the department procured wagons, horses, mules, and oxen and hired teamsters. In the interest of economy, the department had authority to contract for the transportation of supplies. It also procured forage for the animals used on its supply lines and by any mounted troops. If the troops moved by water routes, the department bought or built boats—flatboats, keelboats, steamboats—for use on rivers and lakes. When the army was engaged for the first time in overseas operations during the Mexican War, the Quartermaster's Department chartered seagoing vessels to transport troops and supplies. The department was also responsible for quartering the troops. In the field, it procured all camp equipment and tents. To house the troops at posts, it built barracks, which required the department to procure tools, nails, lumber, and a wide variety of materiel. In time, additional duties were turned over to the department, the most important of which was the estimate, procurement, and distribution of clothing for the troops.

The duties of the quartermaster general, as set forth in his regulations, placed upon him responsibility for an unbelievably heavy workload in view of his small staff. In brief, he was to perform the following duties:

Maintain permanent headquarters in Washington but be ready to go any place his presence was necessary or his services required.

Direct all correspondence of his department (which at times was voluminous).

Acquaint himself with all frontiers — maritime and interior — and with the "avenues leading to the contiguous Indian and foreign territories"; with the resources of the country, particularly in districts on the frontier; with the most eligible place for concentrating troops and supplies in relation to both offensive or defensive operations; with the military force in different sections of the country; with the relative expense of concentrating troops at particular points; and with the prices of all articles of quartermasters supply and the cost of transporting all supplies.

Ensure the construction of barracks and storehouses.

Designate the sites for depots; the routes for transportation and communication between the different posts and armies.

Prescribe a uniform system of returns, reports, statements, and estimates for the department.

Maintain, under the direction of the secretary of war, complete control over his deputies and assistants, and generally over all officers and agents acting in, or making disbursements on behalf of, the department, in all matters relating to the administrative part of their duties and their accountability. (Military control over these men remained with their commanding officers.)

One of the most important features of Jesup's regulations was a system of strict accounting for money and property, a grave deficiency in past supply administrations. All monies for the operations of the department were to be drawn by the quartermaster general and distributed by him to the disbursing officers as needs arose.

Their receipts served as his vouchers or evidence that he had transmitted the money, and the person receiving the funds then became responsible for handling the money. All subordinate officers of the department were required to submit quarterly accounts, both of money and property, to the Office of the Quartermaster General for examination and transmittal to the proper accounting officer in the treasury. In the event the accounting officer suspended or disavowed any voucher, he returned it with a written statement of his reasons for such action, to the quartermaster general, who then ordered the quartermaster concerned to send a proper voucher or give a satisfactory explanation. Whenever practical, the senior quartermaster of each separate army or military department could be required to receive and account for all monies for the service of that army or department. All officers of the Quartermaster's Department were directed to furnish their accounts for settlement at prescribed times; those who failed to do so were to be replaced.

The books and accounts of quartermasters could be inspected whenever deemed necessary by the quartermaster general. This inspection, which was to include property as well as money, could extend to all other phases of department activities, such as contracts, prices of articles purchased, and costs paid for transportation. The books and accounts of the quartermaster general were likewise subject to inspection. The inspectors were to report all orders of commanding officers involving expenditures in violation of the regulations. A later regulation, for example, prohibited an expenditure in excess of five hundred dollars in peacetime for the erection or repair of barracks or quarters at permanent installations unless ordered by the secretary of war.

The system of accountability which Jesup originated and upon which he was willing to rest his reputation made each individual accountable for his own acts and made it mandatory for those who received money or property to show how they disposed of it. To provide uniformity, he also prescribed the report forms. Under pain of dismissal, he made sure that quartermasters furnished all required reports and by close scrutiny assured that their reports were correct in every detail. His responsibility, he believed, was as much to compel subordinates to settle their accounts as to enforce their performance of any other duty. Through orders and instructions, by providing the prescribed blank forms for reporting the varied and expanding operations of his department, and through the periodic issuance of quartermaster regulations, he placed his department on a practical, businesslike basis.

Separate regulations were often issued to cover specific functions, such as the handling of clothing and equipage or transportation. In time, the basic principles of accountability set forth by Jesup were extracted and embodied in the general regulations of the army and became applicable to all supply services. Changes in the army and in the responsibilities of the Quartermaster's Department during Jesup's lifetime and in subsequent years naturally brought some modifications, but the essential characteristics of the system he introduced remained, as a study of army regulations will show.[9]

While Jesup was preparing the regulations for his department, Gen. Winfield Scott was engaged in assembling and arranging material for a project of wider scope. Almost three years later, he completed his proposed regulatory code for the army. Jesup served as a member of an eight-man board of officers to review these regulations and add to, alter, and clarify them as necessary. When the first complete code was published in July of 1821 under the title "General Regulations of the Army," Jesup's regulations, devised in 1818 for the Quartermaster's Department, were, with slight modifications, embodied in it.[10]

Before Jesup became quartermaster general, no uniform system of reporting and accounting had existed. His study of earlier quartermaster operations also convinced him that much of the previous confusion and disorganization had stemmed from the lack of appropriate measures to enforce regulations. When he found even minor errors in the vouchers submitted to his office, he returned them to the responsible quartermasters for correction. He gave the same close attention to the quarterly abstracts and monthly summary statements of the officers, making sure they were correct in every detail. Jesup was a strict disciplinarian and promptly rebuked those who did not abide by the regulations or whose conduct he considered improper. But an acute sense of justice made him just as quick to bestow praise when it was due. His correspondence is replete with examples of both commendations and censures. Little evidence suggests that officers of his department resented his criticism and strict discipline. Perhaps the fact that his officers knew he required of himself the same scrupulous exactitude that he asked of them accounted in part for his outstanding success as an administrator.

His close supervision of subordinates trained them to become competent quartermasters and enabled him to exercise control over the most minute details of his administration. Undoubtedly, Captain Cross, who worked beside the quartermaster general as his deputy in the Washington office, profited most from the supervision during the early months. Cross proved an apt pupil; in a relatively short time, he was able to take some of the heavy load of work off the shoulders of the chief.

Another frequent irregularity encountered by Jesup early in his administration was the unauthorized purchase by quartermasters of items which were the procurement responsibility of other departments. Such actions had long been permitted to go unchecked. Though regulations governing accountability had been prescribed in the past, they had been inadequately enforced, and quartermasters had not been aware of their precise procurement responsibilities. Their purchase of items for which they were not responsible promoted confusion in expenditures. Jesup's concern and persistent overview of the minutia of quartermaster duties kept accounts and thus expenditures in order and maintained control over the disbursements of his appropriation. When such unauthorized purchases came to light in abstracts received in his office, he deleted the items, reprimanded the quartermasters guilty of the infractions, and cited the specific paragraph of the regulations violated. Sometimes Deputy Cross did the reprimanding. When, for example, the assistant quartermaster general at Boston procured drums, fifes, and musical instruments and charged the purchase to the quartermaster account, Cross pointed out that the instruments were classed as ordnance items, since they were a "species of accoutrement and a substitute for arms in the hands of the musicians."[11] They should therefore have been paid for out of the Ordnance Department appropriation.

The quartermaster general could reprove officers of his own department who made such procurements. But when commanding generals ordered the purchase of items they were not authorized to have, his only recourse was to appeal to the secretary of war. For example, when Gens. E. W. Ripley and Daniel Bissell ordered the assistant deputy quartermaster general at New Orleans to purchase unauthorized penknives and spyglasses, Jesup requested Calhoun to hold the two commanders accountable for the amount of the purchase.[12] A commanding officer was responsible for ordering the supplies necessary for his command. But Jesup insisted that to obtain his authorized supplies the officer must apply to the supply department responsible for them and follow the regulations. Enforcement of this concept of quartermaster responsibilities brought some clashes between line and staff, which were resolved only gradually. Jesup was intent on exercising his control, for any diversion of departmental funds from the purposes for which they were appropriated resulted in the development of arrearages — certain to bring congressional criticism during consideration of appropriation bills.

Jesup also made special reports from time to time to the secretary of war. In a report dated 19 October 1818, he noted a sharp increase over the years in peacetime appropriations for the Quartermaster's Department and explained why they would continue to rise. From $165,000 in 1801, appropriations had climbed to $260,000 in 1811 and to $460,000 in 1818. He ascribed the rise to the constant extension of the frontier, increased prices of supplies, and the remote location of many military posts, rather than to the growth of the army. With the population of new states and territories increasing so rapidly that their inhabitants were consuming the greater part of their surplus produce, Army supplies necessarily had to be drawn from greater distances at increased expense.[13]

Only ten months after he became quartermaster general, Jesup found himself actively supervising supply preparations for a military expedition on the western frontier. To control the Indians, promote the fur trade of American trappers, and exclude foreigners from that profitable market, the War Department had begun to build a chain of forts. So rapidly had settlers moved into the area after the War of 1812 and so far-flung were the operations of the fur traders—ranging to the Rockies and beyond—that the existing military frontier provided inadequate protection. When Secretary of War Calhoun proposed to establish a new military frontier farther westward, the War Department organized two expeditions to carry out his plans.

The major expedition was to move up the Missouri River and establish a fort at the mouth of the Yellowstone River—a distance of some 1,800 miles. Along the way the troops were to erect intermediate posts 650 miles above St. Louis at Council Bluffs and, nearly 900 miles further on, at the Mandan village (just north of the modern city of Bismarck, North Dakota). Since the Mandan village was the nearest point on the Missouri to the British Hudson's Bay Company outpost on the Red River, Calhoun considered it the place "best calculated to constrict [British] hostilities to [America] or influence with the Indians." The other, shorter expedition was to ascend the upper Mississippi River to the mouth of the St. Peter's (now the Minnesota) River, and build a fort (near the present city of St. Paul, Minnesota). A strong post there was very important; it would be in the path of the "great thoroughfare of the British trade with the Indians," and would, together with Fort Armstrong at Rock Island, Illinois, constitute one of the most commanding posts on the upper Mississippi.[14]

The shorter expedition was not scheduled to begin until early in the summer of 1819, but Calhoun insisted that an immediate attempt be made to establish the Yellowstone post. On 16 March 1818, he instructed Brig. Gen. Thomas A. Smith, commander of the 9th Military Department with headquarters at St. Louis, to organize a detachment of riflemen to undertake the mission. The assignment came nearly two months before Jesup was appointed quartermaster general and three months before he organized his department, while other staff bureaus were also still being formed. Consequently, the burden of providing provisions and transportation for the detachment fell upon General Smith, while the Ordnance Department and the commissary general of purchases supplied the military stores and clothing. Preparations took much longer than anticipated. Not until 30 August did three companies of riflemen under Lt. Col. Talbott Chambers set out in three keelboats from Belle Fontaine, above St. Louis. Calhoun realized that the late start would prevent the detachment from reaching the Yellowstone before winter, but he hoped the expedition might get as far as the Mandan village. Battling the Missouri current, the keelboats made slow progress. After two months, the men reached Cow Island, only four hundred miles above St. Louis. They could go no farther; ice had formed in the river and they were running out of provisions. Erecting Cantonment Martin for protection against the cold, the 272 riflemen spent a dreary winter hunting game in the wilderness to keep from starving.[15]

This inauspicious beginning made it evident that more adequate preparations would have to be made when the Missouri expedition resumed its efforts to reach the Yellowstone in 1819. The failure of the 1818 expedition had been due in part to the fact that the army supply system was in a period of transition. With the task of setting up staff departments in Washington completed, their officers were taking an active part in the arrangements. However, the newly created office of commissary general of subsistence was not authorized to assume its function of supplying provisions for the army until June of 1819. Rations for the expedition, according to plans, were to be on hand well in advance of that date. Thus subsistence would have to be provided through existing contracts, held by James Johnson of Kentucky, for provisioning troops at various western posts. Early in the winter of 1818, Calhoun had ordered Johnson to deposit 420,000 rations at Belle Fontaine by 21 March 1819; he later directed him to furnish an additional 250,000 rations by 1 May.[16]

Johnson solicited a transportation contract under which he would provide steamboats to transport both troops and supplies for the expedition. He had an influential ally in his younger brother, Richard M. Johnson, who was not only an old friend of Calhoun's but also chairman of the House Military Affairs Committee. Serving as his brother's lawyer and agent, Richard Johnson was instrumental in convincing Calhoun that steamboats should be used on the expedition.

Upon the shoulder of Quartermaster General Jesup rested the responsibility for supervising the transportation of troops and supplies for the expedition. He strongly opposed the use of steamboats by a civilian contractor for such an important undertaking. That the military should have complete control of the venture was vital, he contended. His army experience had led him to have little faith in contractors. Moreover, steamboats were still in the experimental stage; none had yet been tried out on the Missouri River, and he was skeptical that they would be successful. When Richard Johnson, acting in behalf of his brother, submitted the contract to him for approval, Jesup delayed his decision for fifteen days, reluctantly signing it on 2 December 1818, at Calhoun's insistence. But his skepticism persisted. Four weeks later when he informed

James McGunnegle, his assistant quartermaster general at St. Louis, that he had signed the contract "by order of the Secretary of War," he instructed him to retain all transports until it was "ascertained whether the Steam Boats succeed."[17]

At the suggestion of Maj. Stephen Long of the Topographical Engineers, a scientific corps was added to the expedition to explore the country between the Mississippi and the Rocky Mountains. The corps, under Long, was to have its own steamboat, to be built at Pittsburgh with funds provided by Jesup's department. The *Western Engineer* was a seventy-five-foot stern-wheeler mounting three brass cannon. Its grotesque appearance was deliberately designed to overawe the Indians. Its figurehead, carved to resemble the head of a sea serpent, was engineered so that smoke belched ominously through the nostrils. The strange-looking boat was completed in March of 1819.[18]

James Johnson had the contract to furnish steamboats, but he did not have the vessels; they were yet to be built. By 1 March 1819 he was to deliver two steamboats capable of navigating the waters for which they were intended, and they were to be subject to the orders of the quartermaster general. If they proved successful, Johnson was to furnish additional steamboats should they be required. If they failed, he was obligated to provide keelboats. Since steamboats had never navigated the waters in which they were to operate, no rate of remuneration was established. Johnson was to provide the boats on a cost-plus basis, with the government allowing him a reasonable compensation, the amount to be determined later.[19]

While the steamboats were being constructed on the Kentucky River near Frankfort, the War Department ordered more troops to St. Louis. Col. Henry Atkinson, commander of the 6th Infantry Regiment, was designated to command the Missouri expedition. He and his troops were then stationed at Plattsburgh in the northeast corner of New York State. To reach Council Bluffs on the Missouri, they had to travel more than twenty-six hundred miles by way of Pittsburgh and St. Louis. Their journey from Plattsburgh to Council Bluffs constituted the longest American military expedition to date. Jesup later referred to it as the most important and most expensive peacetime operation yet undertaken.[20] Calhoun appointed Brig. Gen. Daniel Bissell commanding officer at Belle Fontaine to succeed Lt. Col. Talbott Chambers. He selected

Col. Henry Leavenworth, commander of the 5th Regiment, to head the expedition up the Mississippi, and ordered Brig. Gen. Alexander Macomb to occupy the post on the St. Peter's when it was established. [21]

Jesup was busy preparing for his first extensive logistical operation since taking office. He requested Quartermaster McGunnegle at St. Louis to assist him in estimating the cost of transporting troops and supplies by furnishing all available information concerning navigation on the Missouri and Mississippi, including distances from St. Louis of all existing and contemplated posts and other pertinent points, obstructions in the rivers, and the prices being paid for transportation. He directed Quartermaster Johnston at Pittsburgh to have transports in readiness for five hundred troops of the 6th Regiment due to arrive there from Plattsburgh about 10 April and for a detachment of riflemen (recruits) who were marching to Pittsburgh from Philadelphia. He wrote to Calendar Irvine, commissary general of purchases, that his department was greatly inconvenienced because clothing and other stores intended for troops on the Mississippi and its tributaries were being deposited at the depot at Newport, Kentucky. He pointed out that stores intended for St. Louis "would go more securely and at much less expense" if they were sent direct from Pittsburgh, eliminating the need for rehandling at Newport. He wrote James Johnson that he expected to see him in Kentucky early in April. [22]

As War Department preparations neared completion, on 27 March Calhoun ordered Jesup to proceed to St. Louis, as soon as official duties would permit, to supervise the movement of troops and supplies. Jesup informed Calhoun that his deputy, Captain Cross, would direct the Washington office during his absence and left the city for the first time in the ten months he had been in office. [23]

Meanwhile, after their long trek from Plattsburgh, Atkinson and his 6th Regiment arrived at Pittsburgh and on 8 May began moving down the Ohio toward St. Louis in ten keelboats furnished by the Quartermaster's Department. Atkinson reached St. Louis on 1 June. On the eighth, he notified James Johnson that everything was in readiness to move up the Missouri upon arrival of the steamboats and their cargoes. Johnson, however, was still not ready to comply with the terms of his contracts; he was having financial difficulties as well as trouble with his steamboats. [24]

Jesup, at St. Louis awaiting arrival of the steamboats, was incensed at the delay and regretful that he had been persuaded to approve the Johnson steamboat contract. Before leaving Washington he had advanced $45,000 for construction of the boats. At Lexington, Kentucky, on his way to St. Louis, he had given Richard Johnson a draft for $10,000 more, upon assurance that the boats were ready and adequate arrangements had been made for the provisions. The contract called for Johnson to have one steamboat ready to move from St. Louis by 5 April, another by 1 May, and a third by mid-May. By 12 June, none of the boats had arrived. Jesup was apprehensive: "If the business be not taken out of the hands of Colonel Johnson, I fear but little will be accomplished this summer." Even if Johnson failed completely, Jesup assured Calhoun he was determined that the posts at Council Bluffs and at the mouth of the St. Peter's would be established before winter. He was on his way to the mouth of the Ohio where, he had been informed, a great part of the provisions and two of the steamboats were detained.[25]

Undoubtedly, Jesup would have been even more incensed had he known that Richard Johnson, writing from Kentucky, was bombarding Calhoun with urgent pleas for—and getting—additional advances for his brother. In justice to the Johnsons, it should be noted that they were experiencing the impact of the 1819 panic. "It is impossible to describe to you the distress of this [western] country. Loans cannot be obtained from Banks or individuals . . . nothing can be purchased on credit," Richard Johnson informed the secretary. His first three letters, written within a week, contained fervent appeals for a further advance of at least $50,000; he further asserted that the government would be perfectly safe to advance $100,000. He enclosed "certificates of honorable men" as proof that Jesup's estimate of transportation costs "upon which [the] advances have been predicated was the ordinary price upon [America's] . . . most frequented rivers." If the additional funds were provided, the expedition would "go on with dignity, honor, success & brilliancy"; if not, his brother would be ruined and the expedition would fail. Nothing the administration had done before had so excited the western people and received "half the interest & satisfaction" as the plans for the expedition. If it failed for lack of further advances, he intimated, the administration might suffer at election time.[26]

Fearful that Richard Johnson might be correct in his contention that the expedition would fail without the additional funds, the secretary granted the $50,000 requested. He also approved two drafts drawn on him by Richard Johnson. Moreover, he instructed the commissary general of subsistence to advance an additional $35,000 on the Johnson subsistence contract—but only if the advance were absolutely necessary to save the expedition. Although it by no means marked the end of their repeated requests for more and more funds, the Johnsons did complete—far behind schedule—four steamboats and headed them toward St. Louis. The *Calhoun* was to be the flagship of the Johnson fleet, but that ill-fated vessel broke down and never reached St. Louis. The *Expedition*, the *Johnson*, and the *Jefferson*, with much difficulty, managed to reach Belle Fontaine, where the contractor was beset by more trouble. The Bank of Missouri had obtained a judgment against him in a civil suit. If he landed his boats at Belle Fontaine for inspection, they would be attached by Missouri authorities, and Colonel Atkinson refused to accept the supplies without inspection. After much wrangling and delay, Johnson moved the boats downstream to the Illinois shore. Inspectors found the provisions he had supplied to be poor in quality and short in quantity.[27]

When Jesup learned of Calhoun's $50,000 advance, he branded as "entirely incorrect" Johnson's claim that the expedition would fail without it. The $55,000 which he had himself advanced "was more than the whole expedition ought to have cost—more than it would have cost, had Colonel Johnson not been employed." The troops had been waiting nearly a month, yet only a small portion of the provisions contracted for had been delivered, and it was "almost reduced to a certainty" that Atkinson would be compelled to purchase additional provisions. If the contract system were abolished, Jesup contended, the army might be supplied more efficiently, at savings of from 10 to 20 percent. He added, "Colonel Johnson is zealous, but he is entirely unqualified for the business he has undertaken. He has neither the requisite energy, nor the talent for arrangements. Had we relied upon him the expedition must have failed."[28]

Jesup was determined that, despite delays, the expedition would reach Council Bluffs before bad weather. He arranged for more keelboats and also for his department to furnish a large quantity of stores to make up for Johnson's deficiencies. Late in

June, the three steamboats finally reached Belle Fontaine. Two weeks earlier the first detachment of troops had started up the Missouri in five keelboats provided by Jesup's department. It consisted of 270 riflemen under the command of Colonel Chambers, who had led the ill-starred expedition the year before. The troops were to go as far as Fort Osage, near the present city of Sibley, Missouri, and await the arrival of the steamboats. They were followed by the 6th Infantry, the main body of troops, who embarked on 4 and 5 July. With steamboats able to accommodate only half the men, four companies had to be placed aboard keelboats furnished by the Quartermaster's Department. On 9 July, Jesup left Belle Fontaine and, in company with Atkinson, made the trip to Fort Osage by land. Leavenworth and three hundred men of his 5th Infantry, who constituted the main body of troops for the Mississippi expedition, had reached Fort Crawford at Rock Island, Illinois, on 30 June after a journey of nearly seven weeks by water. They had sailed from Detroit on 14 May and traveled by way of Lakes Huron and Michigan and then over the Fox and Wisconsin rivers. Another detachment of the same regiment had begun moving up the Mississippi from Belle Fontaine after being detained by the late arrival of recruits and Johnson's delay in furnishing supplies. Since no steamboats were available for either detachment, they, too, had left on keelboats furnished by the Quartermaster's Department.[29]

As part of the cost of financing the Missouri and Mississippi expeditions, Congress had appropriated $190,000 for transportation. Of that sum, $140,000 was for transporting troops and stores and $50,000 for transporting provisions. Before the two expeditions left Belle Fontaine, Johnson had already received nearly $180,000, yet he had been able to provide transportation for only half of the troops of the Missouri expedition. Of the 680,000 rations he had agreed to furnish, he actually supplied about 350,000. Moreover, as Jesup reminded him, he had not informed the quartermaster general of his plans, if any, for furnishing provisions and transportation for the Mississippi expedition. Jesup also accused Johnson of taking "improper advantage" of the quartermaster at Louisville by requiring him to pay three dollars per hundredweight for transporting clothing, stores, and medical supplies from Pittsburgh to St. Louis when the usual freight rate between those cities was $1.75. He refused Johnson's requests for

further advances, declaring that the contractor had already received more than twice what the transportation costs would have
been had the business been left to the Quartermaster's Department.[30]

If Jesup believed that the Johnsons would not be able to
wheedle any more advances, he underestimated the resourcefulness
and persuasive powers of the contractor's brother. When President
Monroe arrived in Kentucky on a western trip early in July, Richard Johnson seized the opportunity to describe to him in glowing
terms how well the expedition was going so far as his brother was
concerned. He impressed the chief executive with the wide popularity of the undertaking and the stoic patriotism of the Johnson
brothers in the face of great adversity; he also suggested that more
money was needed to save the expedition. When Monroe authorized a further advance of $85,000 in the transportation and sub-
sistence contracts and $57,000 more upon delivery of title to the
steamboats, Richard Johnson made no attempt to conceal his
elation. "I shall never be done acknowledging my gratitude to the
President & yourself. I have never met with men so much entitled
to my gratitude & friendship, altho the support rendered is nothing
but what corresponds with justice, liberality, policy, and public
duty."[31]

The president's authorization on top of Calhoun's and Jesup's
earlier liberal advances to the Johnsons dealt a severe blow to the
budget of the Quartermaster's Department. With less than half the
fiscal year gone, its appropriations were nearly exhausted. An
appeal would have to be made to Congress to cover a "very heavy
arrearage." The secretary expressed grave concern in his reply to
Johnson, stating that the War Department would be "exceedingly
embarrassed" before the end of the year. He begged Johnson to
make no further drafts without his consent; a sheer lack of funds
might compel him to refuse payment. Before Calhoun's communication reached him, Johnson had written several more letters to
the secretary. His notes had been protested by the Lexington
Branch of the United States Bank, he told Calhoun, and he had
taken the liberty to draw once more upon the War Department.
He heaped praise upon his brother and the secretary, adding that
Jesup, "this good man this gallant & faithful officer [had] permitted his mind to be poisoned & operated upon" by the enemies of
the Johnson brothers. In his letter of 9 July he enclosed title to

the steamboats, thus enabling him to take full advantage of the president's authorization.[32]

Jesup, busily engaged in supervising the transportation of the two expeditions moving into wilderness country, was unaware of the president's large advance to the Johnsons and the precarious financial status of his department. Calhoun explained the situation in a letter dated 19 July which Jesup did not receive until six weeks later. While the recent drafts of the Johnsons as a result of the president's action had increased the "embarrassed state of funds in [Jesup's] department," the secretary believed other departmental expenditures to be greater than they should be. He had ordered an investigation into the disbursements of several officers of the department, because it appeared to him that they had expended funds which should have been charged to other departments. The "greatest degree of economy and energy will be necessary to prevent very considerable arrearage at the close of the year," he wrote, adding that Jesup should return to Washington "as soon as the state of movement upon the Missouri and Mississippi will permit." He expressed full confidence in Jesup's "vigour & skill to remove any impediment which is in the way of a complete and economical execution of the plans of the Government."[33]

Although Jesup was responsible for all money expended by his department in connection with the expeditions, he discovered that James Johnson was drawing on his funds without his knowledge or consent. Both men were in the same area, but the contractor was simply ignoring Jesup. Such lack of military control over contractors was one of Jesup's objections to the contract system. When Calhoun learned of these unauthorized drafts, he called Richard Johnson's attention to the matter: "You will at once see in what an awkward predicament this places the Department and I do hope it will not again be repeated." Once more he urged Johnson not to draw without his assent and thus subject Calhoun to "the painful necessity of refusing [his] bill." Johnson protested that he would be ruined if the secretary did not make drafts available to him: "The arrival of the President was a day of joy to us all . . . but my joy is of short duration—my money matters are again deranged, my credit affected, and my peace of mind disturbed. . . . I appeal to your friendship to liberality & to your justice for such advances . . . as will meet my bills."[34]

By mid-August, advances to the Johnsons on the transportation contract with the Quartermaster's Department approximated $250,000, not including the $107,000 authorized by the president. Of this amount, Jesup personally had advanced only $55,000. Yet the Johnsons had furnished far less than half of the transportation required for the expeditions, and Jesup's department had supplied the balance. Now, Richard Johnson had appealed for still more funds. Monroe, back in Washington and briefed on the situation by Calhoun, agreed the time had come to call a halt to the endless advances. The president, the secretary wrote Richard Johnson, had concluded that the advances already made were "as great as he can consistently with propriety authorize at the present." He pointed out that, excluding Monroe's authorization and $41,000 for the steamboats, advances from the Quartermaster's Department funds totaled $212,000; if the cost of the steamboats were included, the sum was "upwards of $250,000." The advances, he felt, had been "very ample," and, according to Jesup, would "greatly exceed" the amount due James Johnson at the expiration of his contract the following June.[35]

Upon his return to St. Louis from Fort Osage on 26 August, Jesup found Calhoun's letter awaiting him. Stunned by the large advance the president had made to Johnson from the department's appropriation and the additional $50,000 that was being deposited to Johnson's credit in the Missouri Bank, Jesup wrote the contractor that since all the funds of his department were being placed at Johnson's disposal, the contractor must make the disbursements for transportation: "I have therefore instructed Captain McGunnegle to call upon you for such sums as may be necessary to enable him to discharge the boats which were employed in consequence of the deficiency of your arrangements."[36]

Meanwhile, the Johnson steamboats had proved to be more of a handicap than an asset to the expedition. Even with only partial loads, they lacked sufficient power and sturdiness to make headway against the swift and treacherous Missouri current. One by one the boats had to be abandoned and their cargoes transferred to keelboats sent from St. Louis by the Quartermaster's Department. The steamboats, Jesup wrote Calhoun, "are badly constructed, and the management of them is worse than the construction." The *Expedition*, after its load was lightened, arrived at Fort Osage on 18 August, but the *Jefferson* had bogged down below the fort, and the *Johnson* made it only to a point near the mouth of the Kansas

River. The troops left Fort Osage on 23 August aboard keelboats, and the *Expedition* reached Cantonment Martin at Cow Island in five days. There, the last of the Johnson steamboats was abandoned and the troops, transported by sixteen keelboats, arrived on 29 September at Council Bluffs, where, about seven hundred miles above the mouth of the Missouri, they erected Fort Atkinson. One steamboat did reach Council Bluffs and was there when the main body of troops arrived in keelboats. Colonel Long's grotesque *Western Engineer* had made the long trip from Pittsburgh without mishap, proving that properly constructed steamboats could navigate the Missouri. The Mississippi expedition had achieved its objective a month earlier. After their seven-week journey by water from Detroit, Leavenworth and his 5th Infantry had reached Prairie du Chien on 30 June but had been delayed there more than five weeks waiting for Johnson to deliver subsistence and supplies. Finally, on 8 August, Leavenworth and his men began the ascent of the Mississippi in keelboats furnished on Jesup's orders. They arrived at the mouth of St. Peter's River on 24 August and began constructing the fort that the government had directed to be built there.[37]

Jesup was not surprised to learn from Calhoun that his department's appropriation was nearly exhausted. "I had expected to receive such information at a much earlier date," he admitted, citing numerous reasons for the heavy drain of funds. Despite the "enormous" advances to the Johnsons, his department had had to furnish more than two-thirds of the transportation for the two expeditions. Large sums had also been applied to the service of the Ordnance Department. Congress had made no provision for the sizeable arrearage of the previous year, which had been deducted from the current appropriation. Moreover, the $50,000 which Calhoun had recently placed to the credit of James Johnson in the Bank of Missouri had not been used for the public service as the secretary had intended; instead, Johnson had sent $30,000 of it to Kentucky and the remainder to Illinois. "I cannot consent to be considered responsible for any operations with which Colonel Johnson is connected," Jesup insisted. In response to Calhoun's stated belief that disbursements not connected with the expeditions were too large, Jesup said the funds of his department were expended by commanding officers "as their caprice may dictate, without regard to laws or regulations. The consequence is, that the appropriation remains charged with the amount of improper disbursements until the accounts of the disbursing officer are adjusted."[38]

Jesup remained at St. Louis until he was satisfied that the two expeditions would reach their respective goals for 1819. Before leaving, he outlined plans for resuming the expedition to the Yellowstone the following spring. If steamboats were to be employed, the best interests of the country would be served "by affording a fair competition to the owners of such vessels in the Western waters."[39]

Back at his desk in Washington after an absence of six months, two problems demanded Jesup's immediate attention. First, he must reduce his department's expenditures and exercise strict economy in its operations. All government agencies were reacting to the effects of the Panic of 1819, which was bringing a severe depression throughout the country. Overexpansion of manufacturing facilities in the East and the even more significant extensive purchase of land by settlers on long-term credit in the West as well as general land speculation were suddenly brought to a halt when banks curtailed credits. Payments fell in arrears, some state banks collapsed, and the overall economic situation became extremely critical. Retrenchment was the order of the day. Army expenditures must be cut to the bone, and Jesup was sounding warnings to all officers of his department.

Although retrenchment and economy could reduce future expenditures, the lack of control over its own disbursements was to blame in large measure for the existing financial straits of the Quartermaster's Department. Cross, while serving as acting chief, discovered that departmental funds were being expended without his knowledge and by authority of Calhoun himself. Cross learned by accident on a visit to the Treasury Office on 1 October that of the $200,000 he had on hand as of 26 July, only $32,000 remained. Yet he had issued requisitions for only $61,200. The remainder, nearly $107,000, had been drawn on drafts authorized by the secretary without informing the acting chief. When the War Office followed that procedure, Cross wrote Calhoun, the chain of responsibility was broken. The chief of a department could not be held accountable for the application of an appropriation which he did not control.[40]

The second problem demanding Jesup's attention concerned the entanglement with the Johnson brothers. Settlement of the controversy over the Johnson contracts was to be submitted to arbitrators, and Jesup was responsible for preparing the government's case against the contractor's claims. Late in December 1819, James Johnson presented his bill for service under his transportation contract. It contained other surprises than its size. He submitted a claim of $20,533 against the government for detention of two steamboats at the mouth of the Missouri for cargo inspection. He demanded payment in full for all transportation performed during the expedition, though most of it had been furnished by the Quartermaster's Department when Johnson's steamboats broke down. He charged $15,000, at the rate of $50 a head, for transporting three hundred officers and men in three steamboats to Council Bluffs, despite the fact that none of the boats got within five hundred miles of that place. This total claim was figured to the last penny—$256,818.15. Along with the bill, he sent some caustic remarks about Jesup, Colonel Chambers, Quartermaster McGunnegle, and others. The quartermaster general, he declared, had devoted little time to him and had not afforded him an opportunity to explain his difficulty with the St. Louis Bank.[41]

"The charge for detention cannot in justice be made or allowed," Jesup wrote Calhoun. He maintained that Johnson's failure as a contractor was responsible for the delay. He charged that the contractor, while the other two steamboats were being inspected, had deliberately detained the *Jefferson* below St. Louis with its cargo of ordnance stores and clothing "to put it out of the power of the commanding officer to move the troops." He branded as "extravagant in the extreme" the contractor's charges for transportation between St. Louis and Council Bluffs. In answer to Johnson's complaint against him, Jesup stated that it was not his custom to trouble himself with the private affairs or personal quarrels of any man. He also defended Captain McGunnegle: "It is due to that officer to state that there is not an abler man of his rank in the Army, and that for correctness and attention to duty he is surpassed by no one. . . . " McGunnegle, he pointed out, had acted under the order of Colonel Atkinson and himself; if the course the captain pursued was incorrect, the blame should attach to his superiors, not to him. He surmised that the captain's only "offense" was that he transported public stores for $5.50 per hundred pounds over the same route for which Johnson was demanding from $16.25 to $20.[42]

By this time, opponents of Calhoun were raising questions in Congress regarding the cost of the Missouri and Mississippi expeditions and the amounts still to be spent to attain their objectives. Calhoun asked Jesup to prepare reports answering congressional queries.[43] The secretary had hoped to continue the work of the Missouri expedition in the summer of 1820, but when the House struck $50,000 from the funds allotted to the Quartermaster's Department, the expedition was doomed.[44]

Still to be settled was the matter of Johnson's claims. On behalf of the government, Jesup prepared a lengthy statement regarding those claims and submitted it to arbitrators early in February. Among the arguments he advanced for rejecting the contractor's claims was Johnson's failure to comply with the terms of his transportation contract. In addition to being delivered late, the provisions Johnson furnished had been deficient both in quality and quantity, and a considerable additional supply had to be procured before the expedition could move. His failure as a contractor had not only jeopardized the expedition but had also caused the government to spend $100,000 more than the whole expedition would have cost had he not been employed. The detention of the steamboats at the mouth of the Missouri had not been occasioned by the government or its agents but by the neglect or failure of the contractor himself. When his steamboats proved incapable of navigating the Missouri, he had made no provisions to replace them with keelboats, as his contract required. His charge of $533.33 per day for steamboats was out of proportion to their real value. He was demanding three times as much for his transportation service as the Quartermaster's Department had paid for similar services. Why, Jesup asked, should Johnson's boast of his patriotism have any bearing on the case? "His *Patriotism* is admitted to the fullest extent, but it cannot be allowed to affect the price of transportation; indeed it is believed, that his is the first instance in which *American Patriotism* has been considered a marketable article."[45]

Jesup's arguments were to no avail. For reasons which are not clear, the arbitrators allowed Johnson's claims in full. When a dispute arose over the findings, Jesup was not in Washington, having been sent to West Point to serve on the Board of Visitors. In his absence, Deputy Cross protested the decision, and Calhoun asked the arbitrators to interpret their ruling. Their decision, however, remained final. Nine months later, a House committee, investigating the arbitration findings, passed a resolution requesting the attorney general to use all legal means to set aside the award and "to recover, for the United States, whatever may be due from Colonel James Johnson."[46]

In March of 1820, Congress directed its attention to the War Department budget. The economy bloc soon made it apparent that the army was in deep trouble. Calhoun's request for $1,500,000 to carry out existing contracts for coastal fortifications was sliced in half. Nearly $100,000 was pruned from Jesup's estimate of $526,000 needed for operation of the Quartermaster's Department. The clothing allowance for the army was reduced by one-third. The United States Military Academy came under attack, and several speakers proposed that it be abolished. Charges were made that the army was too large and the troops too widely scattered, and that the number of officers was disproportionately large. As usual, some congressmen maintained that a standing army was not necessary, particularly in peacetime. The discussion came to a climax only four days before summer adjournment, when the House passed a resolution directing Calhoun to prepare a plan, to be submitted at the beginning of the next session, for reducing the army to 6,000 officers and men.[47]

While Congress debated the army's fate, Jesup pointed out in a detailed study that the many disasters suffered by its fighting forces in the War of 1812 were the consequence of the country's neglect of its military establishment in the period following the Revolutionary War: "Thirty years of peace and prosperity had left us without military knowledge—the champions of the Revolution had almost descended to the Tomb; those who survived had become enfeebled by age or had lost by want of practice their aptitude for military service." The energies of the young nation had been directed to politics and commerce, and "little mind was left to be applied to military affairs." General Washington, aware of the importance of military knowledge to the country, had endeavored to form an establishment which might perfect and preserve it and had created a staff suited to the exigencies of the service. John Adams had improved the staff, but the succeeding administration not only abolished it but destroyed the army. At the start of the War of 1812, Jesup noted, the national treasury was "uselessly squandered by the inefficiency of the administrative branches of the staff—the corps were without organization or discipline—their supplies of the worst quality and as bad as they were, not regularly serviced." Consequently, "more than half of the force was generally in the hospital or the grave before the commencement of a campaign," Jesup wrote.

While support of a large military establishment in time of peace was not practicable, Jesup considered it of immense importance to educate and retain in the service a large body of officers who could train soldiers, supply them, and put them in motion. Therefore a staff should be created in time of peace, "with a view to a state of war," and the administrative corps should be so organized that it could be attached to either the regular army or the militia, which would constitute the greater part of the active force in time of war. "The frequent changes and mutilations of the Staff have been a serious evil in the operations of all the departments of the army —one system has scarcely been known before another has been adopted and the consequence has been an ignorance of all . . . ," Jesup charged.

Quartermaster and commissary departments, he asserted, demanded "the most sedulous care and the liberally fostering hand of the government," because success in time of war depended in such large measure upon the "able arrangement and proper discharge" of their duties. "It is truly astonishing that so little attention should have been paid to the organization of corps, so essential to the well-being and efficiency of the army and even the existence of the soldier." This lack of attention Jesup attributed to an "entire absence of military intelligence" on the part of the public and to "false notions of economy."[48]

During the summer of 1820, Calhoun—conferring with Jesup and the other top-ranking officers—worked out his plan for reducing the army to 6,000 men, as the House resolution stipulated. Both the secretary and the officers hoped that the reduction might be accomplished in such a way that the basic military organization would remain sufficiently intact to allow its rapid expansion in the event of hostilities, without having the addition of new regiments or battalions. When he submitted his plan to Congress in December, Calhoun proposed that the staff be retained virtually at full strength and that the reduction be carried out by simply reducing the enlisted personnel in each company to half strength. In case of war, the army could then be returned to full strength by doubling the number of privates in the existing companies, "instead of creating a new army to be added to the old, as at the commencement of the late war." If necessary, the strength might be augmented further by slicing each company in half to form two companies and then adding the required number of officers and recruits. This plan would enable the government to obtain a regular force adequate for any emergency, properly organized and prepared for actual service, with no need to "new-model or create." The secretary also argued that the military organization "ought to be such as to induce, in time of peace, citizens of adequate talents and respectability of character to enter into and remain in the military service of the country, so that the Government may have officers at its command, who, to the requisite experience, would add the public confidence." He argued that if it was worth having an army at all, it was worth having it well commanded.[49]

Calhoun's plan was ingenious and probably as reasonable as any that could have been devised to achieve the reduction; yet while some members praised it, Congress as a whole failed to grasp its logic. The principal objection raised was that the plan reduced only the line and not the staff. Those who objected demanded that reductions be made across the board. Supporters of Calhoun's plan were outnumbered. Consequently, both the secretary's advice and the experience of the War of 1812 were ignored on 2 March 1821 when Congress enacted legislation which not only reduced the army to 6,183 officers and men but also emasculated the staff organization.[50]

The new law was a severe blow to Jesup and his staff. It abolished the eighteen regimental and battalion quartermasters and reduced the number of Jesup's assistants from eighteen to twelve. Of the thirty-seven officers who had served in the department since 1818, only thirteen were retained. At the same time, the department's workload was increased with the reduction of the Purchasing Department to a commissary of purchases and two military storekeepers. Previously, the personnel had included a commissary general of purchases, two deputies, six assistant commissaries of issue, and "as many military storekeepers as the service may require." Lacking sufficient personnel, the Purchasing Department could no longer perform its functions; so Calhoun, of necessity, transferred to Jesup's department the responsibility for distributing, accounting for, and preserving army clothing as well as preparing estimates for its requirements. Heretofore the Quartermaster's Department had been responsible only for its transportation.

Thus the labors and responsibility of Jesup's department were nearly doubled, while his work force was reduced by nearly two-thirds. In addition to himself, his department now consisted of two quartermasters with the rank, pay, and emoluments of majors of cavalry, and ten assistant quartermasters to be taken from the line and paid an additional sum of not less than ten dollars nor more than twenty dollars per month. Congress apparently assumed that the 50-percent cut in army strength would bring a corresponding reduction in the workload of the Quartermaster's Department. Actually, as Jesup pointed out, its workload was not dependent upon the number of troops in service but rather on the number and remoteness of the posts occupied, the extent of the frontier, and the dispersed state of the nation's military resources.[51]

The legislation made one concession designed to compensate the Quartermaster's Department in some measure for its drastic reduction in personnel. It gave the secretary of war authority to order assistant commissaries of subsistence to serve in the additional capacity of assistant quartermasters. The number was not to exceed fifty, and all were to be taken from the line. In practice, this double-duty theory did not provide much relief to the Quartermaster's Department. The assistant commissaries were kept so busy with the duties of their own department that they had little if any time to assist quartermasters. "The experience of every department proves that the only way to insure strict accountability is to confine officers to the duties of their own branches of service, to compel them to perform them, and positively to prohibit their interference with those of others," Jesup pointed out. The number of officers attached to Jesup's department was "entirely inadequate to the proper and efficient discharge of the duties required of them."[52] Jesup made repeated attempts during the years following 1821 to get his staff augmented, but not until 1826, when the workload of his department was once more increased, did he meet with any success.

The new legislation in 1821 also abolished the two divisions into which the army had been divided since 1816, providing for only one major general. As Jacob Brown was the senior officer, he was retained as commander-in-chief of the army. The army was reorganized into an Eastern Department, to be commanded by Winfield Scott, and a Western Department, to be commanded by Edmund P. Gaines.

In consequence of the retrenchment in 1821, Zachary Taylor faced the loss of his commission; only through the efforts of Jesup was he retained in the army. Taylor greatly appreciated Jesup's efforts: "I was not mistaken in attributing my retention to your friendly interference. The numerous acts of friendship I have recd. from you since our acquaintance I can assure you will not be forgotten."[53]

In March of 1820, Taylor had joined the 8th Regiment, then constructing a military road from Madisonville, Louisiana, to Columbia, Tennessee. The costs were heavier than previously calculated and would, he informed Jesup, fall very heavily on his department, particularly for transportation. The 8th Regiment was composed "entirely of recruits without organization, subordination, or discipline, and without harmony among its officers." The part of the regiment assigned to his command numbered about 420 men whom he found upon his arrival to be near starvation, having been for nearly six weeks "on half rations, & in a country where nothing could be procured except beef, of the poorest kind, waiting for supplies from New Orleans . . . with only five days rations on hand." Taylor's quartermaster was without funds, and the credit of the government was nearly exhausted.[54]

Through their exchange of letters, Jesup learned much about conditions in the field, and Taylor was kept informed of developments in Washington. The two officers exchanged views on the growth of West Point. Taylor hoped that nearly all of the officers in the future would be graduates of West Point but was fearful that a military education would be of little service "unless practice was blended with theory." If a choice must be made, it was better to have a "practical" rather than a "theoretical" soldier. Unfortunately, because of the American passion for building roads, fortifications, and barracks, "the ax, pick, saw & trowel, has [sic] become more the implement of the American soldier, than the cannon, musket, or sword."

Taylor, who had seen a copy of Jesup's report on the tragedy of military unpreparedness, called it "able & interesting," and he hoped Congress would "profit by the light [Jesup had] thrown on the subject." He considered Jesup's plan of establishing "large depots in time of peace well supplied with all the munitions of war, on the great avenues leading to the frontiers" much more important than covering the frontiers with fortifications. He was in complete agreement concerning the importance of "educating and retaining in service, officers sufficient in each department to organize and put in operation a respectable army in the event of war."[55]

Although Jesup wrote Taylor in the summer of 1821 that he was contemplating a southern inspection tour, he did not request permission to make the tour until 6 September. He wanted to look into the many abuses at the southern posts in the expenditure of public money and property. He had planned to leave about 20 September to visit posts in Louisiana, Florida, and Georgia, but illness delayed his departure. From Philadelphia on 18 October he wrote that he was "extremely weak from the effects of a severe attack of fever, accompanied by a stricture of the lungs." Three days later he had recovered sufficiently to sail from New York aboard a steamboat bound for New Orleans. During the four months Jesup was on tour over most of the southern section of the country, visiting Georgia and Florida for the first time, Captain Cross was again in charge of the Washington office. As a result either of the "exercise of traveling, or the influence of the mild climate," Jesup's health was restored.[56]

CHAPTER 5

A BACHELOR
TAKES A WIFE

BEFORE RETURNING TO Washington from his southern tour
Jesup visited Locust Grove, the large Croghan estate just outside
Louisville, Kentucky, where George Croghan, now retired from
the army, and his wife were living with George's parents. Croghan
and Jesup had become friends during their military service. Jesup
had been a house guest at Locust Grove on previous occasions and
had soon developed a romantic interest in George's pretty and
popular young sister, Ann. This visit marked a turning point in the
general's personal life, for he and Ann became engaged and made
plans to marry in the spring. The Croghans were well-to-do and
highly respected. Ann's father, William Croghan, Sr., had served in
the Revolutionary War, attaining the rank of major. Her mother,
Lucy Clark, was a sister of George Rogers Clark and the renowned
William Clark, co-leader with Meriwether Lewis of the Lewis and
Clark Expedition.

About 1 May 1822, Jesup, who had returned to Washington to
resume his official duties, requested an extended leave of absence
and set out again for Locust Grove. There, on 19 June, Brig. Gen.
Thomas S. Jesup, thirty-four, and twenty-five-year-old Ann Heron
Croghan were married. General Gaines served as best man, and
Ann's only sister, Elizabeth, was a bridesmaid. Eliza, as Ann's
younger sister was known, was married to George Hancock, a
cousin of Zachary Taylor.

Locust Grove Restoration.

Locust Grove, built by William Croghan, Sr., late in the eighteenth century, was a handsome red-brick house located near the Ohio River.[1] While waterways still afforded the principal means of long-distance transportation, Locust Grove remained a convenient and popular resting place for many public figures, including Presidents Monroe and Jackson. Croghan and Richard Taylor, Zachary's father, were neighbors. After his marriage, Locust Grove became a second home for the quartermaster general. He and his family frequently visited there, and Ann and the children usually took up residence there when Jesup was away from Washington on prolonged military assignments.

Jesup developed a warm, close relationship with Ann's brother, Dr. John Croghan, a congenial bachelor with a sense of humor and strong family ties. Though a practitioner in good standing, he showed little inclination to pursue a medical career, preferring to engage in land speculation and various enterprises. He became best known as the man who established Mammoth Cave in Kentucky as an experimental sanitorium and famous tourist attraction.[2]

With his marriage, Jesup assumed what proved to be a burdensome relationship with Ann's brother, George, who earlier, as a clean-cut youth with high ideals and a charming personality, had achieved national fame for his defense of Fort Stephenson. As he grew older, George developed an astounding propensity for getting into trouble from which General Jesup, more often than not, had to extricate him. Symptomatic of what lay ahead was a memorandum from George to his brother, William, Jr., on the eve of the wedding: "Please pay to Genl. Thos. S. Jesup Twelve hundred and fifty Dollars for this amount most kindly advanced me yesterday & oblige [signed] G. Croghan."[3] Had Jesup been clairvoyant, he might have sensed that this loan was but the first of many he would advance to his brother-in-law in the years ahead.

Thomas and Ann Jesup arrived in Washington about mid-September and took temporary abode at Mrs. Peyton's boardinghouse, where Jesup had lived as a bachelor. Later they moved to the house in Georgetown which was to be their home for fourteen years. While still at Mrs. Peyton's, Ann wrote to Mrs. James Findlay about their trip to Washington by stagecoach and of the exciting plans for the months ahead. "Nothing is talked of here but the ensuing winter. It is to be so gay, so fashionable, so everything that is charming." She was to make her debut in Washington society the next day, calling first on President Monroe and then returning a dozen or more calls on ladies who had called on her. "It is now nearly dark and Genl Jesup has not returned from his office," she wrote. "He is there all day & I am quite alone. Every day he says he will stay more at home, but his business accumulates instead of diminishes, and I have despaired of having more of his company."[4]

Unfortunately, the winter did not turn out to be the gay season Ann had anticipated. By October, the dreaded cholera had struck; sickness was widespread in Washington, and many prominent residents died. In an apparent effort to prevent his expectant wife from being exposed to the contagion, and perhaps with the thought that it might be better anyway if she had her first child at her mother's home, Jesup took Ann to Kentucky for the winter.[5] Lucy Ann Jesup was born at Locust Grove on 17 April 1823.

In the decade following his marriage, the duties of Jesup's office demanded an increasing amount of attention. Ann could only regret that the general had so little time to spend with his growing family. During those years, Jesup's department struggled to perform its duties, handicapped both by the drastic reduction of its personnel to thirteen by the Act of 1821 and by its increased workload. Jesup made repeated appeals for more officers. In November of 1823 he declared that his staff was entirely inadequate to the proper and efficient discharge of its duties. Moreover, the compensation of the assistants, on whom necessarily devolved most of the laborious details of the department, was not in just proportion to their duties and responsibilities. He warned that "unless measures [were] adopted to render their situation more desirable," the men would abandon their tasks and return to their companies. He proposed that his department be authorized three more quartermasters and eight assistants, all to be taken from the line. This increase, along with sufficient inducements (including a forage allowance for the assistants) to attract "men of character to enter and remain in the department," Jesup felt would "better secure a strict accountability than all the restrictive laws on the statute books. It is called for by every consideration of policy as well as economy; for the best guarantee the nation can have for the proper application of its funds will be found in the honor, intelligence, and abilities of its officers."[6] Congress took no action on his recommendation.

The scarcity of officers to perform the growing responsibilities became so acute by the fall of 1824 that Jesup was compelled to break one of his own long-standing rules. Upon becoming quartermaster general, he had been opposed to professional clerks, preferring only men who had seen active service in the field and were familiar with military procedures. After six years, the paperwork had so increased that he was forced to add to his Washington staff of two officers, one of whom was the deputy, two civilian clerks at an annual salary of $1,150 each.[7]

No additional responsibility imposed on the Quartermaster's Department proved more troublesome than the requirement to account for clothing and equipage distributed to the troops. Jesup introduced some improvements in the existing system of accountability in 1821, but he lacked legal authority to enforce an effective system. Such a system would have to include authority to fine soldiers for damages to, or loss of, items of clothing. In a comprehensive report to Calhoun in February of 1824, Jesup explained the necessity for "further legislative provision to render more perfect the accountability" in his department. All officers previously responsible for the preservation and issue of clothing and camp equipage had been discharged from the service in the 1821 reduction of the army, he pointed out, adding: "There is abundant reason to fear that heavy losses have been sustained by the public for want of a proper system of accountability for the Clothing and equipment of the troops. . . . it is a fact worthy of notice, that while our statute books abound with laws relating to *money* accountability, there is scarcely a line in relation to that of *property*. With a view to supply this deficiency and to obtain for the Department an organization better suited to its new and increased duties, I submit a detail of the provisions which I consider indispensably necessary to secure the public interests." Although Congress delayed action for two more years, it finally reached full agreement with Jesup's views. The language of the legislation enacted on 26 May 1826 was taken almost word for word from his 1824 recommendations. The regulations he drafted became the basis of accountability for clothing and equipage in the army and were repeated, with little change, in subsequent regulations until the time of World War I.[8]

Under the new law, the Quartermaster's Department was now legally charged with the additional responsibility of distributing to the army all clothing and equipage required for the use of the troops. Procurement of these items remained the function of the Purchasing Department, but Congress directed the quartermaster general to prescribe and enforce a system of accountability for all clothing and equipage issued to the army. Under the regulations formulated by Jesup, every captain or commander of a company or detachment or other officer receiving clothing and equipage for use of his command must submit to the quartermaster general a quarterly return, on a prescribed form, showing the name of each man in his command and the clothing and equipment issued to each, along with appropriate vouchers. Jesup was to examine these returns and vouchers and, after approval, turn them over to the Treasury Department for settlement. All officers responsible for issuing clothing and equipage were required "carefully to preserve the same from waste or damage." Unless an offender could show that any damage or deficiency which occurred did not result from neglect, the assessed value of the missing or damaged article was to be deducted from his monthly pay.[9]

As directed by the secretary of war, the quartermaster general continued to prepare an estimate of clothing required by the troops, formerly the responsibility of the Purchasing Department. Commanding officers of regiments sent their annual estimates of clothing and equipage needed by the troops to the quartermaster general before 1 July. Jesup reviewed the estimates and, when necessary, modified them to bring them into agreement with the allowances set forth in regulations. He sent the revised estimates to the Purchasing Department, which then furnished the supplies. Jesup used the same regimental estimates to prepare a detailed annual estimate of the clothing and equipage needed by the army during the following year. After approval by the secretary of war, he sent that estimate to the Purchasing Department. It provided guidance for future procurement and became the basis for the monetary estimate which the Purchasing Department submitted to Congress for consideration in enacting the army appropriation bill.

This arrangement continued until 1832 when Secretary of War Lewis Cass, recognizing the need for an officer in the War Department to whom he could submit all clothing problems, established the Clothing Bureau as an appendage to the War Office. Even then, the responsibility for making an annual estimate of clothing requirements for the whole army remained a function of the quartermaster general. The following year Jesup called Cass's attention to the misunderstandings that might grow out of the existing mixed jurisdiction. "I am far from wishing to avoid any duty which may be confided to me," he wrote, but with the establishment of the Clothing Bureau he believed the task of preparing estimates of clothing needs might more properly be taken under the secretary's supervision.[10] Cass concurred, and the function was transferred to the Clothing Bureau.

Jesup assumed still another responsibility, growing out of his determination to serve the troops to the best of his ability. When Lt. John F. Lane, an assistant quartermaster at Boston, made a suggestion to the quartermaster general regarding the use of India rubber cloth in construction pontoons, he found an enthusiastic supporter. Lane believed the pontoons would make possible the quick erection of bridges to provide rapid transportation across rivers and other streams for an entire army, including heavy wagons, artillery, and horses. Jesup was convinced that the rubberized cloth could be used successfully for pontoons; moreover, his active mind foresaw its possibility for other military purposes, such as tents, baggage wagon covers, and waterproof apparel for soldiers. In August of 1835 he requested permission from Cass to conduct experiments to ascertain the adaptability of the rubberized cloth for military items, recommending that Lane be directed to super-intend the tests.[11]

Cass approved the recommendation, and in September Lane began collecting materials for building the Army's first experi-mental pontoon bridge. He made periodic progress reports to the quartermaster general. Because of Jesup's encouragement, sugges-tions, and wholehearted support of the project, Lane persistently referred to it as the "Jesup ponton" [sic]. Much sooner than he probably anticipated, Lane would have the opportunity to test his pontoon bridge under wartime conditions.[12]

To carry out the additional responsibilities for clothing im-posed on his department by the Act of 1821, Congress, in 1826, authorized Jesup to add two quartermasters and ten assistants, all to be taken from the line.[13] Although the number of officers in his department was increased from thirteen to twenty-five, including himself, it still fell far short of the thirty-seven available to him be-fore the 1821 reduction. Despite the growing workload of his de-partment, the number of officers remained unchanged for the next twelve years. His Washington staff was small, and much of the of-fice work, particularly the endless estimates and reports, fell upon Jesup's shoulders. Not only were his duties burdensome and exact-ing, they were also confining, contributing, no doubt, to the poor health which so frequently plagued him.[14]

Executing the department's original functions for transporta-tion and construction also added to the workload. Expenditures for transportation grew to considerable proportion as the military frontier was extended westward. The posts at Council Bluffs and St. Peter's had to be supplied. By 1822 troops were garrisoned at a post six hundred miles up the Arkansas River; others were locat-ed on the Red River beyond Natchitoches; still others were sta-tioned at the falls of St. Mary, 125 miles beyond Mackinac. Because the army was too small to furnish troops at all points needing pro-tection on that extended frontier, frequent troop movements be-tween posts took place—a "showing of the flag" to intimidate any hostile Indians.[15] Quartermasters contracted for steamboat accommodations to transport troops on the Great Lakes and western rivers. Supplies also had to be shipped—usually by wagon—and as supply lines lengthened, costs increased. Regulations granted a transportation allowance to officers traveling on duty without troops. Jesup eliminated earlier confusion by giving his subordinates Melish's *The Travellers Directory*, which showed the distances on the principal roads of the United States, for their use in computing allowances.[16]

Directing surveys and supervising the building of roads and bridges for military purposes was a part of Jesup's responsibility for transportation. For some years before he became quartermaster general, government policy had been to open up essential communications with the different frontiers by building roads, using troop labor for the purpose. Most of those roads were constructed by executive order with funds taken from the general army appropriation. Quartermaster duties were limited to providing necessary tools and paying the sums due for extra pay to the soldiers building the roads. As the frontier rapidly filled with settlers after the War of 1812, roads were necessary not only for their protection but also to provide transportation routes for the products of their labor. The need for internal improvements led Congress, in April 1824, to enact legislation appropriating funds for federal surveys of routes for roads and canals needed for commercial, military, and postal purposes. It directed the Corps of Engineers to carry out this work.[17] Previously, government financing of such projects had been viewed by some as unconstitutional.

Jesup's department continued to be responsible for roads that were strictly military in character. Since assignments were not always clear-cut, responsibilities for road construction tended to overlap between the Corps of Engineers and the Quartermaster's Department. In the 1820s Congress provided for the construction of a number of military roads, but with the army drastically reduced in size, the Quartermaster's Department had to supplement troop labor with civilian laborers.[18] Most of these roads were built in Arkansas Territory and northern and eastern portions of Florida Territory. Little was known about the interior and southern parts of that territory. At Jesup's urging, the department built roads on the southwestern frontier as a defensive measure in the event of war.[19] In subsequent years, a network of military roads was built under departmental supervision in Arkansas Territory as the threat of Indian warfare increased and the disturbed relations between Texas and Mexico underscored the need for them.

Not all roads constructed by the department were strictly military in character. However, since the War Department believed that all roads served both the military and economic needs of the country, Secretary of War Peter Buell Porter could report to Congress in 1828 that the quartermaster general, assisted by other officers and soldiers of the line, was engaged "in the construction of roads and bridges for the citizens at large." Then, with the pride of an old soldier, which he was, Porter added that the army had proved itself to be "a body of military and civil engineers, artificers, and laborers, who probably contribute more than any other equal number of citizens, not only to the security of the country, but to the advancement of the useful arts."[20]

Even some assigned river and harbor improvements were among the projects supervised by the quartermaster general. The most outstanding of these projects was the construction of a breakwater at the mouth of the Delaware River. Although the Navy Department originally had responsibility for that undertaking, President Jackson reassigned it to the War Department in April 1829, and the secretary of war delegated the task of managing and supervising its construction to Jesup's department. During the next seven years, two quartermaster officers selected by Jesup served as overseers of the work. After the outbreak of the Second Seminole War in 1836, Acting Quartermaster General Thomas F. Hunt requested that the department be relieved of this responsibility, and the project was again reassigned, this time to the Corps of Engineers.[21]

While he recognized the commercial and political importance of internal improvements such as roads, canals, and bridges, Jesup believed they were of still greater importance for the nation's defense: "The Military power of a nation consists not so much in a numerous population and great resources, as in the capacity which it possesses of concentrating them at assailable points, with certainty and rapidity . . . it inevitably follows that the nation having the best system of internal improvements, all other circumstances being equal, will be more powerful than any other."

He was especially enthusiastic about canals and strongly advocated that more of them be built. At his direction, quartermasters conducted transportation experiments on completed portions of the new Erie Canal. They ascertained that troops with all their supplies could be moved by boat on a canal at a rate of fifty to sixty miles in twenty-four hours without experiencing fatigue. In contrast, a column marching by land, even on the best roads, could not average more than twenty miles a day, and if a movement continued at that rate for four or five days, troops would require considerable time for rest before they would be fit for efficient operations in the field. The experiments convinced Jesup that canals, as a means of military concentration, were preferable even to the best turnpike roads, "for they will enable the nation possessing them to concentrate its force with more certainty, rapidity, and with less fatigue, than could be done by any other means."[22]

As troops became more widely dispersed on the frontier, the quartermaster general's responsibility for constructing barracks, storehouses, and other facilities was greatly expanded. Following the War of 1812, the War Department had formulated plans for a system of fortifications along the seacoast and a chain of forts along the northwestern frontier. Jesup's responsibility at seacoast fortifications was limited to the construction and repair of storehouses and sheds needed to protect public property deposited there. The Corps of Engineers was given responsibility for all other phases of construction at such fortifications.[23] But the quartermaster general continued to be completely responsible for all construction at posts on the inland frontier. As was customary, the troops felled trees and built the posts; the quartermasters furnished tools and nails. Thereafter, quartermasters made repairs or built new barracks and facilities as needed. Sometimes such construction was required to maintain defensive positions; upon occasions the quartermaster general requested a construction project to eliminate the need to pay rentals for storehouses. To carry out any such work, Jesup prepared an estimate and Congress appropriated funds for an approved project.[24] Quartermasters supervised troop labor, requisitioned tools and materials, and submitted to Jesup their accounts of expenditures. When troop labor was unavailable, they contracted for the services of civilians. When a permanent structure was to be erected, as, for example, at Jefferson Barracks, elaborate plans were drafted, and brick and stone were used. For the most part, the facilities built on the inland frontier were simple wooden structures.

After 1821 line officers and troops of the smaller army (now about 6,000 strong) were spread thinly over the country, with officers of the General Staff stationed in Washington. Some congressmen believed the peacetime army was still too large, with too many officers in proportion to men in the ranks. The House of Representatives adopted a resolution in April of 1828 requiring the secretary of war to submit his views concerning the propriety of reducing the number of officers and of reorganizing the army in conformity with the proposed reduction. Action on that resolution was still pending when Secretary of War John H. Eaton took office in 1829, and he directed Jesup to prepare a report on the subject.

Jesup was firmly opposed to any further curtailment of the armed forces, particularly of officers. He contended that it was imperative for the welfare of the country to retain in service in time of peace the nucleus of an army which could readily be expanded in time of war or national emergency. Officers constituted the basis for this nucleus, because they provided a reservoir of military knowledge so vital in wartime. He looked upon a further reduction of army officers "as a measure fraught with the most ruinous consequences to the service." He presented his views in a lengthy report to Secretary Eaton.

With the experience of the War of 1812 still fresh in mind, he deplored the events that resulted from the nation's lack of timely preparations.

> What American with a single spark of patriotism and material pride . . . can look back to the events of the late war without the deepest humiliation. We had submitted to outrages upon our Commerce and our Citizens until forbearance ceased to be a virtue. The Country was indignant not so much at the conduct of the enemy as the pusillanimity of those who directed our affairs . . . our rulers failing to make those preparations which an ordinary degree of foresight must have demonstrated to be necessary, plunged into War without calculating the consequences, as the Suicide plunges into Eternity . . . they filled the higher ranks of the Army for the most part with lawyers & politicians without the least regard to their military fitness. The consequence was we had no integrated plan of operations . . . in the movement of the different Armies . . . the strength and resources of the Country were wasted in puny & unsuccess-

ful efforts without use or object, on extensive & distant frontiers, and we presented the singular spectacle of a powerful
nation with more than a million men capable of bearing arms,
resources vastly exceeding those of any other nation of equal
population, with two hundred thousand men actually under
arms, invaded at all points, our Capital taken, our Treasury involved in fiscal ruin, compelled at length to close the War without gaining a single object for which it had been declared.

Underscoring the need for retaining experienced officers in the
army, he pointed out that the naval victories in the war were
achieved "by officers who were masters of their profession . . .
Whose victories form the only mantle to cover our national disgrace."

Jesup emphasized that in expressing his opposition to a reduction of army officers he was not to be understood as referring to
his own case. He would leave it to others to estimate the value of
his services "for [he] could not consistently with a proper respect
be induced to offer an opinion on an occasion like the present supporting in the most remote degree the necessity of [his] own official existence."[25] The quartermaster general's communication to
Eaton, which served as the basis for the secretary's report to the
House, apparently accomplished its purpose. At any rate, no further action was taken by Congress to reduce the number of army
officers.

While occupied with matters concerning the expanding operations of his department, Jesup suddenly and surprisingly found
himself at odds with his old friend General Gaines. On 10 January
1824, the general sent him a letter intended for the president: "I
wish you to read, seal and put it into the Post office, or hand it to
the President and consider it was confidential between you and
me." He wrote in great haste but noted that "this day 25 years ago
I was appointed an ensign in the army." He sent his respects to
Mrs. Jesup, signing the letter "Your friend E. P. Gaines."[26] This
letter was probably the last friendly one Jesup ever received from
Gaines.

More than a year later, Dr. John Croghan, writing from Louisville, commented on a report that Gaines had attacked Jesup in
public print for a pamphlet he had written in 1823 on "Rights and

Disabilities of Brevet Rank." Croghan was surprised that at this late date anyone should be making strictures upon Jesup's essay. He hoped the report was in error, for, having entertained a favorable opinion of General Gaines, he "should regret exceedingly his resorting to so pitiful a means to subserve his views."[27] Later events proved that Gaines was without a doubt the source of those strictures.

In an era when open quarrels among high-ranking army officers were commonplace, one officer might easily misinterpret the motives of another. Early in 1823, Secretary Calhoun had informed Jesup that the controversy between Generals Gaines and Scott over brevet rank was a cause of embarrassment to the War Department, and he wanted the matter settled. In order to insure justice, he requested all principal officers of the army to submit their views and interpretations of the laws on the subject. Jesup was reluctant to become involved in what he knew to be a delicate issue. Moreover, his opinions on the question, in the abstract, were adverse to his own interests.

Calhoun was insistent. After making repeated requests for a report, he at length informed Jesup "in the most decided terms" that he expected it. Jesup was thereupon obliged by military duty to make the report, in which he discussed "the abstract principle without reference to any case or any individual."[28]

Among the questions he considered was the relative value of lineal and brevet rank. Was an officer with more years of service entitled to preference over an officer with less service, though the new officer obtained a higher brevet rank than the senior in service? At that time, both Scott and Gaines held the brevet rank of major general. Jesup achieved the same rank on 3 May 1828, three weeks before Alexander Macomb did on 24 May. Gaines and Macomb entered the army on the same day—10 January 1799— and both Scott and Jesup entered on 3 May 1808. Gaines was bitter because, while he had nine years' seniority over Scott and both had advanced to brigadier general on the same day, Scott had been awarded the brevet rank of major general twenty-one days ahead of him. To his dying day, no one could convince Gaines of the justice of any rules or regulations which gave the younger Scott the right to outrank a veteran like himself.

After completing the report written at the insistence of Calhoun, Jesup sent a copy to Gaines. About eighteen months later, he learned to his great astonishment that Gaines considered it as evidence of Jesup's hostility toward him and had made a violent personal attack upon Jesup in an official report to the War Department. The quartermaster general explained his own position.

> That my course was dictated neither by hostility to one, nor friendship for the other, is apparent from the facts . . . and my own position; for as it regards our interests General Gaines' case is emphatically my case, & a strong friendship indeed would induce a man to advance another's interests at the expense of his; and even had I been hostile to him, it could scarcely be credited that I would sacrifice my own views of advancement merely to injure him. Still less reasonable is it that I would be instrumental in promoting the interests of another at the expense of my own, if I were not activated by those immutable principles of justice, which I consider, and hope I ever shall consider, paramount to every personal consideration.[29]

Believing that Jesup had deliberately taken Scott's side, Gaines demonstrated his vindictiveness by seeking in various ways to discredit and disparage his old friend. In the spring of 1829, as commander of the Eastern Department, he registered another complaint against the quartermaster general in an official report to the War Department. He charged Jesup with giving orders to quartermasters and other officers of the general staff without channeling them through him or furnishing him with copies, in alleged violation of General Regulations 489 and 869. Moreover, he attacked Jesup personally, calling him "vain" and "visionary."

General Macomb, commander-in-chief of the army, informed the quartermaster general of the charge and enclosed a copy of Gaines's letter. Jesup, thoroughly conversant with army regulations which he had had a hand in drafting, promptly replied that the paragraphs he was accused of violating related "to *military orders*, not to *administrative instructions*." He pointed out that military orders were indeed communicated through the adjutant general, but administrative instructions always went directly from the chiefs of staff to their subordinate officers. The instruction of which Gaines complained was not a military order; it related to no matter or subject connected with his command. It was, in fact, a letter from Jesup to Quartermaster Henry Stanton in New York. Jesup was irritated that his erstwhile friend had not only erroneously denounced his act as a violation of military principle but had "undertaken to assign the causes and ascribe the motives of that act," charging that Jesup had acted because he was "vain and visionary." Jesup assured Macomb that he was perfectly content to let those who knew both men decide who was the more vain. As to the charge of being visionary, he hardly knew whether to consider it a compliment or a censure. "Men of liberal minds & honorable principles, when compelled to report the acts of others usually leave their motives to be deducted from the acts themselves, and seldom risque the injustice of assigning motives for their conduct. . . ." If he had violated the law, he should be judged by the law, but Jesup protested "the right of General Gaines, or any other person, to assign motives" for his conduct.[30]

About the time Jesup was writing the report which cost him the friendship of Gaines, George Croghan was interested in becoming postmaster at New Orleans, a position that Jesup was instrumental in getting for him in the summer of 1824. Croghan was soon dissatisfied, convinced that he was worthy of a more important position than that of "franking letters."[31] When Congress rejected a resolution to extend him a vote of thanks for the act which had earlier won him a moment of glory, he wondered if its members had been informed of all he had done at Fort Stephenson. In 1818 Croghan had written a threatening letter to Gen. William Henry Harrison, blaming him for statements appearing in Robert McAfee's *History of the Late War in the Western Country* which were "positively incorrect" and damaging to his fame. He maintained that Harrison had given "sanction and authority to the publication."

The controversy was seemingly stilled when Harrison declared that he had in no way disparaged Croghan's defense of Fort Stephenson. In 1825, Croghan rekindled that controversy, dormant for seven years. "Strict justice," he wrote, "has never yet been done to the brave men who served me at Lower Sandusky & I require it for them at your hands." He charged that the general, then serving in the Senate, had failed to keep his pledge to correct the false impressions created in McAfee's history.[32] His accusations initiated an exchange of letters in which Harrison agreed that Croghan "had not been sufficiently noticed & rewarded" for his military efforts. In the face of his threatening and offensive letters, however, Harrison would do nothing until Croghan had withdrawn the charges. When Croghan remained adamant, Harrison proposed that the quartermaster general be named to arbitrate their differences. The arbitration, he said, "could not be in safer hands." Croghan readily agreed.[33]

What went on behind the scenes in Washington before Croghan's letter agreeing to arbitration arrived is not recorded. At any rate, on 31 December 1825, George Croghan was appointed inspector general of the army with the rank of colonel. He thus accomplished his objective—to gain an important post for himself. Harrison was happy to have the controversy end. Apparently neither man gave any more thought to "justice" for the others who fought at Fort Stephenson. From New Orleans, Croghan wrote Jesup: "Mr. Clay, Genl. Harrison, C. A. Johnston & you (more especially) are entitled to & shall receive . . . my formal expressions of grateful thanks." He assured his brother-in-law that his office arrangements were such that he would turn over to his successor everything in "such systematick exactness . . . as can not be found in any other post office establishment in the U. States."[34]

His "systematick exactness" obviously did not extend to his financial arrangements. Jesup and members of the Croghan family were deeply shocked when they learned that George had used post office funds—to the extent of eleven thousand dollars—to pay personal debts. "Borrowing" postal money to pay short-term notes, he had then depended on borrowing enough from friends to restore the public funds before his quarterly reports were due. Before he could replace the funds, an audit uncovered the shortage. Since Croghan had no intent to defraud the government, Postmaster General John McLean was persuaded to refrain from taking action against him, if all the money was repaid. William and Dr. John Croghan, who had guaranteed their brother's bond, made desperate efforts to raise the full amount, but money was so extremely scarce in the face of their other obligations that they were able to obtain only three thousand dollars. Thus Jesup himself had gone into debt to pay the Post Office Department nearly eight thousand dollars. Colonel Croghan was to repay Jesup's loan out of his military pay, but he did not do so for five years, having in the meantime obtained further loans from Jesup.[35]

Three years later, George Croghan was again in serious trouble that could have ended his army career. At New London, Connecticut, he had appeared so intoxicated that he was unable to inspect the command. The commander appealed to Jesup to use his influence with Croghan. Jesup must have lectured his brother-in-law, because the colonel's conduct during the next six months was apparently beyond reproach. But the following spring, reports of his intemperance and gambling again began to circulate.[36]

Thus was established the pattern of George Croghan's life, in spite of which his inspection tour reports to the War Department were so valuable as to be published later.[37] His letters to Jesup often contained comments and suggestions useful to the quartermaster general. Just as he would appear to have conquered his bad habits, he would revert to them—he would become intoxicated, then gamble and lose. While still in a stupor, he would be induced to sign notes, supposedly to cover his losses.

One such incident occurred in 1839; as usual, the colonel appealed to Jesup for financial assistance to get him out of his scrape: "I most unwillingly call upon you who have so often extricated me out of difficulties of the most serious nature (but of my own creation) but am forced to do so sooner than suffer the severe *penalty* that silence might bring upon me." At moments of "too great forgetfulness," he had signed several notes amounting to about two thousand dollars. "How to provide for them I know not unless through you—& to you I now appeal. . . . I am now & hope to continue as *correct* in my habits as you would desire me my best friend, or I would not presume to beg your aid." Jesup complied.[38]

Jesup's letters and other records indicate the heavy drain on the general's finances caused by the countless loans made over the years to his brother-in-law. Why was Jesup willing to sacrifice his own welfare to rescue Colonel Croghan from one scrape after another caused by drunkenness and gambling, both of which the general strongly condemned? He appears to have done so out of consideration for his wife. "You will hear so much of his bad conduct that it will be enough to make you cast him off . . . but my Dear husband he is my brother, one whom I was proud to call my brother & although now disgraced by his habits, I still have a sister's affection for him & for my sake do not cast him off from you entirely."[39]

Jesup's friendship with Henry Clay, a fellow Kentuckian who had been helpful in obtaining the post of inspector general for George Croghan, brought him involvement of another sort. Jesup was called upon to act as second when Clay challenged Senator John Randolph of Virginia to a duel in response to Randolph's charge of a "corrupt bargain" between John Quincy Adams and Clay. The 1824 presidential election had been thrown into the House for a decision when no candidate won a majority of the electoral votes. Clay asked his supporters to vote for Adams. After his victory, Adams appointed Clay as his secretary of state giving rise to Randolph's charge. When on 30 March 1826 Randolph denounced the administration as a "corrupt coalition of the Puritan and Blackleg," Clay could tolerate no more. He requested the quartermaster general to carry to Randolph his note demanding satisfaction.

Jesup's efforts to dissuade Clay were to no avail. Rep. Edward F. Tattnal of Georgia, acting for Randolph, was equally unsuccessful in preventing the confrontation, which took place at 4:30 P.M. on Saturday, 8 April, on the Virginia side of the Potomac River above the Little Falls Bridge. Late the night before, Tattnal had sent a note to Jesup informing him that he had given Sen. Thomas Hart Benton instructions on how to reach the site. The seconds apparently hoped that Benton might talk the principals out of their resolve to duel. The senator, no stranger to duels, rode up on horseback in a last-minute effort to prevent the shooting, but the duel had begun. The two combatants had exchanged shots without effect. The affair ended with Clay and Randolph shaking hands.[40]

By this time Jesup's onerous staff duties had become so burdensome and confining that he hoped to obtain relief by an appointment in the line. Such a prospect presented itself when Jacob Brown died in February of 1828. Before a successor was appointed, Jesup requested Secretary of War James Barbour to consider him for the vacancy that would occur if either Winfield Scott or Edmund P. Gaines were appointed to command the army: "The appointment would confer on me no additional rank but its duties would be more agreeable to me than those I perform, and would besides, be less injurious to my health." To the surprise and chagrin of both Scott and Gaines, Gen. Alexander Macomb was named the new commander-in-chief. For Jesup, the outcome merely frustrated another attempt to rid himself of his laborious and unrewarding duties as quartermaster general.[41]

On 8 May, Jesup was brevetted major general for ten years of faithful service in one grade. Two months later, his health had become so bad that he was granted extended sick leave. While his family remained at home in Georgetown, he went to Kentucky to recuperate. Major Cross, Jesup's deputy, was placed in charge of the Quartermaster's Department. Concerned about the general's illness, Cross hoped that exercise and relaxation from business would soon restore Jesup's health.[42] Part of the general's four-month leave was spent at Locust Grove.

The knowledge that his burdensome quartermaster duties were undermining his health and that he might be compelled to retire probably accounted for Jesup's increased interest in land speculation in the late 1820s and for his determination to acquire a farm to which he could retire. In the fall of 1826, he had bought a 2,600-acre farm in Todd County, Kentucky.[43] The following summer, he had obtained a three-month furlough to go to Kentucky to further his private business interests. His wife, who was expecting another child, had remained in Washington. Before Jesup left the city, the two had signed a legal document which designated Joseph R. Underwood of Kentucky as their attorney and land agent.[44]

Few men knew Jesup more intimately over a long period of years than did Underwood. Their relationship dated back to the early part of the War of 1812, when Jesup was supervising the building of boats at Cleveland for Harrison's army and Underwood was a lieutenant in the 13th Kentucky Infantry Regiment. By 1827, Underwood had served several terms in the Kentucky legislature; in 1828, he was elected judge in the court of appeals. He would later serve in Congress, first as a representative and then as a senator.[45]

During his recuperation at Locust Grove in the summer of 1828, Jesup entered into a business partnership with his brother Samuel to operate the Todd County farm acquired two years earlier. Samuel was to conduct the actual operations; both men were to share all expenses and profits. The general reserved one five-hundred-acre corner of the farm as a homesite for the Jesup family in the event of his retirement.[46]

Jesup's need to supplement his military income in order to support his growing family is evident from the fact that his pay and emoluments as quartermaster general in 1828 totaled a little less than $4,000. This amount included support allowances for three servants—$897 for pay, subsistence, and clothing—and $378 for forage for his horses, which varied in number from three to five. His pay amounted to only $1,248, but he also received $876 for subsistence and $600 for double rations—a figure somewhat smaller

J. R. Underwood, Jesup's attorney and land agent. In the Senate he vigorously defended the general's reputation.

than normal, since Jesup declined to accept double rations for his period of sick leave.[47]

With his health seemingly improved, Jesup once again became absorbed in the routine duties of his office. Suddenly, early in March of 1832, he suffered a severe hemorrhage of the lungs and was unable to leave his room for several weeks. Surgeon General Joseph Lovell considered the attack so serious that he warned the forty-four-year-old quartermaster general that if he desired to live, he would have to quit his post and seek a more active life. By late March, Jesup was feeling somewhat better and was considering the acquisition of a plantation, possibly in Mississippi, to which he could retire if his health compelled him to resign.[48]

In the meantime, when the effects of the attack subsided, Jesup returned to duty. Apparently both the acquisition of a plantation and the doctor's warning were forgotten for the moment, because that spring and summer, with the Black Hawk War in progress, Jesup's attention was focused on providing the necessary support. For three months, Brig. Gen. Henry Atkinson and Col. Zachary Taylor, with a force of army regulars and Illinois militia, pursued Chief Black Hawk and several hundred of his Indian supporters up the Rock River from Illinois into the Wisconsin wilderness. There, at the mouth of Bad Axe River on 3 August, the uprising came to an end when Black Hawk's remaining followers were virtually annihilated and the chief was taken into custody. No longer needed to support an active campaign and with his health still impaired, Jesup took two months sick leave and hurried to Locust Grove to meet Ann, the children, and Mrs. Croghan. He took them all for a sojourn at Warm Springs in the Virginia mountains.

While relaxing there, Jesup wrote to Taylor at Prairie du Chien on 23 September. Taylor's reply focused on the Black Hawk War and Jesup's role in it. He was critical of the leadership of General Atkinson in the field and of General Macomb, commander-in-chief of the army, in Washington but praised Jesup for his energetic support of the troops: "I well knew when it was necessary for you to act, that you would do, not only your duty, but more than your duty; for had you not assumed the responsibilities you did, besides acting with your accustomed energy in supplying funds, there is no telling when the war would have ended."

In Taylor's opinion, army companies as then composed were too small for frontier service, even when all the ranks were filled.

He was critical of company commanders who used soldiers as personal servants to work in their houses and gardens or take care of their livestock. "Let them be prohibited under the severest penalties from making use of them as servants directly or indirectly."

Taylor counseled Jesup not even to consider resigning his post: "You have served the country too long, & too faithfully in peace, & in war from the grade of a Lt. to the highest rank in our army to adopt another profession [and] your rank, & station is equal to any in the gift of the president. . . ."[49]

Relaxation at Warm Springs with his family did much to restore the quartermaster general's health. Secretary Cass, apparently in the belief that Jesup would benefit further if given a little more time away from his confining duties in Washington, designated him to serve again on the board of visitors at the United States Military Academy. This duty meant another absence from his wife and children, who remained at home. Ann's frequent letters from Georgetown give an insight into the deep affection that existed between the members of his family.[50]

The Georgetown house was in need of extensive remodeling, which Jesup planned to undertake. When Dr. Croghan and his mother urged Ann and the family—three girls and two boys—to come to Locust Grove for a lengthy visit. Jesup decided to sell their furniture and take his family in the fall of 1835 to Kentucky, where they were to remain all winter, giving the workmen a free hand in reconstructing the Georgetown house. Jesup returned alone to Washington in January of 1836, after making definite arrangements to revisit Kentucky in April when a survey was to be made to determine the boundaries of his Todd County farm.[51]

Early in April, Jesup awarded a contract for the construction of his new home in Washington; a few days later, the first of the building materials were delivered at the site. About the same time, he received a letter from Ann at Locust Grove, saying she was distressed by his illness. She hoped Congress would soon adjourn. "I wish so much to see you My Dear Love that every day appears longer to me than they have ever done. The children too complain of their long separation from you. . . . We are all well. May God grant that this find you so too is the prayer of your affectionate Ann H. Jesup."[52]

Although Jesup had not anticipated the delay, he would not see his family again for another two years. The War Office was bustling with increased activity, and he was busily engaged in arranging for the transportation of troops and supplies. Army regulars and militia from nearby states had been sent to Florida, where the Second Seminole War had erupted. In Alabama and Georgia, a serious uprising of the Creek Indians was taking place. Jesup was destined to take a leading role in both conflicts as a troop commander.

CHAPTER 6

COMMANDER IN
THE CREEK WAR

THE SECOND SEMINOLE War erupted in Florida while General Jesup was in Kentucky. The conflict was a result of President Jackson's determination to carry out the policy of removing Indian tribes from the East and resettling them on lands west of the Mississippi. Many of the Seminoles had repudiated a treaty[1] signed by their principal chiefs and refused to leave their homeland. Several months before actual warfare began, Brig. Gen. Duncan L. Clinch, commander of the United States regulars in the Florida Territory, was reporting to the War Department that force would be necessary to compel the Seminoles to comply with the stipulations of that treaty. Moreover, the effort was going to require more troops than he had under his command.[2]

By December 1835 the Indians were plundering and burning the homes of white settlers along the frontier. The country between the Suwannee and St. Johns rivers for a distance of fifty miles above the Indian boundary was abandoned by the white settlers who had taken refuge "in a few miserable stockade forts."[3] The situation reached a climax on 28 December 1835 when the Indians murdered Indian Agent Wiley Thompson and Lt. Constantine Smyth at the Indian agency adjoining Fort King. They also massacred Maj. Francis L. Dade and two companies of troops in an ambush during their march from Fort Brooke on Tampa Bay to reinforce the garrison at Fort King, near the present city of Ocala.

In the course of the first month of the war, sixteen large plan-

119

tations, each with from 100 to 150 Negro slaves, were burned to the ground and their occupants forced to flee for their lives. Reports of other Indian depredations and atrocities were widespread. The number of warriors on the warpath at this time was more than nineteen hundred, of whom 250 were Negroes. During the war, the Seminoles, who possessed numerous slaves, captured many more from Florida plantations. In addition, they were joined by both runaway and free Negroes.[4] A wave of terror spread throughout the Florida Territory. Volunteers and militia from the territory and nearby states, along with more United States regulars, were called in to subdue the rampaging Indians and protect the inhabitants. When it became apparent that Clinch lacked the manpower to cope with the situation, President Jackson, on 21 January 1836, ordered Gen. Winfield Scott to take command in Florida.[5]

Jesup was by then back in Washington, but Maj. Thomas F. Hunt, serving during Jesup's absence as acting quartermaster general, had already initiated measures to provide adequate support by reassigning quartermasters to key positions. He assumed that any operations on the west coast of Florida would be supported by supplies drawn from the general depot at Tampa Bay, which in turn would obtain its supplies from the assistant quartermaster at New Orleans. East coast operations would call for supplies from a depot on the St. Johns River, backed up by supplies drawn from Charleston and Savannah. Hunt assigned assistant quartermasters to these depots and ports. At the same time, he directed Capt. Samuel Shannon, assistant quartermaster at Pensacola, to report to General Scott's headquarters to serve as his chief quartermaster. All quartermasters in the field were placed under Shannon's direction.[6] During Scott's campaign in Florida, the department remitted to these quartermasters $612,000 so that they could fill any requisitions for supplies and meet any demands made by the military operations in that territory.[7]

When Jesup resumed his duties, he immediately ordered the procurement of certain supplies that he foresaw would be required. This policy of anticipating demands without waiting for requisitions was continued throughout the war. Otherwise, the lack of lead time necessary for producing new supplies, the distance supplies had to be shipped, and the delay in receiving requisitions from field quartermasters would frequently have resulted in supplies arriving too late for use in the intended operation. Without

Gen. Winfield Scott, whose friendship with Jesup ended in a confusion of letters that plagued Jesup for the rest of his life.

waiting for requisitions from either Scott or his chief quartermaster, Jesup ordered 5,000 bushels of corn to be shipped from Baltimore to Savannah in 2½-bushel bags and directed the purchase and shipment of ten strong wagons with harness for six horses each.[8] To Maj. Trueman Cross he assigned the task of expediting the procurement of wagons, forage, and other quartermaster supplies. Despite the major's best efforts, new wagons could not be obtained in the number required, and used wagons were procured and shipped. Shipment was delayed because troops, provisions, and forage had priority in transportation, and wagons could be sent only when space was available on the vessels. The last of the ten wagons ordered by Jesup did not arrive on the St. Johns River until May.[9]

Reserve stocks of supplies were meager. The army had remained small in size for years, and appropriations had been limited to its peacetime needs. Nevertheless, the Quartermaster's Department made every effort to support the troops in Florida. Between mid-January and late May, when Scott closed his campaign because of the approaching "sickly season," the department had furnished his army 75 wagons, 36 carts, 135 sets of harness, 98 packsaddles, 618 horses, 69 mules, 934,518 pounds of hay and fodder, 49,563 bushels of corn and oats, and 11,882 forage bags.[10]

While Jesup was initiating his first procurement orders, Scott was proceeding to the Florida Territory, making requisitions en route upon the governors of South Carolina, Georgia, and Alabama for volunteers and stopping along the way to order wagons and horses for the theater of operations. Scott had never been to Florida and knew nothing about that unexplored country. John Bemrose, a participant in the war, reveals that Scott took with him to Florida "... a band of choice musicians, with appurtances to match, marquees of furniture, something beyond what had ever entered this wilderness before, giving our surroundings the appearance of sudden refinements. ... He had three large wagons, laden with superb furniture and all things comfortable for his staff."[11]

Scott's general plan of operations was to move at the same time three separate forces from Fort Drane, Volusia, and Tampa in a three-pincer movement designed to funnel all the Seminoles to the vicinity of the Withlacoochee River, where his forces would crush them. Bemrose comments, "The plan proved an utter failure; the general having drawn it upon the carpet before his comfortable fire, allowing for no impassable country, thereby showing a great lack of the tactics needed for Indian bush fighting."[12]

Scott later placed much of the blame for the failure of his Florida campaign upon the unexpected "intrusion" of General Gaines, commander of the Western Department of the Army. Gaines was at New Orleans when news of the Dade massacre reached him, along with a report that Fort Brooke at Tampa Bay was in danger. Since his jurisdiction included that area of Florida, Gaines promptly sent a messenger to inform General Clinch that he would arrive at Fort Brooke on 8 February and would cooperate fully with him. Without learning of Scott's appointment, Gaines embarked from New Orleans with a force of eleven hundred men, arriving at Fort Brooke on 10 February. Three days later, with only ten days' provisions and a complete lack of knowledge of the country, they began their march towards Fort King, where they expected to get supplies and join General Clinch.

Gaines reached Fort King on 22 February. He and his troops had not seen one Indian during their long march. Moreover, the rations they had expected to find at the fort had not arrived, and they were able to obtain only meager provisions. Clinch was absent, and they learned that Scott had taken over the Florida command. Disgusted and disappointed, Gaines decided to return to Fort Brooke.

After two days of marching, the troops reached the Withlacoochee River where they suddenly encountered their first hostile Indians, a force of warriors led by Jumper, Alligator, and Osceola. While the troops improvised a pine-log fort, Gaines dispatched messages to Scott and Clinch, asking for supplies and urging that they move immediately to attack the enemy's rear. He believed the Indians to be gathered in force around his camp and that simultaneous assaults from the front and the rear could destroy them and end the war. His suggestion did not fit into Scott's plan of campaign.

Scott, a large, towering man with a high regard for himself and a low boiling point in temperament, not only contemptuously rejected Gaines's proposal that he dispatch troops, but he also instructed Clinch not to send Gaines any provisions. He was indignant that this "interloper" had disrupted his campaign plans and had used up most of the provisions intended for his own army. Despite Scott's order to the contrary, Clinch sent forty head of cattle to Gaines's camp, and he himself followed with a detachment of troops.

Meanwhile, the Indians continued their siege of Gaines's camp, keeping up a sporadic firing and yelling. On the night of 5 March, the Indians proposed a conference, and a parley was arranged for the next day. Jumper and Osceola told Capt. E. A. Hitchcock, acting inspector general for Gaines, who represented his commander in the talk with the Indians, that they did not wish to fight anymore and wanted to make peace. Just as the conference was drawing to a close, Clinch and his troops arrived and, not realizing what was going on, opened fire on the Indians, who quickly disappeared. The rescue from his plight ended Gaines's adventure in Scott's theater of operations.[13]

Captain Hitchcock was convinced that the Indians sincerely wanted peace and that only the ill-timed arrival of Clinch's forces had prevented an on-the-spot agreement to end the war. Writing to Rep. Francis S. Lyon, a Whig member of Congress from Alabama, he gave a glowing account of how Gaines had "broken" the spirit of the Indians.[14]

In his letter to Lyon, published in the *Washington Globe*, Hitchcock made a special point of explaining why Gaines with a force of eleven hundred men had taken only ten days' rations from his depot at Tampa Bay for a march through an unfamiliar country to a distant fort where he was not expected. The general "had reason to suppose that a large supply of stores was at Fort King," because his quartermaster had shown him an official letter from the quartermaster general, dated 21 January, advising him that 120,000 rations had been ordered to that post. Hitchcock went on to say that "the General, contrary to his reasonable expectation, found no sufficient stores of any kind." He also took pains to point out that his letter could be used "for the information of the public."

General Jesup undoubtedly looked upon that published letter as another effort by Gaines to discredit him. Writing to the editor, he emphatically observed, "[Hitchcock,] in the warmth of his zeal for his chief . . . , attempts to throw the responsibility of the movement on Fort King, with inadequate supplies, upon the officers of the quartermaster's department." He noted that no mention was made that the rations had been ordered from New York and that insufficient time had elapsed for them to reach Fort King "even in the most favorable season of the year, and with the land communication entirely free from interruptions of the enemy."

Moreover, no just grounds existed for supposing that any supplies would be found at Fort King other than those sufficient for its own garrison. "Tampa Bay was the proper depot for General Gaines' division. When he left that post for Fort King, the supplies were abundant; if he chose to leave them there, and allow the enemy to cut him off from them . . . the responsibility as well as the honor, is all his own."[15] Hitchcock kept the controversy alive by writing another letter to the *Globe*, critical of the quartermaster general, but Jesup had by then left Washington and taken the field.

Although he had the largest army thus far assembled in Florida, Scott, after two months of active campaigning, was still unable to put his strategy into operation. By the end of May, at the start of what came to be known among the troops as the "sickly season," Scott was ready to end his campaign. He reported to the War Department that he was ill at St. Augustine and was granted permission to return to New York.

When Joseph M. White, delegate to Congress from the Florida Territory, learned that Scott was abandoning his campaign, he wrote to President Jackson on 28 May, requesting that Scott be relieved immediately of the Florida command. No harmony remained between Scott and the territorial authorities; the feeling was so strong against the general that he had been burned in effigy at Tallahassee, White declared. Even that "infamous proceeding" did not justify Scott's "degrading epithets and insults" to the whole population. White's purpose, he stated, was to "request an inquiry into the manner of conducting the late campaign in Florida, and into the conduct of the major general commanding for having gone into summer quarters . . . leaving the country without defence, and the inhabitants at the mercy of the Indians." President Jackson endorsed Delegate White's letter with the following notation to the secretary of war: "A copy of this letter to be sent to General Scott, with an order to be withdrawn from the command in Florida."[16] His endorsement was dated 1 June 1836.

Scott declared at his court of inquiry six months later that, until White's letter was read there, he had not known that the president had endorsed it with an order withdrawing him from the Florida command. Quite likely, his statement was true since, through an error, the endorsement was omitted when the letter was first published. Also, Secretary Cass had been absent from the city when the document arrived in Washington. Upon his return he apparently, either by oversight or deliberate intent, did not notify Scott of the president's order. The War Department had in fact directed Scott to conduct a campaign against the Creeks in Alabama and Georgia, provided he was recovered from his illness.

With Scott supposedly out of the picture, command of the Florida troops was offered to Clinch, who rejected it; he had decided to resign his commission and return to civilian life. The command then devolved upon Brig. Gen. Richard Keith Call, commander of the Florida volunteers, whom the president on 16 March had named to succeed John Eaton as governor of the territory. Call, well acquainted with the territory, was eager to conduct a summer campaign despite the "sickly season."

In Washington, Francis P. Blair, editor of the *Globe*—the proadministration newspaper—defended Scott in an editorial: "We observe with extreme regret the unmerited censure, which some of the southern presses are casting upon this gallant officer. Without . . . knowing the difficulties against which he contended, they heap invective upon a brave man, because success does not always crown his efforts."[17] This editorial was the last attempt by Blair and the *Globe* to defend Scott.

Meanwhile, at St. Augustine, Scott received an urgent plea from Gov. William Schley of Georgia to send him some United States troops and to come to his aid: "The Creek Indians are in a state of open war, killing and destroying everything in their way. They have crossed to the Georgia side of the Chattahoochie and burnt Roanoke, and an attack on Columbus is daily expected. . . . The people of our frontier are in a wretched condition—their lives and property being at the mercy of the savages."[18]

On 19 May 1836, by direction of President Jackson, the secretary of war ordered Jesup to leave his quartermaster general post temporarily to take command of United States regular troops as well as the militia of Georgia and Alabama who had been called into service because of Creek Indian hostilities. His assigned mission was to suppress the insurrection, disarm the Indians, prevent them from joining the Seminoles in Florida, and force them to migrate west of the Mississippi. His instructions from Secretary Cass emphasized the necessity for prompt action. The orders also stated, "Should Major General Scott . . . proceed to the theater of

Francis P. Blair, editor of the Washington Globe *and a staunch defender of Jesup.*

operations, he will, of course, be entitled to the command, and you will serve under him."[19]

At forty-seven, Jesup was the youngest of the four top-ranking officers in the army; he had been quartermaster general for eighteen years. Scott was fifty, while Macomb was fifty-three, and Gaines fifty-nine. The sudden order to take the field came as a surprise to Jesup, but he reacted promptly. With customary foresight, he spent two days making thorough preparations. He sent instructions to the various quartermasters involved as well as to the chiefs of the other bureaus in Washington to furnish all the supplies he anticipated would be required. Significantly, in light of a charge Scott would make later, among the first of his numerous orders was one to Capt. John Page, acting assistant quartermaster at Fort Mitchell, Alabama, "to take immediate measures to purchase and secure in safe storehouses out of the reach of hostile Indians . . . all the corn which [he could] procure not exceeding twenty thousand bushels."[20] He sent instructions to Lt. John F. Lane, inventor of the rubber pontoons, directing him to serve as his adjutant. Jesup also dispatched a brief note to Dr. Croghan, informing him of his mission and requesting a favor. In order to have sufficient personal funds to take with him, he had been obliged to draw on the Bank of Kentucky; he asked his brother-in-law to make certain he had not overdrawn his account.

The general remained at his office until after midnight on 21 May, working on last-minute details and giving final instructions to Maj. Thomas F. Hunt, who was to serve temporarily as acting quartermaster general. Maj. Trueman Cross, who usually filled that post, was charged with expediting procurement. Jesup boarded a steamboat at 3 A.M. to begin his journey to Fort Mitchell, via Charleston and Augusta.[21] At Augusta he unexpectedly met General Scott, who had just arrived from St. Augustine. Together they went to Milledgeville, Georgia, where they conferred with Governor Schley at his executive mansion. The next day the governor accompanied the two generals in a public stagecoach to Columbus, where Scott established his headquarters and assumed top command. In accordance with his instructions from Secretary Cass, Jesup agreed to serve as second in command. Scott then outlined his strategy. He would command the troops in Georgia; Jesup would have charge of those in Alabama. The two forces would converge along the southern frontier, sweep northward through the Creek country, and overpower the Indians. The juncture was to take place at Irwinton, Georgia, requiring Jesup, with such force as he could raise in Alabama, to move across the area where the hostilities were then centered. Scott expected to have his Georgia troops ready to move by 15 June.

On 31 May, Scott dispatched a message to Alabama Governor Clement C. Clay that he planned to send Jesup to Montgomery to confer with him and to take charge of the Alabama volunteers as soon as a sufficient escort could be provided. "I mean sufficient, in my judgment for General Jesup would be willing to set out with but a small number of men to protect him." He added that Jesup, before leaving Washington, had ordered from New Orleans large supplies, including subsistence for the men and corn for the horses, and that he, Scott, had ordered from the same place 250,000 rations and other supplies.[22]

Four days earlier, while at Milledgeville, Jesup had received another letter from Cass, calling attention once more to the necessity for swift action: "It may be well to mention that you will collect the Indians as speedily as possible . . . and feed them as fast as they are brought together. It seems to me also important that they should be removed with the least possible delay."[23] The fact that he addressed his letters to Jesup indicates that Cass assumed Scott was not on hand to conduct the campaign.

While waiting impatiently in Columbus for Scott to provide him with a suitable escort, Jesup shopped for the numerous items he would need, including three horses, two saddles, eight bridles, a pair of pistols, holsters, and a dirk. He purchased clothing items: a waterproof coat, boots, and a cap—all made of India rubber—and pantaloons. He also bought some bedding and a case for his clothing, paying for everything from his personal funds.[24]

Army Surgeon Jacob Motte wrote a fascinating account of his experiences while serving in both the Creek and Seminole conflicts in which he described the devastation in Alabama resulting from the Indian uprising. Marching south with a company of soldiers from Columbus, Georgia, to an Alabama plantation whose owner had appealed to Scott for protection, he saw nothing for eight miles before reaching Roanoke but heaps of ashes marking the location of homes of former settlers. Roanoke itself was reduced to ashes and "a few charred logs."[25]

An escort of about 120 mounted men, including some friendly Indians, was finally ready on 4 June. While Scott remained in the safety of his headquarters, Jesup dashed through the hostile Indian country in Alabama, arriving at Tuskegee on the evening of 5 June.[26] He passed within three miles of the camp of Eneah Micco, one of the principal leaders of the uprising, where hundreds of bellicose warriors were gathered. At Tuskegee, Jesup learned to his surprise that the Alabama militiamen were opposed to serving under a regular army officer. Disturbed by this unexpected development, he continued on 7 June toward Montgomery to confer with Governor Clay, whom he accidentally met en route at Line Creek. The two returned to Tuskegee. In response to the appeals of the governor, the militiamen consented to serve under Jesup, and on 9 June he assumed the command.

On 8 June, as the command problem was being resolved, Jesup had sent a message to Scott. He had not yet obtained the command of the troops; but, he wrote, "if I obtain it at all, I shall probably enter on duty to-morrow." If Scott would send him two or three companies of regulars, he could begin the removal of the Indians at once. "The hostile Indians are committing the most cruel and distressing outrages on the inhabitants a few miles below." He would have to make a move in that direction to protect the settlements, to hold Eneah Micco in check, and to obtain forage. "If a movement is determined on, I will send you information of it by a runner."[27]

After being installed as commander, Jesup prepared another message, which Scott never received. Jesup had intended to send the message by a runner, but the task was inadvertently overlooked until ten days later. On the surface, Jesup may appear to have been guilty of gross carelessness, but he was operating with no staff officers to assist him. Working hurriedly, with little sleep, he was responsible for innumerable details. Without army regulars available to serve as a nucleus, he had to focus on the task of welding the Alabama militiamen and any friendly Indians he could muster into a force sufficient to combat an insurrection which threatened the lives and property of white settlers.

As the first step toward organizing the friendly Indians, Jesup held councils with Chief Hopoethle Yoholo and others whom he considered trustworthy. After obtaining their promises of support, he directed that a force of one to two thousand friendly warriors be raised. He ordered into the custody of the friendly chiefs all hostile Indians found in the vicinity; among them were about one hundred Indians from Eneah Micco's camp who had come to

Jesup's headquarters, professing to be friendly. When he discovered that thirty-four of them had weapons, he ordered them disarmed and held. As he prepared to lead his force through the hostile Indian country, Jesup left behind a garrison of adequate strength to protect the depot and the inhabitants of Tuskegee. Heavy rains delayed the start of his march for two days.

While waiting for the weather to clear, Jesup wrote Secretary Cass that the rain and the unpreparedness of the Indian warriors had delayed him. He expected to advance twenty-eight miles on 12 June to a position on the Fort Mitchell road and await the arrival of the warriors under Hopoethle Yoholo. He found the country almost without supplies; those he had ordered before he left Washington had not yet arrived. The horses would have to be put on half-rations and the deficiency supplied from the cane swamps. Jesup had received no word from Scott since leaving Columbus under escort: "The communication with Columbus is in the hands of the enemy. . . . This circumstance inclines me to strike a blow at once, though there is some hazard in it." He informed Cass that a corps of artificers and laborers was necessary to the efficiency of the Quartermaster's Department. "Southern militia and volunteers cannot be induced to labor. Such a corps, if authorized, should be employed entirely in the southern States."[28]

The following day, Jesup set out for Irwinton with the Alabama volunteers and 450 friendly warriors. His route took him past the camp of Eneah Micco and that of Eneah Mathla, another prominent leader of the insurgents. Many of the hostile Indians were concentrated at these two camps. Eneah Micco's camp was broken up by the troops, and the chief and his followers were disarmed. During the course of the day, the general wrote another message to inform Scott of his activities and of the fact that Chief Hopoethle Yoholo, with a large number of warriors, was to join Jesup on 16 June. "With that Indian force united to the regular and militia force the war, I think, may be brought to a close in ten or fifteen days. If, however, the hostile force should be larger than we apprehend, our united force will be sufficient to [defeat] them in a month. . . . I would be glad to have a few regular troops; if two companies can be spared, I desire that they should join me as soon as practicable."[29] Ironically, his letter did not reach Scott until 21 June.

While on the march on 15 June, the advance body of Jesup's

force succeeded in capturing Eneah Mathla and his son. They joined the growing list of prisoners now numbering several hundred. In a letter begun that night and finished the next, Jesup wrote Scott about the prisoners, explaining his plans to attack the captured chief's camp, where a large number of the Indian band reportedly were still gathered. Jesup was within fourteen miles of Fort Mitchell and was unable to obtain either corn or subsistence; the Indians had destroyed all they had not taken. If he did not find supplies at the Indian camp, he might have to fall back to Fort Mitchell. He requested Scott to make provisions and corn available to him at the fort, as he had only five days' rations and no corn. "I hope to receive orders from you at that place." He went on to say, "My movement to this point has, I understand from a gentleman who arrived today, tranquilized the frontier."[30]

Jesup's force had grown to formidable proportions. The Alabamians numbered 2,300, organized into twelve companies—seven mounted and five infantry. They were joined by 1,150 friendly Indian warriors under Chief Hopoethle Yoholo. Jesup was encamped within a few miles of his next objective, the camp of Eneah Mathla. On the evening of 16 June, while Jesup was making preparations to attack that camp, he received from Scott the first of a series of highly critical, provocative letters which threatened to end their long friendship.

Jesup, heeding the repeated warnings of Secretary Cass that whatever was done "must be done without delay," had acted promptly and with a marked degree of success to halt the Indian depredations and suppress the uprising. Scott, on the other hand, except for posting guards to prevent the Creek Indians from escaping into Florida, had kept his men inactive at his headquarters at Fort Mitchell, ten miles south of Columbus. He was waiting for more troops, guns, ammunition, and the propitious moment to launch his campaign. In addition to his army regulars, he had 3,300 Georgia volunteers, no more than one-third of whom were armed. He also reported on 12 June that he had been quite sick for ten days but expected to "be on horse-back tomorrow."[31] Understandably, he was annoyed when more than a week had gone by since Jesup's message of 8 June with no further word.

Scott made no attempt to conceal his annoyance in a lengthy letter of 16 June. After scolding Jesup for his failure to communicate and reprimanding him for his "unauthorized" movements, he charged, "The whole letter [of 8 June] is mysterious and enigmatical in the extreme." He had much more to say.

> You . . . tell me that "if a movement is determined on, I will send you information of it by a runner." A movement to be determined on by whom? the Alabama commanders, or those in conjunction with yourself? . . . In the first place you would certainly not determine on [a] scheme of offensive operations without my concurrence and readiness to co-operate; yet without receiving any runner from you, or communication of any kind, since the 8th instant, a passenger in the stage on the upper route . . . reports that you, at the head of about 3,000 Alabamians and 1,000 friendly Indians, was about . . . to commence offensive operations on a grand scale! I have no doubt there is a great mistake in this report. You may, perhaps, have been about to make some defensive movement or operation to clear a frontier settlement of a portion of the enemy—but I will not believe that you have declared your independence of my authority. . . .

He directed Jesup "instantly" to stop all offensive movements until the Georgians were ready to act, on about 21 June. He would begin to assemble his troops somewhere in the neighborhood of Irwinton, and he desired Jesup to meet him "about that time and place" and bring his force. Or, Scott continued, "hold the whole of the Alabamians on defensive positions on the frontier settlements till I shall bring the war into your neighborhood, when you can come into the general line of operations with me."[32]

Jesup presumably was unaware that Scott had not received his earlier communications. Nettled by what he considered unjust criticism, but confidant that Scott, if he knew Jesup's general situation and what he had accomplished would approve of his action, Jesup dispatched a runner to Scott with his reply. He regretted Scott's disapproval of his operations, but he had commenced and continued them "for the purpose of staying the tomahawk and scalping knife, and preventing the devastation of entire settlements . . . on the frontier." They had been successful, he believed, in tranquilizing the frontier and inducing the inhabitants to remain at home. He regretted the unmerited censure implied in Scott's remarks. He had acted in accordance with what he believed to be the spirit of Scott's instructions; but even if his conduct had been in direct opposition, the altered circumstances of the country should have provided full justification: "I consider it so, for I have none of that courage that would enable me to remain inactive when women and children are daily falling beneath the blows of the savage."³³

Scott's order to cease all offensive actions placed Jesup in a difficult situation. The large force of friendly warriors he had recruited would likely lose faith and defect if he did not keep them moving. Moreover, the Alabamians had reluctantly accepted him as their commander; he had no guarantee that he could retain their confidence if he suddenly stopped the operations when they were proceeding so well. He was within five miles of Eneah Mathla's camp. If the Indians were not attacked, they might escape. After serious consideration, Jesup decided to disobey Scott. The next morning he gave orders to strike the hostile camp. His action came too late; the Indians had fled during the night. While Jesup stood in the deserted camp preparing to pursue them, a runner from Scott's headquarters came dashing up with another command to stop all offensive movements.

The message made new charges against Jesup. Scott was "infinitely astonished and distressed" to learn of Jesup's approach, "and in a starving condition." Jesup knew, he stated, that "no supplies should reach even Irwinton from New Orleans earlier than the 21st" and that the Georgian troops were living from hand to mouth. "Under these circumstances, imagine my astonishment, to learn . . . that you had come through the heart of the Indian country, seeking private adventures, which, if successful, could hardly have advanced the war, and against my own plan of operations." Scott's grief and distress were at their utmost height. "All this is infinitely strange, and was the last thing in the world to be expected of you." He directed Jesup to encamp his troops in the neighborhood of Fort Mitchell until further notice, or until Scott could see him.³⁴

Jesup was rankled at the false charge that his force had approached Fort Mitchell in a "starving condition." He also bitterly resented Scott's assertion that he was "seeking private adventures." Knowing that he could not disobey the second order to halt his operations, Jesup determined to go to Scott and explain his actions. Instructing his troops to hold the Indians in check by the use of large reconnoitering parties, he rode the eighteen miles to Fort Mitchell. Once more fate was against him. Scott was not at his headquarters; he had gone to Columbus. Disappointed, Jesup rode back the next day to his own headquarters.

Before leaving Fort Mitchell, Jesup had answered Scott's last letter. He wrote that he had halted his command on the Irwinton Road and had come to the fort, hoping to confer with the general. His troops were not in a "starving condition"; the supplies he had ordered from New Orleans, and which he had been expecting, had arrived by steamboat. Moreover, he had captured nearly a hundred head of cattle in the neighborhood of a hostile camp and had a good supply of rice so that his troops could have reached Irwinton without need of supplies from Fort Mitchell. As for "deranging" Scott's plan of campaign, he replied, "I understood one part of that plan to be the protection of the frontier settlement of Alabama. I may have failed in judgment as to the proper mode of protecting it; but, give me leave to say, the course I have adopted has been successful; that frontier is now secure." He warned that the nearly twelve hundred Indian warriors in his camp would not remain inactive and asked Scott what to do with them.

Jesup pointed out that his duties had made communication impossible. So incessantly had he been occupied that he had not averaged three hours' sleep in the twenty-four for two weeks. He had not thought it necessary to explain his acts: "You knew me; and, from the perfect candor and fairness with which I acted towards you, and the efforts I made to sustain you . . . I had a right to expect different treatment from you. Under the circumstances, the harshness with which you have treated me is the extreme of cruelty."

Jesup appealed to Scott to move promptly; they had important duties to perform. He believed that with their combined forces they could end the war before another night. "I am not ambitious of the honors of Indian warfare. I am content that the whole of them shall be yours; . . . I felt resentment this morning; I feel it no longer. By our former friendship, let me entreat you to act promptly."[35]

When Scott received at Columbus the letter Jesup had written at Fort Mitchell, he answered it immediately. His reply lacked much of the harshness of his previous letters. He even praised his old friend and admitted that the supplies Jesup had ordered from New Orleans before leaving Washington had arrived. But he completely ignored Jesup's plea for prompt action. His troops should perhaps be ready to move within three or four days; he would then proceed with his plan of campaign. He ignored Jesup's question with regard to twelve hundred friendly but restless Indians. He admitted that he had "complained heavily" of Jesup but denied any intent to injure him. "I have the greatest and undiminished confidence in your honor, your intelligence, and capacity for war. You use the word friendship. I have cherished for you, for more than twenty-two years, a warm and sincere affection which I would not part with on any consideration. It has been a little shaken since I last saw you; but one expression in your letter goes far to recall it." He still thought Jesup had been inattentive to his plans and instructions and had erred in failing to report fully. "It will give me sincere delight to put down this war with you, and to give you all the fame which I know you are so capable of winning." Scott would not keep Jesup inactive many more days.[36]

Perhaps Jesup was led to make his decision by the assertions that he was leading a "starving" army and "seeking private adventures" or by the harsh charges which he considered unmerited censure of his conduct—coupled with the continued delay of Scott in taking the field. At any rate, on 20 June, before he had received the commander's two latest letters, he prepared and sent to Scott a lengthy report of his operations, announcing that he would ask to be relieved. He stated his accomplishments in detail, explaining his course of action. He had considered it his duty to put his troops in motion after receiving word of several murders and burnings by the Indians. His objectives were three: to give protection to the citizens of Pike County; to hold hostile chief Eneah Micco in check; and to collect the forage said to remain in the country. The first two objectives had been completely attained; the third had been partially thwarted when the Indians removed a large portion of the corn. "I risked nothing by my movement, as I was in sufficient force to beat any body of Indians in the Creek country. I was on the shortest route to Irwinton, and so near the enemy as to compel them to remain imbodied where they were numerous, and to disperse where they were weak. The effect of the movement has been to put an end to all murders and conflagrations, and tranquilize, completely, the whole frontier of Alabama." Since he had been "placed in this service by the express order of the President," Jesup concluded, "I shall apply to him to be relieved, and shall demand a court of inquiry."[37]

Despite Jesup's expressed desire to be relieved of his command, his explanation to Scott of his actions brought an unexpected result: It led to a reconciliation of the two generals. Scott, impressed and pleased by the report delivered to him by Jesup's aide-de-camp, Lt. John Lane, couched his prompt reply in a conciliatory tone. He praised Jesup's statement as an excellent military report of his operations, adding that he regretted the conclusion and would be sorry to lose Jesup's services in the campaign. He had no objection to Jesup's asking for a court of inquiry nor to his pursuing any other mode of redress against what Jesup might consider an injury at his hands. "I do not think I have injured you. If I should be convinced of the contrary, there is no atonement, public or private, which I should not be ready to make."

Scott enclosed with his letter a copy of his Order No. 15 of 21 June, the language of which indicated his belief that Jesup would reconsider and agree to remain with him. He stated his "great satisfaction" with the report of "the zeal, gallantry, and general good conduct of the Alabama troops" in their march through enemy country "under the able command of Major General Jesup." The order went on to say that Jesup would march his force by the best possible route to a point below the enemy, where, "in a few days," they would come into line with the Georgia volunteers. After a union of the forces, they would march "in concert against the enemy."[38]

Jesup was satisfied with Scott's sudden favorable change in attitude. He believed himself vindicated and felt his operations to be approved by Scott. Their disagreeable controversy seemed happily resolved, and he was willing to continue serving under the general. As he rode to inform Scott personally of his decision, he became ill with a severe attack of gravelrash and was in so much agony that he could not write. The following morning, though he was still unable to ride horseback, he was sufficiently recovered to write to Scott. His report, he explained, had been prepared before he had received Scott's two most recent letters; had he known of those letters, he would not have included his final paragraph. "I will cheerfully go on to the close of the campaign, and afford you every support in my power. . . . I have no personal object in view; my only desire is to serve the country in the best possible manner."[39]

When Scott received that letter from Jesup, his enthusiasm was boundless. "I already feel the return of all my ancient affection for you. As to my confidence in your high honor, intelligence, and capacity for war, nothing has ever shaken that."[40]

That same day, Scott addressed a letter to Adjutant General Roger Jones in Washington. He wrote that his friendship with Jesup had been restored and requested that his letters which had been so critical of Jesup, along with those of Jesup to him, be returned so that any trace of their "misunderstanding" would be removed from the record.

> Permit me to say . . . that my friend, General Jesup, has, by fuller explanations, perfectly satisfied me that he moved from Tuskegee and operated in this direction upon what he deemed an imperious necessity, and although I do not altogether concur with him in that conviction, I am satisfied that it was too strong upon him to have resisted.
>
> Indeed, if I had received his letter of the 9th instant, which, by accident was never sent, or his letter of the 12th, which, by accident again, came to hand (a copy) on the 21st, no unkind remark on his correspondence or operations would probably have been made by me. . . .
>
> I am now further persuaded that, whether his operations were in conformity with my plans or not, very favorable results have followed those operations.[41]

Scott returned to Fort Mitchell, where on 23 June the two generals met for the first time since Jesup had set out three weeks earlier on his perilous trip through the hostile Indian country. About 10 o'clock that night Scott showed Jesup a draft of his proposed letter to the adjutant general. When Jesup objected to some portions of it, Scott must have revised it, informing Jesup the next morning that he would ask to have the offending letters withdrawn.

Jesup, in the twelve days before he received the order to halt all offensive operations, had broken the back of the insurrection while the Georgia volunteers and the regular army troops remained idle, awaiting orders from their commander. It is fair to say that Scott took cognizance of Jesup's achievement and that he magnanimously paid repeated compliments to his fellow officer, who had gone into hostile Indian country to win the loyalty of the reluctant Alabama volunteers, recruit a ragtag army from among the

Creek Indians themselves, and weld all of them into an effective force, without the aid of any army regulars. Jesup's success may explain why Scott never initiated any disciplinary action against him for disobeying a superior officer.

Jesup wrote to Cass, explaining his reasons for disobeying Scott's first order and expressed his willingness to accept the consequences of whatever action the president should decide to take. After declaring that his operation had "broken the power of the hostile chiefs, dissolved their formidable confederacy, and given entire security to the country," Jesup added that he had been severely censured by Scott. He recognized that to disregard the positive order of a military superior was a high military offense. However circumstances had dictated that he take prompt and decisive action, and he had done so on his own responsibility. "I would infinitely prefer to lose my commission for what I have done, than to receive the highest honors of my country, had I remained inactive, and permitted the country around me to have been devastated."[42]

During the two weeks following their conference, the two generals worked in harmony in their efforts to close out the campaign. Then, unexpectedly, on 6 July, Scott received a presidential order from Maj. Gen. Alexander Macomb, commander-in-chief of the army, directing him to turn over the command to Jesup and proceed to Washington. No reason was given. "[The] Creek war, though not yet wound up, may be considered virtually over," Scott declared in his final order, announcing the change in command and praising Jesup as "an able commander."[43] The two men parted on the most friendly terms and might have remained so—except for a certain letter.

When Jesup wrote Scott from Fort Mitchell of his intent to ask the president to recall him, he was deeply hurt by what he considered unmerited censure of his conduct and by Scott's degrading and excessive language in criticizing him. He knew Scott's letters were going to the War Department and would be published in the newspapers. He had also learned that Scott was repeating to members of his staff the same criticisms of Jesup. Such public criticism could be highly detrimental to his reputation and career. The time had come to speak out in his own defense. In this moment of resentment, he had written Scott of his intention to quit the campaign and, in this same mood on the same day, he had posted a private letter to his friend and next-door neighbor in Washington, Francis P. Blair, editor of the *Globe*. He informed Blair that if he were not arrested by Scott, he would ask to be relieved from his command and would demand an investigation of the campaign, because he disapproved of the course of action Scott was pursuing. He was convinced that Scott was making the same mistake against the Creeks that had caused the Florida campaign to fail. "We have the Florida scenes enacted over again. The war ought to have ended a week ago. I commenced operations on the Alabama side, and have succeeded in tranquilizing the whole frontier."

Eneah Micco had surrendered and been taken along with many of his followers to the camp Jesup had formed so that the starving Indians could be fed preparatory to their removal. Another hostile chief, Eneah Mathla, was also a prisoner in the camp. "I was in full march, with a force sufficient to have terminated the war in five days, when my progress was arrested by an order from General Scott. He has censured me in the most unmeasured and unwarrantable manner; and I shall be compelled to have the subject of this campaign investigated." The force at Tuskegee, Columbus, and Fort Mitchell was sufficient within one week after their arrival, Jesup went on, "to have put an end to this war, if it had been properly used; but it was thought necessary to adopt a splendid plan of campaign on paper, and make everything bend to it." He disapproved entirely of Scott's course of action and believed his delay to be destructive of the country's interests. Jesup asked that the president see his letter. "He, I am sure, will approve the promptness with which I have acted, when he shall be sensible that I have, by the movement I have made, tranquilized the whole Alabama frontier."

When Blair showed the letter to the president as requested, Jackson retained the private communication for the War Department files. On the back he wrote his endorsement, instructing the secretary of war to order General Scott to Washington to face an inquiry "into the unaccountable delay in prosecuting the Creek War and the failure of the campaign in Florida. Let General Jesup assume the command."[44]

When he returned to the North and learned of Jesup's letter, General Scott was furious. Only a few weeks before, he had written to Jesup that nothing had ever shaken his confidence in Jesup's "high honor" and "intelligence." Now it had been shaken; everything was changed. All of Scott's "ancient" affection for his old comrade-in-arms had disappeared like a wisp of smoke. He was ready to believe the worst about his "former" friend, and he set out with grim determination to try to destroy Jesup's image in the eyes of the public. Scott charged that his own removal was part of an "intrigue" by Jesup to get himself appointed to the command in Florida. In this intrigue he included the president and Blair, and he looked upon the three in his fury as his most bitter enemies (General Gaines had been forgotten for the moment). Scott launched a vendetta against them not only in the anti-administration papers but, through Whig friends, in the halls of Congress. He made the strange claim that Jackson, the hero of New Orleans, was attempting to destroy the army or bring it into disrepute, as though the fate of the army was somehow dependent upon Scott's glory. Blair was dubbed the "Chief of the Kitchen." As one Whig newspaper phrased it: "It would appear that Jesup is in great favor with Blair, the Chief of the Kitchen, and as soon as he found that Scott had been ordered to conduct the war against the Creeks, determined to use his scavenger friend to procure the recall of his superior officer."[45] Jesup had run afoul of Scott, the Whigs had an issue, and the controversy was to rage in the newspapers and in Congress for years.

Andrew Jackson declared many times that he had decided to recall Scott even before he saw Jesup's letter. In fact, a month earlier, in a directive upon receiving Florida Delegate White's letter demanding the general's removal, he had ordered the secretary of war to withdraw Scott from the Florida command. Why Cass omitted the president's endorsement from the copy of White's letter he sent Scott and why he made no reference to the recall order remain a mystery. Jackson had been displeased with Scott's Florida campaign. While he admired Scott's other qualifications as a general, he had become disenchanted with his ability to cope with Indian warfare. "Genl Scott had ought to know I had no hostile feelings towards him," Jackson said, though he believed that "the shameful proceedings in Florida . . . had tarnished the reputation of the army. . . ." Oddly enough, Blair had demonstrated his loyalty to Scott only a few weeks before in stoutly defending him against what he considered "wanton attack" made by the Whigs upon the general.[46] The records reveal nothing that might implicate

Blair in an intrigue. Nor has any evidence been found to suggest that Jesup either expected or desired to be placed in command in the Creek country or in Florida. On the contrary, every indication suggests that he had gone to put down the Creek uprising at considerable sacrifice to himself and that he had a number of personal reasons—among them a concern over his health—for not wanting to take the field at that time. Once in the field, he sought to end the Indian insurrection as quickly as possible in accordance with his instructions. Characteristically, he placed public duty above personal considerations.

President Jackson, having gone on a vacation trip to his home in Tennessee, was not in Washington when Scott arrived in the North. Secretary Cass was also temporarily absent from the city. Scott used their absence "as a pretense for raising a noise in New York, as if he were denied some essential right," and sought to set up a public clamor by insinuating that Blair had been involved in his recall. If Scott persisted in his accusation, Blair threatened "to make him sick of it."[47] In a *Globe* editorial, Blair said it appeared that Jesup wanted to communicate to the president the motives for his conduct but could not do this through an official channel without implicating Scott to the extent that he must subject him to a court-martial.[48]

The charge by Scott and his partisans that Jesup had maneuvered through intrigue to replace Scott in command struck a responsive chord among the Whigs. They were convinced that if the president and Blair could be made to appear involved in the "plot," they would have an issue to help them vilify the Jackson administration. The Whig newspapers and congressional party members either simply ignored or sought to ridicule Blair's disavowals of involvement. Scott, whose conduct of the Seminole War the Whigs had earlier condemned, had become their "hero," as one Democratic member of the House described him.[49] The Whigs lavishly lauded the general while heaping abuse on Jesup for "dishonorable conduct."

Nettled by what the "knavish editors" of the "journals of opposition" were saying about the president, Jesup, and himself, Blair wrote another editorial. The objective of these opposing editors, he charged, was to injure the president by degrading Jesup and exalting Scott. While such action would be advantageous to the Whig party, Blair was not so certain that all of the Whigs were "so dishonest, so wretchedly depraved, as to be willing to see a brave, modest, patriotic man, like Jesup—who has been cut almost to pieces in the defence of his country, and who has never interfered in its politics—iniquitously sacrificed to the policy affecting the President's popularity." Blair said he had known nothing about the controversy and had no enmity towards Scott.[50]

A month after that editorial appeared, Jesup, still engaged in mopping-up operations in the Creek country, wrote a second letter to Blair, which the editor published in the *Globe*. Jesup had been surprised and disturbed by the clamor resulting from his first letter —a private communication to a friend. After expressing regret that he should have been the cause of bringing Blair into difficulty, he went on to explain his reasons for the earlier letter. He had written upon learning not only that Scott had sent to the War Department copies of his own extraordinary letters to Jesup but also that Scott "was representing [him] in his conversations, as having deranged his plan of campaign, and brought a starving corps of two or three thousand men to consume the small quantity of subsistence *he* had collected for the Georgia volunteers and the regular troops." Jesup admitted that he had written under the influence of exasperated feelings produced by his belief that a wrong had been done him and that his language might have been stronger than was necessary. "But," he added, "the language used expressed my opinion then; it expresses my opinion now." Being occupied with public duties, he had no time to defend himself; as he did not "meddle with the politics of the country," he would not consent to be defended on party grounds.

Jesup had written to Blair as editor of the *Globe*, "in the columns of which [he] expected to see Gen. Scott's letters spread before the public." He had asked Blair to show his lettter to the president "as a measure of defence against the charges contained in General Scott's letters." The results had not been what he expected or desired. With his command halted by Scott while still in the presence of the enemy's principal force, he had expected that the Indians would disperse into small parties, forcing the troops to hunt them through the swamps, as had been the case in Florida. "Having been censured for what I considered the true course of operations, and believing that I could render no useful service to the country in chasing small parties through the swamps, I desired, at the time I wrote, to be withdrawn from the army."[51]

On 3 October 1836, President Jackson directed a court of inquiry to assemble in Frederick, Maryland, "as soon as the state of military operations against the Indians permit the witnesses to attend." The court's purpose was to examine the causes of the failure of General Scott's Florida campaign, to determine why the general had delayed opening and prosecuting the campaign against the Creeks in Georgia and Florida, and to establish the reason for the failure of General Gaines's Florida campaign. Jesup was involved only in the inquiries into Scott's campaign against the Creeks. The court did not convene until late in November and was not finally dissolved until 8 March 1837. The state of military operations made it impossible for Jesup or any of his officers to be present at the hearings.

The court consisted of Gen. Alexander Macomb, who served as president, and Bvt. Brig. Gens. Henry Atkinson and Hugh Brady. Brady and Atkinson "were the friends and special favorites of General Scott,"[52] who used the inquiry as a platform from which to make scathing denunciations of Gaines and Jesup. The general had had about five months in which to prepare his defense, which he conducted with skill and ingenuity. He submitted the bulk of the 268 documents before the court, along with written answers to his interrogatories from friendly witnesses who did not appear in person. He was also permitted to question the testifying witnesses—all of whom were friendly to him. Early in his testimony, Scott developed the theme that all of the delays in opening his Creek campaign stemmed from causes beyond his control. He claimed, for example, that the Alabama force had at the outset acquired virtually all the guns and ammunition available in the area, thus depriving the Georgia troops of them and forcing him to delay his movement. Inasmuch as no one in the courtroom could refute his claims, Scott made the most of what was clearly his show.

With the preliminaries out of the way, and confident that he had proved his innocence, Scott turned his verbal guns on the absent Jesup. The general blamed his "ancient friend" for both his recall and for the court of inquiry itself, citing Jesup's letter to Blair as the source of all his troubles. Until that letter was published, he told the court, he had had not the slightest expression of official disapproval from Washington of his conduct in either Florida or the the Creek country. "[But when] a celebrated letter reached Mr. Blair, the storm thickened, the clouds were rent, and I was struck by the winged bolt on the distant banks of the Withlacoochie . . . ; on arriving in Washington, I saw the treacherous instrument which had stabbed me in the dark."

Scott told the court that Jesup seemed to have the leisure while in the Creek country to write to Blair and the secretary of war "for the eyes of the President" but not to him "who was charged with conducting the war." While the general had heard no word from Jesup between 8 and 17 June, Jesup had written twice to the secretary of war during that period. Scott strongly intimated that he doubted his former friend's veracity in the matter of the letters of 9 and 12 June, insinuating that Jesup had "invented" the letters later when he thought it necessary to do so.

In neither letter to Secretary Cass, Scott declared, did Jesup say a word "of his having commenced operations 'for the purpose of staying the tomahawk and scalping knife, and of preventing devastation of entire settlements or neighborhoods on the frontier;' nothing of his having 'none of the courage that would enable [him] to remain inactive when women and children are daily falling beneath the blows of the savage.'" In Scott's words, "These were flourishes which occurred subsequently—not until I rebuked him for violating my order." Scott contended that "the frontier settlements of Alabama had been tranquilized before [Jesup's] arrival at Tuskegee."

In his indictment of Jesup, Scott intermingled his "factual" testimony with ridicule, sneers, derision, insinuations, and satire. He accused this "great General" of moving too early, without the permission of his commander; of going in the wrong direction, reversing the adopted plan of operations "without the crying necessity afterwards invented, without the 'altered circumstances of the country' in his haste to take the war into his own hands." He charged that Jesup knew when he left Washington that Scott had aroused the displeasure of the president and that he believed himself at liberty to defy Scott's authority, "as often as his vanity might dictate."

The general spoke derisively of Jesup's statement that upon arrival at Fort Mitchell, he found the several thousand bushels of corn he had requested Captain Page to purchase. Scott regretted the absence of Captain Page, who was ill, but asserted that Jesup probably first heard of that corn in Scott's letter to him dated 19 June. Fortunately for Scott, Captain Page was not present at the court of inquiry, for he could have confirmed that General Jesup did, on 19 May, before he left Washington for the Creek

country, write asking the captain to procure the corn. Jesup directed Page, then at Fort Mitchell, "You will take immediate measures
to purchase and secure in safe store houses out of the reach of the
hostile Indians along the frontier of Georgia . . . all the corn which
you can procure not exceeding twenty thousand bushels."[53] That
letter was not shown to the court.

Scott's assessment before the court of Jesup's activities in the
Creek country was in marked contrast to his on-the-scene appraisal
in late June 1836, when he acknowledged that very favorable
results had followed Jesup's operations. In his closing remarks,
Scott acknowledged the one-sidedness of the testimony. "Much, I
know, to be wholly omitted on the other side." He was confident,
however, that no examination of any opposing testimony would
be able to controvert the "ample and overwhelming" evidence he
had presented.

One unexpected development occurred during the inquiry. The
court received a letter, dated 13 December 1836, from Florida
Delegate White, who had written on 28 May to President Jackson
demanding that he immediately withdraw Scott from the campaign
and begin an inquiry into his operations. Jackson had endorsed the
communication, instructing the secretary of war to recall Scott.
White said he was sending this second letter because he had learned
that his letter to the president had been introduced into the testimony. "This places me in an attitude I do not choose to occupy—
that of an accuser of the distinguished officer, into whose military
operations you are now inquiring." White was satisfied "upon a
full and impartial review of the facts and circumstances connected
with the Florida campaign, upon evidence not then before me,
that the failure is not to be attributed to Major General Scott, nor
to causes which it was in his power to control or remove." But, he
added, "I confine the corrigendum to his military operations. I
neither intend to explain or retract anything I said of [Scott's]
'Order No. 48', reflecting on the people of Florida. . . . I can never
think there was any justification for the charge."[54] Scott read this
letter to the court, declaring, "This voluntary and unsolicited
retraction is manly and noble. In my judgment and feelings it
shows the correspondent of the court to be worthy of being called
the honorable Mr. White, by higher claim than that of mere
courtesy."

On 30 January 1837 the court completed its inquiry and was

ready with its verdict. In view of the circumstances under which the hearings were conducted, the decision could hardly be termed unexpected. The court held that, after careful examination of "the abundant testimony," it believed that no delay "which it was practicable to have avoided" was made by Scott in opening his campaign against the Creek Indians. On the contrary, he appeared to have taken "the earliest measures" to provide arms, munitions, and provisions for his forces.

The only surprise came in the verdict's final paragraph. The court ruled that Scott's plan of campaign was "well calculated to lead to successful results," and that it was conducted by him, "as far as practicable, with zeal and ability," until he was recalled from the command upon representations made in Jesup's letter to Blair. This letter, the court stated, was "exposed and brought to light by the dignified and magnanimous act of the President" in placing it on file in the War Department as an official document. "Conduct so extraordinary and inexplicable on the part of Major General Jesup, in reference to the character of the letter, should, in the opinion of the court, be investigated."

The president was furious. If members of the court had hoped to placate Jackson with flattery about his magnanimity, they did not know "Old Hickory," and they were in for a shock. On 14 February he disapproved the verdict and returned the documents to the court with a blistering verbal spanking. The opinion, he declared, was not accompanied by any facts he had required in establishing the court. On the contrary, the facts were left to be deduced from "the mass of oral and documentary evidence contained in the proceedings." Thus a most important part of the duty assigned to the court had not been fulfilled.

The president also charged that the opinion of the court was argumentative and lacking in precision when it stated that *"no delay, which it was practicable to have avoided, was made by Major General Scott, in opening the campaign against the Creek Indians."* The wording implied that some delay had occurred but that it was made by someone other than Scott. The court, Jackson pointed out, failed to specify of what such a delay consisted, when it occurred, how long it continued, or who occasioned it. Moreover, the causes of the recall of General Scott from the command and the propriety of the conduct of General Jesup "were not submitted to the court as subjects of inquiry. The court itself appears to be of this opinion, inasmuch as no notice was given to Gen. Jesup of the pendency of the proceedings nor had he any opportunity to cross examine . . . the witnesses, nor to be heard in respect to his conduct. . . ."

President Jackson ordered the court to reconvene on 2 March 1837, in Washington, to reconsider and review its proceedings. The court's revised verdict differed from its earlier one in only one regard. It made no reference to the recall of Scott upon "representations" by Jesup in his letter to Blair nor to any investigation of Jesup's conduct in writing that letter. The fact that the court's earlier findings had been widely published and that Scott had been cleared provided the Whig newspapers and party members in Congress with more ammunition for their attacks upon the administration and the nonpartisan Jesup.[55]

Jesup, who was still closing out his campaign against the hostile Creeks, learned that at least some of the people in Alabama did not share the views of Scott and his Whig friends when, on 11 September 1836, a delegation wrote to him. Certain citizens, the letter announced, ". . . being desirous of testifying to you the high appreciation of the eminent services rendered by you to the country during the last war with Great Britain; their admiration at the promptitude, energy, and skill you have displayed in bringing the disturbances among the Creek Indians to a close, and effecting their removal from the borders of our State; and their respect for you personally, have appointed the undersigned to ascertain from you, at what time would suit your convenience to attend a public dinner in this town." The letter was signed by a committee of eight, including John A. Campbell, who had served as a colonel of the Alabama volunteers.

The *Montgomery Advisor* published the committee's letter in its issue of 11 September, along with an editorial voicing high praise of Jesup and defending him against those who sought to misrepresent him. "The testimony of the officers and men of our State, who served with General Jesup and under him, has been uniform to his high and chivalrous character, and to the urbanity of his manners, and the purity of his life. That the American people should permit an officer as gifted in mind and intellectual qualities to be sacrificed, is what for one moment cannot be credited."

The committee's letter did not catch up with Jesup for twelve days. He expressed his "grateful acknowledgement" and "warmest thanks" for the flattering terms in which the committee had thought proper to notice his services, but he politely rejected the invitation. Under other circumstances than those in which he was placed, to meet with them would have afforded him great pleasure. "But it has suited the purposes of others, in order to divert public attention from the facts connected with the Creek campaign, to misrepresent my conduct. . . . Until an investigation takes place, and my reputation be rescued from the odium attempted to be fastened upon it, I deem it due to myself to decline all public attentions such as tendered through you."[56]

Removal of the Creek Indians to the West proved to be a formidable task even after their uprising had been suppressed. Surprisingly, the friendly Indians caused more problems than the hostile ones, with whom Jesup had no difficulty. "They had, by their hostilities, forfeited all rights under existing treaties; and, on receiving their submission, I had, as military commander, the right of prescribing the conditions on which their lives should be spared." Those who were captured with arms in their possession were promptly sent to the West along with their women and children. Removal of the friendly Indians was more difficult. Though the chiefs generally favored emigration, a great number of their people were opposed to it; even those who were willing to go desired delay. Article 12 of the Treaty of Washington of 24 March 1832, Jesup pointed out, gave each individual Indian the right to remain in the country or to emigrate; had he attempted to remove the Indians by force, a single writ of habeas corpus would have made him powerless to do so. "I availed myself of the moral influence I commanded; but, in all my conferences with the chiefs, I assured them that it would be used, so far as the friendly Indians were concerned, only to enforce their authority over their people."[57]

Jesup had also to deal with the claims brought by white men against the Indians. In order to protect the Indians' property rights, Jesup had to employ a lawyer to examine all claims against the Indians and defend them in all "vexatious suits." So long as the Indians remained in the Creek country, their renewal of the war was a constant threat. Therefore neither the militia nor the volunteers could be discharged nor could any troops be sent to Florida, where they were greatly needed. By late August, however, General

Call was experiencing so much difficulty in organizing and launching his summer campaign against the Seminoles that he sent Jesup an urgent appeal for aid.[58]

The critical situation in Alabama was finally resolved on 28 August when Col. John Campbell, at Jesup's direction, negotiated a contract with six of the influential Creek chiefs. Under its terms, the United States government agreed to advance to the tribe $31,900 to be applied in the discharge of the Indian debts; to pay $10,000 to the Creek Indians who would agree to remain in military service until the termination of hostilities against the Seminoles; and to pay $2,000 to Chief Hopoethle Yoholo.[59]

The contract paved the way for the actual removal of the friendly Creek Indians, which began on 31 August 1836. On 8 September, Jesup announced that the campaign was officially closed and began the discharge of the militia and volunteers who were eager to return to their homes. The Tennessee mounted force of about 1,200 volunteers, who had served with distinction in the Creek campaign, did not request release but volunteered for duty in Florida; Jesup sent them to aid the hard-pressed General Call. Also transferred to Florida, after conspicuous service in the Creek country, was Col. Archibald Henderson and the detachment of four hundred marines he had recruited from various navy yards.

Although Jesup was not in full accord with Jackson's removal policy, the effectiveness of his own measures is evidenced in the annual report of the secretary of war. The secretary stated, "more that eighteen thousand Indians, of whom four hundred were Seminoles, sixteen thousand nine hundred Creeks, and the remainder Potawatamies, have reached the west bank of the Mississippi on their way to their new homes. . . ."[60] President Jackson and the War Department were impressed with the results of the experiment in the use of friendly Creek chiefs and warriors in suppressing the uprising of hostile Indians in Alabama and Georgia. As early as 11 July, Secretary Cass suggested to Jesup that a corps of two or three hundred Creek warriors be sent to aid General Call in his summer campaign and that they be placed under the command of a white officer who had their confidence. Jesup informed Cass that the friendly Creek chiefs would not consent to sending such a small force and proposed that the number be increased. Jackson finally set the figure at a minimum of five hundred. In addition to the $10,000 these warriors were to receive in pay, they were to be permitted to keep any "property" they took from the hostile Seminoles, with the exception of Negro slaves. Fearful that the Creeks might cause "the destruction of the negroes in place of their capture," Jesup promised a small compensation to the friendly warriors for Negroes captured and turned over to his headquarters.[61] While the Indians were fighting in Florida, their families were to be fed, housed, and protected in Alabama in special camps provided by the United States government.

Jesup chose his aide, John Lane, to lead the friendly Indian regiment. Jackson approved his selection, and Lane was promoted to the rank of colonel. Second in command was Lt. Col. Harvey Brown of the 4th U.S. Artillery. The Creek warriors were mustered into the service as militia and instructed to wear white turbans in battle to distinguish them from the Seminoles. On 20 September, Colonel Lane and his command left Fort Mitchell for Florida, arriving on 5 October at Fort Brooke on Tampa Bay. From the fort they moved inland to join General Call.[62]

Lane had an opportunity while still in Alabama to demonstrate the success of the pontoon bridge he had developed. Jesup appointed a board of officers to witness the first field test of the equipage at Tallapoosa. A fourteen-foot-wide bridge, supported by sixteen pontoons, was erected across the Tallapoosa River, a deep and rapid stream 350 feet in width. On 30 August, Jesup reported the success of the experiment in a letter to Maj. Trueman Cross, who had succeeded Hunt as acting quartermaster general. "A military bridge was thrown across the Tallapoosa at this place, over which Infantry passed in column. Mounted men and wagons also passed. I directed a board to examine the bridge and report upon the adaptation of the invention to military operations."[63]

Secretary Cass had made it clear in several letters to Jesup that he was to accompany the troops to Florida as soon as his services were no longer required in the Creek country. Then the president, in one of his private letters, instructed Jesup to proceed to Florida and take command, "unless General Call is in the field." Thus Jesup's hopes of returning to Washington and demanding an investigation of his conduct were dashed. In mid-September, he made a trip to Tallahassee to confer with Call about the situation in Florida. Learning that Call had made arrangements for a campaign, Jesup declined his offer to take over the command but volunteered to serve under him. "I have had a personal interview with General

Jesup," Call informed Cass, "in which, with great magnanimity, he declined the command of the army in Florida, and proposed to serve under my authority as a volunteer. It is gratifying to me to know that the country will have the benefits of his talents and experience, even though he declines the nominal command of the army."[64]

When Georgia Governor Schley requested troops in Ware or Lowndes counties to round up hostile Creeks who were trying to join the Seminoles, Jesup's departure for Florida was delayed.[65] He finally reached Tampa Bay on 20 October. Much to his consternation, he found that the supplies and transportation he had been assured would be found there were not available. Acting Quartermaster General Cross believed Jesup had been deliberately deceived. "Whoever misled you by the assurance that 'every thing necessary for an immediate movement would be found there in abundance,' must have done so intentionally as there certainly was no grounds for such an assurance." Cross quoted Lt. John C. Casey's report for the third quarter, which listed 109 horses and 32 mules at Tampa Bay. If Jesup had found only 40 horses there, he assumed that Lane's Indian force had taken the others to Fort Drane, "where there was already more than could be sustained."[66]

Until the necessary supplies and means of transportation were procured, Jesup could do little of value except study the countryside. After Jesup had waited impatiently for more than five weeks, everything was finally in readiness, and he left Tampa Bay on 27 November with an escort of four hundred troops. He proceeded across Florida to join General Call at his headquarters in Volusia on the St. Johns River on 2 December.

CHAPTER 7

AN EMBATTLED GENERAL
IN THE SEMINOLE WAR

WHEN LEWIS CASS resigned as secretary of war on 5 October 1836 to become minister to France, President Jackson assigned Attorney General Benjamin F. Butler to the additional duty of acting secretary of war. Jackson had become disillusioned with Gen. Richard K. Call and his campaign. Butler wrote the general an extremely harsh letter, charging that he had, upon encountering a force of the enemy on the Withlacoochee, retreated with his superior army to Fort Drane instead of crossing the river to attack the Indians. The president had directed that Call be relieved of his command.[1] At the same time, Butler wrote Jesup that, because of "the retrograde movement of Governor Call" and the "feeble state" of his health, the president had determined to commit to Jesup the command of the army in Florida and the general direction of the war against the Seminoles.

Butler specified in considerable detail just what Jesup was expected to do. He was to attack the hostile Indians in their strongholds on the banks of the Withlacoochee and drive them from the area between the river and Tampa Bay. He was to establish posts at or near the mouth of the Withlacoochee, at Fort King, and at Volusia. Through these posts and by such means of transportation as might be most economical, he was to make permanent arrangements for obtaining sufficient supplies.

Should Jesup succeed in bringing the Indians to a general engagement and defeating them, Butler believed, with considerable optimism, that the "ready submission of the tribe" could probably be expected. If the Seminoles abandoned their position on the Withlacoochee before Jesup reached it, or should Jesup drive them from their stronghold without entirely subduing them, he was then to take "such advanced positions to the South of Volusia and to the East and South of Tampa Bay, as the nature of the country may admit, and push from them such further operations, as may be necessary to the most speedy and efficient subjugation of the enemy."

These instructions to attack the enemy strongholds and to possess the country between the Withlacoochee and Tampa Bay, Butler stated, were to be regarded as a positive order to be executed at the earliest practicable moment. In other aspects, Jesup was to exercise discretion, adopting such measures as he deemed best suited to protect the frontiers and to effect the subjugation and removal of the Indians. Butler expressed great confidence in Jesup's "prudence, energy and skill."[2]

The ailing General Call was engaged in writing a spirited reply to Butler's letter, which he described as "the most extraordinary document" he had ever received, when Jesup arrived at his headquarters. After expressing to Butler his satisfaction at Jesup's arrival, Call wrote, "Feeling a deep interest in the prompt and successful termination of this troublesome war, I am highly gratified at being relieved by an officer of such distinguished merit."[3] The command was officially transferred to Jesup on 8 December, eight days before his forty-eighth birthday. He designated his command "Army of the South." Call returned to Tallahassee to devote full time to his duties as governor.

The day after he assumed command, Jesup defended Call in a report to the adjutant general in Washington. To have permitted Call to close the campaign, Jesup suggested, would have been preferable. No man who had not been there could have an adequate idea of the difficulties the general had had to encounter. Call had established the post at Volusia and had taken every preliminary step to supply it. Supplies and means of transportation were then rapidly arriving; had he retained the command, "he would soon have struck an important blow."[4]

Edwin C. McReynolds, who later wrote of the engagement, believed that "by comparison with Jesup, Call was an amateur."

According to McReynolds, "[Jesup's] appointment to the Florida command was the result of his record as a fighting officer. He was to have many disappointments in the Seminole campaign but none through personal failure. He was to become a friend of the Seminoles, like Wiley Thompson, through acquaintance with the people."[5]

Though Jesup's army was reputed to number about four thousand, the terms of service of many of the volunteers, among them members of the Tennessee brigade who had performed so well in the Creek country, had ended or were about to expire. In order to take advantage of their remaining time, Jesup decided to move earlier than he had intended and accompany the volunteers to the mouth of the Withlacoochee, where they were to embark for New Orleans on their way home. By 12 December, a sufficient supply of subsistence had been received at Volusia so that Jesup was able to carry twenty days' rations along on the march towards Fort Brooke on Tampa Bay. He arranged his supply depots so that if he were compelled to relinquish one objective, he could readily strike another. According to his intelligence, the principal Seminole chief, Micanopy, Chiefs Philip and Cooper, and the young, influential, and daring militant warrior Osceola—each with from 120 to 200 Indians and Negro warriors—were about a day's march apart from each other. Jesup hoped to strike them in succession, preventing them from concentrating their forces.[6]

Nearly all of Jesup's early reports mentioned his difficulty in finding the Seminoles. He might have been pursuing a phantom enemy. On 17 December he directed the troops under his immediate command—the Tennessee brigade, an Alabama battalion, 300 regulars, and 500 Creek warriors—to conduct a thorough search of the Wahoo Swamp. Not an Indian was found. The next day he decided to erect a depot at the site of the Dade massacre. The Tennesseans assisted in this project, and the depot was named Fort Armstrong, in honor of their commander. When it was finished, Jesup left 150 men to guard it. With the remainder of his force, including the Tennessee volunteers, he proceeded along the Withlacoochee, instructing the troops to scour the country on both sides of the river all the way to its mouth. When they succeeded in capturing a few prisoners, he learned that Micanopy, his brother-in-law Jumper, and Abraham, a Negro interpreter, intended to flee ahead of the army and avoid capture by hiding in the dense hammocks and swamps in the Everglades. Osceola, they said, would never surrender and was determined to remain on the Withlacoochee as long as possible. Jesup hoped to drive out all the Indians remaining on or near the river and to ascertain the feasibility of navigating to the river's forks. If the river was navigable, he believed the Indians could be forced to abandon their settlements in the cove and the swamps of the Withlacoochee.[7]

Brig. Gen. Joseph M. Hernandez, who was to play an important part in Jesup's campaign, was mustered into federal service on 20 December. He had been commander of the 2d Brigade of the Florida militia. A patriotic and influential citizen of Florida, he had offered his services fourteen months earlier but had been informed by Secretary Cass that since Gen. Duncan L. Clinch had more than seven hundred troops, his services were not needed. Now they were needed, and Jesup assigned Hernandez to command the forces east of the St. Johns, while he operated west of it.[8]

After the erection of Fort Armstrong, Jesup directed Lt. Col. William Foster of the 4th Infantry to construct a depot about twenty-five miles above Fort Brooke at the point where the King Road crosses the Withlacoochee. Named Fort Foster, the depot was some fifteen miles south of Fort Armstrong. The establishment of these two forts provided Jesup with eight depots, which he considered sufficient for the time being. Although the terms of service of the Tennessee volunteers had expired, they agreed to escort a wagon train to Tampa Bay to obtain supplies for the new depots.[9]

To safeguard the subdepots of military supplies needed to support the men and animals engaged in this most rugged type of warfare, Jesup early determined that a network of temporary posts must be established and fortified in the primitive Florida wilderness. The erection of such a string of temporary posts and magazines was not a new concept; it had been used in earlier Indian expeditions and in the War of 1812. Advance or subdepots were made more effective by support from base depots from which not only rations, forage, and clothing could be drawn but at which extensive repair of broken-down wagons, harness, and other articles could be made, eliminating the necessity for requisitioning distant replacements. Shortly after his arrival in Alabama, Jesup had requested that a corps of artisans and laborers be sent to perform work that he could not induce southern militia and volunteers to undertake.

Artisans were as badly needed in Florida and were supplied by the Quartermaster's Department. Before the end of the Seminole War, the principal base depots were located at Palatka on the St. Johns River, St. Augustine on the east coast, and at Tampa Bay and Cedar Key on the west coast. Not only did these depots have extensive warehouses for handling and forwarding supplies, but they also had repair facilities—wheelwright, saddler, and smith shops. Cedar Key even had facilities for repairing and constructing boats.[10] This system of base and advance depots, perfected by Jesup, later found a ready application during the Mexican War.

On about 23 December, Commodore Alexander J. Dallas arrived in Tampa Bay with a squadron of warships, and Jesup went there to confer with him. Dallas agreed to help relieve the manpower shortage by furnishing as many sailors as could be spared from the ships to serve as guards at some of the depots. "The Commodore has acted on this occasion with the same . . . magnanimous zeal which distinguished his conduct during the Creek campaign. His co-operation . . . will relieve me from many embarrassments, and will enable me to take the field several days sooner than I had hoped." Dallas also agreed to send an officer with a party of sailors to ascertain the practicability of navigating the Withlacoochee. Maj. Joseph Nelson, with four companies of mounted men from Georgia requisitioned by Jesup from Governor William Schley, arrived at about the same time from Fort Clinch. This brought the number of mounted men at Jesup's command to about five hundred. He kept a portion of them constantly on the move, seeking out the Indians and protecting the white settlers. Brig. Gen. Walker K. Armistead, who Jesup placed in command of the forces on the Withlacoochee, had orders to scour the country between the river and Fort King. Not a sign of the hostile Indians was found, and their trails appeared to lead in a southeasterly direction.

"You shall not be disappointed in my efforts," Jesup assured Butler, "though you may be in their results. The country is so extensive, and contains so many hiding places for large as well as small parties, that the enemy may escape me." Jesup expressed his great embarrassment at the difficulty of obtaining laborers, drivers, and artificers. If the war did not end in a few weeks, he would send to Cuba for mule drivers and to New Jersey for artificers and laborers.[11] On the same day Jesup sent his letter, Acting

Quartermaster General Cross wrote him that after great exertions on the part of quartermasters in Philadelphia and New York, a corps of twenty mechanics of various trades, thirty teamsters, and fifty laborers had been organized for service in Florida, and the vessel in which they were to embark "was only waiting a fair wind to sail from New York." [12]

By 1 January 1837 so many volunteers and regulars had fallen ill that no more than nine hundred to one thousand men were available for active service in the field, and at least one hundred of those were required for convoy duty. The manpower situation would have been even worse if Commodore Dallas had not supplied garrison forces at Forts Clinch, Foster, and Brooke. The friendly Creek warriors were "entirely broken down." Most of them were sick. Expecting little if any service from them, Jesup was considering sending them home. On 12 January he was able to report the capture of some prisoners, including more than fifty Negroes, a portion of whom were from Osceola's band. One of the Negroes, Primus, told him that Osceola was ill on the Withlacoochee with only three warriors and his family there but probably could collect as many as one hundred warriors. Jesup then sent troops down both sides of the river in an unsuccessful effort to flush out any Indians they found. "The difficulty is not to fight the enemy," he reported to Adjutant General Roger Jones, "but to find him." [13]

When he learned from his scouts that Micanopy and Jumper had established strongholds on the headwaters of the Oklawaha, Jesup set out to attack them, moving from Fort Armstrong toward Lake Ohapopka on 22 January with the 2d Brigade under Col. Archibald Henderson. The next day, Lt. Col. D. A. Caulfield assaulted a Seminole force on the borders of the lake, surprising and killing Chief Cooper, his son, and two other warriors and capturing eight Negroes and nine Indian women and children. The prisoners revealed that the principal force of Indians and Negroes had fled southeasterly toward the head of the Caloosahatchee. When the army overtook that force on 27 January near the Great Cypress Swamp, Jesup ordered a swift attack. After a brief but sharp skirmish, the Indian and Negro warriors retreated into one of the large swamps, but the troops captured their horses and baggage, along with twenty-five Indian and Negro women and children. When Colonel Henderson pursued the Seminoles into the swamp, and drove them out, the warriors fled into a denser swamp, where they quickly dispersed.

Indian scouts reported another hostile force about two miles away. A detachment of troops moved swiftly to that point to find a large Seminole encampment with fires still burning and food cooking, but the Indians had disappeared. With darkness coming on, pursuit was considered impossible, so the army encamped on the edge of Lake Tohopekaliga.[14]

The next morning Jesup sent a prisoner with a message to Jumper and the other hostile chiefs, offering them peace on the condition that the Seminoles agreed to fulfill the terms of their treaty. He hoped to confer with them and convince them that further fighting and bloodshed were useless. Most, he knew, were opposed to leaving Florida, but, as commander, he was obliged to enforce the government's removal policy. As early as 20 February, Jesup exhibited his lack of sympathy for that policy. He could make peace within an hour, he stated, if he were not bound by instructions to insist on the removal of the Seminoles. The Indians, he was sure, would renew the war; no peace would occur until all of the principal chiefs and first-rate warriors had been killed. "The policy of removal is one of extremely doubtful propriety as regards the Florida Indians. If small grants of land were made to the Indians they would be satisfied and they would soon be entirely harmless." He would do his utmost to carry out the view of the government, but he was doubtful that his efforts would be successful.[15]

While awaiting word from the Seminole chiefs regarding their reaction to Jesup's proposal, the army moved to a strong position on the lake near Great Cypress Swamp where it captured several hundred head of cattle. On 29 January, Jesup received messages of an encouraging nature from Alligator and Abraham, who visited Jesup for a preliminary talk two days later. On 3 February, Abraham returned with Jumper, Alligator, and two subchiefs, one of whom was Davy, a nephew of Chief Micanopy. The five promised that they and the other chiefs of the nation would meet with Jesup at Fort Dade on 18 February for a peace parley. They also promised to send out runners with instructions to chiefs and warriors that all hostilities were to be suspended pending the outcome of the conference. Somewhat elated, Jesup and his troops began their seventy-mile return march, arriving at Fort Armstrong on 7 February. In the meantime, the soldiers not involved in the military operations had opened a seventy-mile road into the interior of the Indian country—an area which white men had probably never before seen.

Jesup had learned from personal experience of the great difficulties involved in fighting the Seminoles in the extensive Florida wilderness. As a consequence, he concluded his report to Washington concerning his pending conference with the Seminole chiefs, with a frank apology to his predecessors for any derogatory remarks he had made concerning their Florida operations. The difficulties in conducting military operations there, he stated, could be appreciated only by those who experienced them. He acknowledged that he had advantages which none of them had possessed—better preparations and more abundant supplies. Jesup had not been able to operate with any success until he established a line of depots across the country. This service was one that no officer would seek with any other view than a mere performance of duty. The difficulties were such that the best-established reputation could be lost without a fault. "If I have, at any time, said ought in disparagement of the operations of others in Florida, either verbally or in writing, officially or unofficially, knowing the country as I now know it, I consider myself bound, as a man of honor, solemnly to retract it."[16]

Jesup was likely directing his apology primarily to Scott, or so Scott believed. In his memoirs, published many years later, he declared that Jesup, "smitten with remorse," had "retracted his charge of dilatoriness, etc. The *amende* lacked a little in fulness, but Scott, in time, forgave." He referred to Jesup as President Jackson's "pet."[17]

One repeated charge made by congressional Whigs during the Seminole War was that the army and its generals were "disgraced" by their continuing failure to defeat a small band of savages. Undoubtedly, those who made the charge had never set foot in the then-unexplored areas of the Florida Territory and did not realize the many formidable problems the soldiers faced. Nor did they comprehend the Seminoles' grim determination to fight to the death rather than be removed from their homeland. As Jesup pointed out, "We have perhaps as little knowledge of the interior of Florida, as of the interior of China."[18]

The territory was a vast, almost trackless wilderness, with

seemingly endless swamps, morasses, thickets, and dense hammocks in which the Seminoles, familiar with the terrain, could hide from the soldiers or take up concealed positions from which to launch frightful ambushes. The Seminoles craftily avoided fights out in the open, choosing instead battle sites favorable only to themselves. The interior was devoid of food for the men and forage for their animals. Supply wagons, once they reached Florida, had to be "dragged over pathless tracts of spongy pine barren, through almost impassable swamps, and across marshy rivers."[19] Crude maps had to be drawn to guide the men. The soldiers had to depend largely upon their friendly Indian allies to detect the lurking places of the Seminoles and to follow their trails and rapid flights. "Florida presented no field for artillery distinction."[20]

Surgeon Jacob R. Motte had an answer, in one sentence of amazing length, for those who charged that the army and its generals were disgraced by not winning a quick victory over the Seminoles:

> It was the character of the country, not the want of valor or persevering energy in our army; notwithstanding the abusive comments of some civilians, who reclining on cushioned chairs in their comfortable and secure homes vomited forth reproaches, sneers, and condemnation, wantonly assailing the characters of those who alienated from home and kindred and all the comforts of life, were compelled to remain in this inglorious war, checking the depredations of the savage, and pressing forward in the defense of their country; traversing unexplored tracts; marching over burning sands; wading in morasses and swamps waist deep, exposed to noxious vapours, and subject to the whims of drenching rains or the scorching sun of an almost torrid climate, whose mid-day beams burned the skin and fermented the flood; surrounded by the hardships, and privations without a murmur, and of which no one can have the least conception who was not a participant; and finally, when worn out by arduous service, sent home with ruined constitutions, to drag out a miserable existence, to be ended most probably in poverty, if not previously laid under the sod of Florida by an Indian bullet, or midnight dews, whose imperceptible damps imbibed by the thinly-clad-body, soon infected it with the disease that layed many in the silent tomb. [21]

Although Jumper, Alligator, and presumably Micanopy had entered into a truce agreement with General Jesup on 3 February, only five days later he had reason to suspect that the plan was not favored by all the Seminoles. Shortly before dawn on 8 February, a party of two hundred Indians unsuccessfully attacked Camp Monroe (later renamed Fort Mellon) at the head of Lake Monroe, near the site of the present city of Sanford.[22] Either the party had not yet heard of the truce or did not intend to abide by it. The attack was led by King Philip and his twenty-eight-year-old son, Coacoochee (Wild Cat). Under Philip's leadership, the Indians had earlier attacked and destroyed all of the plantations on the east coast south of St. Augustine, capturing many slaves.

When the Indian chiefs failed to appear at Ford Dade on 18 February, the agreed-upon date, Jesup was skeptical of their intentions. He kept the troops in readiness to renew the war but, hopefully, he continued to honor the truce. The day before the attack on Fort Mellon, he had distributed seventy dollars worth of presents among the Indians.[23] A week after the appointed date, he was considerably relieved when Alligator appeared at his headquarters, accompanied by Davy, Micanopy's nephew. The two explained that the Indians were so widely scattered that to bring them together would take more time. All the Seminoles desired peace, they said, but they were noncommital on the subject of migration. Jesup informed them that peace was entirely dependent upon their migration and that Micanopy's presence was compulsory in any peace talk. The chiefs then agreed to hold the council on 4 March. They left twelve Indians with Jesup as hostages in token of their good faith.[24]

Neither Micanopy nor any other chief appeared on 4 March, but the next day, Jumper, Davy, Cloud, and Abraham arrived at Fort Dade to meet with Jesup. The Seminole chiefs again expressed their desire for peace. Jesup demanded cessation of hostilities and immediate emigration in accordance with the Treaty of Payne's Landing. Jumper objected to immediate emigration, contending that the Indians could not leave before fall. The parley resumed the following day with two more Seminole chiefs, Alligator (nephew of Micanopy) and Coacoochee, and a Negro, John Covalo (Cowayya or Cowaya), in attendance. Jesup was still adamant about migration, and, after considerable argument, four chiefs and John Covalo signed the peace pact on behalf of the

Seminoles, while Jesup signed for the United States. Under the terms of the "capitulation," all hostilities were to cease immediately, the entire Seminole Nation was to migrate west of the Mississippi, and all of the Indians were to withdraw at once south of the Hillsborough River. After 1 April, any Indians found north of that river and an imaginary line from Fort Foster east to the ocean, without the permission of the commanding general, were to be considered hostile. The chiefs and warriors were to assemble with their families not later than 10 April at a camp to be established for that purpose near Tampa Bay. Until they migrated, they were to leave hostages in Jesup's custody to guarantee "the faithful performance of their engagements."

On behalf of the United States, Jesup pledged that "the Seminoles and their allies, who come in and emigrate to the west, shall be secure in their lives and property; that their negroes, their bona fide property, shall accompany them to the west; and their cattle and ponies shall be paid for by the United States at a fair valuation." He also stipulated that the United States would subsist the chiefs, warriors, Negroes, and their families from the time they assembled for emigration until they reached their new homeland and for twelve months thereafter. The United States would pay all expenses of the move and would recognize all the advantages secured to the Indians by the Treaty of Payne's Landing. Micanopy, one of the hostages, was to remain near Jesup until his people were ready to move.[25]

Two days after the pact was signed, Jesup wrote Cary A. Harris, commissioner of Indian affairs, that the removal of at least part of the Seminoles within two months was a "fair prospect." Ten days later he was much more optimistic: "Micconopy informed me last night that he had never before consented to emigrate; but that he now believed the Great Spirit had so ordered, that he should leave the land of his fathers, and he submitted cheerfully."

Although Jesup believed the war was at an end, he warned that any interference in his operations by white citizens could rekindle hostilities. Should the whites attempt to seize any of the Indians either as criminals or as debtors, he would not hesitate to declare martial law and send every individual not connected with the public service out of the country. He was holding the troops in such a position as to produce the best military effect. He could operate in any direction from Fort Dade and never be more than from thirty-five to fifty miles from a depot if the Indians did not act in good faith.[26]

In Washington, meanwhile, Martin Van Buren had succeeded Andrew Jackson as president on 4 March 1837. The new secretary of war was Joel R. Poinsett, a former congressional representative from South Carolina who had served as minister to Mexico between 1825 and 1829. B. F. Butler, who for five months had been the acting head of the War Department, took the occasion of leaving that post to write a letter to Jesup, expressing high praise for him: "I desire to make known to you the high sense entertained by the late President and myself for the indefatigable zeal, and the great promptitude and skill with which you have devoted yourself to the arduous duties of your command. . . . I feel it is my duty to place this testimonial on the records of the Department."[27]

Following Micanopy's surrender and approval of the capitulation document, Jesup moved his headquarters to the vicinity of Tampa Bay. A number of the prominent chiefs were in the neighborhood with "detachments" of their people. Micanopy, Davy, Cloud, and Coacoochee, among others, had left Jesup's headquarters to go to the camp about ten miles from Tampa Bay where the Seminoles were to assemble for migration. Permitting Micanopy to go to that camp was probably one of Jesup's most serious mistakes. Coacoochee promised that the elderly Sam Jones, chief of the Mikasukie tribe which had also strongly opposed migration, would come in with his people. Coacoochee himself was returning to the St. Johns to collect his cattle; he gave assurance that he, his father, and their people would go to the camp.

The chiefs entered into an agreement on 8 April to surrender the Negroes they had taken from white men during the war to the commanding officers of the posts on the St. Johns. When the pact resulted in a considerable number of Negroes being surrendered by the Indians, the Abolitionists severely condemned Jesup, claiming that he "possessed no power to bind the Seminole Nation, nor to surrender those persons to slavery." They also charged that this action, sanctioned by the War Department, violated the terms of the capitulation.[28]

Jesup wrote optimistically about the future: "The War, I hope is over; at all events there is but little danger of a renewal of hostilities, if the Troops be held in readiness for immediate action,

Joel R. Poinsett, who served as secretary of war under Martin Van Buren.

and the inhabitants of Florida act with ordinary prudence." He expressed confidence that the greater number of the Seminoles would migrate. His concern was that "strolling vagabonds will remain, probably, and annoy the frontier inhabitants." To restrain them he proposed to reestablish Fort King, and establish a post between Fort Drane and the Suwanee. Because they were in a very unhealthy section of the country, the garrisons at Forts Drane, Mellon, and Call would have to be withdrawn early in June.

When Secretary Poinsett requested him to supply topographical information for use in preparing maps of Florida, Jesup replied that while two Topographical Corps officers had been assigned to his command by army orders, one had been withdrawn without entering upon duty and the other had been recalled within a few days after joining Jesup. He himself had gone to Florida with no knowledge of the country; the only guides from whom he could obtain any correct information were the captured Indians and Negroes. He directed Lt. Thomas B. Linnard, his aide-de-camp, "to collect and arrange such data as are accessible."[29]

In Washington as well as in Florida and elsewhere, optimism ran high that the war was nearly at an end. Commander-in-Chief Alexander Macomb sent instructions to Jesup concerning the disposition of the regulars stationed in Florida should the favorable reports prove accurate. Jesup had visions of employing some of the regulars in exploring and surveying areas of the territorial wilderness.[30] On 5 April, the *Washington Globe* printed an item from the *Savannah Republican* stating, "latest accounts make it almost certain that General Jesup has effected the objects for which he was sent to Florida."

Jesup devoted considerable time and effort to establishing rapport not only with the chiefs and warriors but also with their children. In addition to the gifts he had distributed earlier, he spent nine dollars for a pair of blankets for a warrior he learned was in need of them. He gave five dollars to a group of Indian boys he found engaged in a ball game. From the Seminoles he purchased a horse and a pony. He paid Alligator's son ten dollars for a sword and a similar amount to another Indian for a sword taken from an officer killed in battle; sixteen dollars went toward tobacco for the Indians. All such expenditures were drawn from Jesup's personal funds.[31]

The presence and influence of the Seminole's Negro allies

served as an all-important difference between the removal of the Creeks from Alabama and Georgia and the Seminoles from Florida. To a large extent, the Negroes dominated the Seminoles rather than vice versa. Jesup was quick to realize that they could well be the key to any success he might have in persuading the Indians to migrate. Consequently, he had carefully stipulated in the compact of 6 March that the Seminole "allies" (presumably free Negroes) and those who were their "bona fide property" were to accompany the Indians to the West. Among other issues, this stipulation raised the question of how to prove with any degree of certainty which Negroes were free, which were slaves legally possessed by the Seminoles, and which fitted into some other category. Nearly every problem in regard to dealing with the Negroes was so controversial that any solution satisfactory to everyone was utterly impossible. Thus Jesup was in the line of fire of two opposing factions whose viewpoints were completely incompatible. On the one hand, the white settlers, who were proponents of slavery, were determined to get rid of the Seminoles and gain possession of the Indian lands, but they were equally determined to repossess all the Negro slaves which they claimed the Indians had stolen from them. On the other, Abolitionists, such as Joshua R. Giddings,[32] ignoring the fact that Florida was a slave territory, were bitterly opposed to any action or policy which did not give the Negroes complete freedom. The Abolitionists' accounts of events in Florida were extremely biased and exaggerated for propaganda purposes in their efforts to abolish slavery.

When news of the capitulation spread and the slave owners learned that the Negroes were to accompany the Indians to the West, they rose up in great indignation to condemn Jesup. Newspapers which earlier had praised him for his effective measures now angrily denounced him. A group of citizens sent a letter of protest to the secretary of war. The people of Florida had not acted with the "prudence" that Jesup had hoped they would. Upon receiving complaints from the chiefs that the white people were constantly interfering with the Negroes of the Indians, Jesup did what he had, in effect, threatened to do earlier; he issued Order No. 79, forbidding citizens to enter the Indian territory between the St. Johns and the Gulf of Mexico, south of Fort Drane.[33]

This order brought even louder cries of anguish from the white settlers, particularly those who wished to enter the forbidden area to seize slaves. More condemnation of Jesup appeared in the Florida press. The widespread protest culminated in a public gathering in St. Augustine, attended by citizens from various parts of the territory. A committee, appointed to remonstrate with the general, appealed to him to rescind the order. Their letter contained the rather surprising statement that "the regaining of their slaves constitutes an object of scarcely less moment than that of peace in the country."[34]

Perhaps realizing that he may have acted too hastily and encompassed too large an area, Jesup decided, three weeks after issuing Order No. 79, to modify it to allow citizens to enter the area as far south as the road connecting Volusia with the Withlacoochee. On 1 May he so informed Maj. William L. McClintock, commander of Fort Drane. The next day he notified Brig. Gen Walker K. Armistead that he was to consider the order "so far modified, that citizens will be permitted to visit any of the posts on the St. Johns, and to traverse or remain in any part of the country south of the Withlacoochee" in order to recover their herds of cattle. Now the Abolitionists took their turn at criticizing the general, charging that he was "incapable of resisting the popular clamor" and was making it convenient for claimants to recover their slaves.[35]

While some Florida citizens were finding fault with Jesup, an unidentified officer at Tampa praised him in a letter published in the *Charleston Courier* on 4 May. The Indians were coming in fast, the officer wrote, and Jesup deserved great credit for the delicacy and discretion with which he had acted. "The Floridians ought, of all others, to thank him." [36]

When the Seminoles began turning in their cattle and horses in accordance with the terms of the capitulation, Jesup considered the act an indication of their good faith, as he informed the commissioner of Indian affairs. "The emigration will be tedious and expensive but I think it will certainly take place." Then he added, with a note of skepticism, "The Seminoles, however, have less regard for their promises than any other Indians I have ever known."[37]

Another seeming good sign that the emigration plans were proceeding smoothly was the behavior of Osceola following the capitulation pact. Lt. Col. William S. Harney,[38] commander at Fort

Mellon, where many of the Seminoles were assembling, informed Jesup that Osceola and his family had arrived there early in May. Though not a chief, this young Indian leader of the militant Seminoles, whose record of treacherous killings had made him notorious, now expressed his desire for peace and voiced his willingness to migrate. As a display of his good will, he helped arrange a game of ball to entertain the garrison.[39] Despite his reputation for malicious mischief, no indication has been found that any of the officers, Jesup included, suspected him at that time of duplicity. In fact, on 8 May, Jesup expressed his belief that "Powell [Osceola] will be highly useful in bringing the Indians in, and in hastening their embarkation." He was concerned only about the possibility of imprudent conduct on the part of some of the white settlers. "The officious interference of some of them has already embarrassed the service; and from the public papers I discover that certain citizens of Florida, who, I presume were unwilling to trust their persons nearer to the Seminoles than Charleston, are denouncing me and my measures. I have only to say in reply that I can have no agency in converting the Army into negro catchers. . . ."[40]

Micanopy, Jumper, and Cloud were at the emigration camp while Davy was collecting his followers, who were due in by 20 May. Alligator and his people, who had assembled but fled again when they heard a rumor that they were to be executed, were finally induced to return by assurances that the rumor was not true. A continuing problem was caused by the appearance in the area of white settlers seeking and demanding the return of their slaves. Whenever word spread that the slaveowners were in the vicinity, the Negroes would disappear into the wilderness.[41]

Despite the criticism he had to endure from some quarters in Florida, Jesup retained the complete confidence of the War Department. Secretary Poinsett wrote him on 25 May that the department desired him to continue to exercise great vigilance in protecting the Indians from all violence, both from troops and citizens, and to take all proper measures to prevent any "officious interference" from any quarters. The attacks upon his course of conduct, Poinsett stated, were not worthy of his notice. "It is hoped that you will steadily proceed in the execution of your important duties without regard to them; and rely upon the support of the people and approbation of the Department, to sustain you in your efforts to put an end to the war and to send the Indians, speedily and peaceably, to their new homes."[42]

From all outward appearances, Jesup had terminated the conflict and brought the Seminoles under his control in less than three months since he had assumed command. There had been no sign of hostilities since early in February. Now, at the end of May, travel in the territory was safe once more. Most of the white settlers had emerged from the stockades and blockhouses where they had taken refuge in panic when the Indians went on the warpath in December of 1835. With the frontier quiet and no apparent need remaining for their services, Jesup discharged the bulk of the militia and volunteers, and sent the marines under Col. Archibald Henderson back up north.[43] "It must be admitted," writes McReynolds, "that Jesup had given the most effective display of military power that had been shown in Florida since the active days of General Andrew Jackson."[44]

The Indians' embarkation date had been postponed from week to week because of the pleas of some of the chiefs, who said they were expecting more relatives and friends to accompany them to the West. Otherwise, preparation was proceeding smoothly. Capt. John Page, superintendent of emigration, was busily recording the arrivals of newcomers on the growing list. Micanopy, who had given his promise to leave the country, was directing the preparations of his people for departure. Nearby, in the Tampa Bay harbor, a fleet of twenty-six boats was ready to transport the Seminoles and their Negroes to their new home beyond the Mississippi. Jesup had every reason to believe that the Indians had resigned themselves to peaceful migration. Then, the bubble suddenly burst.

On the night of 2 June 1837, Osceola and Sam Jones, with a band of about two hundred young militant followers, slipped into the emigration camp. They kidnapped Micanopy, forcing him despite his violent protests to accompany them. With a dire threat that no dissent would be tolerated, they compelled the other Seminoles to flee. Jumper and Cloud, who like Micanopy favored migration, were among those coerced into leaving. By dawn the camp was deserted, and the troops could no longer hope to overtake the Indians before they disappeared into the wilderness. Their flight confirmed Jesup's pessimistic prophecy, made nearly four months before, that the Indians would renew the war rather than leave the country.

The sudden disastrous turn of events was a crushing blow to Jesup's hopes. He was now convinced that the Seminoles were determined to fight to the finish to remain in Florida and that the government's removal policy no longer had any prospect of being successful. The warriors had removed Micanopy as head of the nation, replacing him with Sam Jones, the Mikasukie chief. Jesup announced that he would immediately discharge the vessels which had been employed to carry the Indians to the West. Also, he would deposit to the credit of the U. S. treasurer all of the money which had been placed to his credit in the branch of the Bank of Alabama at Mobile and in the Union Bank at New Orleans.[45]

John T. Sprague sheds some light on the attitude of the Seminoles and the reasons why the militants waited so long to make the move which halted the government's emigration program. "The true reason was their indisposition to leave the country, and the determination of the younger chiefs that they never would. . . . Now well clothed for the approaching season, their crops advanced, and the sickness throughout the country precluding the possibility of military movements, they asked for nothing more from the whites, and were determined to enjoy their homes until another emergency should compel them to capitulate." That the war could ever be ended on the government's terms was unlikely.

> No vigilance, sagacity, or forecast, could close a contest with an enemy utterly regardless of integrity and honor, nor could human wisdom defeat a scheme so ingeniously and covertly designed, and so promptly executed. The public mind became highly excited. The press condemned General Jesup without inquiry or investigation. In the escape of the Indians and the renewal of hostilities, their infidelity was lost sight of, and the embarrassments by which the commander was surrounded were completely disregarded. Those removed from the scene of action, could not understand and appreciate his position, even if disposed to listen. . . .[46]

Jesup was not taken by complete surprise. More than thirty-six hours before the flight of the Seminoles, he had received from the chief of the friendly Creek Indians "an intimation that an attempt would be made in a few days by a party of Mikasukies and a small band of Seminoles to kill or abduct those chiefs." Acting on this tip, he had taken what he considered the necessary precautions. He had ordered Maj. William M. Graham, stationed four miles from Micanopy's camp with a mounted company and 120 Creek warriors, to send out spies at night to observe the movements of the Indians. The major had sent two Indians into the Seminole camp on the night of 1 June, and, though he had ordered them to go there again on the following night, they had either disobeyed his order or failed to report. The mounted forces at Tampa Bay and at Major Graham's camp had been held in readiness to move at a moment's warning, but the flight of the Indians was not discovered until the morning of 3 June. The Seminoles had a twelve-hour start, and the extremely hot weather and the nature of the country made it useless to pursue them.

Something of Jesup's character is revealed by what happened when he met in council with the principal chiefs the day before the flight. He could have seized them and captured their camp, "but such an act would have been an infraction of the treaty." He continued, "The capture of a few hundred Indians would have been a poor compensation for the violation of the national faith; the Indians now have no confidence in our promises, and I, as a representative of the country here, was unwilling to teach a lesson of barbarism to a band of savages."

Durable peace with the Indians would have been an easy matter, he contended, had they been permitted to remain in Florida. The Indians felt that they were beaten; they were tired of war and ready to make peace. But the emigration scheme was impractical. "This is the first instance in our history in which we have attempted to transfer Indians from one wilderness to another. On all other occasions the white population has been pressing and crowding them out before we have attempted to remove them." The only way to get rid of the Indians was to exterminate them; was the government ready for such a measure? "Will public opinion sustain it? If so, resort must be had to the bloodhound and the northern Indian." He intimated that he did not favor such a policy and did not believe the public would either.

Believing that the war would probably be renewed under the leadership of the Mikasukies, Jesup informed Poinsett that he was positioning his troops so as to secure the frontier and preserve the men's health during the sickly season. Jesup recommended that the troops should be ready to take the field by 1 October for the fall campaign, but he gave a broad hint that he was leaving the way open for the appointment of his successor to the command: "The depots necessary to the most vigorous prosecution of the war may all be established and filled by the 1st of September. The officer who is to be charged with the operations of the next campaign should be at once placed in command of the army, in order to make timely arrangements for the service."[47]

Convinced that the public had lost confidence in him, Jesup fully expected to be relieved, and he had no desire to retain his command. Although his military operations had been eminently successful, his efforts to remove the Indians from Florida had failed just when it seemed they might be successful. He was aware that the public, particularly the people of Florida, were not satisfied with what he had accomplished. "I hold, that the moment the public confidence is withdrawn from a general, the executive is bound to remove him; for no matter what may be his merits, or how transcendent his abilities, his private and personal interests should not be put in competition with the interests of the nation." He frankly admitted that his views concerning the Indian removal policy were contrary to those of the administration. Therefore, on 5 June, to avoid placing President Van Buren in an "embarrassing" position, he requested through the adjutant general in Washington to be relieved of his command. His application was rejected on the ground that his experience in conducting the operations in Florida was too valuable to be lost by removing him from the command.[48]

At that point, two unexpected developments occurred. First, Poinsett suddenly and without explanation reversed his earlier decision. On 22 June, he informed Jesup that he would be permitted to return to Washington to resume his duties as quartermaster general, provided that on receipt of the letter he still desired to be relieved of the command. Second, great pressure, some from surprising sources, had been exerted upon Jesup to retain the command, and he too had reversed his decision. He explained that a material change had taken place: "The press, either mistaking or misrepresenting my motives, had denounced me, in no very measured terms, for asking to be relieved; and the people of the country, as well as the officers of the army, so far as their opinions were made known to me, seemed to desire that I should retain the command." Jesup's feelings and interests prompted him to retire, but the position he then found himself in caused him to believe that he was not at liberty to do so, and he announced his intention to remain.[49] He was thus committed to conduct a second campaign.

The escape of the Indians caused a general alarm among the white settlers. With volunteers and militia from adjacent states already discharged and the regular troops ineffective because of widespread sickness and a shortage of officers, Jesup had to rely primarily upon armed Floridians during the summer to protect the frontier settlements. He requested Governor Call to furnish 300 men east of the Suwannee River and 400 west of it. After the flight of the Seminoles, Jesup left the Tampa Bay area and crossed over to St. Augustine, where he was engaged in recruiting volunteers and organizing them into mounted and infantry companies. He kept detachments of mounted men on the move to prevent hostile Indians from approaching the settlements.[50]

Jesup believed that the regular troops should be kept as quiet as possible during the hot weather in hopes they would be in good condition for the autumn campaign. In addition to their health, he displayed concern about getting them more pay for the hardships they had to endure. Six months earlier, Jesup had written Butler that the pay of the troops should be doubled while serving in Florida and had urged him to impress upon Congress "the necessity of putting the army upon a better footing." He said, "I wish nothing for myself, and, if justice can be done to my brave companions, I will cheerfully serve out the campaign without pay or emoluments." Four days later he had warned Butler that the army was in danger of disbanding because soldiers were not reenlisting due to the low pay, and that officers were not able to subsist on the miserable pittance allowed them; "they should upon principles of common justice, be placed on a footing with the corresponding grades in the navy." He broached the subject in several subsequent letters to Butler, but no action was taken. On 10 June 1837, he suggested to Poinsett that the "troops and all officers below the rank of Major-General should receive double pay while serving in Florida."[51] Jesup could not anticipate that when the 25th Congress opened on 4 September it would be in no mood to adopt his proposal; the high cost of conducting the war would be a subject of spirited debate between the Whigs and administration supporters in the months ahead.

Jesup acknowledged that removal of the Indians from Florida would be a task of great magnitude: "We have, at no former period of our history, had to contend with so formidable an enemy. No Seminole proves false to his country, nor has a single instance ever occurred of a first rate warrior having surrendered." He urged that all regiments be organized at the full wartime strength of at least one hundred men to a company and that the ranks be filled as early as possible. Jesup also requested that an auxiliary Indian force be made available by September.

While restricting activities of regular troops during the excessive summer heat, Jesup continued to maintain a surprisingly heavy schedule for himself. Official correspondence and preparations for his fall campaign kept him quite busy, yet he often traveled long distances on horseback. One officer wrote, "Gen. Jesup has just left this post [Fort Heileman] for St. Augustine. This is the second time he has been from Tampa this summer; he rides thro' the country sometimes forty or fifty miles a day, as tho' it were his profession."[52] This active, outdoor life, despite its perils, hardships, and frustrations, seems to have been beneficial to the strength and vigor of the quartermaster general whose duties had kept him confined so closely to his desk as to endanger his health.

While administration officials in Washington had complete confidence in Jesup's ability as a military leader, they were disturbed because he did not approve of the removal policy. Consequently, Poinsett undertook to explain President Van Buren's viewpoint. True, the Seminoles "dwell in an inhospitable and deadly climate, and occupy inaccessible swamps and morasses which are not susceptible of cultivation or improvements by the whites." Nevertheless, their presence was a threat to the peace and security of white settlers in Florida. The government's duty was, therefore, "to carry out the same policy with regard to Seminoles which it had adopted in its treatment of other Indian tribes east of the Mississippi." Either the Seminoles must be removed or the settlers must be withdrawn from East Florida and the western part of that territory protected by a cordon of posts and troops. "Every consideration of sound policy required them to adopt the former alternative." For the government to withdraw its forces "would not only tarnish the honor of our arms but violate the sacred obligations of the Government to protect the persons and property of the citizens of Florida from the savage aggressions of the Indian." Poinsett was convinced that that obligation could be fulfilled "without seeking to exterminate the Seminoles."[53] Jesup no doubt knew as well as Poinsett all the arguments for supporting the removal policy; he was not swayed by them.

CHAPTER 8

JESUP'S

SECOND CAMPAIGN

AGAINST THE SEMINOLES

JESUP'S HOPE OF beginning his second campaign by 1 October was rejected by Poinsett late in the summer when he instructed the quartermaster general not to commence active operations before November.[1] Meanwhile, on 19 August, Jesup met at Fort King with a number of Indian chiefs who wished to see him. During the next two days, the chiefs expressed their earnest desire for peace but declared that the majority of the Seminoles were opposed to leaving their homeland. Jesup was sympathetic but informed them that they must first agree to fulfill the terms of their treaty before any peace discussion could be held, warning that he could not confer with them on any other subject. Those who decided to surrender for the purpose of migrating should come in under a white flag so as to be safe from attack by scouting parties as they approached.

Coehadjo, the principal chief at the conference, told the general that although many of the Seminole chiefs were in favor of migration, Sam Jones, the elderly Mikasukie chief, and Osceola, who controlled the young warriors, were adamant in their opposition and had threatened to put to death all who favored the plan. The chiefs of the nation planned to hold a council in a few days on the St. Johns to reach a decision, but he suspected that Sam

Jones would try to prevent the council from being held. Coehadjo promised to return to Fort King in twenty days to report the results. He proposed that in the meantime hostilities should cease on both sides. Jesup agreed to the armistice, provided that "all the Indians should withdraw south of Fort Mellon, and on no account return to the north of that post; that they should neither cross the eastern side of the St. Johns, nor to the western side of the Fort King road; and that the violation of any of those terms should be considered an act of hostility."[2]

Jesup reminded the Indian leaders that the Seminoles, through their principal chiefs, had surrendered to him by capitulation in March at Fort Dade. Consequently, he considered them to be prisoners of war who had violated their parole. Although he could easily have done so, he had made no attempt to hold those who had assembled for the conference. He warned that no Indian in the future would be permitted to enter his camp for any other reason than to remain and emigrate; anyone coming in under a white flag would be considered to have surrendered with full intent to emigrate and consequently would be detained for that purpose in accordance with the treaty. He provided the Indians with strips of muslin to be used as white flags to ensure their safe entry and promised that those who decided to come in would be treated with kindness and consideration.[3]

Experience had taught the general to adopt a strict policy regarding Seminole visits to his camp. The Indians had violated the white flag a number of times. Some had employed it in good faith. Others had come in under such a banner proclaiming their friendship and declaring their intentions to migrate; then, after receiving the supplies they needed and observing the position and strength of the troops, they had left the camp to resume their hostilities. In May, for example, Osceola, accompanied by his followers, had entered Fort Mellon under a white flag and surrendered to Lt. Col. William Harney, declaring himself done with war and wishing to migrate. He solicited subsistence and transportation to take his band to Tampa Bay, where the Indians had been directed to assemble for migration. Harney supplied Osceola with provisions, and relying on his word and apparent sincerity, paroled him to go to Tampa Bay without a guard. At the same time, Coehadjo was given subsistence for his band for the same purpose. Osceola not only failed to take his own band to Tampa Bay, but he also forcibly

Thomas Hart Benton, senator from Missouri, who defended Jesup in Congress and was the grand uncle of the American painter who bore his name.

prevented Coehadjo and his own people from going there as they had planned. Thomas Hart Benton declared later in the Senate that this practice of deception ". . . was making a mockery of the white flag, and subjecting the officers to ridicule as well as to danger. General Jesup resolved to put an end to these treacherous and dangerous visits, which were giving spies and hostile Indians ready access to the bosom of his camp."[4]

Coehadjo failed to return to Fort King as promised. Sam Jones and Osceola had apparently been successful in scaring off most of the chiefs. The few who attended made a pact to punish any of their people who committed depredations against white inhabitants but decided against leaving the country.

Lacking regular army officers and troops, Jesup had been forced to conduct his first campaign with a command comprised predominantly of volunteers and militia. Now, as he was planning his second campaign with the expectation of having a larger proportion of regulars, he was provoked when the secretary of war detailed two regular officers to serve as instructors at the United States Military Academy. "It may truly be said," he wrote the adjutant general on 13 August, "the spirit of the service is gone, or fast going, when officers of respectable standing can be found ready to abandon the high and honorable duties of their profession to become *schoolmasters* at West Point."

The reaction to that statement, obviously made in an unguarded moment of vexation, illustrates again the willingness of army officers in that period to engage in public quarrels with comrades-in-arms even in the midst of a war. It brought indignant and derogatory comments from the "schoolmasters." In letters to the *Army and Navy Chronicle*, some of them severely upbraided the general while defending the academy and their roles as military instructors. One was particularly vicious in a lengthy discourse. His remarks followed the line being pursued by the Whigs, insinuating that Jesup had supplanted "in a very irregular manner, his senior, a general of the army, and once 'an ancient friend.' " On the other hand, an anonymous contributor was "very sorry to see such a disposition to abuse Gen. Jesup and such lukewarmness among his well wishers in his defence. . . . The public will never have a more zealous, active, and faithful public servant, although it gives him little else than reproaches, sneers, or condemnation."[5]

Meanwhile, the term of army service of the friendly Creek Indian warriors ended in September. They were to be reunited with their families and sent to the West to join thousands of other Creeks who had been removed from Alabama and Georgia the previous year. As preparations were made for their departure, Jesup displayed concern for their welfare. He moved his headquarters from St. Augustine to Tampa Bay in time to bid them farewell, and instructed Maj. William G. Freeman to accompany the warriors to Pass Christian and make arrangements to discharge and pay them. On 9 September, he ordered Freeman and Capt. James Boyd to look after the well-being of the Indians while they were in New Orleans, making sure they did not waste their money on useless articles. "I wish you and Captain Boyd to assist them in their purchases, so as to prevent imposition being practiced upon them."[6]

As an inducement to obtain their services in Florida, the Creek warriors had been promised all of the Seminole property they captured. From Tampa Bay on 6 September 1837, Jesup issued order No. 175, which provided that all Seminole Negroes captured by the army would "be taken on account of Government and held subject to the orders of the Secretary of War." He advised the secretary that had compensation not been promised, the Creek warriors would have put to death all the Negroes they captured.[7] Poinsett on 7 October approved this action, which subsequently provided ammunition to the anti-slavery Whigs. Joshua Giddings declared in a fiery speech in the House on 9 February 1841 that neither Jesup nor the secretary of war had the constitutional power or right to make the country "slaveholders." He vilified the general and the administration for all of their policies relating to Negro slaves. The speech, published in the *Washington Globe* on 21 February, later served as the nucleus for Giddings' book, *The Exiles of Florida*, published in 1858, in which he sought to prove that slavery was the underlying cause of the war.

The question of property rights was an exceedingly tangled problem for Jesup to resolve. To pay the Creek warriors for the cattle and horses they captured was easy enough. But to determine the proper disposition of the captured Negroes was not so simple. First, he must ascertain how many were bona fide property of the Seminoles, how many were free, and how many belonged to, and had been captured from, the citizens of Florida. To determine which had been taken by the Creeks and which by the troops was also difficult. Jesup proposed to allow the Creek warriors eight thousand dollars as a fair equivalent for their claims, and they assented to the proposition. This amount was to be paid to them at Pass Christian.

Much to Jesup's surprise, at Pass Christian the Creek warriors refused to accept the money, claiming that the amount was too small. Jesup believed their refusal resulted from influence exercised by certain white men who were eager to make a quick profit by purchasing the captured Negro slaves from the Creek warriors at a price higher than that set by the government. James C. Watson of Georgia, for example, offered the warriors $14,338 for sixty-seven of the Negroes they claimed, knowing they were worth many times that figure on the market. Strangely, he was acting at the suggestion of Secretary Poinsett himself and with the support of the Office of Indian Affairs. "I was apprised of an order to surrender the negroes," Jesup states, "but protested against the measure and probably had some influence in preventing it from being carried out."

Having been criticized by others for his arrangements with the Indians, Jesup later expressed his own views in order that his conduct and motives might be correctly understood. He contended that the commander of an army, like an ambassador or other public minister, acted under the laws and constitution of his own country or the positive instructions to his command. Congress had legislated in regard to captures at sea. But captures on land, including all movable property captured, it had left to be disposed of according to the laws of nations. Therefore, whether Jesup had made any promises to the Indians or not, they would have had a fair claim to their proportion of the captured property. He had not claimed the right to put forth any arbitrary definition of his own as to what constituted property. The prisoners who were free he had recognized as persons; those who were slaves he had viewed as property.

> As the Commander of the Army I was the humble representative of a nation composed of slave-holding and non-slave-holding States. Had that Army been operating on the northern frontier I could not have recognized negro prisoners as property; but operating in a slave-holding community I was bound by the lex loci and could not avoid considering them as property. . . . If I erred I had high authority to sustain me—the distinguished statesmen who formed the commission at Ghent, a majority of whom were citizens of non-slave-holding states,

solemnly recognized & stipulated as property, slaves captured by the British forces in the late war [War of 1812].[8]

To replace the Creek warriors as allies of the army in Jesup's second campaign, Poinsett recruited about eight hundred Indians from northern tribes, including Delawares, Fox, Kickapoos, Sauk, and Shawnees. When word of this reached the House, one Whig member, Caleb Cushing of Massachusetts, condemned the administration for using Indians to fight Indians.[9]

In late September, Jesup received word that Rep. Henry A. Wise of Virginia, a former Jackson Democrat turned Whig, had made a serious charge against him and was demanding the appointment of a congressional committee to investigate his conduct. Wise, a bitter critic of the Jackson and Van Buren administrations, had asserted on the floor of the House that Jesup had made a solemn pledge to the Creek Indian Chief Hopoethle Yoholo that, as a reward for aiding the general in the removal of the Creeks from Alabama and Georgia, the chief would be allowed to remain on the land he claimed, but that when the Creeks were overcome, Jesup had turned upon him and "with bayonet in hand drove him from his possessions." Wise had added, "The most condign punishment should be visited upon a Major general guilty of such conduct towards the Indians within our territory." When Rep. J. R. Underwood pressed Wise for details, the Virginian replied that his information did not enable him to supply them. Underwood knew Jesup too well to believe the story, so he did some investigating. Two days before adjournment of the first session of the 25th Congress, he informed members of what he had learned and read a letter from Jesup, who denied entering into any such agreement with Hopoethle Yoholo or breaking any treaty with that chief.[10] Underwood's defense marked the end of one false accusation, but many more were to be made against Jesup.

Before the end of the summer at least some of the Negroes had become disenchanted with their life among the Seminoles. On 4 September, four slaves captured at a sugar plantation near New Smyrna escaped from the Indians and sought refuge at Fort Peyton, near St. Augustine. The tales they told seemingly refuted the legend that the Seminoles were always kind to their slaves. The escapees complained of a lack of food and charged that they had been severely beaten; they appeared delighted to be reunited with the whites.[11]

Based on information they provided concerning an Indian camp, General Hernandez set out with a detachment of troops. He came upon five more escaped Negroes seeking the protection of the soldiers. One agreed to guide the troops to a spot near where the Indians were encamped. At dawn of 9 September the men surprised and captured King Philip and all members of his party except his eighteen-year-old son, who managed to escape. Among the captives was an Indian known as Tomoka John, who revealed that another Indian camp was in the vicinity. That night the men surrounded the camp and at daybreak captured an important chief, Uchee Billy, his brother, Uchee Jack, and a number of warriors. All were taken to St. Augustine and held at Fort Marion.[12]

King Philip, apparently resigned to migration, received permission from Hernandez to send Tomoka John for his family. Tomoka John returned accompanied by Coacoochee, who, at the urging of his father, agreed to try to bring in members of the family. Coacoochee made it clear, however, that since he had come in voluntarily, he expected to be free to leave. Hernandez was reluctant to let him go and referred the matter to Jesup, who directed that the Indian be permitted to carry out his mission. Coacoochee promised to bring in all the Seminoles in the St. Johns area where his father was the principal chief. Jesup warned him that no one should be invited to come in for any other purpose than to remain and migrate.[13]

The young chief returned on 17 October with a brother of Philip and one of his own brothers. He had succeeded, he said, in rounding up about one hundred Indians and about as many Negroes, who were on their way to St. Augustine. He also brought the surprising news that Osceola and his followers were only a day's march from St. Augustine and that they were planning to come in for a conference.

On 20 October, Osceola made camp with about one hundred of his followers near Fort Peyton and sent John Covalo, a Seminole Negro, into St. Augustine to invite General Hernandez to come to his camp *without an escort* for a talk. Jesup was then at St. Augustine, having returned from Tampa Bay. Keenly aware of Osceola's earlier treacheries while pretending friendliness, and suspecting that this might be another ruse, he gave Hernandez permission to meet Osceola but ordered him to take along a military escort sufficient to cope with any surprise. Jesup believed that

Osceola's motive in asking Hernandez to come into his camp alone was to seize him as a hostage to be exchanged for King Philip and Uchee Billy. Moreover, he was skeptical of any venture in which Covalla was involved, since the Negro had been among those who engineered the escape of the Indians at Tampa Bay. His suspicions were further aroused when several Negroes, formerly with Osceola's party, came to his headquarters and told him that the Indians had "come for no good," that they did not intend to migrate, and that they wanted to obtain powder and clothing. They also informed Jesup that Osceola and his followers only a short time before had killed a white man and that some of the Mikasukies and Tallahassees from Osceola's party had gone to the Alachua frontier to steal horses and cattle.[14]

As a test of the Indians' sincerity and intentions, Jesup prepared a list of seven questions to be asked at the meeting. In general, these inquired into the topics he had discussed with Coehadjo during their earlier conference at Fort King. Coehadjo, who had not returned to the fort as he had promised, was now in Osceola's party. Jesup's instructions to Hernandez were that if the answers of the Indians were not satisfactory, he was to seize the entire group.[15]

The historic meeting between Hernandez and Osceola took place in Osceola's camp, approximately a mile south of Fort Peyton, on 21 October 1837. Hernandez arrived with an escort of about two hundred mounted men under Maj. James A. Ashby of the 2d Dragoons. Osceola's party numbered ninety-five, including Coehadjo and twelve other chiefs, seventy-one warriors, six women, and four Negroes. Hernandez construed the fact that no Indian children and only a small number of women were present as an indication of the party's hostile intentions. The Indians kept their guns, loaded and primed, within arm's reach, hidden under deerskins. According to Assistant Army Surgeon Nathan Jarvis, who was present, Osceola stood beneath a white flag to greet the army officers.[16]

Jesup had directed Lieutenant Peyton to keep him informed of the progress of the conference. When Peyton returned to say that the Indians' answers to the questions had been evasive and that they had evidently not come in with any intention of migrating, Jesup sent a messenger to Hernandez with an order to make them prisoners: "Let the chief and warriors know we have been deceived by them long enough, and that we do not intend to be deceived again. Order the whole party to town—you have force sufficient to compel obedience . . . they must be disarmed—they can talk in town, and send any message out they please."[17]

Hernandez reported to Jesup the following day that the Indians were "perfectly disposed" to bring in the Negroes and the property they had taken from the inhabitants during the war. However, he continued, "[They were] by no means prepared to surrender themselves, and their answers to the questions put to them in regard to their breach of the stipulations made with you at Fort King, I conceived to be wholly evasive and unsatisfactory. Indeed their answers were generally so." Hernandez was convinced: ". . . nothing but the promptitude and efficiency of the troops under my command prevented the effusion of blood; for the arms of the enemy, artfully covered by deer-skins, as if carelessly thrown upon the ground occupied by them, were ready and evidently prepared for action."[18]

All ninety-five prisoners were taken to Fort Marion. Osceola, who complained of feeling ill, Coehadjo, and one other were mounted on horses for the seven-mile trip to St. Augustine; the others were marched between lines of mounted men. Soon after their imprisonment, Osceola and Coehadjo requested permission to see General Jesup and were taken to his headquarters in St. Augustine. They told him that Micanopy, Jumper, Davy, and most of the Seminoles were prepared to migrate but were deterred from coming in by the Mikasukies. They proposed that messengers be sent to Micanopy and Jumper and asked to be allowed to send messengers to their own people, who, they said, would come in if assured their lives would be spared. Jesup complied with their requests and dispatched a special messenger of his own to Micanopy. Five or six weeks later, while Jesup was at Fort Mellon, he received word from Micanopy that he was ready to fulfill the terms of the capitulation and was confident that he could induce other chiefs and the greater number of his people to surrender. About the same time, the messenger sent out by Osceola arrived at Fort Mellon with Osceola's family and people. Jesup sent them with an escort to St. Augustine, where they joined Osceola in Fort Marion.[19]

In his report to Secretary Poinsett, General Jesup stated clearly that he did not consider the flag displayed by Osceola to be a genuine flag of truce. He listed his reasons for ordering the seizure of the Indians.

> As I had informed the chiefs at Fort King [in August 1837] that I would hold no communication with the Seminoles, unless they should determine to emigrate; as I had permitted no Indian to come in for any other purpose but to remain; as they were all prisoners of war, or hostages who had violated their paroles; as many of them had violated the truce entered into at Fort King . . . and as the white flag had been allowed for no other purpose than to enable them to communicate and come in without danger to attack from our parties, it became my duty to secure them, on being satisfied of the fact they intended to return to their fastnesses. I accordingly required General Hernandez to seize them, and take them to St. Augustine; but, notwithstanding their character as prisoners and hostages who had violated their parole, and who according to the laws of war, as recognized by civilized nations, had forfeited their lives, I directed that they should be treated with every kindness, and have every accommodation consistent with their security.[20]

The late Dr. Mark F. Boyd, past president of both the Florida Historical Society and the American Society of Tropical Medicine and author of perhaps the most comprehensive study of Osceola's life, concluded, "It would be difficult to understand how, given the opportunity, Jesup could have done otherwise than to seize Osceola and the other Indians, and not have been derelict in his duty."[21]

Surgeon Motte, who stood on a stump to watch the captives as they were marched toward St. Augustine, believed that General Jesup was completely justified in ignoring Osceola's white flag and in ordering the seizure of the Indians.

> There were some individuals who pretended to condemn the capture of Osceola and his warriors as dishonorable on the part of Gen. Jesup;—as a base violation of a flag of truce. Tis true they had a white flag flying; but they were never told that it would afford them indemnity from capture on this occasion. On the contrary, they had been repeatedly told that the only

terms with which they would be received were those of actual surrender and that no flag would be received in any other terms. . . . Even had they been enticed in under the immunity of the white flag, Gen. Jesup would have been perfectly justified in making prisoners of them, for he was dealing with the very individuals who had repeatedly and treacherously trifled with the flag of truce; had forfeited their plighted faith, and flagrantly deceived him, in forcibly carrying off hostages left by them in his hands; and when we recollect that this interview was sought by them with the worst of motives, public opinion ought not only to justify, but commend him for the transaction.[22]

Surgeon Jarvis noted that the Indians displayed no signs of surprise or fear when the troops surrounded and captured them. On the way to St. Augustine, Jarvis rode alongside Osceola. He observed that although the Indian was obviously unwell, he was not downcast. When Surgeon Samuel Forry in his professional capacity saw the Indians at Fort Marion, he also commented that Osceola was ill, suffering from an intermittent fever. Neither Osceola nor the others seemed to regret their capture but were eager to be reunited with their families.[23]

The news that Osceola and a dozen hostile chiefs had been taken into custody was the cause for jubilation among the white inhabitants of Florida. The Whigs reacted differently. Seeing an opportunity to deal another blow to the administration, they promptly condemned General Jesup for the manner of the capture. It was Jackson—was it not?—who had placed the general in the Florida command; and Van Buren who had kept him there. In both houses of congress and in the party newspapers, the Whigs hurled the charge and repeated it over and over again that General Jesup had committed "perfidy" by capturing the "noble" Osceola through "treachery" and "fraud." They expressed sympathy toward Osceola and nothing but criticism toward Jesup. The Whigs renewed demands for a congressional investigation of the general's conduct, but they did not wait to learn what such an investigation might reveal—they had reached their own verdict. To them a white flag had but one meaning—it was a flag of truce—and they had no hesitancy in passing judgment without a hearing upon the officer they accused of violating it.

Rep. Waddy Thompson of South Carolina asserted that the incident "was the first instance in the history of our country where an American officer had refused to respect a flag of truce." Senator William Preston, also of South Carolina and one of Jesup's most bitter and persistent critics, was among those who extolled Osceola as a hero and denounced his captors. Representative Wise of Virginia confessed, "[Osceola] excites my wonder and admiration. This nation and its army are bound to accord him praise for his great qualities and achievements."[24]

Among those in the House who spoke in defense of Jesup was Rep. Thomas Glascock of Georgia. "This Osceola is here held up to public admiration, as a warrior worthy of imitation and applause whilst many of our own gallant officers are handed over to public indignation and scorn, as violating a flag of truce. . . ." He admonished the Whigs to "recollect the murders" which that Indian "has committed, before they attempt to eulogize; they should recollect the cold blooded murder of General Thompson. . . ." Glascock conceded that Osceola was a brave man, adding, "So are many assassins; so are many murderers . . . but are these men to be held up to public admiration by honorable men on this floor?"[25]

Charles Downing, the delegate from the Florida Territory, declared that only Jesup's vigilance had prevented Osceola from seizing Hernandez as a hostage. "And if he had, did anybody believe that the House would have heard anything of a resolution of inquiry in regard to this conduct of Osceola?" Had he been General Jesup, he would not only have taken those "murderous chiefs" prisoners, but he would have left them "pendent on the crooked limb of a yellow pine."

Rep. Richard Biddle[26] of Pennsylvania stated that he would confine his remarks to the appropriation measure under discussion. Before he finished, however, he had entered into a long discourse about the court of inquiry of General Scott. Scott, he contended, "was a brave and gallant officer, who had been recalled from Florida at the moment he was striking the decisive blow, by the dishonorable conduct of General Jesup, in writing a private letter to the *Globe*, condemning the course of his commanding officer." Biddle concluded with a laudatory account of Scott's "gallant conduct in the War of 1812."

Representative Glascock accused Biddle of "resorting to subjects . . . wholly unconnected" with the one before them, in order to avail himself of an opportunity ". . . to pour forth his bitter feelings against the Administration, and in unqualified terms to denounce Gen. Jesup, and become the eulogist of Gen. Scott."

> A blow, says the gentleman from Pennsylvania, has been aimed at General Scott's integrity, and the sword has been struck from behind. Well, sir, might I not retort upon the gentleman in the same manner, and say that an attempt was now making to do the same with another officer of our army? The gentleman has referred us to the fields of Chippewa and Niagara for the gallant exploits of General Scott, and has told us how his youthful bosom glowed when he heard of the triumph of our arms . . . but has the gentleman forgotten the valorous deeds of Jesup on the same battle field, and that General [Jacob] Brown himself had said that this gallant officer was foremost in the blaze of battle?

Representative Underwood, himself a Whig but also an intimate friend of Jesup, remonstrated against "these *ex parte* trials and condemnation of Generals Scott and Jesup. Did members of the House have all the facts before them?" he asked. They had not, but a letter from General Jesup "justified the capture, for it appeared that Osceola had come in with a perfidious intention." He then read the letter in which the general requested "a most full and ample inquiry into all his transactions, both in the Creek and Seminole campaigns."

Following the debate, a call was made in the House for a vote on Wise's amendment to cut in half the appropriation for support of the war. It was overwhelmingly rejected.[27] The administration had won that skirmish, but the debate in congress over the war and the charges against Jesup would continue for years.

Meanwhile, Jesup was about to launch his second campaign in Florida. Although nearly one hundred and fifty Indians, including some important chiefs, were imprisoned in Fort Marion, many others remained ready to carry on the war. Sam Jones, the head of the Mikasukies, was believed to be concentrating his main force—about fifteen hundred—on the upper St. Johns. In addition, several roving bands were still to be found north of Fort Mellon and Tampa Bay; still others were scattered over the country to the southernmost part of the peninsula. So vast was Jesup's theater of operations that he had to establish and garrison forty posts and operate "from a base extending from Charlotte Harbor, by way of the Suwannee, to St. Augustine, upwards of 300 miles." Before the end of his campaign, he would set in motion at least nine columns which would penetrate virtually every section of Florida, but his plan first called for four major divisions. One, under Hernandez, was to move from St. Augustine and scour the country between the St. Johns and the Atlantic Ocean. Brig. Gen. Abram Eustis, at the head of another, was instructed to operate in a southerly direction on the western side of the St. Johns. Col. Persifor F. Smith, with a regiment of Louisiana volunteers, was ordered to enter the peninsula through the Caloosahatchee and comb the area below that river as far as Cape Sable at the southern tip of the Everglades. Col. Zachary Taylor, a newcomer to Florida, was directed to open a road in an easterly direction from Tampa Bay, establish posts at the head of Pease Creek and on the Kissimmee, and attack the Indians in that region.[28]

Taylor arrived at Tampa Bay on 8 November with his 1st Infantry Regiment in company with the Louisiana and Missouri volunteers. Before leaving Kentucky, he had spent an evening with Mrs. Jesup, her children, her mother, and Dr. Croghan at Locust Grove. In a personal note to the general, he assured Jesup that all were in good health. Ann, he wrote, was bearing "with fortitude" his separation from her, as well as the "puerile & public attacks," made on him by "envious & cowardly assassins" who had assailed him through the newspapers.[29]

While Taylor was preparing to leave Fort Brooke on his assigned mission, Jesup accompanied General Eustis's column to Volusia on the other side of Florida, where he had taken command nearly a year earlier. He then joined a mounted force moving down by land to Fort Mellon on the St. Johns. There he found the messenger he had dispatched to Micanopy. The chief sent word that he would abide by the arrangements made at Fort Dade and was confident he could induce the chiefs and the greater part of his people to surrender.[30]

About the middle of November, a deputation of five Cherokee chiefs arrived in St. Augustine. At the invitation of Poinsett, they had been selected by their principal chief, John Ross, to serve as mediators of the war. Jesup received them at Picolata and expressed his appreciation of their motives and courage in undertaking their perilous mission, for the more militant Seminoles had threatened to kill any white or Indian emissaries who dared to suggest migration. The general made arrangements for the Cherokees to confer with the prisoners in Fort Marion.[31]

Following that conference, Jesup met with the delegates. When he asked to see a copy of their proposed "talk," prepared by Ross, he discovered that it did not conform with his own instructions from the government. "It held out to the Seminoles the promise of a new treaty; but I was required to enforce the provisions of an *existing treaty*, not to make a *new treaty*." He informed the Cherokees that unless they modified their talk, he could not allow them to present it. Jesup permitted them to proceed on their mission only after they had consented to change the objectionable parts.[32] He allowed Coehadjo to accompany the Cherokees as a guide, designating him as his own messenger to the Seminole chiefs. The delegates left Fort Mellon, on horses furnished by Jesup, for Chickasawatchee Creek, a distance of about forty miles, where Micanopy had promised to meet them.

Evidence suggests that the Cherokees in their council with the Seminoles did not adhere to their modified "talk" as they had agreed to do. Auguste, a Seminole Negro interpreter, later made a formal sworn statement to one of Jesup's officers in which he stated that the Cherokee mediators had told the Seminoles that the general's "time was out"; that he lost so many men "he was afraid to go home to Congress"; that he did not want to make peace but "could not help himself now that the paper made by the President" had been sent to them. In addition, they promised that when the Indians came in all the provisions in the fort would be given to them. Moreover, the Cherokees would take four Seminole chiefs to Washington, where the president would give them "whatever land they might call for."[33]

When the Cherokees and Coehadjo returned to Fort Mellon on 3 December, they were accompanied by many of Coehadjo's people and Chiefs Micanopy, Cloud, Tuskegee (nephew of Sam Jones), and Nocose Yohola, along with about a score of their followers. Jesup was disappointed that Sam Jones was not among them. At Fort Mellon a dispute arose as to the status of the Seminole chiefs. Jesup maintained that they were still prisoners of war or hostages and that in coming into his camp they were surrendering. He had stated repeatedly that no Indians were to come in for any other purpose than to migrate. The Cherokees claimed they should be considered as having come in under a white flag. Jesup reiterated his position to Poinsett: "I authorized no assurances to be given to the Indians that they were to come to my camp and be permitted to return. I promised them protection and kind treatment. If the Cherokees promised more, it was on their own responsibility, and without my authority."[34]

The dispute appears to have been largely academic, for on 5 December, when Jesup held a council with the chiefs, Micanopy informed him that his people would come in and migrate. The other chiefs made similar pledges. Under pressure from Jesup, Micanopy assured the general that Sam Jones and his Mikasukies would come in. Jesup gave him ten days to make good on his promises. All of the chiefs then designated messengers and dispatched them with orders to round up and bring in their followers, along with Sam Jones and Alligator.[35]

The Cherokee delegates, accompanied by these messengers, continued their mediation efforts while the Seminole chiefs remained at Fort Mellon as hostages. Jesup held out little hope that they would succeed and was not surprised when the Cherokees returned on 14 December to report their mission a failure. The general then sent the chiefs he had held as hostages, along with Coehadjo and his people, numbering seventy-two in all, by steamer to St. Augustine to join the other prisoners in Fort Marion. Jesup's report to the secretary of war held a trace of disgust. He had lost fifteen "most important" days because of the Cherokee negotiations, a delay "the consequences of which no subsequent effort could retrieve; for, in the meantime, the Seminoles had dispersed, and the water in the St. John's had fallen so low as to compel [him] to use the boats propelled by oars and poles, to transport supplies to the depots which [he] found necessary to establish further south on that river."[36]

The Cherokee mediators blamed Jesup for the failure of their mission, apparently never realizing that their task was doomed from the start because they were working at cross-purposes with the commander in the field. They were sympathetic to the Seminoles and made them promises they were in no position to keep, such as a new treaty which would permit them to remain in Florida. Ironically, Jesup, too, was sympathetic to the Indian cause, but as commander he was obliged to carry out his orders calling for removal of the Seminoles. When the Cherokees reported to John Ross upon their return to Washington, he lodged a protest with the secretary of war, claiming that Jesup's seizure of the Seminoles was a violation of the agreement they had made with the chiefs at Chickasawatchee Creek. Ross gained no sympathy in Washington; in fact, he declared that he found "the door of communication with the Executive Department closed" against him.[37]

While the Cherokee mediators were still in Florida, the *Georgia Constitutionalist*, on 27 November, published a letter to the editor which gives a vivid verbal picture of General Jesup encamped in the field with his troops. The paper withheld the writer's identity, but the letter was written at Fort Mellon, "in great haste," and would appear to be from a soldier.

> [Coehadjo], the great Seminole chief, is here, a prisoner at large, and living in the [military] family of Gen. Jesup, who, by the way, is beloved by the whole army. No officer in the army is now so popular as Gen. Jesup; his strict discipline, coupled with kindliness and attention to all under his command, has won the hearts of officers and soldiers. He will come into their tents at night to inquire if all is well, visit the sick soldier and give him comfort, and will send from his own table any little luxury which will add comfort to the sick. His keen eye is all through the camp, and his gigantic mind is constantly pondering on his country's good. The public will soon know how to appreciate a General of so many good qualities, and reward him for his past services, which will never be forgotten by a grateful people.[38]

Among those taken prisoner with Osceola was the young chief Coacoochee, son of King Philip, who was captured in September of 1837. In accordance with his father's wishes, he had brought various members of the family to join him. Coacoochee was then permitted to leave. Later, however, he had joined Osceola's party and was now highly incensed at being imprisoned at Fort Marion. On the night of 29 November, he and nineteen other Seminoles made a spectacular escape through a narrow casement window from the old Spanish stronghold at St. Augustine. Not until the next morning was the precipitous flight discovered. Osceola reputedly sent a message to Jesup that he and his people could also have escaped but had scorned to do so.[39]

Coacoochee's imprisonment at Fort Marion proved to be one of the major mistakes of the war. At the time of his escape, the only other important chiefs still at large were Alligator and Sam Jones, who with their people were reportedly on their way to surrender. Coacoochee is believed to have intercepted them and prevailed upon them to renew the fight. Embittered by what he considered unjust treatment, he replaced Osceola as the leading war spirit of his nation. With the collaboration of the other two chiefs, he succeeded in rallying a formidable force of militant Seminoles and Mikasukies, who proved capable of prolonging the war five more years.[40] Thus, once more, just when Jesup seemed to be on the verge of ending the conflict, another unpredictable incident led to its renewal.

After Coacoochee's escape, Jesup ordered the other 203 prisoners transferred to Fort Moultrie on Sullivan's Island in the harbor at Charleston, South Carolina. In accordance with his instructions, the prisoners were treated with kindness, allowed complete freedom within the fort's enclosure, and permitted to have visitors. The artist George Catlin, who went there to paint portraits of the Seminole chiefs and became friendly with all of them, was particularly attracted to Osceola.[41]

The potency of the Indian force Coacoochee had brought together was demonstrated less than a month after his escape when it engaged Taylor's command in the hardest-fought battle of the war. Jesup called the encounter "one of the best actions known in our history."[42] Taylor was at Fort Gardner, which he had erected on the Kissimmee near Cypress Lake, when Jesup sent word that the Cherokee mediation effort had failed and directed him to move against any Indians within striking distance. Since Jesup's forces were operating to the east of the Kissimmee, Taylor proceeded down the west side of that river towards Lake Okeechobee, where, on Christmas Day 1837, he came upon the Indians led by Coacoochee, Alligator, and Sam Jones concealed in a dense hammock near the northern tip of the lake. In crossing a large swamp to attack the Indians posted on the far side, the Missouri volunteers, leading the attack, came under a galling fire. The troops succeeded in driving back the Indians, who scattered, losing three hundred head of their cattle and about one hundred horses, some with saddles. For distinguished service in the Battle of Okeechobee, the future president was brevetted a brigadier general after nearly thirty years of service in the army.[43]

Far to the south, Jesup was moving his own army. When news

of Taylor's conflict reached him days later, its site proved his contention that the principal force of the hostiles was heading for the southern part of Florida. He was anxious to communicate with Taylor to coordinate the movements of their armies. Moving his army into unexplored wilderness required extensive planning and preparations. Rations and other supplies, including forage for the animals, had to be transported long distances from St. Augustine through difficult terrain to places unfamiliar to the troops. From his long experience as a supply officer, Jesup knew he must create an adequate chain of new posts and depots at least as far south as Jupiter Inlet. With only crude maps of the country to guide him, he decided to move troops and supplies southward along two routes—down the Indian River along the Atlantic Coast and inland down the St. Johns to the head of the river.

To support Jesup's army as it moved southward, the troops erected a depot at the head of Lake Harney; built a fort, called Fort Christmas because work on it had begun on 25 December 1837, at Lowell's Town on the St. Johns about eighty miles north of Lake Okeechobee; and constructed another post, Fort Taylor, further up the river, about one hundred miles south of Fort Mellon. Jesup ordered the exploration of the St. Johns to determine whether it could be navigated to Fort Taylor.[44]

On the Atlantic coast, General Hernandez, with a force of Florida militiamen, had established depots at New Smyrna and at the haulover on the southwestern end of Mosquito Lagoon. He had then returned to Fort Mellon, where he was joined by the Tennessee volunteers, commanded by Maj. William Lauderdale. After the collapse of the Cherokee mediation effort, Jesup had directed Hernandez to proceed to the head of the St. Johns and Lt. Col. Benjamin K. Pierce, with several companies of his regiment, to move by barges down the Indian River to Indian River Inlet and build a post in that area. On 2 January 1838, Pierce erected a blockhouse—named Fort Pierce in his honor—about four miles south of the inlet. His troops were then employed in transferring supplies across the mile-wide lagoon from the river to the fort, from where they could be transported further south as needed. Meanwhile, on 26 December 1837 Lt. Levin N. Powell of the navy, with about two hundred sailors, army regulars, and volunteers, set out in thirty-three small boats to explore the lagoon of Indian River from the haulover as far south as Jupiter Inlet.[45]

Jesup accompanied General Eustis, who commanded the main force of about fifteen hundred regulars, on their tedious march from Fort Mellon to Fort Christmas. On 6 January 1838, after abundant supplies had arrived in barges, Jesup decided to make another attempt to contact Taylor. Instructing Eustis and his slower-moving force to follow, he advanced with about five hundred mounted men, dragoons, and volunteers, crossing Big Cypress Swamp on 7 January. Discovering fresh Indian trails leading south, he sent out scouting parties to reconnoiter. One group encountered a small party of Indians and captured a warrior whom the general employed as a guide to locate Taylor's route. When Jesup reached the head of the St. Johns, he was joined by Hernandez and his mounted men who had, with extreme difficulty, found their way through the unfamiliar wilderness. Baffled by his inability to locate Taylor's route, Jesup at length reluctantly gave up the search and headed for Fort Pierce to make certain that sufficient supplies were reaching that post from the north. He arrived at the fort on 14 January after leaving a part of his detachment at Fort Floyd, which Taylor had constructed earlier thirty miles west of Fort Pierce and eight miles north of Lake Okeechobee.[46]

On 15 January, Hernandez, who had served with much distinction in the army after his plantation had been destroyed by the Indians at the outbreak of the war, now asked permission to resign his commission, because his private affairs demanded his attention. With much regret, Jesup accepted his resignation and agreed to discharge with him all members of his brigade of Floridians. "I speak not in the language of idle compliment when I assure you of the high estimation in which I hold your services. The cordial, constant, and efficient support which you have invariably given me, has made an impression on me not easily to be effaced."[47] The next day, Lieutenant Powell's command arrived unexpectedly at Fort Pierce in a state of shock, one of its three units having been repulsed in a battle with a much larger force of Indians. It suffered the loss of five killed and twenty-two wounded, including all but one of the officers.[48]

Jesup ordered his mounted men to prepare at once to move to the Jupiter River region in hopes of locating the Indians. At daylight on 17 January, he and his detachment left Fort Pierce and set out on a westerly course for Fort Floyd, where he would assemble his army for its march to the south. On the second day, they arrived at Fort Floyd, where they found Eustis with ten companies of the 3rd and 4th Artillery and a train of ambulances and baggage wagons. Exposed to scorching sun or drenching rain, they had marched two hundred miles through the wilderness, cutting roads through swamps and hammocks and bridging streams to permit the passage of wagons.[49]

At dawn on 20 January, Jesup's army moved from the head of the St. Johns and began its arduous march to the south. It numbered about fifteen hundred, of whom six hundred were dragoons, four hundred artillerymen, and approximately five hundred Alabama and Tennessee volunteers. The troops advanced in three columns, with wagons, artillery, and pack-mules in the center. Riding in single file on the right flank about one hundred yards from the middle column were the dragoons; on the left, at the same distance, were the volunteers. When the troops encamped the first night near a marshy bog they were joined by thirty-five friendly Delaware Indians sent by General Taylor, whose command was moving southward much farther to the west along the edge of Lake Okeechobee.

Surgeon Motte, who rode with the dragoons, left a record in his diary of the severe hardships suffered by the troops and animals on their journey into the unexplored wilderness region, declared uninhabitable by their Indian guides. The country beyond Fort Pierce "was one unbroken extent of water and morass; like that of a boundless rice-field when inundated . . . exhibiting a picture of universal desolation." At times the foot soldiers had to make their way through water nearly up to their middle; the water rose to the saddle-girth of the mounted troops. At intervals of several miles, they passed small clusters of trees on slightly elevated spots. These afforded somewhat drier ground, but only with much difficulty could the troops find such islands of sufficient size for them to encamp at night. Upon occasion, the troops were forced to take to the water to avoid the dense growth of scrub and saw palmetto. The spiny-toothed leafstalks of the saw palmetto cut gashes into the legs of the horses and tore to tatters the outer garments of the men, who patched their clothing as best they could with old corn bags. Mud, water, and saw grass also ruined shoes; many of the troops were soon barefooted, with their clothes torn off and their flesh badly lacerated. They saw "more snakes, mosquitoes, and other venomous 'critters' than one can shake a stick at. . . ."[50]

Surprisingly, despite their hardships, the troops apparently re-mained cheerful. Motte described the camp scene after the mules were unpacked, the horses unsaddled, the tents pitched, and wood gathered for the fires. "Soon the cheerful blaze would crackle in all directions, and around each fire might be seen groups of men, cracking their jokes, and speculating on the probability of soon coming up with the enemy." Motte also wrote of the camp after the men had retired for the night.

> Frequently have I deserted my blanket to wander through the tented avenues and canvass streets when midnight has thrown its deep shadows o'er the sward, and the sounds of camp are all hushed; when nothing is heard but the piping of the wind through the branches of the trees. On one side . . . a long line of horses fastened to ropes stretched from tree to tree, and extending from one extremity of camp to the other. In another direction . . . innumerable wagons drawn up in solid squares; their white and clean looking tops glancing in the light of the camp fires, which every where threw up a flickering blaze. All around are the temporary abodes of hundreds of human beings; here today; gone tomorrow.[51]

On 23 January Jesup's army crossed the headwaters of the St. Lucie River and soon came upon the site of a large Indian camp abandoned only recently. The many Indian trails all led south. When the march resumed at daylight on 24 January, progress was slow; roads had to be cut through thick hammocks and heavy growths of saw palmetto. Shortly before noon the advance guard of dragoons, riding about four miles ahead, sent back word that a strong force of Indians, prepared to fight, was posted behind a dense hammock. Jesup immediately issued orders for the mounted men to ride forward at full speed and attack. As usual, the Indians had selected the battle site with care. To reach their hiding place, the troops had first to penetrate an almost impassable cypress swamp, about half-a-mile in width. The horses of the mounted men splashed and floundered in mud and water up to their saddle girths and stumbled on the various cypress knees. The dragoons dismounted, left their horses with guards, and charged into the hammock. The artillery soon joined in the conflict, and a howitzer at the edge of the hammock began throwing grape and shells into the bushes. "Congreve rockets also contributed their terrible whizzing toward increasing the stunning uproar that raged on all sides."[52]

When the soldiers reached the center of the hammock, they found their advance impeded by the Loxahatchee River that emptied into Jupiter Inlet. From behind trees on the other side, the Indians were spraying a deadly fire across the water. The dragoons promptly plunged into the river and managed to reach the opposite bank, though some had to swim because of the unforeseen depth. This unexpected maneuver so surprised the Indians that they retreated to a new position. The Tennessee volunteers, meanwhile, appeared reluctant to enter the hammock. Observing their hesitancy, General Jesup dismounted from his horse and drew his pistol. Ordering them to follow, he dashed into the hammock and continued all the way to the bank of the river, then looked back to see if the Tennesseans had obeyed his command. As he turned, an Indian bullet struck him in the face, breaking his spectacles and ripping a gash in his cheek just below the left eye. Although stunned by the impact, he carefully searched the ground and picked up as many pieces of his broken glasses as he could salvage. Spectacles were a precious commodity in the wilderness. Then he moved to the rear to have a surgeon examine and dress his painful, disfiguring wound.[53] The battle ended quickly after the soldiers had penetrated the hammock and crossed the Loxahatchee River. The Indians, their hiding place overrun, scattered and disappeared before the pursuing troops could capture them.

Ironically, on the same day that Jesup was wounded in that desolate and remote region of Florida, he was being subjected in Washington to a scathing denunciation by the Whigs in the comfort and security of the halls of Congress.

Some of the participants in the battle on the Loxahatchee estimated that as many as three hundred Seminoles were engaged in the fighting. In Jesup's opinion they numbered no more than one hundred, but in view of their "almost impregnable position," they "ought to have held it much longer than they did." His army suffered rather heavy casualties—seven killed and thirty-one wounded, including himself. His severe wound did not prevent him from remaining with the troops. Jesup was not critical of the behavior of the Tennessee volunteers, merely stating that some confusion had occurred among them, "in consequence of which they suffered severely; but order was readily restored. Many of them behaved with the greatest bravery, and all of them as well as raw troops usually behave in their first encounter with an enemy." Five of the Tennesseans were killed and twenty-three wounded, some so severely that they died later.[54]

After the Indians fled, Jesup ordered the troops to encamp on the battlefield, where a search was made for the dead and wounded. The army remained at its encampment the following morning until a bridge could be erected, then crossed the river and marched southward five miles to Jupiter Bay. The general ordered a stockade—named Fort Jupiter—built there to serve as a depot for supplies sent down from Fort Pierce.[55]

Although the fort was completed on 28 January, the army had to remain there eight more days because of the denuded condition of the troops after their rough journey through the wilderness. Hundreds of the men were without shoes; many wore tattered clothing or none at all. The troops could not take the field until new shoes, clothing, and other needed supplies arrived from Fort Pierce. The dragoons, who were not as badly off as some of the other men in regard to shoes and clothing, were kept on the move. On 29 January Jesup dispatched Major Ashby and 150 dragoons on a scouting mission. They returned the following day with twenty head of cattle and thirty ponies but no word of the foe. On 1 February two guides reported that they had located the Seminoles concealed in another cypress swamp about twenty-eight miles further south. That night a messenger from Taylor announced that his division was encamped at the head of the St. Lucie, some twenty-one miles to the north of Fort Jupiter. Jesup promptly sent a company of the Alabama volunteers and 150 dragoons to strengthen Taylor's command.[56]

With the arrival of new shoes and clothing, the army resumed its southward march on 5 February toward the cypress swamp where the Indians were reportedly hiding. That night, Jesup related, General Eustis urged him to terminate the war by an agreement with the Indians whereby they would be left in the southern part of Florida, believing, as Jesup did, "from the nature of the country in which [they] were operating," that no permanent advantage could be obtained except by peaceable means. "The general expressed the most decided opinion that the [War] department would approve the measure. I promised to consider it."[57]

On 6 February the column moved within a few miles of the swamp where the Indians were concealed and encamped. Fresh moccasin tracks led in a westerly direction, and the commander sent a detachment of dragoons and Shawnees to reconnoiter. During their absence, Col. David E. Twiggs and other principal officers on his staff came to Jesup's headquarters with the same suggestion Eustis had made the previous evening. They assured him that "most, if not all, the officers of the army entertained similar views." Those views coincided with the conviction Jesup had expressed twelve months earlier,[58] and that night he decided to offer the Indians a peace settlement on terms he hoped the administration would sanction. He made it clear to Poinsett that while Eustis, Twiggs, and others had urged him to end the war by allowing the Indians to remain in the Everglades area of Florida, he accepted full responsibility for any blame attached to the action taken.[59]

Surgeon Motte declared, "Florida is certainly the poorest country that ever two people quarreled for. . . . It is in fact a most hideous region to live in; a perfect paradise for Indians, alligators, serpents, frogs, and every other kind of loathsome reptile." If the Indians wanted it, then "why not in the name of common sense" let them have it?[60] He probably expressed the sentiments of Jesup and thousands of other soldiers who marched, fought, and suffered in the rugged Florida wilderness.

Early in the morning of 7 February 1838, Jesup sent a Seminole Negro named Sandy into the swamp to find the Indians and invite the chiefs to a conference. Sandy's mission brought a quick response from the eager Seminoles. Several Indians with a white flag asked to see Jesup, and the general moved forward at once to greet them. Young chief Hallec-Hajo spoke of the "wretched condition" of the Indians and their ardent desire for peace but declared that the greater part of them wished to remain in the country. They would be willing to accept any part of their homeland, however small, that the government would assign to them. Jesup asked that Tuskegee, the principal chief of the party, join in the conference. The next day Jesup, Tuskegee, and Hallec-Hajo arranged that the Indians would assemble within ten days in a camp near Fort Jupiter and await the decision of the president as to whether they would be permitted to stay. Jesup promised to recommend that a small district in the southern part of the peninsula be assigned to them.[61]

The conference concluded with handshakes all around, and the Indians returned to the swamp. When Jesup's troops broke camp on 10 February and began their march back to Fort Jupiter, they were followed by the Indians, who encamped about a mile from the soldiers. They could be seen constantly "wandering about our camp like domesticated animals; the men begging . . . tobacco . . . the squaws engaged in the less dignified employment of picking up corn which our horses dropped from their mouths." The squaws presented "a most squalid appearance; being destitute of even the necessary clothing to cover their nakedness; many having nothing around them but the old corn bags we had thrown away."[62]

Some two weeks earlier this same band of Seminoles had battled Jesup's army and inflicted a disfiguring wound on his face. Now, the general was asking mercy for them, obviously touched by their story of hardships suffered from the relentless pursuit by his troops. He was convinced that the time had come to stop this senseless war and to change the government's removal policy. His decision demonstrates the courage of his convictions and his strength of character, for he knew he was risking a rebuke from the War Department and a possible recall. On the day he returned to Fort Jupiter, he wrote a long, eloquent plea to the president and directed Lt. Thomas B. Linnard, his aide-de-camp, to hand-carry his letter to Washington.

Jesup pointed out that in the past no Indians had been removed to the West until their land was actually needed for agricultural purposes by the whites. But the case of the Seminoles was different. "We exhibit, in our present contest, the first instance, perhaps, since the commencement of authentic history, of a nation employing an army to remove a band of savages from one unexplored wilderness to another." He was aware that his duty as a soldier was not to comment on the policy of the government but to carry it out as instructed. He had endeavored faithfully to do so, but little prospect remained of terminating the war in any reasonable time. Unless the emigration policy was abandoned immediately, the war would continue for years to come, at mounting expense.

Jesup suggested "with great diffidence" that the Indians be allowed to remain and be assigned to a specific area. "That would satisfy them; and they might hold to it on the express condition that they should forfeit their right to it, if they should either commit depredations upon the white inhabitants, or pass the boundaries assigned to them without the written permission of the military commander or agent." He was recommending that measure for the consideration of Secretary Poinsett and the president "as the only means of terminating, immediately, a most disastrous war, and leaving the troops disposable for other service.[63]

During the truce, Jesup set up headquarters in the artillery section of the camp at Fort Jupiter. The dragoons were encamped nearly a mile away; about the same distance further on was the assembly place of the Seminoles. On 24 February the Indians visited the general's camp for a ceremonial council. Tuskegee and Hallec-Hajo arrived at the camp with their warriors. Dressed in all their finery, the warrior danced about until they reached the general's headquarters, where they seated themselves in a ring. After the calumet was smoked, the council was opened by an old squaw, who pleaded for peace.[64]

Jesup insisted upon one stipulation, to which the chiefs reluctantly agreed: The Seminole Negroes who had taken up arms during the hostilities were to be sent immediately to the West. Consequently, on 27 February, about 140 Negroes and the Indians who had surrendered unconditionally left under escort for Tampa Bay, the embarkation point. The attitude of the Indians in the camp was influenced, it appears, by Micanopy's nephew, Halatoochee, the number two chief of the Seminoles. Halatoochee had come from New Orleans to join Jesup at Fort Jupiter, hoping to prevail upon more of his people to migrate. Tuskegee assured the general that he and his people would migrate even if the government gave him land in Florida. Hallec-Hajo stated that he was ready to obey any orders that came from the great white father in Washington, but at all events he would not be separated from his Negroes.[65]

While the troops and Indians were awaiting the president's decision, inventor Samuel Colt arrived at Fort Jupiter to demonstrate his single-barreled repeating rifle with a multi-chambered rotating breech. On 3 March, Jesup appointed a board of seven officers to examine the structure, reliability, and accuracy of the rifle. Some of the officers remained skeptical of the new arm, but Col. William S. Harney, who was impressed with it, was allotted fifty of the weapons for his dragoons to replace their carbines.[66]

When no reply concerning his proposal had been received from Washington by 14 March, Jesup sent a second letter by regular mail to the secretary of war for the eyes of the president. He sought to reinforce the arguments for the course he had recommended. By reason of the more rapid and reliable system of communications which Poinsett had established between Florida and Washington, he expected the document to reach the capital in about five days or so.[67] Extracts from this second letter indicate the depth of his feelings.

> It has been said that the national honor forbids any compromise with them—can there be a point of honor between a great nation and a band of naked savages, now beaten, broken, dispirited and dispersed? I think those who believe so form a very low estimate of national honor. But admit that our national honor could be tarnished by giving up the contest entirely, and forming a new treaty with different provisions from those of the existing treaty. We are surely at liberty, without compromising our honor, to adopt those measures whether of direct hostility or of policy which shall promise the greater possibility of success. . . .
>
> The Seminoles . . . have been as completely beaten as the Western Indians were by General Wayne or General Harrison—and were I permitted to make a treaty on the terms which those Generals treated, permanent peace could be secured in a week. I, as well as my predecessors in command in Florida, have failed to catch and remove the Seminoles to Arkansas; but it should be remembered that we are the only commanders who have ever been required to go into an unexplored wilderness, catch savages, and remove them to another wilderness. Search all history and another instance is not to be found. . . . To persevere in the course we have been pursuing for three years past would be a reckless waste of blood and treasure; and I sincerely hope that I may soon receive instructions to adopt the course I have recommended, or if I should act without instructions, that my measures be approved.[68]

On 17 March, three days after he dispatched his second plea to Washington, Jesup received a response to his first letter. His proposal, on which he had pinned such high hopes for ending the conflict, had been rejected. President Van Buren refused to budge from Jackson's Indian-removal policy. The tone of Poinsett's reply was kindly but firm. The subject was one "of great interest," and he had given it "the most diligent and respectful consideration." But "in the present stage of our relations with the Indians residing

within the States and Territories East of the Mississippi, including
the Seminoles, it is useless to recur to the principles and motives
which induced the Government to determine their removal to the
West." The president and Congress "evince a determination to
carry out the measure, and it is to be regarded as the settled policy
of the country."[69]

The president's decision meant that the bloody, costly, and
frustrating war could continue for years. Discouraged, disturbed,
and reluctant to inform the Indians, Jesup waited until 19 March
before directing the Seminole chiefs to meet him in council at
noon the following day. Tuskegee sent word that he did not care
to attend; he and his people had already decided to go to the West.
When none of the other chiefs came to the council, Jesup instructed Colonel Twiggs to make prisoners of all the Seminoles in camp.
The general's report to Washington stated that 513 Indians and
165 Negroes had been taken into custody but that 15 Indians had
escaped.[70] His detractors charged that Jesup violated the confidence of the Seminole leaders by seizing them before notifying
the assembled Indians of the president's adverse decision. That
charge has questionable validity. The principal chiefs, Tuskegee
and Hallec-Hajo, had previously agreed that they and their people
would abide by the president's decision, and Jesup did not take
them into custody until after they had failed to attend the council
at which he intended to inform them of it. The general's implicit
orders from Washington were to force the Indians to migrate or to
destroy them. If they were allowed to return to the swamps, either
he or some other commander under the same orders would have to
hunt them down again, with more bloodshed on both sides. Since
he was opposed to their extermination, it seems reasonable to
assume he considered it preferable that the Seminoles at least have
the opportunity to begin a new life beyond the Mississippi rather
than be pursued endlessly like animals and perhaps be killed in
Florida.

Because he had the temerity to recommend to the president
that the war be terminated by permitting the Indians to remain in
Florida, Jesup now found himself attacked from an unexpected
quarter. His usually faithful defender, Editor Blair, rebuked him in
the *Globe* for making such a recommendation when he "had every
reason to know that such an idea was inadmissable."[71]

Residents of the Florida Territory were greatly relieved when they learned that Jesup's proposal had been rejected. The Florida newspapers, highly critical of the general's suggestion, praised the administration for its decision.[72] The *Florida Herald* on 15 February, claiming to speak for all Floridians, declared, "The breach is too wide between the Indians and the Floridians, ever to be healed. The people of Florida will not submit it, and it has cost too much blood and treasure for the government to give up the war in this style."

In Washington, meanwhile, the House had been engaged in a debate over an appropriation measure for support of the war. During the proceedings on 24 January, the same day Jesup was wounded, he was subjected to ruthless attacks by Whig members. This time, their criticism centered on his conduct in relation to the Cherokee mediators and his seizure of the Seminole chiefs the Cherokees brought to his camp to negotiate. "General Jesup holds those chiefs as his prisoners. And how did he get them?" Horace Everett of Vermont asked rhetorically. "By the act of double perfidy; first to them and then to the Cherokees who brought them in. Is not this the true cause of the continuance of hostilities? Is it not the obvious and sufficient cause? The Indian can no longer rely on General Jesup's flags of truce."

Henry Wise of Virginia charged that the war had been conducted in a manner morally wrong: "It has been marked on our side by perfidy after perfidy. Was there no perfidy in the capture of the young chief, Wild Cat, a son of Philip, whom you used as a spy to bring in Micanopy and Osceola under the white flag of truce, and then seized him and carried him as a prisoner to St. Augustine?" He charged that the Cherokees had been abused for acting as mediators. Had it not been the government itself who sent them? They had brought in the head chiefs, unarmed, and no ambuscades had occurred. Did that not contradict the assertion that the Cherokees acted a double part in mediating for peace while telling the Seminoles to hang on until spring when Congress would not appropriate money for continuing the war? He intimated former-President Jackson was responsible for these orders: "There is an old chief, well known here, who writes from his wigwam in Tennessee, who originates these instructions."

Richard Biddle of Pennsylvania characterized the appropriation bill as another of General Jesup's "pretexts" of an "emergency" to force a bill through the House and declared he would vote no more money for the war "until some satisfactory explanation had been given to its object." Despite all the vehement attacks by the Whig members upon the appropriation, the war, the administration, and Jesup, when the roll was called, the measure was approved by an overwhelming vote, with only two nays cast.[73]

In late February of 1838, when Chief Micanopy and the other Indians who had been confined at Fort Moultrie on Sullivan's Island left Charleston harbor in the brig *Omar* for New Orleans on their way west, Osceola, the most famous of them, was not among those making the trip. He had died on 30 January—not of a broken heart, as many have been led to believe because of a myth perpetuated even by some modern-day historians, but from a severe attack of quinzy.

Dr. Mark F. Boyd, the first American to receive the Prix Emile Brumpt for research in tropical medicine, expressed his belief that Osceola's vitality had been weakened by a chronic malaria infection from which he had been suffering since 1836. During the summer of that year, Osceola and other Indians occupied Fort Drane, which had been abandoned by the soldiers as unhealthful after one-third of the garrison became ill of malaria and the commanding officer, Lt. Col. Julius Heileman, had died of the disease. "It is noteworthy," Dr. Boyd pointed out, "that most observers who subsequently commented on Osceola's appearance, stress an aspect which one would expect to observe in a sufferer from chronic malaria. . . . We conclude that at the time of his capture he was an enfeebled, ill, and tired man, perhaps not overly averse to the prospect of capture."[74]

Osceola did not die alone and neglected, as myth would have us believe. An army doctor, Dr. Frederick Weedon, and a civilian consultant, Dr. B. B. Strobel, professor of anatomy at the Medical College of South Carolina, were with him during his fatal illness. Both tried to treat him, but Osceola would accept only the care of an Indian medicine man. At his bedside were both of his wives, his two children, and some of his band. Artist George Catlin spent much time with him, as did others during his illness. On the night of 27 January, when it was believed that he might not live until morning, Catlin and some of the army officers sat up with him throughout the night. Osceola survived that crisis but died three days later at the age of about thirty-five. He was buried near the main entrance to Fort Moultrie.[75] Although he was not interred in the soil of the Florida homeland for which he fought, Osceola is probably the only Indian partisan of that war whose gravesite is marked and identifiable today. Covered by an engraved marble stone, the plot enclosed by an iron fence, his grave still attracts visitors to Sullivan's Island.

Drs. Weedon and Strobel issued detailed statements concerning the circumstances surrounding Osceola's fatal illness, which were published originally in the *Charleston Patriot*. Reproduced in the *Washington Globe* of 14 February 1838, these statement were preceded by a brief editorial: "The sympathy expressed by the Federal press for the fate of Osceola is entirely exaggerated and misplaced. There is not a court and jury in Christendom by which he would not have been condemned to death for the assassination of General Thompson, for private revenge. . . ." The paper's intention was not to "chronicle his crimes," it stated, but "simply to refute the story of his having died of a broken heart."

In the meantime, in Congress, Senator William Preston of South Carolina, a bitter critic of the war, was among the Whigs who extolled Osceola as a hero and denounced his captors for their alleged mistreatment of him. In an outburst of oratory, he exclaimed: "The great master chief, Osceola, has been captured, but how captured, let the history of our times speak. That great and daring man ended his days on a deserted island, in a state of utter destitution and misery, without any of those sympathies which the conduct and noble daring of so great an aboriginal chief should have challenged from his captors." Senator Robert Strange of North Carolina retorted: "The warm imagination of the Senator from South Carolina" had presented a picture based not on truth but on fancy. Osceola "was not a noble savage battling for his rights, but a miserable half breed, a traitor, and violator of everything held sacred among all races of men, whether civilized or savage."

Senator Clement C. Clay[76] of Alabama rebuked Preston for making "insinuations unfavorable to the character of an American officer of high grade, merely upon the authority of doubts and suspicions." So far as he had been able to judge the conduct of General Jesup ". . . in the management of the several campaigns under his direction, he had seen nothing to censure. . . . If that General had erred in any thing it had been . . . on the side of humanity, and forbearance towards his savage enemy; certainly not in cruelty or treachery."[77] Thomas Hart Benton also replied to Preston: "The collector of Indian curiosities and portraits, Mr. Catlin, may be permitted to manufacture a hero out of this assassin, and to make a poetical scene of his imprisonment on Sullivan's Island; but it will not do for an American Senator to take these same liberties with historical truth and our national character."[78]

With most of the important Seminole chiefs now in custody, Jesup focused his efforts on capturing the two most formidable Indian leaders still at large—Sam Jones and Alligator. Confident that Sam Jones was in the area to the south, he detached Maj. William Lauderdale with a company of the 3d Artillery and two hundred Tennessee volunteers to explore that region and erect a post at New River. About fifty miles below Fort Jupiter, they constructed Fort Lauderdale on the site of the present city of that name.

Upon learning from the Indians who came into Fort Jupiter during the truce that Sam Jones and his band had taken refuge on islands in a remote area of the Everglades near New River, Jesup ordered Eustis to augment his force and proceed to that region. But before Eustis could carry out the orders, his mission had to be changed. Word had reached Jesup that some marauding bands of Mikasukies had eluded the troops in the south and had gone to the north, where they were committing atrocities in middle Florida— which had long been peaceful. He directed Eustis and his command to hurry to that area and stop the depredations.

Replacing Eustis on the expedition into the Everglades was Lt. Col. James Bankhead, who, like Eustis, was a veteran of the War of 1812. With six companies of the 1st and 4th Artillery, Bankhead set out for Key Biscayne, from where he was to move his troops by barges up New River in search of Sam Jones.[79] Efforts to meet in conference with the Indians were unsuccessful. As Bankhead and his men continued their pursuit of Sam Jones, the swampy land became such a mass of tangled mangroves and roots that the soldiers could not carry even their cartridge boxes. They had to place them, along with their muskets, in light boats which they slowly pushed before them through the mud. When they finally came upon the Indians, a brief skirmish occurred, whereupon the

Indians suddenly scattered and disappeared so quickly that the troops were unable to pursue them.[80]

On 24 March, while Bankhead was in the Everglades, Jesup sent Halatoochee and Abraham to join Taylor's command with instructions to locate Alligator and prevail upon him to migrate. When they found him, west of Lake Okeechobee, he and his followers agreed to surrender and were influential in inducing others to do the same. As a result, 365 Indians and Negroes capitulated to Taylor, among them 100 warriors.[81] Alligator had fought against Taylor at the Battle of Okeechobee.

Jesup ordered Lt. Col. William Harney to take up the search for Sam Jones in the Everglades, which the Indians called Pay-Hai-O-Kee (River of Grass). He relieved Bankhead, who was directed to join the other forces in the troubled area in northern Florida. Harney and his dragoons left Fort Jupiter on 30 March. By 20 April, his search for Sam Jones had taken him to Biscayne Bay. Some of his troops encamped on Key Biscayne; he established his own headquarters on the mainland, probably near the site of the Deering Estate in the present city of Miami. A few miles to the north at the mouth of the Miami River was Fort Dallas, another in the extensive chain of posts and depots erected on Jesup's orders.

Hoping to surprise Sam Jones at night, Harney and one hundred men embarked in fifteen canoes on the evening of 21 April and proceeded down along the coast. By daylight they had reached a point some twenty miles below Cape Florida without seeing any Indians. Two days later, when they first came upon an Indian camp, a skirmish lasted more than two hours before the Indians retreated and seemed suddenly to melt away. Sam Jones, fearing capture, reportedly had fled at the start of the shooting. Exhausted, their rations gone, Harney and his men returned to camp, where Harney received orders to proceed to the headquarters of Gen. Winfield Scott at Athens, Tennessee. He and his troops were to assist in the removal of the Cherokees who were resisting efforts of Scott's troops to force them to the West.[82]

Jesup, in the meantime, had crossed the Florida peninsula from Fort Jupiter to Tampa Bay. His objective was to attack the Mikasukies and Tallahassees (another branch of the Seminole tribe) who had taken refuge in the swamps near the mouth of the Withlacoochee. He was in the process of assembling troops when

General Order No. 7 of 10 April 1838 arrived from Washington, instructing him to transfer a large portion of his troops to the Cherokee country as soon as practical. He was also ordered to turn over the Florida command to Taylor and resume his duties as quartermaster general in Washington.

With mingled emotions, Jesup prepared to leave Florida. Ten months earlier when he had asked to be relieved of the command, he had written Adjutant General Roger Jones, "It is known to members of the late Administration that I was placed in command not only without solicitation, but contrary to my known and expressed wishes." But circumstances had changed. After fifteen months as commanding general, during which he had on several occasions been near success, he was reluctant to depart before achieving the purpose for which he had been sent to the territory.[83] He was surrendering his command with a feeling more of regret than of relief. At the same time, he was eager for an opportunity to appear before a court of inquiry or a congressional committee to clear his name and justify his conduct, which had been so severely attacked. He looked forward to a reunion with his wife and five children; he had seen none of his family for nearly three years.

On 15 May 1838, Jesup completed all arrangements for the transfer of responsibility, turned over the command to Taylor, and left for Washington. Shortly before his departure he received a letter from Capt. John R. Vinton, who, because of ill health, had had to leave Florida without seeing his commander. Vinton was a graduate of West Point, an army veteran of twenty-five years, and a talented artist; like Catlin, he had painted landscapes and portraits of Indian chiefs. His letter had words of praise for Jesup: "Whatever measures you might have adopted, you would have seen them condemned by one party or the other. But such is generally the price that public men have to pay for their position. There is, notwithstanding a large portion of the community, as I confidently believe, who will justify your acts, approve your views, and applaud your unwearied devotion to the public service, but first your own story must be told."[84] General Jesup hoped to do just that when he arrived in the nation's capital.

CHAPTER 9

BETWEEN TWO WARS

AT THE END of May 1838, Jesup returned to his office in Washington as quartermaster general, after an absence of two years. His first thoughts were of his family, still at Locust Grove where he had taken them in the fall of 1835. He hurried off a letter to Ann, urging her and the children to join him in Washington. Ann was eager to rejoin her husband but, upon the advice of her brother, Dr. John Croghan, reluctantly agreed to await his arrival in Kentucky.[1] Jesup's duties prevented him from going immediately to Locust Grove. Among other tasks, he had to submit an official report of his operations in Florida as required by a Senate resolution. Reunion with his family would have to be delayed until after Congress had adjourned for the summer.

On 6 July 1838, Jesup sent his lengthy report to President Van Buren, who transmitted it to the Senate three days before the second session of the 25th Congress adjourned. The report, with the accompanying letters of Poinsett and the president, was published as Senate *Document 507*. In the main, Jesup summarized the principal operations of the army under his command and explained his measures. He reserved the right to present a more detailed report as soon as a release from his other duties afforded him time to prepare it. Chiefs Coehadjo, Tuskegee, Hallec-Hajo and many others had declared that the Cherokee deputation assured them in council that the Indians were to remain in the country and that Jesup was carrying on the war contrary to the orders of the president. "This accords with the information received through the negro chief Abraham, in December, and the negro Auguste, in February." He

213

pointed out that during his command in Florida, the number of Indians and Negroes who surrendered or were captured totaled nearly twenty-four hundred, of whom more than seven hundred were warriors. "The villages of the Indians have all been destroyed, and their cattle, horses, and other stock, with nearly all their property, taken or destroyed. The swamps and hammocks have been everywhere penetrated, and the whole country traversed . . . ; the small bands who remain dispersed over that extensive region, have nothing of value left but their rifles. . . ." If his accomplishments fell short of public expectations, it should be remembered that he had been attempting what no other armies of the country had ever before been required to do. "I, and my predecessors in command, were not only required to fight, beat, and drive the enemy before us, but to go into an unexplored wilderness to catch them. Neither Wayne, Harrison, or Jackson, were required to do this; and unless the objects to be accomplished be the same, there can be no just comparison as to the results."[2]

Poinsett assured the general that the War Department was aware of the obstacles he encountered and fully appreciated his untiring efforts to carry out its policies. He had accomplished all that could be expected under the "peculiar and difficult" circumstances under which he had been placed. "In withdrawing you from Florida, the Department was actuated by no want of confidence in your zeal or ability to carry on the war to successful issue, but from a belief that you might now return to the performance of the appropriate duties of your department without injury to the public service."[3]

Jesup viewed his removal in a different light. He believed that "the terms and manner" of his abrupt recall implied "the deepest censure," for, he continued, "I dared to propose the only measure which in my opinion offered the slightest prospect of terminating the war in any reasonable time." After the conflict in Florida had finally ended and Poinsett was out of office, he made his feelings known in 1844 to then-Secretary of War William Wilkins. He wrote to request that brevets be awarded to more than a score of officers for their "gallant and meritorious service" while serving under him in Florida. He attached to the letter a summary of the contributions of each officer. Jesup had not acted earlier in this matter, he explained, because of the extraordinary circumstances he had encountered upon his return to Washington "to vindicate

[his] conduct—personal and official." His efforts to make his side of the story known to the public had led to great frustration. He had planned to make a detailed report that would do justice to all who had been associated with him but "soon found that [his] measures had been misrepresented and false issues made before the public." He had sought a military investigation, as well as an investigation by Congress, but was unable to obtain either. Moreover, since the country was in the midst of the 1840 presidential campaign (won by William Henry Harrison on the slogan "Tippecanoe and Tyler Too"), no subjects unconnected with politics could command any public attention.

Jesup stated that his report, though called for by a resolution of the Senate and printed by its order, had been published in no more than half a dozen papers and had been read by only his personal friends. The times seemed unfavorable "to the cause of truth"; he had thought it best to postpone a more detailed report to a more propitious period. "Whether that report will even be presented is now problematical, but justice to my gallant followers, as well as regard for the Military character of the country, makes it proper that the public mind be disabused of the errors into which it has been led by the misrepresentations of political partisans."[4]

Even in this matter of brevets, the quartermaster general was destined to be disappointed. His recommendations were subject to the approval of the commander-in-chief of the army—Winfield Scott, who had succeeded to that post upon the death of Alexander Macomb. Whether Scott's vindictiveness towards Jesup figured in his decision is not clear. At any rate, in responding to the secretary of war, Scott wrote: "Brevets are the cheap and peculiar rewards of military prowess. But it does not follow that they are to be *cheaply* won. . . . Considering the great number of brevets which have been conferred within a few years, and that some sixty nominations yet remain to be acted upon by the Senate . . . , I beg leave, at least for the present, to decline presenting a new list of officers for brevets."[5]

Poinsett himself had blocked Jesup's efforts to appear before a military court of inquiry. The general had submitted a formal request to the War Department that such a tribunal thoroughly investigate his conduct, both personal and official. In rejecting the application, the secretary stated that Jesup's conduct had been entirely satisfactory to the War Department and that his "reputation as a soldier and a man stands unimpeached." Poinsett added that "anonymous publications in newspapers or denunciations made in Congress during the heat of debate, without any specific charge," did not constitute grounds for a court of inquiry. "On receiving your report immediately after your return from Florida, the department, with the best means of ascertaining and judging all circumstances connected with your military operations in Florida, expressed to you its entire satisfaction with your conduct. . . ." He concluded, "Your request cannot be granted."[6]

The political attacks upon Jesup in Congress and in the anti-administration press did not discernibly abate after he was relieved of the Florida command. With the tenacity which marked their behavior, the Whigs endlessly repeated their charges against the officer who had become their favorite target. His most persistent critic in the Senate continued to be William C. Preston of South Carolina. Among those who rose to the defense of the administration and the nonpartisan general were Senators Wilson Lumpkin of Georgia, Robert Strange of North Carolina, Clement C. Clay of Alabama, and Thomas Hart Benton of Missouri. While Jesup was writing his official report in the early summer of 1838, he read almost daily in the newspapers what was being said for and against him.

On 8 June, Senator Benton delivered his spirited speech in defense of Jesup in direct response to Preston, who had made remarks disparaging the efficiency of the troops in general and of one general officer in particular. Preston had charged Jesup with the violation of a flag of truce and the commission of a "perfidious act" in imprisoning Osceola. "There was great error and great injustice in all these imputations," Benton responded; as chairman of the Committee on Military Affairs, he felt it was his duty to reply to them. In his characteristic dramatic style, the senator answered in detail these and other charges made against the general.

Benton devoted much of his speech to a rebuttal of the charge that Jesup had been guilty of perfidy and violation of a flag of truce. He rejected this accusation, declaring Jesup's "whole conduct in relation to [the] Indians to have been justifiable under the laws of civilized or savage warfare." Osceola's capture was expedient because of his "previous treacheries and crimes." The Indians had been making a "mockery of the white flag." General Jesup, the senator declared, "has been guilty of no perfidy, no violation of flags. He has done nothing to stain his own character, or to dishonor the flag of the United States. If he has erred, it has been on the side of humanity, generosity, and forbearance to the Indians."

Benton answered the charge that Jesup had written a letter disparaging his predecessor, General Scott, by pointing out that the general had apologized "publicly and officially" for "a private and unofficial wrong." He added, "Such are the amends General Jesup makes—frankly and voluntarily—full and kindly—worthy of a soldier towards brother soldiers; and far more honorable to his predecessors in command than the disparaging comparisons which have been instituted here to do them honor at his expense."[7]

Congressman William Montgomery, a physician from North Carolina, advocated disbandment of the regular army because its performance in Florida demonstrated that it had "become useless and totally inefficient." He continued, "We have one million and a quarter militia. Drill them, and put arms in their hands, and the combined civilized world cannot conquer us." He ridiculed Jesup's statement that he had been sent to Florida to "catch" the Indians, not to kill them: "Great God, Mr. Chairman, what will this nation and the world say when they hear this declaration made by this high officer? . . . Great God! what sympathy for a bleeding frontier, and what patience and forbearance for the Indians! Sir, my blood boils in my veins, when I think of such conduct."[8]

While Congress quarreled over the war in progress, its attention was diverted by the threat of another one. Controversy over the country's northeastern boundary might, it feared, lead to a third conflict with Great Britain. To meet this danger, on 5 July 1838 Congress had authorized an increase in the personnel of the Quartermaster's Department for the first time since 1826, and the creation of new grades for its top officers. Under the new authorization, twelve officers were to be added, making a total of thirty-seven, including the quartermaster general. The new grades created were those of colonel for the two additional assistant quartermasters general and of lieutenant colonel for the two additional deputy quartermasters general. Also added to the staff were eight assistant quartermasters with the rank of captain.[9]

Jesup filled the top four staff positions with veteran quartermaster officers he had trained. Trueman Cross was selected for one of the two posts of assistant quartermaster general. The other went to Henry Stanton, who had been with the general in both the Creek and Seminole campaigns. Thomas F. Hunt and Henry Whiting were appointed deputy quartermasters general. On 7 July, two days after the enactment of the legislation, Cross and Stanton were promoted to the rank of colonel and Hunt and Whiting to that of lieutenant colonel.[10] No other changes in the organization of either the Quartermaster's Department or the army occurred until the outbreak of the war with Mexico in 1846.

After reorganizing his expanded department, Jesup prepared to depart on his long-delayed trip to Kentucky. Since his return from Florida he had been living at a boardinghouse in Georgetown. Completion of his new home in Washington had been delayed during his long absence. He was eagerly looking forward to a reunion with his wife and five children after a separation of nearly three years. He was anxious, too, to reach Kentucky to attend to his personal real estate ventures there, neglected during his service in the field. His army pay and emoluments were inadequate to support his large family. The two years he had spent in command of troops had also been costly to him financially.

During his campaigns he had purchased nine horses and two Indian ponies at a cost of nearly sixteen hundred dollars. When he sought reimbursement from the government for two of his horses lost in the service in Florida, he was no more successful than he was in his requests to appear before a court of inquiry or a congressional committee to answer charges and justify his conduct. Peter Hagner, third auditor of the Treasury Department, could find no law which would permit him to collect his minor claim, even when Secretary Poinsett noted that Jesup was "certainly equitably entitled to remuneration for these horses."[11]

On 17 July, Jesup, laden with gifts for his children, left Washington by stagecoach for the long journey to Kentucky.[12] His oldest daughter, Lucy Ann, was now fifteen. Mary was going on thirteen, Jane was eleven, William, five, and Charles Edward, three. During his service in Florida, Ann's mother, Lucy Croghan, had died. The considerable amount of land she left to her daughter added substantially to Ann's property holdings, which the general assumed their children would eventually inherit. Jesup insisted, however, that under no circumstances would he ever use a dollar of Ann's inheritance.[13] His purpose now was to build up his own income, which had suffered during the two years he was in command of troops.

The general's leave from official duties stretched out much longer than anticipated. He remained in Kentucky for six months, traveling by stagecoach over the state to engage in land speculation and other private business affairs, and he renewed with his brother Samuel, by then a Kentucky state senator, the partnership arrangement for operating his farm near Elkton in Todd County.[14]

In Congress, Senator Benton had introduced a bill for the armed occupation and settlement of Florida, and on 5 January 1839 he sent a copy to Jesup, requesting his comments. Under the proposed legislation, the government would grant 320 acres of Florida land to each of as many as ten thousand white settlers who would agree to remain there and cultivate it until the Indians were forced from the territory. They would live in colonies, would be protected by troops while erecting blockhouses, and would be supplied with provisions for a year, seeds for their first crops, and ammunition until peace was restored.[15] The only doubt he entertained for the plan's success, Jesup replied, arose from "the apprehension that the quantity of good land south of 28° of north latitude [was] not sufficient to induce settlers to occupy it. . . ." He added that the Seminoles would never leave Florida until they found the white man in their way. "Let them be crowded by settlers, and that which has invariably occurred thoroughout the whole history of our settlements will occur again; they will not only consent to remove, but will desire it." The Senate approved Benton's bill, but the House defeated it. More than three years later, a modified version of his bill was finally enacted into law.[16]

While Jesup was in Kentucky, the Washington correspondent of the *New York American* published a libelous attack upon him. He charged that the general was delinquent in his public accounts and was unable to make a satisfactory report of his disbursements. The writer may have misconstrued the reason for Jesup's long absence from his office; obviously, he did not consult Treasury Department auditors or other responsible public officials to verify his report before it was printed. Neither did the other antiadministration newspapers which circulated it to their readers.

Probably none of the many accusations made against him for political purposes angered Jesup so much as this one because, in addition to being a malicious falsehood, it cast a reflection upon his character and integrity as a public official—a reputation he had established and carefully guarded over the years. He immediately addressed a letter to the editor of the *Louisville Journal*: "I owe it to myself to say that the statement is utterly false. I have accounted for every cent of public money that ever came into my hands, as my accounts at the Treasury will show." He requested the editors who had published the erroneous statement to insert a copy of his denial. Upon his return to Locust Grove, where preparations were being made for Christmas, he and Ann discussed the advisability of his filing a libel suit.

When the story was published in Washington, William A. Gordon, chief clerk in the quartermaster general's office, having ascertained that far from being in default the general was actually a creditor in the amount of several hundred dollars, drafted an article for the *Intelligencer*, the opposition paper. His article proved unnecessary, for on 31 December the *Globe* published "with sincere pleasure" the general's letter to the *Louisville Journal*, and on 3 January the *Intelligencer* also published it, along with a short editorial, which, Gordon said, "has gratified your friends here." That same day, 3 January, the *Globe* stated in an editorial: "[the *Journal of Commerce*] relieves itself . . . from all further participation in the recent heartless attacks upon Gen. Jackson, Gen. Jesup, and Governor Cass, upon the subject of public defalcations."[17]

On 2 February, Jesup boarded a stagecoach for his trip back to Washington. Because the cold weather and bad roads would have made the journey difficult for his wife and children, they remained at Locust Grove with Dr. Croghan. Jesup promised to return for them in the spring or early summer. That he was still considering legal action against the author of the libelous article is evident from Ann's letter written to him a short time after his departure. Her writing also reflects her great love for him: "Five days only have passed since you left here . . . ; it appears like five weeks, so much I feel the loss of your society." She had thought over their discussions and believed she had not properly advised him. She wished the author of the falsehood every ill but, on due reflection, thought him beneath the general's notice. "Knowing how undeserving you are of everything like censure or blame, it all most kills me to hear a word against you. . . . This day twelve months [ago] I heard that you were wounded in battle. The idea of all I then suffered makes my heart ache."[18] When Jesup discovered that even the usually antagonistic Whig newspapers discredited the story, some taking the unprecedented step of apologizing for publishing it, he apparently abandoned his intention of suing the author.

Soon after Jesup's return to Washington, Poinsett ordered General Macomb, commander-in-chief of the army, to Florida to seek an end to the war through negotiation. The secretary's instructions of 18 March 1839 authorized Macomb to enter into a truce with the Seminoles. The general arrived in Florida early in April. After about six weeks, he announced that a truce had been arranged; the Indians were to withdraw south of Pease Creek and remain there for sixty days under the protection of the troops until further arrangements were made. "I did not think it necessary," Macomb wrote Poinsett, "to enter into a formal written treaty. . . . Nor did I think it politic, at this time, to say anything about emigration"—which was the crux of the problem. He proposed leaving the subject open to future arrangements as the government might think proper.[19]

Many in Washington's official circles rejoiced over the news, believing that the war was over. Poinsett gave his tacit approval to Macomb's arrangements, thus endorsing what was, in effect, the same proposal he had rejected nearly two years earlier when it was made by Jesup. Jesup, given the same authority possessed by Macomb in 1839, could probably have ended the conflict in the summer of 1837. The *Globe* commented jubilantly: "It gives us great pleasure to announce the arrival at the seat of Government of Major General Macomb, who has succeeded in pacifying the Indians of Florida, and has made such an arrangement with them as will effectively put a stop to the further effusion of blood in that Territory."[20]

The rejoicing was premature by three years. The temporary peace that followed Macomb's truce was shattered early in July by a new outbreak of Indian depredations. Poinsett conceded in his annual report in November that the only result of Macomb's negotiations ". . . has been the loss of many valuable lives. . . . The experience of last summer brings with it the painful conviction that the war must be prosecuted until Florida is freed from these ruthless savages."[21]

Before leaving for Kentucky on 20 April to bring his family to Washington, Jesup leased from Col. George Bomford, chief of the Ordnance Department, one wing of Kalorama, Bomford's beautiful home, as a temporary residence for the summer and fall. Finally, on 26 November, the family moved to their newly completed house on F Street in downtown Washington. This house became the family home; for more than fifty years after the general's death, it continued to be known as "the old Jesup Homestead."[22] Jesup once more resumed his close supervision of his children's education and religious training. The children attended the theater and the opera, and their father encouraged them to read, particularly the Bible. The family attended St. John's Episcopal Church, near the White House, where they sat together in a reserved pew.[23]

Although the war in Florida continued with no end in sight, Jesup's department experienced no serious problems other than the heavy financial burden that the conflict imposed upon it. The system of supplying the army which he had devised two decades earlier was functioning efficiently, as Gen. Zachary Taylor attested in his report to the adjutant general in Washington on 20 July 1839: "Notwithstanding our operations have extended over more than fifty thousand square miles no want of transportation or supplies have been experienced, owing to the judicious arrangements of Colonel Cross, assistant quartermaster-general and his able assistants."[24] Cross had been serving on Taylor's staff since the fall of 1838 to direct quartermaster operations. On 21 April 1840, Taylor was relieved of the command, to be succeeded by Brig. Gen. Walker Keith Armistead.

Jesup himself had been highly pleased by the way his department performed while he was in command of troops: "I had, under the most difficult circumstances, an opportunity of testing the high efficiency of the system, an efficiency which I had never before witnessed when serving in the field. I never found the slightest difficulty from the working of the Regulations."[25]

The advent of 1840 could scarcely be said to usher in a happy period for Jesup. He was embarrassed and victimized by the disgraceful behavior of Col. George Croghan, yet he could do little about it without offending his wife, who wanted to save her brother from public disgrace. The general had met with one frustration after another for nearly two years, ever since being relieved of the command in Florida, as he sought in vain to tell his story to the country. Political attacks upon him continued in Congress and in the Whig press. One of the most exciting presidential campaigns in history was nearing a climax, with the election only months away; as political oratory increased in fervor, Whig attacks upon the administration's management of the war and, strangely enough, upon the nonpartisan former commander also picked up momentum.

In the Senate, Preston of South Carolina continued to lead the Whig attack by reviving the accusation that Jesup had been responsible for Scott's removal from the Florida command. Moreover, he made the astonishing assertion that Jesup, after having operated in his own way for some time, had finally concluded that the original plan devised by Scott for dealing with the Seminoles was ". . . the true and only one which could be effectual. . . . the people generally fell into the notion that if Scott had not been superseded, the war would have been terminated at most by one or two campaigns." Thomas Hart Benton responded by noting that Jesup was "still the selected object of attack." The senator from South Carolina was not content, he declared, "with extolling to the skies the officers of his own complexion," but had sought to degrade another officer in order to enhance their praise. Benton did not object to having Preston make demigods of "his Federal or Whig heroes," but he did object to invidious comparisons which placed General Jesup below their level when he had "the advantage in merits." Jesup was the only commanding general, he said, who brought a scar from Florida; "he has done three times as much, in half the time, as all the rest put together have done in that Territory." Yet he was the only one selected for attack; he was the only one "assailed and disparaged by unjust comparison." Was this, he asked, because of Jesup's friendship for General Jackson?[26]

Spearheading the attack in the House were such loyal Whigs as Richard Biddle and Charles Ogle of Pennsylvania, Waddy Thompson of South Carolina, and Hiram P. Hunt and James Monroe of New York. Monroe, a nephew of the late president, had served twice as an aide to Scott. With an eye on the approaching election, the Whigs rehashed the old familiar charges, apparently assuming that constant repetition would bring conviction.

Surprisingly, not merely the Democrats alone came to the defense of the quartermaster general. Alexander Duncan of Cincinnati, who had been elected to Congress as a Whig, proved to be an ardent admirer and supporter of Jesup and a critic of Scott. If any disgrace was attached to the conduct of the war, he declared, it must attach to General Scott. Reviewing the events of the Creek war, he asserted that if Scott's orders had not been opposed by Jesup at the precise time that they were, that conflict in all probability would have turned into another long and costly war like the one in Florida. Had Jesup obeyed Scott's order to cease all operations, ". . . his volunteers would have abandoned him . . . cursing him for a *coward*. The [friendly] warriors . . . would have dubbed him with the title of squaw, and would have dispersed and joined the hostiles."[27] Tilghman Howard of Indiana decried the treatment given returning officers: "Instead of being welcomed home with honors and rewards, we see the Jesups and other distinguished officers . . . treated as if they had returned in disgrace."[28]

William O. Butler[29] of Kentucky, making his maiden speech in Congress, took the floor of the House to vindicate the administration and Jesup. He declared that Jesup's success in the Florida war was "at least five times as great as [that of] all the other generals together" who had participated in it. Under these circumstances, he thought it reasonable to hope that Jesup be permitted to return to his family and rest in quiet. The general, though he had not asked for fame in this war, had won "reputation enough to satisfy the ambition of a moderate man." Jesup had the misfortune, however, to derange one of Scott's "splendid plans" of an Indian campaign, Butler said derisively. "True, he succeeded in seizing the Indians, and preventing a war with the Creek nation, but not on a scientific plan; and that has called down the heavy vengeance of Gen. Scott's friends on this floor." The congressman rejected the charge that Jesup had disgraced the flag in his capture and detention of Osceola; he had done too much "to elevate the flag of this nation in war, ever to tarnish it in peace or war."

To those who criticized the army for not ending the war, Butler replied: "Produce the foe, and, my word for it the war will be ended in an hour; but sir, unless the enemy can be found, how idle is your command to conquer him; you had as well bid your army smooth down the ruffled mane of the deep, or bind the restless wings of the wind, or pluck a star from the coronal of night, as conquer a foe that you cannot find."[30]

Editor Blair of the *Globe*, who corresponded frequently with Jackson at the Hermitage, wrote the former president on 12 July: "Genl Scott through his friend Biddle in Congress, is baiting Jesup most basely. . . . One of the things harped upon is, that you recalled Scott in consequence of my interference." Blair asked Jackson to give him recollections so that he might answer the critics. The aging Jackson reiterated: "The charge that either you or Genl Jesup had any thing to do with the recal [sic] of Genl Scott is entirely groundless. It was the evidence laid before me, satisfactory to my own mind that he was inefficient & unfit for such a service, that produced the recal [sic]."[31]

Joseph Underwood of Kentucky had listened with growing annoyance to the criticism leveled by his fellow Whigs at Jesup. Through many years of intimate association with the general as business agent and friend, he knew better than any member of Congress the true character of the man. He finally rose to speak on 13 July, only seven days before Congress adjourned. Few congressmen, he pointed out, were qualified to decide the merits of military movements. Moreover, the officers who were being assailed were not present to defend themselves, which should have induced the congressmen to proceed with great caution. To disprove the charge that the general "intrigued for command," Underwood reviewed the circumstances surrounding Jesup's departure from Washington on the night of 21 May 1836. So sudden was Jesup's departure, he related, that he knew nothing of the general's intentions to go until after he was gone, although pending business transactions required instructions from Jesup.

Taking up the charge that Jesup's letter to Blair had "poisoned" the mind of Jackson against Scott, he contended that "General Jackson's mind had been operated on long before the Blair letter was written"; the president had ordered Scott's removal from the command in Florida in his endorsement on Delegate Joseph M. White's letter dated 28 May. "When White's letter was written, General Jesup was on his way to assume the command in the Creek country, and could not possibly know any thing in regard to that letter, much less to be the instigator of it." Jesup's letter to Blair was not written until 20 June 1836.

Underwood believed that the facts showed that the Indians, and not Jesup, had been guilty of an act of treachery in the Osceola incident. If Jesup's assailants were seeking the truth, why, he asked, did they not set up a congressional investigating committee or a court-martial? Jesup would not shrink from either tribunal.

Underwood made his two-hour speech more than four years after the quarrel between Generals Scott and Jesup, thirty-one months after the capture of Osceola, and more than two years after Jesup had been withdrawn from the Florida command. So tenaciously did the Whigs cling to their political issues that the Whig version of the Osceola episode and other events of that period gained, through tireless repetition, wide credence. The country was so deeply engrossed in the hotly contested presidential campaign that the newspapers could find no space to report Underwood's speech until nearly four months later, and it was never widely publicized. In contrast, the charges which provoked the speech received extensive press coverage.

Jesup's reputation, Underwood said, had been ". . . made to suffer, by attacks for political purposes, through a thousand channels, when, if the real truth was known, the country would perceive very little, if any thing in his conduct worthy of censure, and much to admire. . . . He is a soldier, and the servant of his country, and does not interfere with the scrambles of politicians for civil offices."

The great compassion which Underwood felt as he delivered the following passage on the floor of the House can be sensed even today.

> Meet General Jesup, and shake hands with him, and you grasp a hand mutilated in the service of his country. Look him in the face, and you see the scar of an Indian bullet. Sir, he has been upon more bloody fields, and received more wounds in battle, than any of your generals; and these wounds are trumpet-tongued, crying shame! shame! shame! upon those who assail his character without knowing the facts, or knowing, disregard them.[32]

Despite the Whigs' unmerciful attack and the defense by the Democrats, Jesup steadfastly refused to become a political partisan. He made his feelings clear in the fall of 1840 when he declined to accept an invitation from Democratic leaders in Michigan to attend a political reception in Detroit for Vice President Richard M. Johnson: "I cannot, consistently with my own view of my duty, accept an invitation so kindly given." His opinions regarding the obligations of military men were perhaps peculiar to himself, but he held it to be "utterly repugnant to the principles of [American] institutions" for them to take part, either directly or indirectly, in political conflicts. The army, to be useful, must be national, and would become dangerous to the public liberties only when its members, abandoning the national standard, "shall rally under the banners of party."[33]

Political excitement was running high in Washington in the fall of 1840. General Harrison's election, Jesup wrote to Dr. Croghan, seemed to be conceded on all sides. Although he and Harrison were on the most friendly terms, he felt the new president would probably be surrounded with men who were his enemies. "It will be impossible for me to act [with them]," he wrote. "Either Preston or Waddy Thompson will have the War Department. The appointment of either will be the signal, necessarily, of my separation from the service."[34]

Jesup's personal embarrassments and frustrations seem not to have interfered with the performance of his official duties; the annual report of the secretary of war provides evidence to confirm this. Poinsett stated that experience in 1840 proved the correctness of his contention that the increase in personnel and proper organization of the staff would produce a more economical administration of its different branches. In particular, he said, the Quartermaster's Department had made a considerable reduction in expenditures. While the decrease was in some measure the result of lower prices, it was due in a much greater degree to the increased efficiency and better administration of that department.[35]

Excitement over the election had finally subsided by the time the second session of the 26th Congress convened. The scheduled opening date was 7 December 1840, but a fifteen-inch snowfall had made most of the roads into the city impassable, delaying the arrival of so many members that neither the House nor the Senate could muster a quorum. One familiar Whig figure was missing in the House when the second session began a day late. Richard Biddle had resigned after the election to resume the practice of law in Pittsburgh. His resignation removed one of the thorns from Jesup's side, but neither his departure nor the sweeping victory of the Whigs in the national election marked the end of verbal assaults upon the general. On 9 February 1841 Abolitionist Joshua Giddings, the antislavery Whig, delivered his long speech on the House floor, denouncing the general's policies regarding slaves during his command in Florida and accusing Jesup of making "slave-catchers" of the men in his army. The report of his speech filled eight columns in the *Globe* on 21 April 1841.

About the time Giddings made his speech, Jesup was preparing a petition to Congress for redress from an injustice he claimed had occurred while he was in command of troops. It pertained to the often-repeated charge that his letter to Blair nearly five years earlier was responsible for the removal of Scott from command both in Florida and in the Creek country. The false charge still weighed heavily on his mind. But how could he prove its falseness? During the summer of 1840, while searching through the records, Jesup made a surprising discovery. In October of 1837, the House had adopted a resolution calling upon the War Department to submit copies of all official documents and correspondence relating to the recall of Scott, which were then printed as House *Document 224,* 2d session, 24th Congress. Included was Florida Delegate White's letter to President Jackson demanding the immediate removal of Scott as the Florida commander. Jesup found that the president's endorsement, ordering Scott's removal from the command in Florida, had been omitted from White's letter as published in *Document 224.* Moreover, that letter, with the endorsement missing, had been submitted as evidence at Scott's court of inquiry at Frederick. Scott's testimony indicated he assumed that White had withdrawn his original letter when he triumphantly displayed to the court White's second letter, which modified the earlier accusations. But White had never requested its withdrawal, as Jesup's search revealed. The letter bearing the endorsement was still on file in the adjutant general's office when White died in St. Louis on 19 October 1839.[36] No satisfactory explanation has been found as to why the endorsement was omitted from official documents. Scott, during his admittedly one-sided testimony, placed so much emphasis upon Jesup's letter to Blair as the reason for his removal that members of the court simply accepted it as the true cause for Scott's dismissal.

After his discovery, Jesup wrote to Poinsett, calling attention to the omission. He asserted, "[The endorsement] is an important part of the document, and was as positively called for as any other portion of the report. My conduct has been questioned and it was due to justice, if not to me, that the entire document should have been furnished. I have now respectfully to ask on whose authority, and in what office, testimony so important to me has been suppressed?"[37] The secretary of war denied, as did the adjutant general, any knowledge of, or responsibility for, the omission. Jesup then turned to Congress.

A great injustice, he declared in his petition, had been done to him by the wide circulation of the charge that he had engaged in an intrigue to bring about the removal of his superior officer from the command of not only the army operating against the Creek

Indians but also the army operating in Florida. The injurious charge, he believed, had been caused by the omission in official documents of the president's endorsement on White's letter. He was prepared to prove, as he would have done had his request for a court of inquiry been granted, that he had "no agency whatsoever in the recall of General Scott from the command of either army."

Among the points Jesup developed in his lengthy petition were these: he had not aspired to the command of any army in the field; he had been much concerned about his health and the welfare of his family at that time; and he had, without any application on his part, been assigned by President Jackson to command the army in the Creek country because he was the only available officer of the rank superior to that of the militia and volunteer officers who would serve there. He had, in fact, agreed to serve under Scott when the latter had arrived unexpectedly in the Creek country. Insofar as the Florida command was concerned, Scott had been informed, as early as 24 June, that that command had been committed to Call. Jesup relieved Call on presidential orders in December 1836, nearly seven months after Scott had left Florida.

With great surprise, he found himself charged by members of both houses of Congress with having intrigued for command and with having caused the withdrawal of his superior. He understood the charges when he discovered the president's endorsement had been omitted from the printed report of the court of inquiry proceedings. His purpose was not to charge anyone with intentional omission of the president's order but merely to set himself right before Congress and the country. The Senate referred his petition, dated 18 February 1841, to the Committee on Military Affairs, which ordered it printed on 3 March 1841.[38]

The next day William Henry Harrison was inaugurated as ninth president of the United States. Perhaps because of his friendship with the sixty-eight-year-old general, Jesup "and ladies" received an invitation to attend the "Tippecanoe Inaugural Ball" at Carusi's Saloon. The following day, President Harrison announced his replacement for Poinsett as head of the War Department. Jesup's earlier dire prediction that the president would appoint either Preston or Thompson proved wrong. The new secretary of war was John Bell, a Tennessean from Nashville, Andrew Jackson's home area. First elected to the House as a Democrat in 1826, Bell had switched to the Whig party two years later and had been elected to six more terms under that banner. One of Bell's first acts was to issue, on 23 March, what might be termed an 1841 version of the modern Hatch Act. He prepared and distributed a circular which contained a warning from President Harrison that any officers or agents of the federal government engaging in "partisan or active interference in elections" or making contributions for party purposes would be removed from office. Jesup circulated a copy among officers of his department without comment.[39]

The hero of Tippecanoe died on 4 April, one month after his inauguration, the first president to die in office. Jesup marched in the funeral procession and sent a message of condolence to the widow, with whom he had long been acquainted. John Tyler, the fifty-one-year-old vice president, took the oath as the tenth president on 6 April, though many thought he should have been designated as "acting president."

On 25 June Maj. Gen. Alexander Macomb died. He had been general-in-chief of the army since the death of Jacob Brown in 1828. The selection of a successor raised again the question as to which of those bitter rivals—Gaines or Scott—was the senior officer in the army. Much to the consternation of Gaines, Scott was appointed general-in-chief on 6 July. While that decision was pending, Jesup had written Secretary Bell requesting that he be considered for the vacancy that would arise in the field command if either Scott or Gaines were chosen for the top post. If successful in his bid, he would at last be freed of the laborious duties of quartermaster general. "After these two officers I am the next Senior of the Army, and for the last twenty-three years have been senior to all the other officers now in the Army."[40]

Once more the quartermaster general's hopes were dashed. Brig. Gen. John E. Wool, who had entered the army four years after Jesup, was selected to fill the vacancy. The appointment undoubtedly was subject to the approval of the new general-in-chief, and Scott more than likely still nurtured animosity towards his "ancient friend." In a *Globe* editorial, Blair was highly critical of the choice. Wool, he observed, had been promoted over the heads of Gens. Hugh Brady, Henry Atkinson, John R. Fenwick, Jesup, and Nathan Towson—and upon what ground? Age, infirmities, and wounds might be alleged to have disabled the first three named, but not Jesup or Towson. "No officers of our army were more distinguished by the number of battles in which they were engaged, the number of wounds received, or the brevets conferred. . . . Both are entitled, by former promotions, to higher rank than General Wool, and are now in the full vigor of their lives, and capable of the most arduous service."[41]

Early in May of 1841—three years after he had been relieved of the command in Florida—the quartermaster general learned that promises he had made in good faith to the Seminoles to induce them to surrender and move to the West had not been kept. John Ross, chief of the Cherokees, wrote to Secretary of War Bell that when he and his people arrived at their new home in 1839, they found Seminoles encamped at various places around Fort Gibson on land assigned to the Cherokees. He was preparing to head a delegation to Washington when he was approached by Alligator, the Seminole chief, who asked him to convey a message to the secretary of war "for the ear of the President." Alligator told him that General Jesup had promised him and his warriors new guns, plows, hoes, axes, and kettles to replace those left behind in Florida, and had also promised that they would have an agent. Ross quoted the Seminole as saying, "I have no gun to kill squirrels and birds for my children; no axe to cut firewood—no plows or hoes with which to till the soil for bread—and no agent . . . to represent my wants and grievances. . . . I am perplexed to perceive the true cause, why these fair promises have not been fulfilled—or, whether they were made only to deceive me."[42]

When Secretary Bell called his attention to the letter, Jesup replied, "The statement of Mr. Ross is substantially correct, and I consider the public faith pledged, as far as a military commander had the authority to pledge it, that the articles left by that band in Florida be replaced." Alligator's band, he explained, was among those that fled upon learning that President Van Buren would not consent to their remaining in Florida. In their hasty retreat the Indians had left plows, axes, kettles, and other property scattered over a wide area. Alligator had sent a message that he would surrender as soon as his people could collect their property. Jesup promised to replace in Arkansas all of these articles. The claim is just, he stated, "but apart from its justice, the highest considerations of policy demand that it be acknowledged and satisfied."[43]

Commenting on this episode, Edwin C. McReynolds observes

that General Jesup, with the pressure of military and political necessity long since removed from his shoulders, still considered justice for the Indians a matter of first importance. "It is a view of the General that has seldom been presented because the current accounts were kept by antislavery men, or proslavery men, or Indian haters, or the speculators in land or chattels. None of these groups found Jesup's policies quite to their liking. They seized upon his mistakes and magnified them, and they did not hesitate to misrepresent his views." McReynolds also summarizes the reasons why Jesup was subjected to criticism for his conduct of the war.

> General Jesup's reputation has suffered from an accumulation of causes. His course in Florida ran counter to the wishes of many local politicians who had influence. He would not engage the army in the work of catching runaway slaves, but only the Negroes who were the allies of the hostile Seminoles. He did not lend his influence to the fraudulent seizure of Negro prisoners on claims of doubtful validity. But, as the responsible military agent of the United States, he attempted to carry out the policy of removal by force, and quite naturally failed to gain the good will of the Seminoles. His very effectiveness as a soldier made enemies for him among those who had strong sympathy for the Indians. The need of thoughtless persons to find a scapegoat for the failure of American society and American government in dealing with the Seminoles, has led a great many critics to heap blame upon the shoulders of Thomas Sidney Jesup.[44]

When word reached T. Hartley Crawford, commissioner of Indian affairs, that Jesup had verified the truth of Alligator's claims and fully supported them, he recommended the appointment of a subagent for the Seminoles. He also ordered Maj. William Armstrong of the Choctaw Agency to purchase farming implements and other articles for Alligator's band, if they would agree to remove from Cherokee land and settle in the country assigned to the Seminoles.[45]

The old question of justice for the Seminole Indians removed to the West arose again in the spring of 1844 when a delegation of the tribe's chiefs, headed by Coacoochee and Alligator, appeared in Washington. Jesup once more championed their cause by calling the attention of administration officials to their presence and purpose. They were in the capital, he stated, to seek fulfillment of the provisions of their treaties and of the promises which he and other army commanders had made to them. Specifically, the chiefs complained that the treaty entered into at Fort Gibson on 14 February 1833 stipulated that they were to have a permanent and comfortable home on a part of the land assigned to the Creek Indians, but that when they arrived they found all of the land occupied by the Creeks. On their behalf, Jesup wrote to William Wilkins, who had been appointed secretary of war on 15 February 1844 by President Tyler.

> The Seminoles are here supplicants for justice. They ask to be put in possession of the territory secured to them by the Supreme law of the land; and they cannot believe that the Government of a great and magnanimous people will refuse them the justice to which they are entitled. As the Commander of the Army in Florida I assured them in good faith, that the country set apart by the treaty was ready for their reception. I consider it due to my honour, as well as that of the Country, most respectfully but earnestly to urge upon the government the prompt fulfillment of the treaty by placing these unfortunate people at once in possession of their lands.[46]

This time administration officials heeded the appeal, and in 1845 a new treaty was signed by the Creeks, Seminoles, and the United States. Under its terms, the Creeks were to permit the Seminoles to settle in any part of the Creek Nation, either in a body or separately, and to make their own town laws, subject to the general approval of the Creek Council, in which the Seminoles would be represented. The United States agreed to abide by the terms of the Treaty of Payne's Landing, which included the payment of $15,400 to the Seminoles as soon as they settled on the Creek lands; an annuity of $3,000 for fifteen years; and $2,000 per year in goods suited to their wants, to be divided equally among all members of the Seminole tribe. The United States also agreed to compensate the Seminoles, at the rate of $1,000 per annum for five years, for the agricultural implements left behind in Florida. Moreover, subsistence for six months was to be provided for all Seminoles who agreed to settle on Creek lands.[47]

Other pledges had gone unfulfilled. John Caulfield Spencer became secretary of war, succeeding John Bell, who resigned on

12 September 1841 after only six months in office. In his annual report for 1841, Secretary Spencer made an urgent appeal to Congress and the administration to honor Jesup's pledge to the Creek Indians. Jesup had promised the friendly Creek warriors who had fought with the army against the Seminoles in Florida in 1836 and 1837 payment of eight thousand dollars for the Negroes they had captured and turned over to his headquarters. Although the warriors had rejected the sum as too small in 1837 when they were mustered out of the service, Jesup considered the government's continued failure to pay the money a violation of the pledge he had made in good faith on behalf of the country. "Infidelity to our engagements, and a refusal to remunerate faithful service," Spencer wrote in support of the general, "will not increase either the confidence or respect of the Indians who have relied on our honor."[48]

In his last annual report as secretary of war on 26 November 1842, Spencer made another fervent appeal to Congress to honor the pledge: "The earnestness with which a gallant soldier pleads for the faith and honor of his country and for justice to a helpless tribe . . . will find a hearty response in every bosom." It appeared for a time that this latest appeal might bring results. W. L. Goggin, chairman of the House Committee on Military Affairs, requested more information on the subject. The quartermaster general hopefully prepared a lengthy review of the circumstances which he submitted along with pertinent documents to the committee on 17 January 1843. A letter Jesup wrote two years later reveals that his pledge to the Creek warriors had not yet been redeemed.[49] So far as can be determined, it never was.

The question of the status of the Seminole Negroes living in the West also remained unresolved. As late as 1844, Jesup was seeking justice and protection for those he had sent west. He called their plight to the attention of President Tyler and William Wilkins, then-secretary of war. More than nine-tenths of those Negroes, he pointed out, had surrendered under the assurance of freedom on certain conditions. He had employed many of them in Florida as guides and messengers. Some of their compatriots had been killed in the service of the army. As commander and the representative of the government, he had pledged the national faith that their families would not be separated nor any of them sold to white men or to others. Jesup had learned that some citizens of the

United States and Texas, and even Creeks and Cherokee Indians, were attempting to obtain possession of them. "I cannot remain passive and witness the illegal interference with the rights of these people," he wrote to the secretary of war. "I earnestly hope that the Executive will not permit the national faith then solemnly pledged . . . to be violated; but that all of the negroes who surrendered to me and have been sent to the West, be protected from capture by, or sale to, either Citizens, foreigners, or Indians; and that measures be taken to recover all who have been separated from their families and sold."[50]

When the new treaty with the Creeks and Seminoles was ratified in 1845, President James K. Polk referred the question of the status of the Negroes to the attorney general. The matter was still pending when Isaac Toucey took over that office on 29 June 1848. His legal opinion was, in effect, that the commander in Florida did not have the authority to grant the Negroes their freedom; therefore, their status as slaves was unchanged by Jesup's promises. Consequently, on 2 January 1849, the Negroes were returned officially to their Seminole masters.[51]

In 1841, when the Seminoles first raised the issue of claims, the costly and unpopular war in Florida was entering its seventh year. Col. William J. Worth, a War of 1812 veteran and a former commandant at West Point, had replaced Brig. Gen. Walker K. Armistead as commander of the troops in Florida on 31 May 1841. In a basic order, he set forth a policy similar to the one Jesup adopted in 1837 that no Indians were to come into his camp except for purposes of emigration. More all-inclusive, Worth's order read: "Any Indian presenting himself at any post will be seized and held in strict confinement."[52]

By February of 1842, when Worth had become convinced that removal of the Indians by force was utterly impractical, he submitted a proposal to the War Department reminiscent of Jesup's recommendation four years earlier. Worth reported that of the 300 Indians still in Florida, no more than 112 were warriors, but that "every diminution of numbers adds to the difficulty of taking the remainder." He proposed, therefore, that the size of the force be limited to the number needed to protect the settlers and that the Indians be permitted to plant crops and come into any post unmolested but that efforts be continued to persuade them to go West. The citizens of Florida were as enraged by his proposal as they had been by Jesup's. Referred to a council of high-ranking officers by Secretary of War Spencer, Worth's proposal was rejected. Only Jesup supported Worth; he had long contended the war could end only when the Seminoles were allowed to remain in Florida.[53]

Three months later, President John Tyler took a hand in the matter. He recognized, as did Jesup, the wisdom of Worth's proposal; in fact, the quartermaster general may have exercised sufficient influence to help sway the president. On 10 May, the chief executive sent a message to both branches of Congress, announcing his decision to bring the war to a close on Worth's terms. He declared that "the further pursuit of these miserable beings by a large military force seems to be as injudicious as it is unavailing." He was authorizing Worth to declare, as soon as expedient, that hostilities against the Indians had ceased. The commander was to provide the necessary protection to the inhabitants and to establish friendly relations with the Indians while trying to persuade them to join their friends and relatives in the West.[54]

Reduction of the military force was to begin as quickly as possible, but at least two regiments were to be retained to form a line of protection for the white settlers. The quartermaster general would instruct his senior officer in Florida regarding the disposal of public property. Three months later, in August 1842, Secretary Spencer declared the Second Seminole War officially ended, though hostilities did not cease completely until some months later.[55] The terms upon which the war concluded were basically the same as those Jesup had recommended in 1838—only to have them rejected by President Van Buren. Had the government heeded Jesup's advice, the war would doubtless have ended four years earlier, and the nation would have saved millions of dollars as well as numerous lives of soldiers and citizens.

The indispensible services performed by supply officers generally go unnoticed by historians, but Sprague's account of the Seminole War pays tribute to the efficiency, skill, and integrity of the twenty-five quartermaster officers who served at one time or another in the Florida conflict. Their "varied and complicated duties," he noted, required "unceasing activity and attention, and an intimate acquaintance with all branches of business, civil and military." Large sums of money were entrusted to them and they were responsible for "its safe custody and its judicious application to the wants of the service." Their "rigid accountability" in the handling of vouchers and returns (a system devised by Jesup) imposed a "laborious task, requiring care and method, more resembling the order and regularity of a bureau, than a place where duties are to be performed with brevity and dispatch." The transportation of all supplies was also dependent upon the quartermaster's experience and ability. The duties of the Quartermaster's Department, "being more numerous and complicated than any other, involving pecuniary responsibility, renders it more imperative that the officers of this corps should possess the highest qualities both of the soldier and the citizen. He has at stake the honor of his country in the efficiency of the soldier, as well as being a trusty sentinel over the coffers of the nation." Sprague had special praise for the ability and zeal of Assistant Quartermaster General Trueman Cross and Deputy Quartermasters General Henry Whiting and Thomas F. Hunt, each of whom directed quartermaster operations during a tour of duty in Florida. Cross, who was chief quartermaster throughout the two-year period of General Taylor's command, was relieved in 1840 by Whiting, who was replaced by Hunt on 12 March 1842.[56] Florida was a valuable training ground for many quartermasters who served with distinction a few years later in the Mexican conflict, as well as a proving ground for Jesup's depot system.

Jesup supported the retrenchment program initiated by Worth in 1841 to curtail the expense of conducting the costly war. This program involved not only the sale of surplus horses, mules, wagons, and other items, as well as the withdrawal of certain army units and the closing of some depots, but also a sharp reduction in the number of civilian employees. Up to that time more than one thousand civilians had been on the payroll in Florida, including clerks, mechanics, laborers, teamsters, blacksmiths, and various other types of workers. On 23 June 1842, Hunt submitted a report that Quartermaster's Department savings in the twelve-month period ending 30 April amounted to $174,923. By 14 August, the official closing date of the war, the figure had reached $206,423. A portion of this savings resulted from the departure of three regiments and five companies of the 2d Dragoons. After their withdrawal, proceeds from the sale of surplus property and supplies from several depots were sufficient to defray the expenses of the army remaining in Florida.[57]

The retrenchment program was not confined to military operations in Florida. The Clothing Bureau, which had been separated from Jesup's department in 1832, was again merged with it on 29 November 1841 by order of Secretary Spencer, netting an annual saving of $1,500. The quartermaster general again became responsible for estimating the clothing requirements of the army. An act of Congress on 23 August 1842, which abolished the office of commissary general of purchases and transferred the purchasing function to the Quartermaster's Department,[58] brought a saving of $3,000 a year. Jesup placed Deputy Quartermaster General Henry Stanton in charge of the clothing depot and quartermaster office in Philadelphia. The depot was responsible for the procurement and production of army clothing and shoes. Through judicious arrangements, coupled with a small reduction in the size of the army, Stanton was able to trim yearly expenses at the depot and quartermaster office by more than $2,600. Congress was so insistent upon stringent economy in the government that one of its measures bordered on the ridiculous. Staff officers were forbidden to use public funds for the purchase of newspapers and other publications useful to them in the procurement of supplies. Jesup cancelled subscriptions to the *National Intelligencer, Globe, Madisonian, American Jurist,* and purchase of books for his law library, resulting in an annual saving of forty-six dollars.[59]

As has been true after every war in which the United States has been involved, Congress turned its attention after the Second Seminole War to the question of reducing its military force. Agitation for a reduction in troops began as soon as it became known that the administration was taking measures to end the conflict. As usual, some congressmen argued that the militia was preferable to a standing army. After a spirited debate, the House passed a bill containing provisions to reduce the army to the size of the peace establishment in 1821 (fewer than 6,000), to eliminate the 2d Dragoons, and to lower the pay of general staff officers. The Senate, however, struck out all of those provisions. The legislation finally enacted on 23 August 1842 retained the 2d Dragoons, converting it from a cavalry to a rifle unit as an economy measure, and reduced the size of infantry companies from fifty to forty-two enlisted men. Otherwise the army remained about the same. Its actual strength in November of 1842 was 10,628, a decrease of only 541 from the previous November.[60] With the war officially ended, the command in Florida was designated as the 9th Military Department.

By 1842, Jesup had become so nationally prominent and popular a figure that pressure was brought to bear upon him to seek the Democratic nomination for president. Approached in August by John H. Sherburne, at the instigation of the president of the Democratic Central Committee of New York,[61] Jesup replied that although others had urged him to run for office, he had constantly resisted the pressure. "I am not now, & cannot be, a candidate for either [the presidency or the vice-presidency]." He did not believe that anyone who had spent three-fifths of his life in the military service was "qualified to administer the government of this Great Nation in all its important departments & details." Experienced statesmen, he believed, should be selected for both offices. He admitted, "[I am] of the old democratic school, though as a matter of military propriety I never meddle with the party operations (nor concern myself with party interests) and shall not so long as I wear a uniform." If he were not a soldier, he would "take an active part in public affairs," without expecting or desiring anything for himself.[62]

Sherburne apparently accepted Jesup's rejection as final. He expressed his approval of "that modesty which impels you to defer your claims whether military or civil, to those of more 'experienced and practised statesmen.' Such sentiments . . . are worthy of being placed in strong contrast to those given to the world, by other men who like yourself 'wear a uniform.' "[63] Doubtless he referred in particular to Maj. Gen. Winfield Scott, who early in September had stated that if nominated by a regular national convention for the presidency, he should certainly accept the honor if he got "not a vote in the Union," but that nothing could induce him to think of the second place.

Assuming that Jesup would be willing to become a candidate for the vice presidency, James L. Cantis of New York wrote him on 20 January 1843, asking that he forward ". . . any Documents you may have in your possession relative to your personal History, as well as any Suggestion you may have to make." Jesup did not see that letter until two months later. In his reply on 22 March, he apologized for the long delay in answering; he had not had the time or inclination to arrange the documents requested. "Indeed my personal history possesses so little to interest my fellow citizens at large, that were I to thrust upon their notice the incidents of a life so unimportant as mine to any but my family circle, I fear I should incur, and perhaps justly, the charge of an undue degree of arrogance and vanity." He was not a candidate for office, he said, and gave his reasons for not engaging in politics: "[The reputation] of a military man, unlike that of a statesman, belongs not to a party, but to the nation; and so far as my public acts have been misunderstood or misinterpreted I shall vindicate them in the proper manner and at the proper time, but I cannot permit it to be done in a political canvass."[64]

Migration to the Far West was beginning in earnest, as Secretary of War Wilkins noted in his last annual report. Over the years since the Lewis and Clark expedition, many travelers had "crossed the Rocky Mountains, until at last the emigrant's trail in the rich valley of the Willamette is now traversed by every kind of conveyance. Entire families, with their household furniture and domestic stock, cross these mountains in search of a new home."[65]

One of the many functions of the quartermaster general was to visit military posts to inspect and supervise officers of his department engaged in constructing barracks, storehouses, hospitals, and other military buildings. Other duties kept Jesup so busy that he rarely assumed this responsibility personally but delegated the task to assistants. In the spring and summer of 1845, however, so many important public works were being erected or planned at Forts Jesup, Towson, Washita, Smith, Scott, Des Moines, Snelling, and Gibson on the western frontier that he decided to make the inspection tour himself, believing he could "make such arrangements on the spot, as would not only benefit the service, but reduce considerably the public expenditures." The trip would also enable him to stop off in Kentucky to attend to private affairs long neglected under the pressure of official duties.

Jesup's proposed western tour was delayed until after the inauguration of James K. Polk in March 1845. Polk selected William L. Marcy, a former newspaper editor from Troy, New York, a Democrat with an impressive background, to succeed Wilkins as secretary of war. Marcy was an associate justice of the New York Supreme Court when he was elected to the United States Senate in 1831; he had resigned in 1833 to become governor of the state. Secretary Marcy had been in office less than a month when Jesup requested permission not only to make the tour of posts but also to be absent from duty for six weeks to two months before or after visiting the posts.[66]

Marcy assented, with the understanding that Col. Henry Stan-

William L. Marcy, lawyer and newspaper editor who became secretary of war under James K. Polk.

ton, assistant quartermaster general on duty in Philadelphia, would have charge of the department during Jesup's absence, while Maj. Daniel D. Tompkins would take over Stanton's Philadelphia duties. Jesup leased his home on F Street to Secretary of State James Buchanan for the period he expected to be away, and on 22 April the Jesups departed from Washington for Locust Grove. Dr. Croghan, who had returned recently from the Mammoth Cave property he had acquired in the fall of 1839, welcomed them warmly. His plan of converting the cave into a sanatorium and health resort for tubercular patients had proved impracticable, but the cave remained an attraction for visitors,[67] and the Jesups lived in it during a part of the summer of 1845.

Jesup took occasion upon his arrival in Kentucky to engage in some private land transactions. He was disturbed to discover during his travels that the old Whig charges of a decade earlier, which he believed to have been scotched, had been revived. "To put them down & to defend successfully my reputation from the reiterated slander of my enemies," he wrote from Louisville to the ailing former president Andrew Jackson at the Hermitage, "I have no other recourse & have to appeal to you for a statement of the facts as you know them to have existed at the time, as well as in regards to the removal of General Scott from command."[68]

In his prompt reply, Jackson refuted the charges. He repeated earlier statements he had made exonerating Jesup from all intrigue in obtaining the Florida command or in causing the removal of Scott.[69] The letter dated 3 June 1845 which he signed was undoubtedly dictated to his ward, Andrew J. Donelson; it was one of Old Hickory's last letters. Five days later, Andrew Jackson was dead.

In late June, Jesup set out from Kentucky on his tour of military posts. Early in July he arrived at Fort Smith on the Arkansas River in the immediate vicinity of the Indian tribes whom the government had removed from Alabama, Georgia, Florida, Mississippi, Tennessee, and North Carolina. He had believed the War Department to be in error when it first occupied the site of Fort Smith; he had been equally certain that to abandon Fort Gibson, as had been contemplated, would be a mistake. "If a post be withdrawn from the Indian country, no matter from what cause, the Indians invariably ascribe it to fear of them. . . . I am opposed to withdrawing Fort Gibson as well as any other posts established in the Indian country." He added, "[If the 1st Regiment had been] left in Louisiana, and the 4th Regiment in Florida, twelve or fourteen years ago in place of establishing two regiments at Jefferson Barracks, the Florida War would never have taken place."[70]

After visiting Fort Smith and learning that steamboats could ascend the river to it ten months of the year, Jesup modified somewhat his views regarding its location. But he remained skeptical about the need for a building program so extensive as that which Congress had ordered for the fort. Since the "highest functionaries" of the government had decided "both as to the military propriety and the policy of that measure," he was precluded from espressing an opinion. But as to the Indian frontier generally, he wrote, "I am decidedly of the opinion that works so extensive, and involving so much expense in their construction, are not required by existing circumstances, or any that are likely to occur." He reported that much of the labor at Fort Smith as well as at Forts Jesup, Towson, Washita, Scott, and Des Moines was being performed by the troops.[71]

By October Jesup had returned to Kentucky, where he was detained by the sickness of his eldest son. "[William] has been for the last thirteen days dangerously ill of congestive fever," he advised the adjutant general. From reports he had received, he added, "This fever prevails throughout Illinois, Missouri, Iowa, and extends into Wisconsin, in consequence of which information I have decided to return to Washington without visiting in those states and territories."[72] But he was detained much longer than anticipated, for not until early December was the Jesup family back in Washington.

Much to the "heartfelt satisfaction" of the Blair family, Mary Jesup, daughter of the general, and James Blair, youngest son of the *Globe*'s editor, had become engaged. The editor wrote to Ann Jesup to express his family's pleasure, adding, "From the war I learned to honor the name of Jesup and a personal intercourse with the General of long continuance has increased that consideration & superadded a strong family attachment."[73]

Blair had lost favor in the eyes of Polk during the 1844 campaign and election, and the new president had made clear his desire that the *Globe* not be the official Democratic paper during his administration. Reluctantly, the veteran editor agreed to sell his newspaper to Thomas Ritchie of Richmond, Virginia. Ritchie changed the name of the paper to *The Union* and began publication on 1 May 1845.

CHAPTER 10

SUPPORT OF TAYLOR
IN THE MEXICAN WAR

IN MARCH OF 1845, shortly after President Polk took office, Mexico broke off diplomatic relations with the United States. The act was in protest of a joint resolution of Congress, in the closing days of Tyler's administration, calling for the annexation of Texas. Although Texas had won independence a decade earlier and leaders there were seeking admission as the twenty-eighth state, Mexico still laid claim to her "ancient province." Mexican authorities had warned President Tyler in 1843 that war was inevitable if he attempted to annex Texas. Tyler was unsuccessful in his efforts to obtain Texas by treaty; because of Mexico's open hostility, he dispatched Brig. Gen. Zachary Taylor to Fort Jesup on the western boundary of Louisiana in the spring of 1844 to take command of an "Army of Observation."

Jesup was still in Washington when the Mexican minister left the country in angry protest over the annexation resolution. For more than six weeks Jesup had waited in the city to determine the consequences of the severed diplomatic relations. Then, apparently convinced that war was not imminent, he had departed on his western tour. He planned to visit Fort Jesup, where Taylor and his command were then assembled. Before leaving Washington, Jesup directed Stanton to strengthen the quartermaster organization in the Southwest.

The angry reaction in Mexico to the annexation resolution by Congress led the War Department on 28 May to instruct General Taylor to hold his troops in readiness. On 15 June the secretary of war ordered him to station his troops at some port where they could readily embark for the Texas frontier. As soon as Taylor learned that Texas had accepted the terms of admission, he was to take a position on or near the Rio Grande "best adapted to repel invasion."[1] Taylor accordingly concentrated his force at New Orleans to await further orders. When official word reached him that Texas had agreed to annexation, he moved his forces in late July to Corpus Christi on the Nueces River, on the southwestern border of Texas, to protect the new state from any invasion attempt by Mexico. In the weeks and months that followed, Taylor's little army gradually expanded to a strength of about four thousand men and officers—nearly half of the entire United States Army—but no enemy appeared to challenge it.

William Gordon, chief clerk in the Washington quartermaster office, wrote Jesup on 3 September that the concentration of troops in Texas seemed to be merely a measure of precaution: "The impression is rather general here that Mexico will not declare war. Some embarrassment is anticipated from General Gaines. He appears determined to have something to do with affairs in that quarter. In the event of extensive operations, you are, so far as I have an opportunity of judging, looked to as the person to conduct them."[2] He advised Jesup of the reassignments of personnel that Acting Quartermaster General Stanton had made to meet any eventualities. Capts. George W. Crosman and Osborn Cross, son of Col. Trueman Cross, were already in Texas, while Colonel Cross, along with Capts. William Ketchum and Abraham Myers, were under orders to go there. Stanton, he noted, was endeavoring to fill some of the vacancies in the department, but so far without success.

Acting on instructions Jesup gave him before leaving on his western tour, Stanton transferred Lt. Col. Thomas F. Hunt, deputy quartermaster general, from Florida to the key post at New Orleans to strengthen the quartermaster organization in the Southwest. Hunt was familiar with the supply resources of the area by reason of his years of prior service there. Assistant Quartermaster General Cross, who had been on duty at New York, was assigned to

Taylor's headquarters as the general's chief quartermaster. Stanton made it clear in his letter of 9 September to Cross that Jesup personally had selected him for that post: "You, Colonel, are designated, in accordance with the views and wishes of the War Department, and those of the quartermaster general, heretofore indicated, to take immediate direction and control of the various concerns of the quartermaster's department within the range of the command exercised by Brevet Brigadier General Taylor, at whose headquarters you will report in person with as little delay as possible."

Cross left Washington the morning of 13 September on his ill-fated assignment. He arrived at Corpus Christi on the evening of 9 October and promptly wrote to Stanton the next day. Much remained to be done, he said, before an adequate train could be formed "to enable the army to move to the Rio Grande, should anything occur to make that necessary."[3] By then, ten quartermaster officers, approximately one-third of the total number on the roster in Jesup's department, were on duty in the Southwest, and nearly all of them had gained valuable experience in the Seminole War. Although the authorized strength of the Quartermaster's Department was thirty-eight, six vacancies remained.

Soon after he arrived back in Washington from his western trip, Jesup wrote Colonel Cross that the Navy Department would return the steamer *Colonel Harney* to the Quartermaster's Department "in perfect repair." Cross was to use it as a dispatch boat between the army in Texas and the ports on the Gulf of Mexico and the Mississippi River: "She will be under your control and that of General Taylor." His letter gave Cross sweeping authority. "Whatsoever General Taylor may consider necessary to the efficiency of the corps under his command, you are authorized to furnish or to do; and you will consider yourself clothed, within the sphere of action, with the whole authority which the department possesses here."[4]

In the meantime, President Polk had sought to restore friendly relations with Mexico through negotiation. Assured through a confidential agent that President José Joaquin de Herrera's government would welcome an American minister, he dispatched John Slidell of Louisiana, a lawyer and Spanish scholar, as minister plenipotentiary to Mexico with instructions to offer as much as $40 million for a satisfactory boundary and the cession of New Mexico and California. The year came to an end without any word on the success or failure of Slidell's diplomatic venture. The question of whether the two unprepared countries would actually go to war was still unanswered.

Word reached Washington on 12 January 1846 that Herrera's government had refused to receive Slidell. President Polk sent orders to Gen. Zachary Taylor the next day to move forward from Corpus Christi and occupy a defensive position on the east bank of the Rio Grande del Norte. Jesup hurried off a letter to Col. Trueman Cross that same day. He had just been informed of the government's intentions, he wrote, declaring, "Whatsoever may depend upon our Dept. must be done to the extent of its credit as well as of its means."

He directed Cross to keep him constantly informed of Taylor's plans and all other pertinent matters. If Taylor's intention was to move into Mexico, extensive wagon trains would be required to insure the troops "a constant and abundant supply." On the other hand, if Taylor had only to hold in check any force at Matamoros, troops could be supplied by boat from existing depots. Was it possible, Jesup asked, for supplies to be taken by water from New Orleans through the Brazos de Santiago and thence to the troops? If so, what kind of vessels would be needed? The department had gained much useful experience in the use of water transportation for supply support during the Seminole War; that knowledge could be applied in aid of Taylor's army, if need be, Jesup wrote. "I will take measures to have added to the Department, if possible, an enlisted Corps of Teamsters, laborers & mechanics." The general had found need for them when he was in command of troops in Alabama and Florida.[5]

Polk was unaware when he ordered Taylor to the Rio Grande that the Herrera government had been overthrown late in December by Gen. Mariano Paredes, who was inaugurated as president early in January. Paredes had frequently expressed his hostility towards the United States and had threatened to retake Texas by force. All hope that Slidell might be able to restore friendly relations between the two countries through negotiations vanished when the new Mexican government gave the minister no opportunity to present his proposals.

Jesup's letter took a month to reach Cross at Corpus Christi via Galveston, as did Polk's original instructions to Taylor, though

Zachary Taylor, whose reputation as commander of U.S. Army troops in the Mexican War led to his election as president of the United States in 1849.

Taylor had already received a duplicate copy by another route. Cross reported that the movement to the Rio Grande would not begin before the first of March and assured Jesup that the army would not be delayed by any lack of transportation. Although all of the wagons he had requisitioned in September had not yet arrived (in mid-February), he was able to muster nearly 300 — about one for every ten marching men in the army, which he said would not exceed 3,000. He had designated 110 wagons for baggage and the hospital department, leaving 190 for a supply train. Despite the presence of six army engineers in camp since October, little reconnaissance had occured. Cross had examined sixty miles of the road towards Matamoros in dry weather and had dispatched an experimental wagon train to test its practicability in wet weather. He had ". . . not received a line of instruction whatever" from Taylor "with respect to the means of transportation to be provided, or other preparations in [his] branch of the service."[6]

Not all of the supplies for Taylor's army were to be transported by wagons. Before the troops arrived at Corpus Christi, they had been quartered temporarily on St. Joseph's Island in Aransas Bay. A depot had been established there under the supervision of Capt. George Crosman of the Quartermaster's Department.[7] With the advance of the troops to the Rio Grande, a new depot was to be erected at Point Isabel on the inlet Brazos de Santiago. Supplies from the depot at St. Joseph's Island were to be moved by water on boats furnished by Lt. Col. Thomas F. Hunt at New Orleans. Maj. Charles Thomas was directed to conduct the transports to Point Isabel and superintend the construction of a depot there.

Taylor's forces began their march to the Rio Grande on 8 March with a train of 307 wagons, 84 of them drawn by ox teams. The army carried twenty days' subsistence for the troops and sixteen days' grain for the animals — 1,900 horses and mules and 500 oxen — which Cross and his assistants had succeeded in rounding up from the countryside. Taylor, with a small part of his command, reached Point Isabel, a distance of 188 miles from Corpus Christi, on 24 March, the same day the transports from the depot at St. Joseph's Island arrived. The men began the burdensome work of getting the supplies ashore as boats drawing more than 4½ to 5 feet of water could not approach within five miles of the landing site. The cargoes had to be shifted first from the seagoing transports to light steamers, then from them to flatboats and other small vessels, and finally from the latter to land.[8]

Meanwhile the troops resumed their march, continuing without further incident, and on 28 March arrived at a position near the mouth of the Rio Grande, directly opposite Matamoros, where Taylor ordered the construction of Fort Brown. After getting the army settled in opposite Matamoros, Cross had planned to return to Point Isabel to supervise the establishment of the depot there, but fate intervened. On 10 April he rode out alone from the fort on an exploratory mission and failed to return. Five days later Taylor reported to the War Department that all attempts to trace Cross had proved fruitless. Not until 23 April was his body discovered in the chaparral about four miles from the American camp. Taylor informed the War Department that it revealed "marks of violence, leaving no doubt that he was robbed, and cruelly murdered" by bandidos. Cross was buried the following day with military honors and reinterred in the Congressional Cemetery at Washington some six months later.[9]

Cross's untimely death was a matter of personal grief for Jesup, as well as a severe blow to his department. Filling the unexpected vacancy presented a problem, but the supply organization he had founded was flexible, and a number of veteran quartermaster officers were on duty in Texas. Jesup appointed one of them, Maj. Charles Thomas, to fill the position temporarily but instructed him to remain at Point Isabel to supervise the establishment of the depot there. Jesup selected another, Capt. George H. Crosman, as the senior assistant quartermaster with responsibility for the quartermaster operations with the marching force.[10] Both officers served with distinction throughout the Mexican War.

The War Department instructed Taylor to adopt a conciliatory attitude towards the Mexicans and not to fire unless fired upon. On 24 April, the day of Cross's funeral, Gen. Mariano Arista assumed command of the Mexican troops at Matamoros. The next day he sent a cavalry force across the Rio Grande into Texas. They encountered and surrounded a small squadron of American dragoons under Capt. Seth B. Thornton—killing or wounding sixteen, and capturing the rest. Taylor sent a message to Washington which read, "Hostilities may now be considered as commenced."[11]

On the same day that Cross was buried in Texas, Ann Heron Croghan Jesup, for twenty-four years the devoted wife of the quartermaster general, died in Washington after a short illness at the age of forty-eight. Although she had been in feeble health at various times during her married life, her death was unexpected. The grief-stricken general, stunned by the loss of his wife, declared, "I now live only for my children; and their happiness is far dearer to me than my own life." The six children ranged in age from Lucy Ann, twenty-three, to Julia, six, born 10 July 1840. The Rev. Smith Pyne, who three months before had united Mary Jesup and James Blair in marriage, conducted the funeral services.[12]

Just two weeks after Ann Jesup's funeral, Taylor's dispatch concerning the beginning of hostilities arrived in Washington. By then, his command had already won the first two battles of the war—Palo Alto (8 May) and Resaca de la Palma (9 May).

When he received Taylor's dispatch, President Polk began preparing his war message to Congress, delivering it before a joint session on 11 May 1846. Mexico, he declared, ". . . has invaded our territory, and shed American blood upon American soil . . . ; war exists . . . notwithstanding all our efforts to avoid it, exists by the act of Mexico herself." Two days later, Congress enacted legislation authorizing the president to issue a call for fifty thousand volunteers to serve for one year and appropriating $10 million for war purposes. It also empowered the president to expand the regular forces by increasing through volunteer enlistments the number of privates in each company of dragoons, artillery, and infantry to not more than one hundred. The response of citizens was so enthusiastic that a battalion from Washington and a regiment from Kentucky were mustered into service before the end of May.[13]

Although Congress sharply increased the army strength, it made no provision—until the war had been in progress ten months —to add to the staff of the Quartermaster's Department which, along with its other heavy responsibilities, had the task of moving the army. On 18 June, Congress did authorize the appointment of additional regimental quartermasters from the line to assist the staff officers in the field. For the eight years previous, the department had an authorized strength of thirty-seven staff officers, but its actual strength in 1846 was far less. The murder of Cross created the seventh vacancy; of the thirty officers remaining, one was completely disabled and two others were partially so. Two staff officers served with Jesup in the Washington office; another was permanently located at Philadelphia as superintendent of the clothing and equipage depot. The number of available officers was inadequate even for a peacetime army, yet in mid-April, when war with Mexico appeared inevitable, an urgent appeal by Jesup to the secretary to fill at least six of the existing vacancies in his department was rejected. When Congress finally recognized the need to increase the overburdened staff of the department in February of 1847, it authorized the president to appoint "from the Army, four quartermasters with the rank of major, and ten assistant quartermasters with the rank of captain."[14]

War with Mexico or England or both had loomed as a distinct possibility for a number of years, yet the United States entered the Mexican conflict unprepared. After hostilities with the Seminoles officially ended in 1842, Congress had wasted no time in taking steps to make the small army still smaller. Moreover, Congress adopted such a stringent program of economy during the following years that the Quartermaster's Department had been unable to accumulate any reserve stocks of military supplies. As early as October 1845, while Taylor's army was still at Corpus Christi, the department was severely hampered by lack of funds.[15] Not until seven months later, after Taylor's forces had fought two battles, did Congress vote an adequate appropriation.

In May of 1846, Washington became the scene of feverish preparation as President Polk, Secretary Marcy, and Commander-in-Chief Winfield Scott belatedly planned for the war Congress had just declared. The hastily formulated strategy called for the invasion of Mexico by army forces over two overland routes, a naval blockage of Vera Cruz and other ports in the Gulf of Mexico, as well as a New Mexico and California expedition and a blockage of the Mexican west coast. Jesup and the chiefs of the other supply bureaus in Washington were busily making their own arrangements accordingly. Jesup's function was to provide as promptly as possible quartermaster supplies and the means of transportation for three separate armies—Taylor's forces on the lower Rio Grande; Wool's forces at San Antonio, Texas, under orders to mount an expedition against Chihuahua; and Col. Stephen W. Kearny's regiment, the 1st Dragoons, at Fort Leavenworth on the Missouri River. Kearny was to arrange with the governor of Missouri to augment his force with volunteers, move into New Mexico and capture Santa Fe, and then proceed west to California.[16] To accompany these armies, Jesup selected as quartermasters men known to him to be efficient and who would utilize to the greatest extent possible the resources of the country through which they moved.

Although the outbreak of the war found it suffering acute shortages of nearly everything else, the army did not lack for manpower, untrained though much of it was. Volunteers responded so quickly that they arrived at Point Isabel in numbers that overwhelmed Taylor and the supply departments. The first influx occurred soon after the start of hostilities in April when Taylor, acting on earlier instructions from Secretary Marcy, requisitioned the governors of Texas and Louisiana for four regiments each—a total of five thousand men. At the same time, he requested Gen. Edmund P. Gaines, commander of the Western Division, to assist in organizing the regiments. Gaines, acting on his own responsibility, extended the call to other states and accepted more than eight thousand volunteers for an enlistment period of only six months.

These volunteers began arriving about the time Taylor crossed into Mexico on 18 May 1846 and occupied Matamoros without opposition. When the recruits came in without equipment or means of transportation, Taylor complained to Washington: "This force will embarrass rather than facilitate our operations." Secretary Marcy denounced Gaines' action as illegal, relieved him from command, and ordered him to report to Washington "without delay." Since these volunteers could not be accepted unless they reenlisted for twelve months, as prescribed by Congress, Jesup's department had to transport the men back to their homes without their having performed any military service, at a time when transportation facilities were in exceedingly short supply.[17]

The twelve-month volunteers from other states who enlisted after Congress declared war on 13 May responded in such large numbers during June that they added to the already difficult supply problems. By then, Taylor had moved his army to Camargo, where he established his principal depot some three hundred miles from the mouth of the Rio Grande. In moving against his next big objective, Monterrey, he left behind a large part of the volunteer force because of insufficient transportation and the uncertainty "in regard to the supplies that may be drawn from the theater of operations." The remainder of the volunteers were kept at Camargo to undergo training and drilling. Taylor's army now numbered more than six thousand, comprising two divisions of regulars and one of volunteers. He wrote the president that the rapid influx of volunteers had even impeded his forward movement, "by engrossing all the resources of the Quartermaster's Department to land them and transport them to healthy positions."[18]

At Washington, Jesup was summoned to the White House on 24 June. "I directed him," President Polk records, "to make ample provision for the troops called out to prosecute the war . . . & told him I should hold him responsible for any failure in this respect. I directed him to provide as well for the irregular forces called out by the unauthorized act of Gen'l Gaines as for the forces ordered out by the Government." Polk had called in Col. George Gibson, commissary general of subsistence, the previous day for a similar discussion.[19] Likely these long-experienced and conscientious officers, each of whom twenty-eight years earlier had established the department he headed, needed no such prodding from the president.

Although all volunteers who enlisted in the summer of 1846 were required to furnish their own clothing, for which each was given a monthly allowance of $3.50, the army had to feed, equip, and transport the troops to Mexico. Their rations were procured by the commissary general of subsistence but transported by Jesup's department, which was responsible for all army transportation. Both departments were understaffed, and their officers were hard-pressed to handle their suddenly increased workloads. Equipping the volunteers as well as the regulars was another responsibility of the Quartermaster's Department. Jesup had anticipated that a large quantity of camp and garrison equipment would have to be expedited to Deputy Quartermaster General Hunt for issue to the volunteers at New Orleans before they left for the Rio Grande. Three days before Congress declared war, he had instructed Assistant Quartermaster General Henry Stanton to ascertain the state of supplies at the Philadelphia depot and to "strengthen [himself] in such articles as [he might] not have an abundance on hand." A week later, based on General Scott's estimate of an army of twenty thousand men, Jesup sent procurement orders to Stanton for quartermaster items to equip that number of men.[20] His communications with quartermaster officers in Baltimore, Philadelphia, and New York were speeded up by the use of the telegraph. Because the invention was in an experimental stage, Jesup, as a precautionary measure, supplemented each telegraphed order with a follow-up letter the same day.[21]

Congress realized the futility of depending on the clothing depot in Philadelphia to clothe the volunteers, since its limited facilities were geared to meet only the needs of a small peacetime army. Instead, it made provision in the law for the volunteers to buy their own clothing. The depot at the Schuylkill Arsenal was hard-pressed at first to meet just the clothing requirements of the growing number of regular troops. This war was the first in which Jesup's department had full responsibility for procuring, storing, and distributing army clothing. The clothing depot, operating under the immediate supervision of Colonel Stanton, purchased cloth from the manufacturers. Government workers at the arsenal cut the cloth into garments which were issued to seamstresses and tailors who returned the finished clothing items to the arsenal for inspection and acceptance. When Jesup ordered immediate expansion of the depot facilities, the number of seamstresses and tailors employed increased from about four hundred to ten times that number. Before the end of the war, the monthly output of the expanded clothing operation at Philadelphia was more than eighty-five thousand assorted garments. In addition, a clothing branch was established in New York about the end of 1846, and early in 1847 the department was in a position to meet not only the requirements of regular troops but could fill requisitions for some of the volunteers, who by then had become destitute for clothing.[22]

In anticipation that Congress would act favorably on a measure to provide clothing for the volunteers, Jesup in December of 1847 ordered a supply from Philadelphia sufficient to clothe both regulars and volunteers. Acting on his own responsibility, he diverted $368,000 of departmental funds that had been appropriated for other purposes. At the same time, he directed the use of credit to cover the cost, confident that Congress would authorize the necessary money to meet the bills when they came due. Although the House much earlier had passed a resolution providing for the issuance of clothing to volunteers, not until 26 January 1848, only a week before the signing of the peace treaty, did the Senate approve the legislation, making it law.[23] Six more months elapsed before Congress appropriated the funds.

In contrast to the system of clothing manufacture, shoes for the army had always been procured by contract. By the summer of 1847, the Quartermaster's Department was still obtaining bootees, as they were called, exclusively by that method, but with so many complaints regarding deficiencies, delays, and losses, some action had to be taken. Jesup decided to establish a bootee-making factory at the Schuylkill Arsenal in Philadelphia. Its output reached 12,000 pairs monthly before the end of the war. So successful was the operation that the War Department continued it after hostilities ended, completely abandoning the contract method of procuring shoes.[24]

Typical of other wars, an acute shortage of tents and of duck from which they were made existed at the outbreak of this conflict. A tent-making section had been established at the Schuylkill Arsenal even before shoes were made there. In addition, some tents were procured from manufacturers by contract. With the threat of war in the spring of 1846, Jesup appealed to Congress to appropriate money for camp equipage, but his request was rejected, which meant that he could not legally apply a cent for such items as tents until after the legislation of 13 May provided funds for war purposes. Even then, neither government nor industry could manufacture good tents without duck. The tents furnished to Taylor's troops at Corpus Christi had come from the meager supply of stock at the arsenal. Anticipating a long wait for duck, Jesup directed that cotton canvas tents be made, which he hoped would give some shelter to the soldiers. Taylor was as aware as Jesup that shortages of supply were due to the country's lack of preparedness for war. Nevertheless he wrote to Marcy from Camargo that his "crying deficiency of camp equipage had been partially relieved by the issue of cotton tents of indifferent quality." By the close of the war, with duck available, the monthly output at the Schuylkill Arsenal was more than seven hundred tents of the common, wall, and hospital types. Additional tents were being procured by contract.[25]

Except for tents, no items of camp and garrison equipment were fabricated at the busy Philadelphia depot. The Quartermaster's Department procured these items by contract from manufacturers in the large centers of population which had the facilities to produce them. Jesup directed quartermasters in such places as Pittsburgh and Cincinnati to contract for knapsacks, canteens, camp kettles, and mess pans and send them direct by water route to New Orleans for issue to the volunteers.[26] To avoid delays and shortages, he advised Colonel Stanton in the fall of 1846 to maintain during the war a supply of these items sufficient to equip at least twenty-five thousand men and of surplus clothing (except uniform coats and caps) for at least ten thousand men.[27]

Determined to provide Taylor with the most experienced quartermaster officer available after the death of Colonel Cross, Jesup assigned Lt. Col. Henry Whiting, deputy quartermaster general, to the Army of Occupation on 3 June, with orders to proceed to his post by way of the Ohio and Mississippi rivers. Jesup placed no restrictions on Whiting's authority: "You are authorized to employ clerks, agents, conductors, teamsters, laborers, mechanics and any other description of persons or force which may in your judgment, or that of the general commanding, be necessary to the efficiency of the department; and you will leave nothing undone which it is possible to accomplish to insure the success of the army."[28] Strong gales on the Gulf of Mexico delayed Whiting's arrival at Taylor's headquarters until 3 July.

The quartermaster general was greatly handicapped by Taylor's failure to inform the War Department of his supply needs—an important function of a field commander. For instance, Jesup in Washington received no information regarding the feasibility of using wagons for transporting troops and supplies in Mexico. If they could not be used, then pack mules could carry supplies; a plentiful supply of them was readily available to Taylor. Colonel Cross had assembled a train of three hundred wagons to transport the army from Corpus Christi to the Rio Grande. Would the Mexican terrain permit the wagons' use once the army crossed the river? Taylor's communications to Washington supplied no answer to this or other pertinent questions; apparently he was depending on the War Department to guess what he would need to fight in far-off Mexico. Cross's complaint that he lacked instructions from Taylor on transportation requirements was echoed later by other supply officers.

Although he had received no requisitions for them, Jesup acted promptly to procure wagons as soon as Congress appropriated funds to prosecute the war. He knew that both Taylor and Wool would need them, at least in Texas, as would Kearny on his march from Fort Leavenworth. He directed quartermasters at Cincinnati, Philadelphia, and Pittsburgh to purchase or have constructed seven hundred wagons together with the necessary harness for mules and oxen. He emphasized that delivery should be made as soon as possible.[29] Upon learning that large numbers of wagons were not readily available in those places, and that much time would be needed to build them, he sent quartermasters scouring other sections of the country for them.

They encountered unforeseen difficulties. Besides having to

cope with a scarcity of both the skilled wheelwrights (some of whom had enlisted in volunteer units) and the seasoned timber required for wagon construction, many of the manufacturing firms were small and could produce only a few wagons at one time. Returning from a search at York and Shrewsbury, Pennsylvania, formerly wagon-producing centers, Assistant Quartermaster Samuel B. Dusenberry at Baltimore reported that the wagon business in that part of the country was greatly diminished since the railroad had begun operation. "I saw not a single wagon with a suitable body," he informed Jesup. After finding wagons scarce in St. Louis, Capt. Abner R. Hetzel had little success at procuring any at Memphis, Vicksburg, or Natchez. And so the search went.[30]

Once the wagons were procured, the big task of transporting them to Mexico still remained. Some were taken apart for shipment, requiring the additional work of reassembling them when they reached their destination; others were sent intact aboard vessels. Despite all the problems and frustrations, by late August wagons were being delivered in sufficient numbers to meet immediate needs, and Jesup called a halt to procurement. If more wagons were required later, he advised that manufacturers would be invited by notices in newspapers to submit bids.[31]

Ignoring the fact that he had been negligent by failing to keep Washington informed of his needs, Taylor complained to the War Department that, while his army had increased fivefold, his wagon train was smaller than when he left Corpus Christi: "I wish it distinctly understood that our ability to move is due wholly to means created here, and which could not have been reckoned upon with safety in Washington." That he was wrong in that assumption is apparent from instructions Jesup had sent to Whiting more than two months earlier, and from a conversation between the president and Jesup at the White House before Taylor's letter reached Washington. On 17 June, Jesup had directed Whiting: "Take measures, immediately, to obtain all the mules you can get from Mexico. By paying cash for them, they can be obtained, I am informed, in very great numbers."[32] In his diary of 5 September, Polk wrote that he had summoned Secretary Marcy and General Jesup to the White House to discuss the proper means of transportation for Taylor's army. He acknowledged that he had had no military experience but had a strong conviction that the use of immense baggage trains would impede the progress of an army. He asked Jesup if it were not true that in all previous wars in Mexico, baggage and munitions had been transported by mules. "Gen'l Jesup gave it as his decided opinion that baggage wagons should be dispensed with and mules employed, and added that such had been the mode of conducting all the wars which had occurred heretofore in Mexico." Polk then asked Marcy and Jesup why a similar means of transportation had not been provided in this instance. "Gen'l Jesup replied that he had received no communication from Gen'l Taylor or the War Department on the subject."[33]

Polk noted that Taylor gave no information on resources available to him which would aid administration planning. He feared that while Taylor was brave, he was not the man to command the army, but Polk did not know whom he could substitute: "Public opinion seems to point to him as entitled to the command." Polk was correct about the general's popularity. Taylor, a Whig who had been brevetted a major general by Congress in June, had already caught the public fancy in a way that would lead to his election to the presidency three years later. "Our old friend Zachary has gained for himself distinguished renown," Doctor Croghan observed in a letter to Jesup on 1 July. While he found the use of his name in that connection very flattering, Taylor wrote to a friend in mid-July: "I am not and shall never be an aspirant for that honor." His views at that time coincided with those of Jesup. "My opinion has always been against the elevation of a military chief to that position."[34]

Tremendous pressure was placed upon Jesup in 1846. He was suddenly called upon to support a wartime army with only meager reserve supplies on hand and with no funds available until after the first two battles had been fought. One of his most important responsibilities was to get the men, equipment, and supplies —including guns, ammunition, and subsistence as well as quartermaster items—to the theater of operations in Mexico. The movement required many more vessels than the army had ever before needed, because this war was the country's first "overseas" conflict. The flood of volunteers rushing to join Taylor's army after the declaration of war created an immediate demand for vessels to transport them and supplies to the Rio Grande. The principal point of assembly and embarkation for the volunteers was New Orleans, where most of them arrived after moving down the Ohio and Mississippi rivers on riverboats; others reached the Rio Grande by traveling on ships along the Atlantic coastline and then across the Gulf.

At New Orleans the volunteers waited for Colonel Hunt to provide them transportation to Point Isabel. Suitable ships in adequate numbers were extremely difficult to find, and the Quartermaster's Department had to canvass port cities all over the country for vessels that could be chartered or purchased. The search took considerable time and money. Even when the ships could be had, purchase and charter prices frequently were exorbitant. The government's change in strategy in the fall of 1846, calling for General Scott's expedition to Mexico City by way of Vera Cruz, created such a big demand for more water transportation that Jesup's department had to construct ten light-draft schooners to insure a constant flow of supplies to the troops and had to increase the number of ships chartered or purchased. During the war the department acquired through construction or purchase a total of thirty-eight sailing vessels and thirty-five steamboats. Accidents, wrecks, and deterioration took a heavy toll of the boats before the conflict ended.[35]

Because of the dangers from strong gales and shifting sandbars, Jesup advised that no troops should be sent by sea steamers without the approval of their commanding officers; in the absence of sanction, sailing ships were to be furnished. He listed the qualifications that sea steamers to be used in the Gulf should possess. They were to be sturdy enough to withstand stormy weather and heavy seas. Their boilers and machinery were to be of suitable construction for the service required of them. They should be provided with masts and sails to enable them to ride out a gale or reach harbor in case of accident to their machinery. They were to carry sufficient fuel for six days. Unless constructed of iron, their bottoms were to be of copper, and their draft must be no more than seven feet. The decision as to whether vessels sent by quartermaster officers to New Orleans were suitable for the Gulf rested with Colonel Hunt. He was also directed to establish a coal depot at New Orleans of adequate size to provide fuel for transporting an army of from twenty to twenty-five thousand.[36]

To keep Taylor's wagon train free to move with the troops during his march from Monterrey, supplies from Point Isabel for his army would have to be transported up the Rio Grande to the principal depot that the commander was to establish at Camargo. Obviously, this move required boats, but nothing in the records shows that Taylor did any advance planning to meet that situation. Though he had been encamped on the Rio Grande since March, he still had taken no action two months later to determine the feasibility of using the river as a supply line. At last, on 21 May, in response to a query from Washington, he assured the War Department that he would lose no time in ascertaining the "practicability" of the river for steamboats. If Taylor on the Rio Grande did not know how many and what types of boats he would need, Jesup could hardly be expected to have reliable information on the subject. Yet Taylor complained to the War Department in June about the "extraordinary delay" of the Quartermaster's Department in forwarding steamboats for use on the Rio Grande. At the same time, he blamed the government for sending a flood of volunteers without the means of transportation.[37] Gen. William J. Worth, who served with distinction in the first war under Taylor and later under Scott, stated privately that Taylor was to blame for any lack of transportation; he described the general's complaints "as intended to ward off responsibility in case of failure and augment glory in case of success."[38]

Meanwhile, Major Thomas, depot quartermaster at Point Isabel, had reported to Jesup in May that two of the four boats the department had been using there and earlier at Corpus Christi were so worm-eaten as to be useless. He pointed out the need for one or two good riverboats of moderate size. When apprised of this need, Taylor issued the necessary requisition, and Thomas on 18 May instructed Hunt to purchase a good, substantial riverboat. Six days later, as though suddenly aware of his own lack of foresight, Taylor increased his requisition to four steamboats. Dissatisfied when the Quartermaster's Department did not immediately succeed in finding the boats he had belatedly requested, Taylor ordered Capt. John Sanders of the Corps of Engineers to New Orleans to assist Hunt in procuring the steamboats. By then, Hunt had decided that Taylor's requisition for four boats should be doubled. Jesup not only approved of this change but authorized a still further increase if necessary. Because Hunt discovered after an exhaustive search that the boats were not available in the New Orleans area, he sent Captain Sanders up the Mississippi and Ohio to canvass river towns for light-draft steamboats.[39]

When Jesup learned on 17 June that Col. Joseph Taylor, assistant commissary general of subsistence and a brother of General Taylor, was leaving Washington for the theater of operations, he authorized him to assist Sanders in procuring a sufficient number of riverboats to insure the speedy transportation of supplies on the Rio Grande. He asked Colonel Taylor to confer with Sanders and with the quartermasters at Pittsburgh and Cincinnati. If the number of boats "which you, and Captain Sanders particularly, shall consider necessary, have not been purchased and sent forward, I desire you to supply any deficiency. If, on consulting Captain Sanders, you should consider more than eight light draught steamers necessary, you have authority to purchase them, or to direct their purchase." Jesup personally had chartered a light-draft steamer for the Rio Grande and had instructed Major Tompkins to purchase and send to Hunt at New Orleans three light-draft steamers then operating on the Ohio.[40]

Writing from Pittsburgh on 21 June, Sanders informed Jesup that on his own responsibility he had purchased a light-draft steamer and charged it to the account of the Quartermaster's Department. Jesup promptly expressed his approval: "It is my desire, as I believe it is that of every one here to render the most efficient aid to General Taylor's operations. . . . You are acquainted with the Rio Grande, and I desire you to purchase or charter such boats as you are confident will render efficient service. If you consider pilots necessary, employ them."[41]

On 2 July, Captain Sanders reported that he had completed his purchases of light-draft steamers on behalf of the Quartermaster's Department. He had praise not only for the "cheerful assistance and hearty co-operation" Jesup had kindly extended to him, but also for that which he received "from the hands of those . . . highly zealous and active officers, Colonel Hunt and Major Tompkins" of Jesup's department. "I shall most assuredly take the liberty of reporting the same to my commanding general," he added.[42]

There was no assurance that the steamboats would reach their destination in safety. Once the light-draft river vessels arrived at New Orleans, they still had to make the hazardous journey over the Gulf of Mexico to the Rio Grande. An unusually fierce gale that had delayed Colonel Whiting's arrival at Taylor's headquarters also prevented the scheduled early arrival of some of the steamboats. By 23 July, Jesup's department had twelve steamboats carrying men and supplies up the Rio Grande to Camargo, and more of the vessels were on their way from the north. The small, weak-powered steamboats faced another peril in navigating the winding, swiftly flowing river and were hampered by the scarcity of dry wood for fuel due to the drenching rains in July.[43]

The country's lack of preparedness placed a particularly heavy burden upon the Quartermaster's Department because of its wide and varied functions. The necessity for procuring everything immediately and simultaneously resulted in exceedingly heavy expenditures. Moreover, once Congress belatedly authorized money to prosecute the war, it arranged the appropriations so badly that Jesup was compelled to divert funds from purposes for which they were earmarked in order to carry out his military responsibilities. He mentioned this diversion of funds in his reply to Captain Sanders:

> Apart from all considerations of duty I am disposed to sustain General Taylor to the utmost; and as far as the means, the energies, and the credit of the department shall enable me, he may reply on all that I can accomplish for him. I sustained him for more than two months by using appropriations for the service of his army which the President would have been impeached for using. It was contrary to law to divert them from the objects to which Congress intended they should be applied, but I considered the situation of the army caused an overwhelming necessity which justified the course which I adopted. I shall never forget how faithfully and ably General Taylor sustained me in Florida.[44]

Seven months later, the reference to the diversion of appropriated funds caused President Polk and Secretary Marcy a bit of apprehension when Jesup's letter to Sanders came to their attention. Marcy noted Jesup's words while assembling all correspondence relating to transportation of the army, in compliance with House resolution. With some misgiving, he promptly instructed his own requisition clerk and the comptroller of the treasury to make a careful check of their records. Their reports convinced Marcy that no irregularities had occurred. He then requested an explanation from Jesup, who was in New Orleans directing supply operations.[45]

Jesup was surprised that his letter had caused such a stir in Washington, particularly after such a long time had elapsed. He replied immediately, assuring Marcy that the diversion was legal: "The appropriations for the active service had most been exhausted. There were large balances of other appropriations subject to my control. Congress was not in session, and the President could not make a transfer. Without consulting you, I applied large amounts of those balances to the active service." Since he did not have access to his records in Washington, he could not give a complete accounting, but he did know that Colonel Hunt had received $105,000 of those balances which had been applied to the support of Taylor's army. Jesup had intended no reflection on the president or Marcy. "I wished to convince a brother officer, with whom I had been on the most friendly terms for years, that the impressions which I supposed he entertained were unfounded, and that in his case I had a personal as well as public motive for sustaining him to the utmost."[46]

Jesup's determined efforts to sustain Taylor in Mexico were neither acknowledged nor apparently appreciated by his long-time friend. For some ill-defined reason, Taylor's attitude toward the quartermaster general had undergone a marked change. Relations between President Polk and Taylor had become strained, and distrust existed on both sides. As a consequence, it seems, Taylor had grown suspicious of everyone in official circles in Washington. Lieutenant Colonel Whiting, soon after he replaced the late Colonel Cross as chief quartermaster, informed Jesup that Taylor tended to be "unjust" in his criticism of the department whenever misfortunes or unavoidable delays occurred. "The department cannot control the elements nor prevent unavoidable accidents, much less resist a torrent of volunteers which overwhelm, for a time, all of its means," he added.[47]

A few weeks later, on 1 September, just before he left Camargo to march into the interior of Mexico, Taylor made a formal complaint against Jesup's department in a letter to the War Department. "I beg leave to place on record some remarks touching on an important branch of the public service, the proper administration of which is indispensable to the efficiency of a campaign. I refer to the quartermaster's department. There is at this moment, when the army is about to take up a long line of march, a great deficiency of proper means of transport, and of many important supplies." He claimed that only by his own repeated efforts had suitable boats been procured for the Rio Grande. "I hazard nothing in saying that, if proper foresight and energy had been displayed in sending suitable steamers to navigate the Rio Grande, our army would long since have been in possession of Monterey [*sic*]." Among his other grievances, Taylor noted that his cavalry had "been paralyzed by the want of horse shoes, horse-shoe nails, and even common black-smith tools," while many other deficiencies were daily brought to his notice. He requested the adjutant general, in justice to himself and the service, to lay his statement before the general-in-chief and the secretary of war.[48]

Just two days after Taylor dispatched that letter, Whiting wrote to Jesup: "Most of the small supplies, of which we have for some weeks stood so much in need, and the want of which threatened seriously to embarrass the movement on the interior, have come in." He also reported that their means of transportation consisted of 1,900 pack mules and 180 mule and horse wagons, which he said was sufficient to carry the army to Monterrey, and no doubt to Saltillo. Taylor would leave Camargo on 5 September for Cerralvo; 200,000 rations had already been sent there. Whiting was convinced that pack mules could be the answer to the army's transportation problems, provided the army could bring itself to make war as the enemy made it. "But this is probably out of the question. We have customs which neither the officer nor the soldier will forego, excepting in cases of extremity. Our camp equipage, so comfortable and yet so cumbrous, our rations, so full and bulky, all must be transported."[49]

As soon as he received Taylor's letter, Marcy sent a copy to Jesup, along with some remarks. Taylor's avowed purpose in presenting these accusations, he commented, was to make them a matter of record.

> I am extremely unwilling, and I presume you cannot be less so than myself, that they should remain there without explanation or investigation. I am fully aware of the great difficulties unavoidable in the management of the quartermaster's department on the sudden occurrence of a war, when the country was not prepared for such an emergency. General Taylor must be presumed to be as well acquainted with all the circumstances of embarrassment attending the quartermaster's department as any other person, and yet his arraignment of it is not qualified by any allusion to them.

The inference, he concluded, was that, with all proper allowances, Taylor still considered that the management of the department deserved censure. If the censure was really warranted, those responsible should be ascertained and dealt with as they deserved. "But, if, on the contrary, it shall be found that the officers of the quartermaster's department have done their duty in a proper and efficient manner, as I trust will be the case, steps must be taken to remove the erroneous impression and vindicate their official conduct."[50]

Jesup's immediate personal reaction to Taylor's complaints is not recorded. Undoubtedly, he was surprised and reluctant to believe that the officer he had so often befriended would insist upon placing on public record such unfair accusations, particularly since Taylor himself was guilty of the lack of foresight which he sought to blame upon the Quartermaster's Department. At the same time, Jesup was disturbed. Perhaps he had been unwise in relying upon subordinates at so great a distance from Washington to make the proper provisions for the army. He decided to request permission to go to the seat of war and take personal charge of the operations of his department there. The tour would also give him an opportunity to investigate and perhaps refute Taylor's charges. His presence would eliminate the need for waiting on instructions from Washington. Though his brevet rank of major general made him the senior of every officer then serving in Mexico, Jesup stated his willingness to waive his seniority, as he did not desire military command. Instead, he proposed to go in his capacity as a staff officer, ready to obey the orders of Taylor or any other officer sent by the government to command the army. "My only object is to benefit the country by securing the most efficiency to the measures of my department, and by that means giving effect to the whole service."[51]

CHAPTER 11

QUARTERMASTER GENERAL AT THE WAR FRONT

O<small>N</small> 2 OCTOBER 1846, Jesup left Washington for New Orleans and the Mexican frontier. Mindful, perhaps, of Colonel Cross's fate, he drew up his will before departing. Its first provision was that in the event of his death, his debts "of every description" were to be paid; and the second, that sufficient funds must be provided from his estate for the education of his two young sons and his six-year-old daughter Julia.[1]

Family as well as official matters were much on Jesup's mind as his duties took him on the long trip to the war zone. His wife's recent death, still so fresh in his memory, had brought an even closer union between him and his children. And now, compelled to leave them and haunted by the thought that he might never see them again, he was much depressed and was "entirely unfit for business." Fortunately, he was accompanied to New Orleans by Capt. Abner R. Hetzel, a man Jesup described as one of the ablest officers in the army. An 1823 graduate of West Point, Hetzel had supervised construction of the Delaware Breakwater when that project was assigned to Jesup's department. Hetzel's wife, Margaret, moved into Jesup's home in Washington to help look after the general's family while he was at the war front. Hetzel, Jesup wrote,

267

helped him through that agonizing period. "The captain is most diligent; and he discharges every duty with so much energy that he relieves me greatly. . . . I could not have gotten along without him."[2]

Low water in the Ohio River—a recurring difficulty encountered in moving boats and supplies to the troops in Mexico—was responsible in part for delaying his arrival in New Orleans. Twenty-five days after he left Washington, he reached the city and took quarters in the St. Charles Hotel. He had stopped briefly at Pittsburgh, Cincinnati, Louisville, and Memphis to transact official business. At Pittsburgh, he had directed Capt. Edward Harding to employ for six-month service in Mexico, ten carpenters and ten blacksmiths, harness-makers, and wheelwrights; instructed Capt. William Wilkins to have 100,000 horse- and mule-shoes made; and ordered Agent Alex Gordon to purchase up to 50,000 bushels of oats, ten sets each of carpenter, wheelwright, and saddler tools, and twenty sets of blacksmith tools, all for shipment to New Orleans. At Louisville, he had requested Col. Stephen H. Long of the Topographical Engineers to supervise the construction of the boats to be built there for use on the Rio Grande and to send them to Hunt in New Orleans at the "earliest possible day." He also asked Long to go to Cincinnati to inspect three available vessels and to purchase the one he considered best adapted to the service. From the steamship *Homer* near Memphis, he wrote to Stanton on 20 October that the water was so low that coal he had ordered earlier in the month could not be moved down the river until it rose, which might not be before Christmas; the fuel would have to be shipped by the ocean route.[3]

A number of important events had occurred by the time he reached New Orleans. Santa Anna, who had been deposed as president and exiled to Cuba in 1844, had been permitted to return to Mexico to take over the government. He had taken steps to organize and train an army in hopes of defeating the advancing American forces. Taylor, after three days of fighting, had captured Monterrey. Although the Mexican defenders had capitulated, Taylor entered into an eight-day truce with the Mexican general, permitting him and his troops to leave without surrendering their arms in the vain hope that war would end.

The victory enhanced Taylor's popularity with the American people; he apparently was beginning to take himself seriously as a

Whig candidate for president and was growing increasingly suspicious of Polk. When the president instructed him to terminate the armistice and not advance beyond Monterrey, Taylor was furious and more than ever convinced that the Democratic administration was trying to discredit him for political reasons.

The other two American armies were on the move. Wool had begun his advance from San Antonio for Chihuahua, Mexico, on 23 September. Supplies for his expedition had to be shipped from New Orleans to a depot established at Port Lavaca on Matagorda Bay and then moved 160 miles by wagon train to San Antonio. Before Wool started on his march, 1,112 wagonloads of supplies had been transported from Port Lavaca to San Antonio. Jesup, who had served on the southern frontier as a young soldier and was familiar with the terrain, knew that Chihuahua could not be reached by a wagon train over any direct route because of the mountains; he had expected Wool to use pack mules. Wool, however, took a circuitous route and utilized nearly 500 wagons. Jesup was exasperated when he learned that Quartermaster Thomas had diverted to Wool more than 150 wagons which had been intended for Taylor.[4] Wool and his army of about 2,700 men arrived at the Rio Grande on 8 October, and on 29 October captured the town of Monclova.

General Kearny, in command of a force of about sixteen hundred, had left Fort Leavenworth at the end of June for operations against New Mexico and California. After a rugged march of nearly nine hundred miles, he had reached Santa Fe in less than fifty days and taken military possession of New Mexico without resistance on 18 August.[5] Supplies for his expedition had been obtained primarily from Missouri and other nearby states and transported by steamboat from St. Louis to Fort Leavenworth. At that point, the troops were furnished rations and means of transportation for their long overland journey. Hostile Indians added to the difficulty of keeping the troops supplied by attacking the wagon trains, killing many of the drivers and driving off cattle. Kearny remained at Santa Fe until he was convinced the situation in New Mexico was stabilized; he then decided to split up his force. On 23 September, he set out for California, leaving behind Col. Alexander W. Doniphan and his regiment of Missouri volunteers. Doniphan, after reinforcements arrived, was to march to Chihuahua, where he was expected to join Wool. Kearny and his men departed from Santa

Fe with a wagon train but soon had to abandon it and resort to pack mules for the trek of more than a thousand miles across rugged mountain ranges and trackless deserts to San Diego. Jesup had selected the highly competent Maj. Thomas Swords, a graduate of West Point, as chief quartermaster for Kearny's expedition. Swords accompanied Kearny to California and then returned with him in 1847. To transport men and supplies for the expedition, including Doniphan's, Jesup's department furnished 1,556 wagons, 459 horses, 3,658 mules, 14,904 oxen, and 516 packsaddles.[6]

After inspecting the condition of his department in New Orleans, Jesup was gratified by his findings: "We are prepared for the most searching investigation. If the army has wanted anything due from our department which we had the means of furnishing, it is because it has not been required by the commanding general. Everything required by him, and infinitely more, has been accomplished." He intended to make a full report to the secretary of war regarding Taylor's complaints as soon as he could obtain in an official form the information he already possessed. Two days later, in a letter to Colonel Whiting, he offered to join Taylor's army as a staff officer: "I desire his success, and will do all in my power to insure it."[7]

Taylor apparently did not take the offer seriously. "I told General Taylor of your liberal offer to join his head-quarters, if he desired it," Whiting responded. "He seemed to appreciate the compliment, but I suppose he would find it even more unpleasant than you to see his former senior subordinate to him. It would be a great relief to me to have you here, as the burden I bear is a heavy one." Whiting did not think that Taylor imputed any blame to the department at Washington: "He knows very well that the requisitions are made here, and not there. I infer he regards the government at fault in having crowded such an additional force upon him in advance of all the means to use them to advantage. Thousands of troops were at the Brazos before we had the means of moving them up the river."[8]

Jesup's inspection soon convinced him that the officers of his department had been unjustly criticized. "No provident foresight" had been exercised by anyone in command. Thus, Jesup wrote, "Officers of the department have, like myself, been obliged to guess what might be wanted, and risk an over supply of some, and not a sufficient supply of other articles." He found that quartermasters were being called upon to perform duties that were the responsibility of other branches of the staff, particularly the Ordnance and Topographical departments. Jesup declared that if a proper topographical survey had been made of the Rio Grande and of the bays and harbors through which army supplies had to pass, much inconvenience and expense would have been spared. Either the Topographical Department should be required to furnish the information necessary to the various supply agencies, he maintained, or a topographical corps should be attached to the Quartermaster's Department. Two or three of these officers, he observed, might have been employed to great advantage in surveys and construction works, especially in building a railroad between the Brazos and the Rio Grande. He had spoken the previous summer to Col. John J. Abert, Chief of the Topographical Engineer Corps, concerning the need for the railroad, but nothing had been done about it. Such a railroad, he claimed, would have saved at least half a million dollars.

Many of the steamers and other vessels engaged in transporting supplies from the depot at Point Isabel to the mouth of the Rio Grande were disabled, and bad weather hampered navigation. Jesup therefore ordered the depot quartermaster to form a train of two hundred wagons to keep up direct communication by land. Although the distance was only ten miles, the route involved crossing the Boca Chica bayou which had to be ferried until his department built a bridge which should have been constructed by topographical engineers. He also cited the need for a corps of enlisted ordnance men under a competent ordnance officer at every depot of the army in the field. Colonel Bomford had sent such a corps to Jesup in Florida. "Artificers and laborers can be hired for service at arsenals, but they cannot be readily hired for service in the field," he noted. "Enlisted men only should be sent to the army."[9]

Jesup's reference to the shortcomings of the Topographical Corps brought a protest from Colonel Abert, who thought his service had not been treated fairly: "Without a dollar to buy a pound of nails, a stick of timber, or hire a mechanic or laborer, how could either bridges or roads be made? . . . you would not think well of a remark that you had failed in transporting supplies, if you had not a dollar, to hire a horse or wagon or a boat." In reply, Jesup denied that he had treated Abert unfairly. Taylor had made serious charges against his department relative to transportation shortages.

Without knowledge of both water and land routes, which Topographical Engineers alone could furnish, Jesup could not determine what class of boats was most suitable or whether wagons could be used at all. He recalled that at a meeting of supply chiefs in May the secretary of war had asked him about the condition of the bays, bars, and harbors. "I referred to you as the officer who alone could furnish such information," he wrote Abert. The $10 million appropriation was available to both officers, and Abert could have utilized part of it for survey purposes. Jesup added, "I meant and still mean to throw from my own shoulders all responsiblity that properly attaches to others."[10]

Abert's response was sympathetic and apologetic in tone: "The fault finding propensity has, I have no doubt been extended to your Department unjustly. A war without preparation for it, would of necessity have to encounter deficiencies." He had made several small drafts for survey against the appropriation, only to be informed that he was to have no share of it. Too many, he pointed out, thought that war consisted only of fighting and that all the preparations and supplies necessary for troops to fight were unimportant matters.[11]

As Jesup continued his inspection, he became concerned about the large number of vessels that were being wrecked or otherwise disabled. "Had we foreseen the nature of the navigation of the Mexican coasts and harbors, and of the Rio del Norte, and built suitable steamboats several months ago, a million dollars might have been saved by this time," he reported, referring primarily to the difficulty and danger of navigating the Gulf of Mexico with boats adapted to shallow rivers. At the mouth of the Rio Grande, where extensive storehouses and workshops had been erected, he ordered that special arrangements be made to repair steamships and other vessels. Results were discouraging. "There is so little energy in all mechanical operations . . . that it is impossible to calculate with any degree of certainty when even the most trifling job can be finished." Jesup was annoyed and puzzled when he observed that boats which seemed to perform admirably when chartered from private owners were grossly neglected after his department purchased them. He cited the case of the *Edith*; her boilers were burned out because her captain and engineer had allowed them to fill with salt.[12]

Jesup recommended to Marcy that changes be made in the

packaging of subsistence and ordnance supplies to save the added heavy expense incurred by having to replace articles damaged in shipping or by exposure to weather and the necessity for repacking in the field. Much damage could be prevented, he suggested, by packing flour, bread, sugar, coffee, and bacon in India-rubber sacks and pork, vinegar, and similar products in half-barrels. The ordnance stores ought to be in kegs or boxes, covered with India-rubber or waterproof leather cases. No package should exceed eighty pounds—at most, a hundred pounds—in weight. Packages should be of a convenient size for packing on mules. Delays often occurred when quartermasters had to reduce the size of packages when loads were transferred from wagons to mules. He urged that instructions on the subject be given to the Ordnance and Subsistence departments.[13]

Jesup's inspection strengthened his belief that any inefficiency in quartermaster operations was due to the lack of business experience on the part of political appointees designated by the president to serve as quartermasters and assistant quartermasters. "The Department must break down if the Executive makes any more appointments like nine tenths of those heretofore made in the Department." He was apprehensive that frauds might have been committed in the field, not with the concurrence of these inexperienced officers but in spite of their "best exertions." When he complained to Marcy about the appointees, the secretary assured him that the men appointed had been presented by politicians to the president "with the highest testimonials of qualifications." Jesup replied that his objections "were not to the character, talents and respectability of the gentlemen appointed, nor to their zeal, but to the want of business qualifications required to enable them to take at once upon themselves the responsible duties of their present stations."[14]

His repeated pleas for more officers with military experience to promote efficiency and economy in field operations finally brought results. Through the combined efforts of Marcy and Senator Thomas Hart Benton, chairman of the Military Affairs Committee, Congress enacted a law on 11 February 1847 permitting an increase in the staff of the Quartermaster's Department. It authorized President Polk to appoint from officers in the army four more quartermasters with the rank of major and ten assistant quartermasters with the rank of captain.[15]

Despite his persistent efforts, Jesup was unsuccessful in obtaining permission to establish a military service corps to provide support for combat troops. He had long considered the lack of such a corps a basic weakness of the army. Throughout the war, great difficulty was experienced in procuring the laborers, teamsters, mechanics, and other types of specialists needed for carrying out the diversified operations of his department. The various armies were too small to permit the detailing of troops to perform the assorted tasks, so civilians had to be hired at high rates of wages and transported to the points where the work was required. Few were willing to contract their services for more than six months; when that time expired, they insisted upon being discharged, often during the most critical operations and where their replacement was impossible. The only solution, Jesup contended, was to organize the corps that he had proposed. He was far ahead of his time. Nearly a century after he first foresaw need of them, Congress, in 1912, authorized the activation and training of military supply units.[16] They were first employed on a large scale in World War I.

Jesup had contended that mules were plentiful in Mexico and could be procured in any number required by Taylor's army. Mexican horses, however, he considered as inferior and unsuitable for dragoon and artillery purposes. Consequently, thousands of horses had to be procured in the United States and shipped to Mexico. He was disappointed that officers of his department had not procured more ox teams in Texas for draft purposes. "They go further without water and subsist on what the woods and prairies afford."[17]

Early in November, Commodore David Conner led an American expedition against Tampico, a major Mexican seaport on the Gulf of Mexico, and took possession of it on 15 November. When he learned that Tampico was in American hands, Jesup directed Capt. Edwin B. Babbitt, an assistant quartermaster at New Orleans, to go there to supervise the erection of a depot and other facilities. Babbitt hired a force of civilian laborers, mechanics, and teamsters and took them by boat to Tampico, arriving on 3 December. In a relatively short time, he had constructed storehouses for subsistence, ordnance, engineer, and quartermaster supplies, as well as a hospital and quarters for men and officers. Tampico became an important base for operations against Mexico City.[18]

Meanwhile, Polk and his cabinet had decided in October that

an attack upon Mexico City by way of Vera Cruz might bring a quicker end to the war. But who would command the expedition? Polk had no confidence in either Taylor or Scott. Finally, on 18 November, he reluctantly selected Scott to command the Vera Cruz expedition. "If I had the power I would certainly select some other," he wrote in his diary, "but I am compelled to use the officers provided by law." Until Scott arrived at the Brazos and explained his strategy, which required Taylor to remain on the defensive, the two officers had been on cordial terms. At that point, the suspicious Taylor suddenly reversed his attitude toward the commander-in-chief, as he had earlier toward Jesup.[19]

After spending six weeks investigating quartermaster operations in the war zone, Jesup made a formal reply to Taylor's accusations against the Quartermaster's Department. Though initially apprehensive that some neglect or omission had occurred on the part of one or more of his subordinate officers, he was, after looking into the matter, "bound in justice to say that no class of officers, not even General Taylor and the distinguished men around him, have better or more faithfully performed their duty."

In conducting a war, he pointed out, the government's duty was to designate the objective to be accomplished; the duty of the general conducting the operations was then to call for the means of accomplishing that objective. If he failed to do so, he was responsible for the consequences. Taylor had complained of the lack of water and land transportation, camp equipage, and shoes for cavalry horses. As to water transportation, Taylor had called for only one light-draft steamer by early May, a request that Hunt complied with as soon as possible. By late May or early June, Taylor considered four boats necessary and appointed his own agents to obtain them. At that time Jesup was under Scott's orders. Believing that Taylor's agents possessed the requisite knowledge, he preferred that they should execute Taylor's orders. Jesup had limited his actions to doubling the number of boats called for by Taylor and authorizing a further increase, if necessary. He noted that the steamers from Pittsburgh that Taylor complained had not arrived until 1 September were the vessels his own agents had procured. While in Pittsburgh on his way south, Jesup had inquired into the delay of the boats. In justice to Captain Sanders, Taylor's agent, no effort had been spared to get them into service as fast as possible.

Jesup pointed out that no information had been received in Washington to enable him to determine whether wagons could be used in Mexico. Taylor had a wagon train sufficient for a force twice the size of the one he commanded before the arrival of the volunteers. Also, he had captured General Arista's means of transportation and was in a country abounding in mules — the means of transportation best adapted to Mexico, and the only means employed by the enemy. "A general is expected to avail himself of the resources of the country in which he operates. If General Taylor failed to do so, and was without the necessary transportation, he is alone responsible."

He remarked that Secretary Marcy was aware that the tentage appropriation he had requested the previous year had been stricken out, and he could not legally apply a cent to tentage before 13 May. After Congress appropriated the money, officers of his department were compelled to obtain whatever materials they could. He had no doubt that some of the material was of the quality described by Taylor but, under the circumstances, that was unavoidable. The officers had obtained the best material they could find.

Jesup was at a loss to understand why the deficiency of shoes for dragoon horses was made a subject of complaint against his department. Every troop of dragoons was allowed, by law, a blacksmith. The duty fell to every commander of a troop to have his shoeing tools complete and to have the necessary shoe and nail iron; the duty of the regimental commander was to see that timely requisitions were made. "Now, if these officers failed to have what was necessary . . . let General Taylor hold them accountable."

He believed that every officer of his department had performed his duty faithfully, and that Taylor's charges were unjust and unmerited: "As regards myself, I feel that I have performed my whole duty, both to the country and to the army; and, if the slightest doubt remain on that subject, I owe it to myself to demand an immediate and thorough investigation of my conduct, and that of the department."[20]

Taylor had insisted that his accusations be made a matter of public record. In view of the widespread attention his charges received, it is not surprising that the quartermaster general's reply was read in the Senate, by Senator Lewis Cass. Although what

Jesup had written was merely a defense of himself and his department against Taylor's accusations, the general interpreted the statement as an "indirect attack" upon him. In a letter to his brother Joseph, Taylor declared that he had not considered Jesup "entirely sane since he wrote that unfortunate Blair letter." This statement was obviously sheer nonsense. Taylor's warmhearted correspondence with Jesup for years after the Blair-letter episode of June 1836 reveals that he did not entertain such a view of his old friend until he himself became politically minded.[21]

Why Taylor turned against the old friend whose many kindnesses he had repeatedly said he would never forget is unclear. He may have become so obsessed with the idea that Polk and Marcy were scheming to destroy him that he became suspicious of everyone even remotely associated with the administration and thus assumed that Jesup was in on the "plot." Or, strangely, he may have looked upon the quartermaster general as a potential rival for the presidency. In a letter to his brother, he lists both Jesup and Scott as "aspirants for the high office."[22]

For whatever reason, Taylor had many more unkind statements to make about Jesup as well as about Cass, Scott, Marcy, and others in letters to his brother: "[Jesup has been] a courtier & time-server his whole life. . . . Cass is certainly one of the most unprincipled demagogues in the country. . . . Scott will be used by certain discerning politicians who are wolves in sheep clothing to defeat any Whig for the office [the presidency] . . . . I do not think there is a more unprincipled editor in all the land . . . than Ritchie of the *Organ.*"[23]

About six weeks after Jesup's reply to Taylor's accusations, a New York paper published Taylor's famous letter to General Gaines. Although Taylor had written it primarily as a defense of his operations and a criticism of the administration, it was also, in effect, another attack upon Jesup. Taylor complained that his army had been delayed by the lack of sufficient transportation and supplies, and he was being blamed for the deficiencies of the Quartermaster's Department. He had not intended the letter for publication and had advised Gaines to "commit it to the flames." Yet he had addressed it to an officer he knew had long been unfriendly to Jesup. The temptation to make the letter's contents known to the public was too strong for Gaines, and he had it inserted in the *New York Morning Express* on 22 January 1847.

Other papers over the country copied it, causing something of a sensation, particularly since Taylor was regarded as a candidate for president. Moreover, the document revealed information concerning military matters which could be helpful to the enemy. Marcy characterized the correspondence as "disgraceful," accusing Taylor of violating army regulations in criticizing his superiors. Taylor replied that he had written "only for private perusal" by "an old army friend" and that the letter had been published "without my knowledge or consent." The document became an issue in Congress. Gaines hurried down from New York to explain to Polk that more of the letter had been published than he intended and that the letter was accompanied by partisan comments of which he did not approve. Polk reprimanded him, commenting in his diary: "Gen'l Taylor is in the hands of political managers, and this letter is another of the many evidences that I have that he is wholly unfit for the chief command of Mexico." [24]

When Jesup left Washington for the war front, his department was geared to provide support for Taylor's army in northern Mexico, Wool's thrust to Chihuahua, and Kearny's expedition to New Mexico and California. President Polk's decision to strike at the heart of the enemy by invading Mexico City required the establishment of still another army, commanded by Scott. Preparation involved the calling-up of more volunteers and the transfer of a large number of troops from Taylor's army. The plan also entailed the country's first large-scale amphibious operation, since Scott's forces were to move by water to Vera Cruz and land on the beaches. This change in strategy greatly increased the already heavy workload of Jesup's undermanned department. Not only would it have to provide transportation for about half of Taylor's army, scattered over much of northern Mexico, but also for Scott's expedition to rendezvous points in the Gulf of Mexico. In addition, supplies, equipment, and transportation would have to be furnished for the eight new divisions mustered into service.

After selecting Scott as commander, Polk requisitioned the governors of various states for the additional volunteers required. Jesup, then at New Orleans, took the responsibility for furnishing quartermaster supplies and transportation for recruits from Louisiana and the nearby states of Mississippi and Texas. At Washington, Stanton directed arrangements for the volunteers from Massachusetts, New York, Virginia, Pennsylvania, and North and South Carolina. Because the Topographical Engineers were without funds, supplies from that department had to be furnished by Stanton along with the transportation of troops, ordnance, subsistence, and other stores ordered from posts on the Atlantic.[25]

Following his arrival at New Orleans, Jesup had been engaged primarily in measures to improve the efficiency of quartermaster operations. When Marcy informed him of the change in strategy, he turned his attention to preparations for the Vera Cruz expedition. Since both Brazos and Tampico were important to the success of the strategy, Jesup arranged to inspect facilities at both places. On the way he was to stop off at Port Lavaca to issue orders for supplying the new regiment of Texas volunteers and to direct the transfer of a portion of Wool's wagon train to the Rio Grande. He had planned to leave New Orleans on 1 December on the steamer *Alabama*, but as the vessel was about to leave port he had an opportunity to obtain valuable information concerning harbors and towns on the coast of Mexico. Accordingly, he sent Captain Hetzel forward to the Brazos and delayed his own departure until 5 December, when he boarded the steamer *Fashion* for Lavaca.[26]

The Lavaca depot on Matagorda Bay, vital earlier in supplying Wool's army, had now outlived its usefulness. Jesup directed Capt. James R. Irwin to send the horses and mules that were still fit for service to San Antonio for the use of a Texas regiment. All forage, tarpaulins, wagons, and parts of wagons still serviceable were to be shipped to the Brazos or Tampico. Horses, mules, and other property not worth removing were to be sold.[27]

On the morning of 13 December, Jesup left for the Brazos aboard the *Fashion*. A few hours after leaving Matagorda Bay, the sidewheel steamer became disabled and was compelled to anchor about fifteen miles from shore. The wind was blowing a strong gale, the sea was extremely rough; for a time the ship appeared to be in serious danger. Throughout the remainder of the day and all night, the anchored vessel was buffeted by huge waves that swept over its deck. By the following morning, the crew had made sufficient repairs to enable the vessel to reach the base in Aransas Bay, where Jesup spent his fifty-eighth birthday on 16 December while the ship was being restored to service.[28]

His experience aboard the *Fashion*, it appears, led Jesup to order stricter regulations concerning steamboats and the personnel employed on them. Only men of approved character and competency were to be employed as officers, engineers, sailors, firemen, or laborers.[29] He was convinced that the *Fashion*, which he had purchased along with the *Alabama* for his department, was not suited to rough weather and should be employed during the winter in the bay of Tampico and on the Panusco River. He considered the *Alabama* an excellent sea vessel. Every steamboat was to be inspected upon arrival at Fort Ogden, Texas, and any captain or engineer who neglected to take immediate action to put his boat or machinery in proper order was to be discharged. Card-playing and gambling were to be prohibited on all boats, whether publicly owned or chartered.[30]

When Jesup arrived at the Brazos, Scott had established temporary headquarters and was completing his preparations. The two generals met to discuss plans for the campaign and the supply problems involved. Their meeting was on the friendliest of terms, their quarrel during the Seminole War period a decade earlier seemingly forgotten for the moment. In contrast to Taylor, Scott had requisitioned supplies in advance and given considerable thought to other preparations. He preferred an army of ten to fifteen thousand but, rather than risk exposure of the men to yellow fever usually prevalent on the coast after mid-April, he was willing to embark with an initial force of eight thousand. All ships to be used in transporting men and supplies were to be afloat and beyond the Rio Grande by 15 January 1847, or by 1 February at the latest. He estimated he would need 140 surfboats to put men, equipment, and artillery ashore from transports at Vera Cruz. Colonel Stanton had the responsibility of having them built and sent from Philadelphia. Scott agreed that the number of officers in the Quartermaster's Department was insufficient for the heavy burdens of war; he endorsed Jesup's letter to the War Department requesting additional quartermasters and assistant quartermasters—the increase authorized by Congress on 11 February 1847.[31]

Before leaving Washington, Scott had requested Marcy to send out a number of large ships in ballast from eastern ports, because he believed it would be impossible to obtain a sufficient number of vessels from New Orleans and Mobile for his expedition. He estimated that about fifty ships each from five hundred to seven hundred tons would be required to transport fourteen thousand men with their horses, artillery, stores, and surfboats. On 11 December,

Marcy, alarmed when he discovered the exorbitant cost of procuring transports from the Atlantic Coast, asked Jesup what portion of the transportation for the expedition could be obtained from New Orleans and Mobile. The quartermaster general assured Marcy that he could provide transportation for all the troops to be withdrawn from Taylor's army and for all the supplies to be taken from either the Brazos depot or New Orleans. He estimated that government-owned vessels under his control could carry three thousand men and all of their supplies and that any additional vessels required could be chartered at New Orleans on favorable terms.[32]

Without waiting for Jesup's reply to his inquiry, Marcy on 15 December sent him a synopsis of the means of transportation that would be required and information concerning embarkation. Regiments from Massachusetts, New York, Virginia, and North Carolina were to embark from Boston, New York, Old Point Comfort, and Wilmington, respectively. Those from Pennsylvania, Mississippi and Louisville would proceed via New Orleans, and the regiment from South Carolina would reach the Brazos via Montgomery and Mobile. Marcy estimated that three ships would be required to transport each regiment with its ordnance and stores, so that twelve ships would be needed for the regiments leaving the Atlantic Coast. He assumed that five ships would be required to transport the one-hundred and forty surfboats and ten more for those to be sent in ballast, basing his estimates on the presumption that Jesup's department would furnish fourteen ships, making in all forty-one ships for Scott's expedition.[33] After receiving Jesup's optimistic assurances as to the amount of transportation that he could provide from New Orleans, Marcy countermanded his order to Stanton for the ten ships to be sent in ballast. He neglected, however, to apprise either Scott or Jesup of the change.

Scott charged later that his expedition "was delayed in whole or in part, at the Brazos and Tampico, from the 15th of January to the 9th of March" because the ten ships in ballast on which he had relied were not furnished. Although Marcy was negligent in not informing Scott and Jesup of his cancellation of those ships, the delay was caused by factors other than the lack of vessels. When Jesup replied to Marcy's inquiry concerning the transportation he could provide, he, too, was relying on those ships. Then the weather became so bad that he thought it unsafe to depend on their arrival. Consequently, he made other arrangements without counting on the ships, and so informed Scott. The amount of transportation provided for the expedition proved to be far in excess of Marcy's estimates. Instead of the twenty-seven vessels expected to be needed for transporting troops and supplies from the Atlantic Coast, Stanton actually dispatched fifty-three, and, in place of the fourteen ships Jesup had been expected to furnish, he provided 163 vessels at New Orleans, the Brazos, and Tampico. Some of these made several voyages.[34] Meanwhile, on 3 January 1847, Jesup left the Brazos for New Orleans aboard the steamer *Alabama* to complete preparations for Scott's operations.

After an unsuccessful attempt to confer with Taylor at Matamoros, Scott returned to his headquarters at the Brazos, where he wrote the War Department on 12 January that his return had been delayed by low water and heavy gales. Northers, he stated, were "again blowing with such violence as to prevent all communication with vessels lying off this place and the mouth of the Rio Grande." Jesup, he noted, was in New Orleans to procure additional lighters "for this terrible coast." Many of the old had been lost; many more were likely to be wrecked. Two weeks later, though the original date set to embark for Vera Cruz had passed, he expressed satisfaction with the state of preparations: "The quartermaster general (brevet Major General Jesup) at New Orleans, has, I find, taken all proper measures, with judgment and promptitude, to provide everything depending on his department for the despatch and success of my expedition."[35]

In New Orleans, where huge quantities of forage were being loaded onto vessels for Scott's army, rumors were rife that the contractor was defrauding the public by short measure. Jesup directed the superintendent in charge of loading the vessels to pay particular attention to the quantities put on board. When he reported that the sacks of corn and oats appeared to be small and that the alleged deficiencies were the subject of common remark among shipmasters and crews, Jesup was so convinced that fraud was being perpetrated that he took drastic action. He stopped payment to the contractor, detained all the vessels that had not yet sailed, and ordered every sack of corn and oats measured and the quantity and quality recorded. The investigation proved that the rumors were false; the contractor had indeed given full measure. Although some sacks were a little short of measure, they were balanced by others that overran. The contractor was cleared and restored to good standing, and the detained vessels were permitted to proceed. Jesup ordered that in future contracts, bushels of grain were to be gauged by weight: corn, fifty-six pounds; oats, thirty-two pounds.[36]

Aware that the extensive publicity given Taylor's letter to Gaines had placed his department in a bad light, Jesup expressed his determination to see that all of his responsibilities were carried out in a timely manner. "I do not intend," he informed Stanton, "to be in arrears with any thing that depends upon me or my Department." Since the department had considerable stocks on hand, Stanton questioned the quartermaster general's order to have four hundred more wagons made for Scott's expedition. Jesup replied that he wanted his order executed with as little delay as possible. "I intend to give orders in time for every thing necessary, and unless the President and Secretary of War interfere to prevent the execution of my orders they must be carried out. . . . I care not how soon the Govt. or Congress may put me out of service, but as long as I remain I will do my duty to the army and to the country, by ordering that which I know to be necessary."[37]

Jesup was under a severe strain during this period, as seems obvious from his uncharacteristic behavior on an early morning visit to Hunt's office. Hunt was absent when Jesup excitedly charged that office with "inefficiency." Hunt thought Jesup must have been under "some misapprehension" because he could see no reason for any charges against him; he felt "duty bound" to demand an investigation of his conduct of the office.[38] As soon as he received Hunt's note, Jesup wrote him a humble apology. He had been, he said, "much harrassed and annoyed" by the failure of many vessels to depart on schedule and by the rumored deficiencies of the forage contractor. He added, "You have more to do than should have been imposed upon any man; and you have certainly done it as well as any one under the circumstances could have done it."[39] Later he wrote to his daughter Mary: "Nearly the whole responsibility for the operations rests upon me, and the whole of the reputation resulting from these operations is gained by others. I get nothing but abuse, and am made to bear the [brunt] of all the blunders of every dunderhead in the army."[40]

On the day Jesup left New Orleans for the Brazos, Taylor was preparing to fight what proved to be one of the bloodiest battles of the war. The Battle of Buena Vista resulted when Santa Anna intercepted a letter ordering Taylor to transfer half of his army to Scott. Taylor was joined by Wool's force. After two days of hard fighting, Santa Anna withdrew, and the Americans claimed a victory over a force four times as large as their own. The battle was the last of the war in the northern part of Mexico.

By coincidence, the same day that Santa Anna launched his attack upon Buena Vista, Scott arrived at Lobos Island—selected as the rendezvous point because its protected harbor was spacious enough to accommodate the large fleet of ships being assembled for the Vera Cruz expedition. The island was about seven or eight miles off the Mexican coast, some fifty miles southeast of Tampico. Scott had complained to Marcy on 12 February that not one of the ships Jesup had promised would be on their way by 24 January had arrived at the Brazos; his expedition was already delayed nearly a month. Now, two weeks later, he wrote from Lobos that two-thirds of the ordnance and ordnance stores and half of the surfboats "are yet unheard of." Also, he was still awaiting the ten transports Marcy was to send him in ballast. Everyone he had relied upon, he said, "knew from the first . . . that it would be fatal . . . to attempt military operations on the coast after . . . the first week in April."[41] It was already the end of February.

Scott must have been aware from his own experience that the northers were responsible in large measure for the delays. There had been no lack of foresight, energy, or planning on his part, and his requisitions were timely and ample. Nor had proper arrangements been lacking on Jesup's part; he was just as annoyed and distressed by the delays as was Scott. He and his department had made adequate provisions for boats and supplies; the difficulty was in getting them to the place of rendezvous in the face of almost incessant storms and other obstacles which no human effort could prevent. Of over two hundred transport vessels furnished for the expedition, more than forty, or approximately 20 percent, were lost in the storms which also delayed many of the others.[42] Because of the drenching rains throughout January, the ships chartered at New Orleans could not be prepared for service as rapidly as planned. The same storms impeded the transfer of troops from Taylor's army, as well as the arrival of the staging area of the ships carrying troops and supplies from the eastern ports.

Numerous other unavoidable delays occurred. When the vessels chartered at New Orleans were ready to leave, crews to man them were scarce. Several crews quit after they had been hired, and valuable time was lost before others could be found.

Each transport was expected to carry fuel and water sufficient for at least sixty days. A shortage of water casks developed, and ships had to be detained while all available coopers, "black and white," were put to work constructing a new supply. Stalls which agents constructed on ships for the transport of horses were "so badly secured, and the work so negligently done" that Jesup ordered the vessels entirely refitted by experienced carpenters before a horse was put on board. Construction of the ten light-draft schooners he had ordered built at Philadelphia was greatly retarded because all ship carpenters there had to be employed in constructing the 140 surfboats which Scott wanted completed in thirty days. Stanton called the order one of the most difficult ever imposed on him, but the task was completed in the specified time. Arrangements for the surfboats' transportation proved almost as difficult as their hurried construction. Few ships were capable of carrying the boats (thirty-five to forty feet long) on their decks, so it became necessary to purchase and open the decks of a number of vessels to make room for them in the holds and between decks. Stanton sent along six experienced boatbuilders and ship carpenters to serve in the field. He dispatched the ships promptly, but because of bad weather only 65 of the 140 surfboats were delivered in time for the landing.[43]

Despite all the obstacles and delays, the fleet transporting Scott's army of about ten thousand men and supplies sailed from the harbor of Lobos Island on 2 March 1847. It headed for Anton Lizardo, the next rendezvous point a dozen miles below Vera Cruz, where a Navy squadron under the command of Commodore David Conner was waiting to give assistance in the amphibious operations. After a rough and stormy passage of two hundred miles, the ships arrived there on the fourth day. The next two days were spent in final preparations for the assault. Jesup was on his way to Tampico when the fleet departed from the Lobos anchorage, but he joined the expedition when it left Anton Lizardo.[44]

On 9 March, the landing was made on a beach three miles southeast of Vera Cruz, opposite Sacrificios Island. Plans for this largest amphibious operation ever attempted by an American force had been worked out in detail by Scott and Commodore Conner, and the maneuver was executed with precision by the army and navy. The first troops ashore were the regulars of General Worth's brigade, quickly followed by Gen. Robert Patterson's volunteers—the division Jesup accompanied. About a mile from shore, the troops left the transports and crowded into the surfboats, each of which was conducted by a naval officer and rowed by sailors from the navy squadron. Upon reaching shallow water, the men, each carrying a two-day supply of bread and cooked meat and holding his gun over his head, leaped from the boats and waded ashore. The entire force landed without serious opposition. The landing of horses and mules was accomplished by forcing the animals overboard near the beach and making them swim ashore. One eyewitness reported seeing between one hundred and two hundred drowned horses that had been washed up on the beach from a transport wrecked off the harbor.[45]

No port facilities were available at the landing site; no wharf could be erected that would withstand the force of the recurring northers. Consequently, all supplies of every kind had to be brought in from the transports riding at anchor a mile or so offshore by surfboats and stacked on the open beach. Storms that followed the successful landing of the troops delayed the unloading of heavy mortars, large shells, wagons, and other cumbersome items until the sea became more tranquil. Ship carpenters were busy repairing the many damaged surfboats. As more supplies arrived, the beach became covered with piles of stores and crowded with men and animals. Large mounds of wagon bodies, axles, tongues, and bows were surrounded by many men engaged in fitting the parts together.[46]

During the landing of troops and the unloading of supplies, thirty vessels were wrecked with a heavy loss of animals, wagons, harness, and numerous other supplies. Of the animals Hunt had shipped from New Orleans, 335 horses and 503 mules were lost in storms. Complete statistics are not available, but the total loss of animals from storms alone in the course of the war was undoubtedly much greater. During a stampede at Vera Cruz, between 1,500 and 1,600 horses ran away; only a few were recovered. "I have never witnessed anything like the destruction of public property in the storms which have occurred during the winter," Jesup wrote from a camp near Vera Cruz. Because of the serious losses incurred, he considered it his duty to the army and the country to trust as little as possible to chance. "Duplicate supplies as well as means of sea transportation were in some instances, accordingly provided."[47]

Scott devoted the week following the landing of his army to strengthening the beachhead and making tactical plans for the capture of Vera Cruz. By 16 March he had completed the investment of the city and was awaiting the arrival of heavy guns to attack its fortifications. Twice during the siege Jesup went to Tampico to speed up the movement of troops, supplies, and the means of transportation for the army.[48] On 22 March, when the defenders refused to surrender, Scott began a bombardment of the city. On 29 March the Mexicans stacked their arms, the American army took possession of Vera Cruz, and Scott set up his headquarters in the governor's palace.

Ten days before the surrender he was already making plans for his march into the interior of Mexico. He sent a memorandum to Jesup stating that for the first division of 10,000 men he would require from 800 to 1,000 wagons with five-mule teams, 2,000 to 3,000 pack mules, and 300 to 500 draft animals for a siege train. Requirements would be similar for the second division in April. Five hundred wagons were still aboard the transports, and Jesup ordered 100 more from the Brazos and 300 from Tampico. The storms had taken a heavy toll of the mules; only 300 remained at Vera Cruz. At Tampico, 700 waited to be shipped, and he ordered 500 from the Brazos. Jesup was skeptical of the need for so many wagons: "I never before saw any troops with so enormous a quantity of baggage . . . as the army in Mexico." On 5 April, Scott protested to Marcy that his army was being delayed at Vera Cruz because of an insufficient number of wagons and animals. Captain Hetzel, his senior quartermaster at that time, had informed him that only 180 wagons and teams were ready for the road, while 300 wagons, without teams, were still afloat. Hetzel feared that large numbers of wagons and teams, along with many artillery and cavalry horses, had perished in the storms that plagued the expedition.[49]

In their meeting at the Brazos in December, Scott and Jesup had agreed that the army could rely on the country through which it would be passing for two-thirds of the draft animals needed, while one-third would have to come from the United States and the northern part of Mexico. These expectations were well founded, because the country about Vera Cruz, Alvarado, and Tlacotalpan abounded in horses, mules, and cattle. Unfortunately, the situation changed. After the surrender of Vera Cruz, Scott sent a joint expedition under Brig. Gen. John A. Quitman and Commodore Matthew C. Perry against the other two cities to neutralize the Mexican residents, acquire a harbor for Perry's small vessels, and open up and secure the resources of the area. An uncoordinated movement by the commander of a navy ship resulted in the capture of both Alvarado and Tlacotalpan, but without securing the resources behind them. Scott's main objective in sending out the expedition was defeated, and Jesup's department had to procure nearly all the horses and mules for the army from New Orleans, Tampico, and the Brazos. The Mexican forces, rather than the American army, could avail themselves of the resources.[50]

While Scott at Vera Cruz was loudly complaining that his army was being delayed by the shortage of wagons and teams, President Polk in Washington was vehemently protesting the shipment of wagons, horses, and mules to Scott's army. Polk summoned Stanton to the White House and called his attention "most emphatically" to what he termed the "unnecessarily heavy" expenditures of the department for Scott's military operations. He was "much vexed at the extravagance & stupidity" of purchasing mules in the United States and transporting them at vast expense to Mexico where "they could be had for one-fourth the price." Polk was unaware of the change in the situation regarding mules in Mexico.[51]

Two days after the surrender of Vera Cruz, Jesup left there for Tampico, the Brazos, and New Orleans to hasten forward the transportation needed by Scott's army for the inland march that would eventually take it to Mexico City. The vigorous measures he adopted brought results, and on 11 April Scott reported that his means of transportation was slowly increasing. The first elements of the army, under Gen. David E. Twiggs, had departed for Jalapa on 8 April, followed the next day by two brigades of General Patterson's division. Jalapa was about seventy-five miles from the coast. Mules, forage, and subsistence should be available in that area. Scott had praise for the energy displayed by Capt. James R. Irwin, the chief quartermaster with his army.[52]

On orders from Jesup, Capt. Edwin B. Babbitt, the assistant quartermaster at Tampico, expanded his work force, divided them into shifts, and kept men busy day and night loading ships. By the end of April he had dispatched seventy-eight vessels with troops and army supplies. During 1847 he purchased and shipped to Vera Cruz 5,226 mules, 548 wagons, and 1,410 horses (including 700 for the Tennessee cavalry). Hunt reported that by early July he had sent 336 wagons and 2,444 horses to Vera Cruz from New Orleans.[53]

By 10 April, Jesup was back in New Orleans after conferring with quartermasters at Tampico and the Brazos concerning measures to speed up shipments of wagons, animals, and supplies to Vera Cruz. Having accomplished all that he thought he could in the war zone, he prepared to return to Washington after an absence of more than six months. He directed Hunt to consider himself authorized to do in his absence all that he could do were he present.[54] On 15 April Jesup departed by steamboat for Washington by way of Louisville, Cincinnati, and Pittsburgh.

While Jesup was en route home, Scott's army advanced half of the distance to Mexico City. Despite stubborn resistance from Santa Anna, who had hurried south after the battle of Buena Vista, the Americans had captured Cerro Gordo, Jalapa and Perote and were preparing to advance to Puebla. At Jalapa, Scott had to wait for essential supplies and for reinforcements; he was losing one-third of his army with the expiration of the period of service of 3,700 volunteers. He released them early so they could avoid the yellow-fever season at Vera Cruz. Upon Jesup's department fell the responsibility for transporting the volunteers back to their homes in the United States as well as moving the remainder of the army forward in Mexico. Adding to the other difficulties of getting supplies from Vera Cruz over roads heavily covered with sand were the attacks upon wagon and mule trains by Mexican bandidos and ranchers. Troops from the small cavalry force were assigned to protect supply trains. The biggest obstacle to delivery, Scott discovered, arose not from the lack of wagons and animals but from a severe shortage of experienced teamsters and conductors. By mid-May the Americans occupied Puebla, the last important city between Vera Cruz and the Mexican capital. The army was by then so reduced in effective strength by illness, fatigue, and casualties that Scott abandoned Jalapa and concentrated all available forces at Puebla to await reinforcements. He spent ten dismal weeks at Puebla before his forces were strong enough to move forward and attack Mexico City.[55]

Jesup returned to duty in Washington on 6 May. On 24 May he learned that Congress had made no appropriation for Scott's operations. More than a million dollars had been expended from his department's appropriation for the transportation of the army in Mexico and its ordnance and engineer stores. Less than $70,000 was left to his department's credit in the treasury, and appropriations for the new fiscal year would not become available before 1 July. He explained the situation in a letter to Hunt at New Orleans: "In paying the claims upon the government you must use drafts upon this office at as long sight as possible; and your purchases when possible must be made on a credit of, say, sixty days, so as to enable us to make payment from the appropriations for the next fiscal year."

Congress had appropriated $500,000 for the care of disabled soldiers being discharged from the service. Jesup ordered the appropriation transferred to Hunt: "You will apply it to any legitimate objects within your administration, but as sparingly as possible, so as to meet the most pressing demands until next year's appropriation be available." He directed Hunt to place in the hands of an officer designated by the Medical Department any sums requested for the relief of disabled soldiers discharged from the service in New Orleans, or who arrived there from the army. If necessary, a hospital was to be provided, and the disabled were to be furnished camp equipage and transportation to their homes.[56]

A charge of "extravagance and waste of public property" was made against the Quartermaster's Department on 17 June by the *Philadelphia Saturday Review.* The newspaper's comments were based on an article by an unidentified correspondent which had appeared in the *New Orleans Delta* on 25 May. The correspondent claimed that since the surrender of Vera Cruz, government-chartered vessels, varying in number from fifty to eighty, employed at prices ranging from $40 to $100 per day, had been anchored at New Orleans, Sacrificios, Lobos, and Anton Lizardo. These vessels, the article stated, were loaded with supplies; some had been at anchor as long as three months. Demurrage on each amounted to at least $60 per day. The Philadelphia editor noted that Jesup had visited Mexico during the winter "to regulate the extravagance and waste of public funds in his department" but had, for some reason, returned to his Washington office. The editor added, "We hope he will, before it is too late, draw a *tight rein* on his inexperienced deputies, who are, it is said, dipping a little too deep into the treasury during these warlike times, at the expense of the People's pockets."

The *Saturday Review* editorial was sent to Jesup by John H.

Sherburne, a Philadelphia literary figure, who stated his intention to make a suitable reply, unless the quartermaster general objected. Jesup had seen the original item in the *New Orleans Delta,* but so many irresponsible stories about "abuses" and "extravagances" were published in newspapers in time of war that he had declined to respond. He explained to Sherburne that he was not in the habit of noticing anonymous statements and could not respond to them without neglecting important public duties: "Aiming always to do that which is right, I feel perfectly indifferent to what . . . prejudiced individuals may think or say. I am not, however, indifferent to public opinion; but having an abiding confidence in the ultimate justice of the American people, I am willing to trust my reputation with them." He would explain his department's operations in his annual report and was willing "to trust the result to the unbiased judgment of [his] countrymen."

Jesup admitted that the correspondent probably told the truth about the number of vessels on demurrage but was either ignorant of all the facts or had intentionally suppressed them. Scott's operation was so vast that nothing could be left to chance; because of the incessant storms and the danger of heavy losses, more vessels and supplies had been ordered than would otherwise have been the case. Without wharves or dock facilities where cargoes could be discharged and stored, many of the transports were necessarily detained. The choice was between incurring the demurrage on them or delaying Scott's army. "I have in all my arrangements looked to successful results, confident that no amount of money saved would compensate the country for the loss of a battle or the failure of a campaign."[57]

Jesup's views, with the fate of an army at stake, were in decided variance with Polk's, whose paramount interest appears to have been focused on strict economy at all times. The president seems to have labored under the delusion that a war could be fought on foreign soil without a heavy drain on the treasury. During the summer of 1847, he summoned Jesup to the White House on various occasions to discuss the general's "reckless extravagance," as Polk referred to it in his diary, and to hear charges of "abuses and frauds" allegedly committed by subordinates in his department. These unverified rumors tended to confirm Polk's belief that corruption was more or less rampant in the army. One Saturday evening in July, Jesup was called to the White House to listen—

over his strong objections to anonymity—while the president read excerpts of letters from two officers (whose identities he refused to reveal) describing "enormous abuses" in the Quartermaster's and Commissary departments at New Orleans and Vera Cruz. Gen. George Gibson, chief of the Commissary Department, had also been summoned to hear the letters. One of these "trusted" informants turned out to be Gideon Pillow, Polk's former law partner, whom Polk had appointed as a major general in the army a short time before. Pillow was nearly as devoid of military experience as was the president himself.[58]

Undoubtedly, some abuses, and possibly some frauds, occurred during the war, but Polk apparently never considered that they might have been perpetrated by the inexperienced political appointees he foisted upon the Quartermaster's Department over the protests of Jesup rather than by qualified veterans. Captain Irwin, Scott's chief quartermaster, complained bitterly about the political appointees: "I am embarrassed more than I can tell you by the appointments in the Dept. Men without experience and judgment, and sometimes without zeal or industry have been thrown into situations which bewilder them."[59]

A victim, though not a perpetrator, of abuse was the highly qualified Lt. Colonel Hunt, who occupied the key post at New Orleans. The calumny against this respected officer became so abusive that Jesup decided to recall him, in the best interests of the service, and replace him with Maj. Daniel D. Tompkins. Hunt had complained to the quartermaster general on 25 July about the slanders directed against him. Jesup replied that Hunt was mistaken if he thought he had been singled out by anonymous and other writers: "The attack upon the Department is general. Some of the writers have assailed me in the most unmeasured terms for permitting you to *enrich your relatives with the public money.*' This is the precise language used in one letter . . . and it is the substance of many." He assured Hunt that he believed the story to be "a base and cowardly slander" but considered Hunt's presence in Washington for the purpose of closing his accounts to be absolutely necessary —"not only for your own vindication, but for that of the Department, and indeed of the Executive."[60]

In mid-August, while Jesup was in New York on official business, he received a telegram, sent on orders from the White House, directing his immediate return to Washington. Owing to the serious illness of Marcy, the president had appointed Navy Secretary John Y. Mason to serve as acting secretary of war. Since Polk planned to call out five thousand additional troops, he had asked Mason to examine the amount of unexpended balances under each head of the War Department appropriation to determine if adequate funds were available for that purpose. Mason was quite agitated the following morning when he arrived at the White House. Unless a check was put upon Jesup's expenditures, he informed the President, the whole fund appropriated by Congress for the fiscal year (which had begun on 1 July) would not last another month. Polk became alarmed. When he looked over Mason's financial report, he was astonished that the greatest expenditures had been made by the quartermaster general—hardly a cause for astonishment, since the nature of the department's functions required the biggest outlay of funds. He assured Mason he certainly would put a check on the quartermaster's "reckless extravagance" and instructed the acting secretary to send the telegram. Without waiting to learn all the facts, Polk recorded in his diary that General Jesup was "wholly unfit for his place."[61]

The commotion caused by Mason's report turned out to be a tempest in a teapot, when, upon his return, Jesup informed the president that he had withdrawn $4 million of his unexpended funds and put them in the hands of disbursing officers at New Orleans and in Mexico. Scott had estimated that his operations would cost a million dollars a month, and Jesup had placed the funds where they would be readily available to meet the requisitions of the army in Mexico. As to the relatively small sum remaining in his hands, Congress had reduced Jesup's estimates for his department and appropriated less than he had requested. Polk said he would delay his call for more volunteers until the quartermaster general made a careful study of the financial situation and reported to him that sufficient money was available to defray the expense of the additional force.

That night the president wrote in his diary: "Gen'l Jesup is a gallant officer, but I consider him unfit for the office of Quartermaster General." Polk, it seems, had little faith in any officers of the regular army. He applied the same term—"unfit"—to both Generals Scott and Taylor, neither of whom lost a battle in the war. Although he was probably one of the hardest workers ever to occupy the presidency, Polk had little confidence in anyone but himself. He boasted that he could operate the government without the aid of his cabinet. "I have made myself acquainted with the duties of the subordinate officers, and have probably given more attention to details than any of my predecessors."[62] Jesup must have thought at times that, in Polk's case, a little knowledge concerning military matters was a dangerous thing.

On 24 August, three days after his return from New York, Jesup called at the White House to inform Polk that a careful check of his records showed he had $2 million more in unexpended funds than he had reported earlier. That sum had been withdrawn from the treasury but had not yet reached the disbursing officers at New Orleans and elsewhere. Polk displayed no elation at the news. Instead, he criticized the manner in which records were kept in the Quartermaster's and Treasury departments, expressing displeasure that the information had not been immediately available to him when he requested it. Jesup pointed out that both he and one of his clerks had been out of the city, and that such information could always be obtained from the Second Comptroller's Office. Polk was not satisfied. He declared that the War Department should keep its own accounts as a check on the accounting officers in the treasury. This "looseness" of keeping accounts must be corrected at once, Polk said, even though he realized that more clerks would have to be hired. Polk had delayed the start of a cabinet meeting to talk privately with Jesup; after the general departed and the cabinet meeting had adjourned, the president sent for Treasury Chief Clerk McClintock Young to question him concerning the whereabouts of the $2 million. When he got no satisfactory answer, Polk directed Young to telegraph Treasury Secretary Robert J. Walker, who had been out of the city for a month because of illness, requesting his immediate return to Washington.[63]

Jesup called at the White House early the next morning to make a confidential report. Since their meeting the day before, he had been trying to trace the $2 million, since it had been withdrawn from the treasury on 17 June. On that date, the chief clerk of the treasury had called on him, in company with Mr. William W. Corcoran of the banking house of Corcoran and Riggs, and requested him to draw a requisition on Quartermaster's Department funds for $2 million to be transferred to New Orleans, with Corcoran and Riggs as the transfer agents. Jesup had learned, he told Polk, that $400,000 had been paid over to the quartermaster at

New Orleans on 27 July, and $500,000 more was to be paid at the end of August. The other $1,100,000 was still in the hands of the bankers. Jesup had just discovered that the money was being used for stock speculation. Polk, greatly upset by this revelation, declared that he would launch a thorough investigation. He was sure his administration had become involved in a big scandal.

Treasury Secretary Walker returned to Washington later that day and hurried to the White House to learn why his presence was demanded. When Polk repeated what Jesup had told him, Walker assured the chief executive that the transaction was neither illegal nor unusual. War Department funds might be transferred to the war zone in three ways, he explained. The first was by authorizing bills to be drawn at New Orleans on New York, but, if these bills could not be sold at par, then second, by carrying the actual specie from New York to New Orleans at great risk and expense. The third way was by arranging to pay the specie in New York to capitalists who, under contract, would place the specie in New Orleans at specified times. He had adopted the third method, which he considered the least risky. The present contract, he stated, required Corcoran and Riggs to make the final payment at New Orleans on 17 September; the amount would definitely be paid on that date. The guarantee of capitalists made the funds more secure, Walker declared, than they would be if the actual specie was transferred by a messenger or an officer of the government.[64]

On 14 September 1847, three days before the quartermaster at New Orleans received the final payment, Scott's reinforced army defeated Santa Anna's forces and took possession of Mexico City. The American troops remained quartered in the "Halls of Montezuma" for more than four months before Mexico finally signed the Treaty of Guadalupe Hidalgo on 2 February—nine days after John Sutter's discovery of gold in California. The ratification of the treaty by both governments officially ended the Mexican War and extended the western boundary of the United States to the Pacific Ocean. General Kearny had completed the conquest of California months earlier. On 6 November 1847, when President Polk granted Taylor's request for a six-month leave of absence from the army, "Old Rough and Ready" returned home to campaign for the presidency. He was succeeded in command by General Wool.[65]

Representing the War Department in Marcy's absence, Jesup addressed a public gathering at the Fuller Hotel in Washington on 1 January 1848 at a dinner honoring Generals Quitman and Shields, who had just returned from Mexico. In no war in two hundred years, the quartermaster general declared, had any nation accomplished so much in such a short space of time with so small a force and at so little cost as the United States had in the Mexican War: "With our nearest depots further from the source of supply than Algiers is from Toulon or Marseilles, we have accomplished more in any six months of the war, than France has in Africa in 17 years. That we have been able to do this, we owe solely to the general education of our country." Scott, he said, "has more educated military men [Grant, Lee, Sherman, McClellan, Beauregard among others] in the small army he commands than Napoleon had in any army he commanded." The nation's power was derived, he said, from its institutions—a free press, general education, and a good mail establishment.[66]

Although Scott's campaign was an unqualified success, his propensity for getting into trouble reached a climax as the war was drawing to a close. He engaged in a quarrel with some of his top officers, which led President Polk to relieve him of his command. Scott wrote a lengthy letter to Secretary Marcy in which he cited "the neglects, disappointments, injuries and rebukes" which had been inflicted upon him by the War Department. His wrath was directed primarily at the secretary of war. He did not mention Jesup by name but claimed that the Quartermaster's Department was responsible for many of the delays he encountered.

Marcy, in a reply that was equally lengthy, adroitly used much of Scott's own language in refuting in detail all of the accusations. He accused Scott of assailing the president through him. The decision for an expedition against Vera Cruz had been made, he noted, some time before Scott was assigned to take command of it, and General Jesup had gone to New Orleans to be in the best position to make the necessary preparations: "From his great knowledge, and long experience in military affairs, not only in his appropriate department but as a commander in the field, the government thought it fortunate that you could have the advice and assistance of so able a counsellor." Marcy added that Jesup had been with Scott at Vera Cruz, had observed his means, and was capable of making an estimate of their sufficiency. The quartermaster general, he said, was "disposed to be just, and even generous to your fame."[67]

Jesup admitted that "most vexatious" delays did occur in the movement upon Vera Cruz but contended that they were not occasioned by any neglect or omission on his part or on the part of any officer in his department. Scott, he said, was "one of the best informed military men now living; but it would puzzle him to show a single instance in military history of the last two centuries in which an army, whose personnel and material had to be collected from so vast a territory, was as well appointed and supplied as his army has been." He added that the "glorious results of his campaign are sufficient answer to all of his complaints."[68]

So extensive, detailed, and complex had the operations of his department become as a result of the war that Jesup found his small office force entirely inadequate for the heavy duties that devolved upon it. Moreover, the burden was soon to be increased by demobilization, disposal of surplus property, settling of accounts and contracts, and all the other paperwork of winding up the war. He requested Marcy to apply to Congress for authority to hire six additional clerks to serve on a temporary basis.[69]

When peace was restored, the troops began evacuating Mexico City and returning to Vera Cruz for the trip back to the United States by sea. Both land and water transportation had to be provided by Jesup's department for an army of more than forty thousand, including some five thousand civilian employees. Volunteers and civilian workers were returned to their homes and regulars were sent to the posts and stations assigned to them in the United States and in the territories acquired by the war. Under an economy measure adopted by the administration following the landing at Vera Cruz, vessels that had been chartered to transport troops and supplies to Mexico were discharged from the public service. Now, a year later, Jesup's department had to charter and assemble another fleet of transports to remove the troops from Vera Cruz, Tampico, and the Brazos. Major Swords, selected by Jesup as general superintendent of embarkation, reported that by August the last vessels had been loaded and Vera Cruz had been evacuated by the United States Army.[70]

Considerable quantities of surplus property were in the hands of quartermasters in Mexico at the close of the war. Jesup directed them to sell at Vera Cruz and other posts in Mexico all property that was damaged or could not be readily transported to the United States, excepting animals and wagons. All serviceable wagons and sound, well-broken horses and mules were to be brought back for use at the various posts and stations. As did all its other operations, the disposal of surplus property subjected the Quartermaster's Department to unjust criticism. Many false rumors and reports were circulated. For example, when Maj. Osborn Cross, who was in charge of the sales at Vera Cruz, reported that he had disposed of some teams for $137,799, rumors were widely circulated in New Orleans that the sale had netted a mere $7,000. Cross noted, "I mention these facts to show that unprincipled persons are ever found ready to spread reports prejudicial to the character of government agents."[71]

Although most of the ships participating in the evacuation program were chartered, the Quartermaster's Department still owned a large fleet of vessels that had been required for its far-flung operations during the war. Only a limited number of them would be needed by the army in peacetime, and there was little prospect of selling them at even half their value. Consequently, Jesup recommended that after selecting those adaptable to military needs, the best of the remainder be transferred to the Navy and Treasury Departments. The others were to be sold. The disposition plan was adopted by the War Department. Previously, on orders of Marcy, the steam propellors *Massachusetts* and *Edith* had been sent to the Pacific with troops and stores, along with four sailing vessels to be used as transports on the coast of California and Oregon. The quartermaster general retained for his department five steamers for operations on the coast of Florida, three for service on the Rio Grande, and three schooners for transports on the Gulf of Mexico. Twenty-two steamers and nineteen sailing vessels were transferred to the Navy, one schooner to the Treasury Department for coast survey, and one bark and two schooners to the Topographical Engineers.[72]

Casualties among officers in Jesup's department were unusually severe during the war. Five died of disease, three were killed, one lost an arm; most of the others suffered from the effects of yellow fever and other diseases caused by exposure to the climate. The health of several officers was so impaired that they could no longer perform useful duty but were carried on the rolls until they died, since no retirement system for age or disability had yet been established. In addition to Col. Trueman Cross, those killed were Capts. William Armstrong and Benjamin F. Graham. Among those who died was Captain Hetzel, who accompanied Jesup to Mexico, assisted him in preparing for Scott's campaign, and organized the depot at Vera Cruz. When Scott began his march into the interior, Hetzel remained in charge of the depot "until worn out by labor and broken down by disease, he was obliged to quit his post, and died [20 July 1847] on his way to join his family." Maj. Henry Smith, who took charge of the depot when Hetzel became ill, died of yellow fever a short time later. Captain Irwin, chief quartermaster with Scott's army, also succumbed to the fever on 10 January 1848. The other quartermaster officers who died of disease were Capts. William Churchill and Robert Fenner. Jesup recommended that Secretary Marcy appeal to Congress to assist the families of those who lost their lives in the war.[73]

Three new states—Iowa, Texas, and Wisconsin—were admitted to the Union during the war; Florida had been added in 1845. The new territories created from the area ceded by Mexico vastly expanded the United States. In the period following the war, national defense became primarily a matter of protecting frontier areas and the wagon trains of emigrants joining the westward movement. As army troops moved in to protect the distant frontiers, the long lines of communication and supply through undeveloped regions greatly increased the problems and responsibilities of General Jesup.

CHAPTER 12

LAST YEARS
OF A LONG CAREER

BEFORE THE MEXICAN War, the furthermost western army posts extended from the Gulf of Mexico to Lake Superior, and they were located on or near navigable water. All were easy of access; because they were in or close to populous, well-cultivated areas, they could be readily and cheaply supplied. In 1844, the entire cost of transporting army troops and supplies had amounted to less than $120,000. With the acquisition of Texas and the Territories of California and New Mexico and the stationing of troops in them and in Oregon, the new outposts were on the Rio Grande, the Gila River, the Pacific Coast, the Columbia River, and on Puget Sound. The agricultural resources of the new frontier had been only partially developed. Further development was hampered by the hostile disposition of the Indians in some areas and by the discovery of gold in California in 1848, which led many to desert their land in search of the precious metal. Consequently, supplies as well as troops for the new frontier had to be transported from older parts of the country over long land and water routes at enormous expense. Long wagon trains were constantly on the move through undeveloped areas to new outposts, while vessels traveled around Cape Horn from Atlantic ports with troops, building materials, forage, and other supplies for California and Oregon. By 1850, the cost of military transportation had increased to more than $2 million, or 1,500 percent more than in 1844, though the army's size had increased only about 50 percent.[1]

Military construction costs also soared as more and more troops arrived to garrison the numerous posts on the new frontier. Records in the adjutant general's office show that in fiscal year 1850, 6,385 officers and men were stationed at sixty-seven posts west of the Mississippi, as compared to only 2,109 at thirty-three posts east of the Mississippi. The ratio of troops on the western frontier to those in the East became greater each year during the remainder of Jesup's life. Expenditures by his department for the erection of barracks, storehouses, and other military buildings increased proportionately. In fiscal year 1851, more than $451,000 was spent on construction and repairs—three times the amount appropriated for military structures in fiscal year 1844. In fact, the entire amount expended by the Quartermaster's Department for all of its operations in that prewar year was only $871,000. By 1850 these expenditures had increased fivefold.[2]

In his annual reports, Jesup called attention to these rising costs and the urgent need for larger appropriations to meet them. He pointed out that Indian hostilities in Florida and Texas as well as New Mexico required constant and active employment of troops as though a state of war existed, thus adding to the heavy expenditures. He recommended that, as a means of promoting efficiency and economy, prompt action be taken to improve rivers and harbors and to construct good roads on the shortest and best routes to and between frontier posts. Such measures, he observed, "would be worth infinitely more, in the defence of the frontier, than any system of fortification." Military activities resulting from the extension of the frontier, he noted, required the utilization of many laborers, teamsters, mechanics, and other classes of workers. They were being hired, in some instances, at exorbitant wages; with no legal means of controlling them, they often performed their work badly. He proposed, once more, that legal provision be made to enlist these workers in the army for at least two years so that they could be brought under military regulations.[3]

Congress displayed little interest in, or appreciation of, the problems Jesup and his department faced in providing support for troops on the distant frontier. It was more concerned with returning the army to its prewar status and in reducing, rather than increasing, War Department expenditures. Between November 1847 and November 1848, Congress trimmed the size of the regular army from 21,686 officers and men to 10,035. With such a vast territory to be defended, so many more remote posts to be garrisoned and supplied, and hostile Indians to be combated, the troops were spread dangerously thin by the sharp reduction. President Polk shared the views of the economy-minded Congress. In his last year in the White House he reduced Jesup's estimates of expenditures for fiscal year 1850 by more than $900,000, despite the quartermaster general's insistence that the figures he had submitted were based on minimum requirements. As a result, Jesup's appropriation was all but exhausted three months before the fiscal year ended, and he warned that without additional funds he would be unable to meet the large drafts of the quartermasters in New Mexico and on the Pacific Coast. His warning went unheeded; Congress did nothing about a deficiency appropriation. The fiscal year closed with large arrearages.[4]

The financial status of Jesup's department was destined to grow worse before it improved. On 4 November 1850, the quartermaster general presented his estimates for fiscal year 1852, along with a letter explaining the requirements. A week later, at the request of the secretary of war, he submitted another report showing the yearly expenditures of his department from 1844 through 1849, along with estimates for 1851 and 1852. The House Ways and Means Committee of the 31st Congress, apparently misled by a mistake on the part of a member who misinterpreted the data supplied by Jesup in the two reports, cut in half his estimates for the fiscal year ending 30 June 1852.[5] Since the funds appropriated by Congress were based on the estimates as reduced by the committee, this error resulted in another large deficit.

Aroused by what he considered an unmerited rebuke and by the continued failure of Congress to appropriate sufficient funds to cover the mounting costs, Jesup determined to bring the problems of his department more forcefully to the attention of Congress and the public in his published annual reports. Since he had no control over the purposes for which the money was being spent, he pointed out, he could exercise little control over the expenditures. Reducing estimates did not reduce the requirements nor the amount of money needed to meet them. Unless the government revised its objectives and lessened the demands upon his department, he emphasized, to reduce his estimates was an exercise in futility, for the reduction merely produced deficits and embarrassed the service without saving any money. He explained in detail the reasons for the growth of his department's activities and skillfully analyzed the various factors contributing to the increased costs. He was aided in this analysis by the full reports he had requested from his principal subordinates in the field. So adroitly did he present the facts that before the end of his administration he was gradually winning the battle of appropriations.

In the face of reduced appropriations, Charles M. Conrad, appointed secretary of war by President Fillmore in August 1850, exercised a much tighter control over expenditures than had been the case in previous years. He prohibited Jesup and the heads of other disbursing agencies from making any contract for more than $2,000 without his approval. When the assistant quartermaster at Benicia, California, submitted an estimate for military structures requested by commanding officers in the Pacific Division (California and Oregon) that would cost more than $2 million, the secretary termed it "reckless extravagance." He promptly issued a directive that no barracks or other buildings were to be constructed without his specific order, "except such as are indispensably necessary for the immediate and temporary accommodation of the troops," and that barracks were to be of the "cheapest kind." He called for the zealous cooperation of all officers to accomplish a more rigid economy.[6]

Jesup, too, was deeply concerned over the sharply mounting costs. He made concerted efforts to reduce expenditures consistent with the requirements of his department. Early in 1851 he dispatched Assistant Quartermaster General Henry Whiting on a tour of inspection of the 8th Military Department (Texas) with instructions and authority to correct all abuses or extravagances that he might find there. He sent Lt. Col. Thomas Swords to the 9th Military Department (New Mexico) on a like mission, and he issued similar instructions to quartermasters in California and Oregon. None of these officers uncovered any such abuses as Secretary Conrad suspected might exist, but they did recommend certain economies. At their suggestion, and with the cooperation of the commanding generals, Jesup ordered the discharge of civilian mechanics and laborers and the detailing of soldiers to perform their duties. Among other changes instituted was the adoption of new packaging methods to reduce the weight of supplies shipped. Clothing, for example, which formerly had been shipped to western posts in ironbound wooden boxes and tierces, was now baled and transported in bundles. Jesup also ordered rents reduced wherever possible. Some savings did result from measures such as these, but they were of a relatively minor nature.[7]

The greatest economy was achieved in the field of transportation—the most costly item in the department's budget. After closely scrutinizing transportation costs, Jesup was convinced that to hire contractors to transport military supplies in civilian wagons would be cheaper than to continue using government-owned wagons. The system would also be less complicated and troublesome. The army had always found it difficult to obtain qualified wagon-masters and teamsters, and those it hired often demanded exorbitant wages. Moreover, the men were undependable, since no military control could be exercised over them. New wagons had to be constantly procured and old ones repaired. Equipment required replacements. Animals had to be fed and cared for year-round whether they were in use or not, and extra animals must be kept on hand to replace exhausted ones. The cost of forage—the counterpart in that era of gasoline in the motor-vehicle age—was high. As Jesup had foreseen, the system of contract freighting proved much more economical than the overland transportation of military supplies by army wagons, and it was adopted on a wide scale.[8]

Jesup also concluded that to hire privately owned ships for water transportation was more economical than to maintain government transports. Consequently, he directed early in 1851 that most of the steamboats and sailing vessels owned by his department be sold and that military stores be transported by public conveyances. Little need remained for the vessels which had been operating in the Gulf of Mexico and on the Rio Grande now that the Mexican War had ended and the threat of Indian hostilities in Florida was diminished.[9] Some of the transports owned by his department had been sent to the Pacific Coast following the war, but they were soon found to be too expensive to operate. The lure of the gold fields made it extremely difficult to hire crews, even at fantastic wages. As a result, Jesup instructed quartermasters to charter vessels for coastwise transportation, as was done in the case of ships carrying troops and supplies to California and Oregon from Atlantic ports.

The shift from government wagons to those furnished by contractors greatly reduced the number of public teams needed at army posts. Strangely, it did not reduce the number of animals that had to be procured. Between 1845 and 1851, the mounted force of the army nearly doubled, and the number of animals (horses, mules, and oxen) in the Quartermaster's Department increased nearly tenfold, from 846 to about 8,000. Some of these animals were required for transporting baggage, rations, and supplies when troops were transferred to new stations, as they frequently were, and on marches against marauding Indians. Horses were also used for escort duty and express messenger service. Although fewer draft animals had to be purchased for pulling wagons, the big increase in mounted troops required the purchase of more horses. So constantly were mounted troops employed in pursuing Indians and protecting settlements on the new frontier that from one-fourth to one-third of their horses had to be replaced each year.[10]

This hard usage and careless handling of horses by the troops was a source of concern to Jesup. Again he exhibited his foresight. In November of 1853, he proposed the creation of a veterinary corps to serve under the surgeon general. (His suggestion came sixty-three years before such a corps was eventually established on 3 June 1916.) The amount of money spent each year for replacing horses and mules lost through the lack of proper veterinary aid, he contended, would finance the operations of such a corps for two or three years. In 1856, he again recommended the establishment of such a corps, and also of a veterinary school where candidates for the corps, as well as dragoon officers, mounted riflemen, and light artillery officers, could receive instruction in the care, management, and diseases of horses and mules.[11] Neither the secretary of war nor Congress was ready for that innovation.

For many years, Jesup had strongly advocated the building of canals and better roads as well as the dredging of rivers to improve lines of communication. By 1852, he recognized that the nature of the country to be traversed made railroads the only practical system for better and more rapid transportation to the West. He proposed that a central railroad be constructed from some point on the Mississippi through Arkansas to the western frontier of Texas on the Rio Grande. He recommended also a line from the frontier of Missouri westward at least as far as Fort Riley on the

Kansas River. Other railways, he suggested, should be built eastward from the Pacific Coast to connect with those projected westward from the Mississippi. "In a military point of view, apart from all other consideration," he declared, "these works would be more important than any other in which the government should engage. They are national; are necessary to bind our distant possessions together to enable us, in the advent of war with a great maritime power, to supply our troops and defend our possessions on the Pacific." [12]

Jesup was not the first to advocate a transcontinental railroad. For several years, there had been considerable agitation for such a project. The North and South agreed on its necessity, but their views regarding the route were nearly as divergent as those over the slavery question. On 3 March 1853, Congress added a special fund to the army appropriation bill to finance an extensive survey of the country between the Mississippi and the Pacific Coast to determine the region through which a railroad could be most easily built. Jesup's department furnished the supplies and transportation for the military and scientific parties. [13] Although they surveyed five routes and obtained valuable geographical and scientific data, no decision was reached because of the great sectional rivalry. Not until after the southern states seceded was the impasse resolved.

The nomadic Indians presented a constant source of danger to army troops and emigrants in the settling of the West. These Indians had followed and subsisted upon the great herds of buffalo that once roamed the plains east of the Rocky Mountains. Now, by the wanton destruction practiced by white hunters, the number of buffalo was rapidly diminishing, though in the summer of 1847, Quartermaster Thomas Swords and Gen. Stephen W. Kearny on their way back from California saw large numbers of them at the junction of the north and south forks of the Platte River. "It was estimated a million could be seen in one view," Swords reported. [14] As their accustomed means of subsistence grew scarcer, the Indians became more warlike and were compelled to fight or steal to avoid starvation. Supply trains were particularly vulnerable to their attacks. Jesup, who at various times had fought with and against Indians, was sympathetic to their plight but foresaw no improvement in the situation "unless we feed or exterminate the Indians, or prevail upon them to settle down as cultivators of the soil." He expressed his concern for the Indians when he authorized the construction of new barracks at Fort Washita, Arkansas. If it were necessary to go into the Indian country to obtain timber for the buildings, he advised, "the Indians should be consulted, their consent obtained, and a fair compensation paid to them."[15]

Problems involved in supplying the new frontier, failure of Congress to provide him with adequate funds for his greatly expanded operations, and the crippling effect of the rigid economy program were all causes of vexation and strain for Jesup as the decade of the 1850s began. His difficulties were heightened by the impact of the "spoils system" upon his department. In addition to being a strict advocate of rigid economy in War Department operations, Secretary Conrad was also a believer in dispensing patronage to faithful supporters of the Whig party. In the days before government employees were protected by civil service regulations, the practice of rewarding loyal party workers with lucrative positions had been rather common. In many cases, party service was often their only qualification. Those who occupied the positions in question were removed without regard to their capabilities or length of service. Jesup's department had been remarkably free from the effects of the spoils system. The politically minded Conrad, however, was quick to discover the potentials at the Schuylkill Arsenal near Philadelphia, the large quartermaster clothing and equipage center with its manufacturing facilities. Soon after taking office he ordered the removal of four veteran employees there and their replacement by Whigs.[16] Since none of these positions had been created by law, Jesup was helpless to do anything about it.

Deputy Quartermaster General Henry Stanton, longtime director of quartermaster operations at Philadelphia, complained bitterly about the replacement of his highly qualified workers "by inexperienced party favorites." The loss of skilled employees through "political barbarism," he declared, would create chaos in his operations. "Who could or would attempt the labor of instructing these upstarts?" he asked. When Conrad became aware of Stanton's protests, he reacted angrily. He ordered the veteran officer removed from the key post at Philadelphia and transferred to St. Louis. The transfer was, in effect, a "demotion" for Stanton. Jesup had no choice but to relieve Stanton. He instructed Maj. George H. Crosman to replace him. Jesup was distressed by the transfer order, which gave him "infinite pain." Fearful that this loyal officer who had been one of his most trusted assistants for thirty-two years might resign from the army, he urged Assistant Quartermaster General Whiting in New York to counsel Stanton not to act hastily. Whiting obviously was successful in that mission, for Stanton wrote from New York late in February that he would leave for St. Louis as soon as he had finished settling his accounts.[17]

The only major military operation during the last decade of Jesup's administration was the Mormon expedition, which began in 1857 when the Mormons, led by Brigham Young, refused to obey federal laws. This undertaking demonstrated the difficult logistical problems involved in campaigning on the western plains at this early period. President James Buchanan ordered a force of about twenty-five hundred to assemble at Fort Leavenworth under Col. Albert Sidney Johnston and march to the Utah Territory. Jesup's department furnished the supplies and transportation for the expedition, and Jesup selected the quartermasters to accompany the troops. He also sent Assistant Deputy Quartermaster General Charles Thomas to St. Louis and Fort Leavenworth to superintend supply arrangements. The objective of the expedition was to establish a military department in the Utah Territory and subdue the Mormons by a show of force. But when the troops approached the territory on 4 October, the Mormons made an unexpected attack upon their trains, destroying seventy-five wagons carrying rations and other supplies.[18] This loss and the lateness of the season compelled Colonel Johnston to take winter quarters at Fort Bridger, Wyoming, thirty-five miles distant. A heavy snowstorm raged for days, so impeding the movement of the troops that they did not arrive at the fort for fifteen days. With forage unavailable, horses, mules, and oxen died by the hundreds from starvation and cold. Faced with a scarcity of food as well as other hardships, the troops spent a grim winter.

Before any movement could be undertaken in the spring, they had to be resupplied and reinforced. Animals and reinforcements for the expedition were obtained from New Mexico by Capt. Randolph B. Marcy of the 5th Infantry and about forty volunteers who made an incredible winter's journey for that purpose. Jesup's department in the meantime had arranged for the transportation of men and supplies from Fort Leavenworth to Utah and to depots at Forts Kearny and Laramie.[19] When the expedition, adequately equipped and provisioned, resumed its march to Salt Lake City in

June of 1858, it met with no resistance. Peace commissioners appointed by President Buchanan had obtained a pledge from Mormon leaders to obey federal laws and not resist the army. By then, two important logistic developments had occurred: army wagons were being constructed with interchangeable parts, and army supplies could be transported to St. Louis by railroad from such eastern cities as New York and Philadelphia.

Under Jesup's guidance the Quartermaster's Department functioned smoothly. In the years following the Mexican War, the number of reports the quartermaster general had to prepare and the amount of paperwork required for efficient and meticulous operations apparently placed a heavy burden on an understaffed department. Jesup never spared himself in carrying out his workload. As early as the winter of 1850–1851, his fatiguing work schedule kept him so closely confined to his desk that his health was again being undermined. "I have been too much occupied to take my accustomed exercises," he wrote to his daughter, Mary Blair. "I am compelled to be at my office every night and every Sunday."

He was disturbed, too, by reports from West Point that his eldest son, William, appointed a cadet by President Taylor, displayed no interest in an army career and was determined to resign from the Academy. The seventeen-year-old youth had become "a source of the greatest anxiety as well as mortification" to the general.[20] When his son's resignation was accepted, Jesup obtained a leave of absence. He wanted a few months away from his official duties to go to Kentucky to regain his health and take care of personal matters. Leaving his office in charge of Deputy Quartermaster General Charles Thomas, Jesup, accompanied by William, left the city on 28 May 1851 for a trip that was to last most of the summer.

In contrast to the long and tedious journey by riverboat and stagecoach in the earlier days, much of the journey to Kentucky could now be made by railroad, for great strides had been made in improving the country's transportation system. Jesup and his son took a leisurely and restful trip to the north, going first by railroad to New York and then on to Albany and Buffalo. From Buffalo they traveled to Cleveland by water on the most luxuriously furnished steamboat the general had ever seen. The lounge was adorned with mirrors; the chairs, sofas, and ottomans were covered with rich velvet. He had especially desired to see Cleveland, where near-ly four decades earlier he had directed the construction of boats to transport Harrison's army across Lake Erie. He was amazed at the growth and the "almost magical" changes that had taken place since he was last there. The two stayed in a "splendid" hotel five stories high. Their parlor and the two bedrooms opening into it were furnished in the "best" manner. While serving in a command post at Cleveland with Harrison's army, "the only room I could obtain for quarters and office was the attic of a one story frame building, about fifteen feet square, and this was given me as a per-sonal favor, as well as a mark of distinction, I being the command-ing officer," he wrote his daughter.[21]

From Cleveland they traveled to Cincinnati by railroad, with a stop-off at Columbus to change trains. The "cars," as trains were then called, left Cleveland at 11 A.M. and arrived in Cincinnati at 11 o'clock that night, making the trip of nearly three hundred miles in twelve hours—an almost incredible speed in those days. Jesup and his son took passage on a river steamboat for the last leg of their trip, reaching Louisville on 12 June.

On previous visits to Kentucky, Jesup's first destination had been Locust Grove. Now, those who had made such visits enjoyable were gone. The familiar figure of Dr. John Croghan, who had always been waiting to greet him, was missing. He had died early in 1849, only three days after his brother, Col. George Croghan, had succumbed to cholera in New Orleans.[22] William, the last of the brothers, had died the following year at his home in Pittsburgh. For Jesup, their passing marked the end of an era dating back more than twenty-eight years to his courtship of Ann Heron Croghan.

Aside from restoring his health, Jesup had two major objec-tives during his long stay in Kentucky. He wished to settle on behalf of his children the affairs of the estates they had inherited from members of the Croghan family, including their share of the Mammoth Cave property. Jesup met with his attorney and agent, Senator Joseph Underwood, who had been appointed a trustee under the terms of Doctor Croghan's will.[23] Jesup obviously was concerned with putting all family affairs in good order. At the same time, he looked into the possibility of enlarging his own estate through the purchase of additional property.

His other objective was to provide a means of livelihood for his son William. With this goal in mind, he entered into a five-year partnership on 30 August 1851 with James E. Jesup, the son of his brother Samuel. James was to operate the general's large farm in Todd County, near Elkton, Kentucky, under an arrangement similar to the one which formerly had existed between Jesup and his brother. William was to live with James and serve as his assistant, "for the purpose of being instructed in the business of planting and farming."[24] During his stay in Todd County, the general divided 650 acres of land adjoining his farm among the six children of his deceased brother William and arranged to pay for the schooling and other expenses of his brother's two youngest daughters. He also obligated himself to provide a 150-acre farm for his widowed sister, Mrs. Sarah Jesup Wilson, and her children.[25]

Jesup arrived back in Washington on 15 September, after an absence of 111 days. There, leaders of the country still hoped that the bitter debate over the slavery question would be tempered by the provisions of Clay's Compromise of 1850. Yet that measure did not quiet sectional strife. Northern Abolitionists were becoming increasingly active and Southern radicals were still talking about seceding from the Union. Opposing viewpoints were aired wherever people gathered. On board the train returning from Kentucky, Jesup had found himself in the midst of a group of South Carolina secessionists. While the quartermaster general owned a few slaves and was a strong believer in states' rights, he shared the view of the late President Taylor and many others born in the South that the Union had to be preserved at all costs. He debated the subject with the South Carolinians. Secession, he told them heatedly, was "the doctrine of cowardice."[26]

Jesup apparently believed that Clay's Compromise of 1850 had prevented a civil war. He expressed his views in a letter to the Society of Tammany, founded in New York after the Revolution to preserve the new experiment in democracy. Official duties prevented his attending in 1852 the anniversary celebration of the society's founding. Providence, he wrote, had confided in the American people the mission of demonstrating that man was capable of self-government. "In the severe ordeal through which they have recently passed [that is, the debate culminating in the Compromise of 1850] they have shown themselves worthy depositors of that high trust. Recognizing the broad principle which lies at the bottom of our institutions, the Union can be maintained successfully only in the spirit in which it originated; . . . the constitution has come out of the conflict strengthened by the shocks to which it has been subjected."[27]

Jesup's belief, shared by many at the time, that Clay's Compromise of 1850 had prevented any serious rupture between the North and the South, was shaken early in 1854 by the enactment of the Kansas–Nebraska Act which repealed the Missouri Compromise of 1820, with its restrictions on slavery. This act precipitated a desperate struggle, reviving all the sectional bitterness over the extension of slavery that had been moderated four years earlier. Tensions continued to mount throughout the rest of Jesup's lifetime.

Through the decade of the 1850s, Jesup administered the Quartermaster's Department under the last four presidents before the Civil War. Millard Fillmore, who succeeded to the presidency upon the death of Zachary Taylor, was denied his bid for a full term in office, and the Democrats returned to the White House with the election of Franklin Pierce. A dejected Winfield Scott, who had been the standard-bearer for the Whigs, moved his army headquarters back to New York.[28] Pierce appointed Jefferson Davis as his secretary of war. Two decades earlier, Davis, a graduate of West Point, had been in Jesup's department as an assistant quartermaster at Fort Winnebago in what was then Michigan Territory. It was he who sought to lessen transportation costs in the Quartermaster's Department by attempting to use camels to carry military supplies across the arid regions of the Southwest—an experiment that failed.[29] The Democrats rejected Pierce's bid for reelection in 1856, selecting instead a prominent conservative bachelor, James Buchanan. Upon his election, Buchanan appointed John B. Floyd of Virginia to succeed Jefferson Davis.

Oddly, the last four secretaries of war under whom Jesup served joined the Confederacy. John B. Floyd was a brigadier general; George W. Crawford, who had served under President Taylor, presided over the Georgia State Secession Convention in 1861; Charles M. Conrad served in the first and second Confederate Congresses; and Jefferson Davis was president of the Confederacy. Jesup himself, though Southern born and a states'-rights advocate, would no doubt have remained loyal to the North, had his life been spared. Years later, in 1872, Henry C. Wayne of Georgia, who served in the Quartermaster's Department during and following the Mexican

War and then as a brigadier general in the Confederate army, wrote to Col. Lorenzo Sitgreaves, Jesup's son-in-law. Wayne outlined the plan he said the quartermaster general had devised for combating secession, which he so strongly opposed: "His plan, as he repeatedly detailed to me, was to have guarded the line of the Susquehanna, blockaded the Southern ports, raised an army of three hundred thousand men, and with a powerful fleet at Cincinnati and elsewhere in the West, descended the Mississippi river to New Orleans, thus cutting the confederacy in two—breaking its backbone . . . and then reduce the Atlantic States." The course of the war, Wayne wrote, demonstrated the wisdom of Jesup's plan: "Not until Hallecks's fine strategy threw Sidney Johnston from Kentucky upon Corinth [was] any serious impression . . . made upon the Confederacy."[30]

As a strong supporter of the Union, Jesup was disturbed by the growing tensions engendered by the controversy over slavery during the closing years of his life. He was also concerned with the need to provide security for his family, and the Panic of 1857 brought additional strain. It rendered his property in Louisville "almost worthless."[31] The burden of his official duties was made no lighter by the failure of Congress to recognize the activity of the army and Jesup's responsibility for supporting it. Army troops were constantly in action by reason of the continued hostility of the Indians on the southern and Mexican borders. "To call ours a peace establishment," as Congress was given to referring to the army when considering appropriation measures, "is a mere abuse of terms," Secretary Floyd declared in his annual report in December of 1859. The army strength at that time was approximately seventeen thousand five hundred, but only about eleven thousand were available for duty at the 130 permanent garrisons, posts, and camps scattered over an area of three million square miles. By then, officers in Jesup's department were limited to four years of duty at one station or on an assignment, unless "the interest of the public service make a change advisable."[32]

During the last decade of his life, as the country drifted toward war between North and South, Jesup wrote a number of letters to friends concerning his views on public questions, some of which were published in the newspapers. A friend, Henry D. Gilpin of Philadelphia, a former solicitor of the United States treasury and later U.S. attorney general, expressed regret that their publication was restricted to newspapers. He thought that because they were "free from party spirit or personal prejudice," the letters should be preserved as a valuable contribution to the political history of the country: "Your opportunities have been so many and your candour towards individuals so much a part of your nature, that I hope the few articles we have seen . . . from your pen, are evidence that you have been preparing many other memorials."[33]

One letter appeared in the Washington *Daily Union* in October 1856 under the heading, "General Jesup's Letter on the Restriction of Slavery in the Territories." It discussed the historical events in the highly critical period leading up to the Missouri Compromise, which Jesup referred to as the "Missouri Capitulation." As a firm believer in strict construction of the Constitution, Jesup maintained that in enacting the compromise, Congress had exceeded its constitutional authority.

His letter reviewed the situation during President Monroe's administration when Missouri had applied in 1818 for admission to the Union. Any attempt to expand the country in that period, he observed, became entangled with the slavery question. If Missouri was admitted either with or without restriction on slavery, her admission would destroy the even balance that then existed between the number of free and slave states. It could also determine the fate of slavery in the remainder of the territory purchased from France in 1803. Louisiana had been admitted as a slave state in 1812. North and South could not agree upon a settlement; neither could House and Senate. During the long and spirited debate, Maine, then a part of Massachusetts, requested admission as a free state. So intense and bitter was the sectional strife that it brought forth open talk of dissolving the Union.

Jesup described the excitement as greater than any he had ever witnessed either in or outside of Congress: "Timid men . . . were quailing; the representatives of foreign nations at Washington, as well as many of our own people, believed our confederacy was to be broken up in a few months; and even some of the boldest and ablest statesmen doubted whether the ship of State would be able to weather the storm then raging."

At the height of this alarming crisis, "when all but a few gallant spirits were desponding," Senator Jesse B. Thomas of Illinois proposed an amendment to the Missouri bill which came to be known as the Missouri Compromise. The bill, as finally approved, admitted

Missouri without restriction but excluded slavery from all territory in the Louisiana Territory north of latitude thirty-six degrees and thirty minutes not included within Missouri. As a part of the compromise, Maine was admitted as a free state, making twelve free and twelve slave states. Monroe, according to Jesup, was opposed to the bill and inclined to veto it, but members of his cabinet, "though they differed as to the constitutional right of Congress to pass such a bill," advised that it be approved as "the only measure by which civil war could be averted." Following its passage, Jesup wrote, "There was a temporary lull in the fierce excitement aroused by the attempt to restrict a State—an excitement which, had the people become as rash and unwise as some of their representatives . . . would have shattered the Union into fragments."

The settlement of the question, Jesup declared, was a capitulation forced by the North upon the South. In his view, if Congress had the right to pass the Missouri Compromise, it became a mere act of legislation that could be repealed by a later Congress. Any other view would have made it an amendment of the Constitution, which would have required the approval of two-thirds of the states. Arguing from his states'-rights view, Jesup held that the compromise was not binding upon anybody, because "it was a subject not within the sphere of national legislation." On the other hand, viewed as a compromise, he considered it "an interpolation into the constitution, by an incompetent body of a principle not sanctioned by the States and the people." From either viewpoint, he considered the Missouri Compromise void. All territories possessed by the United States had been acquired by treaties, he said, which provided for their admission into the Union according to the principles of the Constitution. Thus they would enter on an equal footing with the original states and with such constitutions as the people of the respective territories presented, whether or not they authorized slavery. If the territories were republican, he contended, they should be admitted as states. If not, the spirit of the Constitution would be violated.[34]

On the day Jesup's letter was printed, the *Daily Union*, in an editorial, directed the attention of its readers to this "very interesting and instructive" document. The editor pointed out that Jesup's long connection with the government and his intimate relations with all the distinguished statesmen of the country since 1812 had presented him opportunities which few had enjoyed:

"He possesses, therefore, a rich store of information derived from personal observation, and from his associations with the distinguished political actors, from which he has drawn the materials for the letter."

At the time of the Missouri Compromise in 1820, John Marshall was chief justice of the Supreme Court, a position to which he had been appointed in 1801. Since he served until his death on 6 July 1835, he was chief justice for the first seventeen years that Jesup was quartermaster general. Marshall was a broad constructionist of the Constitution. Thus his beliefs ran counter to those of the quartermaster general and other strict constructionists. Jesup expressed his opinion of Marshall in a letter in December of 1856 to William Henry Chase.

> Chief Justice Marshall, in his admiration of the English constitutional system, went to his grave, I believe, without fully comprehending ours; and I think he did more in his long judicial course than any other man who has lived to give a wrong direction to our institutions. His great abilities, undoubted patriotism and purity of character have clustered such a prestige about his name as to sanctify all his errors. Had he been a rogue like Bacon and Coke, the bar and the courts would have taken his law in the purity of its principles, and have discarded his errors; but now such is the influence of his name, that place his opinions on the one side, and the ten commandments on the other, and the chance is the gentlemen of the law would take his opinions as their guide, and repudiate the ten commandments.[35]

Jesup wrote Chase that his paper on the "Missouri Capitulation" had been published at the urgent request of many of his friends. His views on the powers of Congress under the Constitution would not, he was sure, be acceptable to latitudinarians anywhere. "But," he added, "I am satisfied with them myself; and as they express the opinion which I held in my youth, and have held through a tolerably long life, I shall probably carry them to my grave, for I am too old now to change them."

Jesup's views, like those of many another westerner, embraced contradictory positions. On the one hand, he was a firm believer in states' rights; on the other, he was a strong supporter of the Union.

Though he favored strict construction of the Constitution, he rejected vigorously any thought of secession. As a western expansionist, he strongly believed throughout his career that the United States should acquire Cuba—by one means or another. As a young officer in 1816, he had wanted to lead an expedition to take possession of Cuba by force, insisting that Cuba would be a valuable acquisition, because "it constitutes the key to all western America." Many years later, President Polk sought to buy Cuba, but Spain rejected his offer. During the 1850s, attempts were revived to acquire the island. This late recognition by public officials of the value of Cuba recalled to the minds of some of Jesup's old friends the views the quartermaster general had long held on the subject. One, Robert Patterson, a former comrade-in-arms in the War of 1812, commented, "It seems strange that after a lapse of near forty years, some of our distinguished statesmen should now come to the conclusion that you did then—and take some credit to themselves for their forethought."[36]

As has often been true of military officers in their later years, Jesup developed a keen interest in history. But when someone proposed in 1843, after he had been quartermaster general for a quarter of a century, that he write an autobiography, he declined. He had no desire to write the story of his life. He did not wish to incur, "and perhaps justly, the charge of an undue arrogance and vanity."[37]

More than a decade later, he decided to write not an autobiography but "two or three small volumes, memories of [his] own times, to consist of [his] correspondence on professional and political subjects, with enough of narrative to enable readers to understand the matters referred to." In a letter to William H. Chase in 1856 he noted that he had had advantages which few other men still living possessed. He had been so young when he entered public life that for many years he had worked with men who were fifteen to thirty years older than he. As a result he was perhaps "the only depository remaining of much of the most interesting portions of [America's] history from 1810 to the close of Mr. Monroe's administration." During the administrations of John Quincy Adams and Andrew Jackson, he had been in a position to make himself "acquainted with the concealed as well as the avowed motives and causes which have controlled public measures, as well as the course of public men." Jesup had earlier conceded that during the time of Monroe and of Jackson he had "had some influence," but none thereafter.[38]

Chase believed that Jesup ought to be relieved of the rigorous official duties which confined him to his "badly ventilated" office in the War Department so that he might devote time to his memoirs. "I should think that the admirable system which you have established for the administration of the great supply Department, not only for our present small army, but for future large ones, . . . ought to bring, in its perfection, comparative rest for you."[39]

Preparation of his proposed memoirs would depend upon his health, Jesup wrote in December of 1856. "The difficulty is I have materials enough for thirty volumes, and I hardly know how to select from such a mass . . . the most interesting or useful." Because of illness, he had been confined to his house for about six weeks, but was "as well now, perhaps, as [his] shattered lungs admit of [his] ever being again." About eighteen months later, in June of 1858, he informed his daughter, Jane Nicholson, that he was in communication with "Mr. Appleton" in New York relative to his memoirs; if he received encouragement, he would commence the arrangement of his papers at once but would not publish them without the prospect of realizing a reasonable profit: "I am too old to write for reputation merely." He continued to give thought to publishing his "memoirs," but the task appeared increasingly burdensome. In May of 1860, less than three weeks before his death, he wrote to a friend that although he had been careful to preserve his papers, "it would require many months of constant labour to collect and arrange them."[40] The valuable contribution he might have made in this field was lost.

Although time ran out before Jesup could record his "memoirs," he had always realized the importance of historical study. In educating his children, he had emphasized its value. When his two sons were teenagers, and he thought they had advanced beyond their elementary schooling, he wrote them a series of lengthy letters in the form of history lessons — "for your instruction, as well as for my own amusement." The letters, he felt, would "afford . . . some variety and in that way render the road to knowledge, if not shorter, at least more pleasant." No study was more instructive or more useful than history, he told his children. "It enables us to contemplate man in every situation and relation of life, to trace the improvements of society through every age from the most remote antiquity to the present time, to examine into the rise, progress and decline of nations; and often to discover the causes which have produced the astonishing changes and revolutions." A person well versed in history, could, without the infirmities of advanced age, avail himself of the accumulated experience and knowledge of all past ages and make them subservient to the improvement of his country and his times.

In a free country such as ours, he noted, every citizen has rights to defend and important duties to perform, and should qualify himself to understand his rights and perform his duties. In the United States, where the doors to public honors and public offices were thrown open to all "upon the broad principles of equal liberty," a profound knowledge of history was perhaps more necessary than in any country on the globe. "A careful study of history will convince you that the freedom as well as the prosperity of nations has from the dawn of history always been in proportion to the general diffusion of knowledge among them."[41]

The quartermaster general's interest in, and writings on, historical subjects came to the attention of officers of the Historical Society of Pennsylvania in Philadelphia. On 9 April 1855 they elected him a member of that society.[42]

Though his son William never profited from his suggestions, Jesup's younger son, Charles Edward, was studious and ambitious. "My dear boy," he wrote Charles when the latter was enrolled in a private school in New Haven, Connecticut, "I have every confidence in your principles, and I look forward to you as my hope and comfort of my old age, and if God spare your life, as the protector of your sisters when I am gone."[43] Charles entered the United States Military Academy at West Point on 1 July 1854 and was brevetted a second lieutenant in the 10th Infantry upon his graduation four years later. "There is a singular coincidence," Jesup wrote him, "between the commencement of your military career and mine. I was an applicant of the dragoons & appointed in the Infantry; and my first station was Newport, Kentucky. General George Rogers Clark was an officer of Infantry as was Colonel Croghan, and so were both of your grandfathers."[44] How heartbroken the general would have been had he known that nine months after his own death, one of his fondest dreams would be shattered when Charles was forced to resign from the army on account of an illness that proved fatal eight months later.[45]

By the end of 1856, death had overtaken the four distinguished officers Jesup had appointed as his chief assistants when he became quartermaster general in 1818. Trueman Cross had been killed by bandits in Mexico in 1846. Henry Whiting had died in 1851, and Henry Stanton and Thomas F. Hunt in 1856. All four were veterans of the War of 1812, as had been many of the other old-timers in the Quartermaster's Department. The younger officers who replaced them, nearly all graduates of West Point, would participate in the Civil War, some of them on the side of the South. Many of the junior officers doubtlessly looked with awe at the venerated General Jesup, who had headed the department for two score years and was still functioning in that capacity. Of the original bureau chiefs appointed in 1818 when Calhoun reorganized the War Department, only Generals Jesup and George Gibson remained. Gibson, thirteen years older than Jesup, continued to head the Subsistence Department until his death in 1861 at the age of eighty-six.

By 1856, Jesup's health was definitely impaired. During the next four years he was frequently away from his office for periods varying from a few days to three months. Nevertheless, he kept in close touch with the affairs of his department and continued to direct its operations. In the fall of 1859, he developed serious eye trouble and, accompanied by his daughter Julia, went to New York to undergo an operation. During most of the next three months, from October through December, he was confined to his room with the curtains drawn. Almost daily one or the other of his two chief assistants in the department, Majs. Ebenezer S. Sibley and Henry Wayne, brought him dispatches and correspondence which required his decision or recommendation, and in that manner he directed operations from his home.[46] Except for one short period during the next five months, Jesup was actively engaged in the duties of his office, as he had been over a span of forty-two years. He also resumed his normal social activities and attended the opera with Julia in March and again in April. He signed his last official letter on 6 June 1860. On Saturday, 9 June, Jesup suffered a severe stroke at his home. At 8:45 the next morning he died in his seventy-second year, ending his long stewardship of the Quartermaster's Department and fifty-two years of army service.

"Thus has departed," Secretary Floyd announced to the army, "one of the few veterans remaining in the Regular Army of that gallant band who served in the War of 1812. A man long known, respected and beloved, alike for his sterling integrity, untiring devotion to business, constancy in friendship, and genial social qualities." Floyd instructed all military posts to fire "thirteen minute guns" at noon on the day after the receipt of his orders and to display the national flag at half-staff. He also directed all military officers to wear the prescribed badge of mourning for thirty days.[47]

"This brave officer, whose name is found conspicuous in our military annals," the *Daily National Intelligencer* noted, "was not more admirable as a soldier than he was estimable for his domestic and social virtues. . . . A grateful country must ever bear in honorable remembrance the services of the veteran soldier and gentleman, whose name and fame will go down to posterity as a portion of our brightest military records."[48]

Abbreviations

A&IG	Adjutant and Inspector General
AG	Adjutant General
AQMG	Assistant Quartermaster General
CGP	Commissary General of Purchases
CHS	Cincinnati Historical Society
DA	Department of the Army
DAB	*Dictionary of American Biography*
LC	Library of Congress
OIA	Office of Indian Affairs
OQMG	Office of the Quartermaster General
Ord	Ordnance
OSW	Office of the Secretary of War
PHS	The Historical Society of Pennsylvania
RG	Record Group
SW	Secretary of War
WCL	William Clements Library

Notes

Chapter 1
A Resolute Young Soldier

1. Lewis, Collins, *History of Kentucky*, (revised ed., two vols. in one, Covington, Ky., 1874), II, p. 586. [Hereafter cited as Collins.]
2. H. G. Jesup, *Edward Jessup and His Descendants* (Cambridge, 1887), pp. 108–09, 117, 149.
3. Collins, *History of Kentucky*, II, p. 586.
4. Painted by Samuel King, this portrait of Jesup was presented by his granddaughter, Mary Jesup Sitgreaves, to the Jesup–Blair Library on the grounds of the Washington Cathedral, Washington, D.C., where it hangs today.
5. Collins, *History of Kentucky*, II, p. 586.
6. 2 *Stat.*, 481 (Act of 12 Apr. 1808).
7. RG 107, OSW, Letters Received, J–44 (4) (3 June 1808).
8. Jesup Papers, vol. 1, f. 101 (To Eustis, 8 Feb. 1812). [Unless otherwise noted, all references to Jesup Papers are to those in the Manuscript Division, Library of Congress.]
9. CHS, Torrence Papers, Box 13, No. 12 (Jesup to James Findlay, 20 Feb. 1812).
10. Jesup Papers, vol. 1, f. 102 (To Judge Ethane A. Brown, 17 Feb. 1812). Brown was later governor of Ohio.
11. *Ibid.*, Box 15 (undated, no addressee shown). Likely Jesup was referring to the war with Mexico.
12. Edison V. Westrate, *Those Fatal Generals* (N.Y., 1936), p. 124.
13. Jesup Papers, Box 12, "Narrative of the Campaign which Terminated in the Surrender of Detroit," n.d. [Hereafter cited as Jesup, "Narrative."]
14. Richard B. McAfee, *History of the Late War in the Western Country* (Lexington, Ky., 1816), p. 53. [Hereafter cited as McAfee.]
15. Benson J. Lossing, *The Pictorial Field-Book of the War of 1812* (N.Y., 1869), p. 258. [Hereafter cited as Lossing.]
16. For his subsistence problems, see (1) Samuel Williams, "Two Western

Campaigns in the War of 1812," Ohio Valley Historical Series, *Miscellanies*, pp. 11–12. (2) Erna Risch, *Quartermaster Support of the Army: A History of the Corps, 1775–1939* (Washington, D.C., 1962), p. 155.

17. Jesup Papers, vol. 1, ff. 106–08 (draft of letter to an unidentified friend, 2 Aug. 1812).
18. Jesup, "Narrative."
19. *Ibid.*
20. *Ibid.*
21. Lt. Col. James Grant Forbes, *Report of the Trial of Brig. Gen. William Hull* (N.Y., 1814), p. 91.
22. WCL, Jesup Papers (Jesup to Brock, 18 Aug. 1812).
23. Alexander C. Casselman (ed.), *Richardson's War of 1812* (Toronto, 1902), pp. 70–76.
24. Jesup Papers, vol. 1, f. 109.
25. *Ibid.*, vol. 1, f. 113.
26. CHS, Torrence Papers, Box 13 (Jesup to James Findlay, 15 Dec. 1812).
27. Jesup Papers, vol. 1, f. 117 (To Gen. James Taylor, 28 Dec. 1812).
28. *Ibid.*, vol. 1, ff. 120–21 (4 Jan. 1813).
29. *Ibid.*, vol. 1, f. 122 (5 Jan. 1813).
30. *Ibid.*, vol. 1, f. 124 (26 Jan. 1813).
31. *Ibid.*, vol. 1, ff. 127–28 (To Col. William Duane, 5 Mar. 1813).
32. RG 107, OSW, Letters Sent, vol. 6, f. 310 (9 Mar. 1813).
33. (1) Jesup Papers, vol. 1, f. 131 (To Armstrong, 27 Mar. 1813); f. 143 (To Monroe, 28 Apr. 1813). (2) WCL, Jesup Papers (Mason to Jesup, 8 May 1813). John Mason was commissary general of prisoners.
34. Jesup Papers, vol. 1, f. 144 (To Dr. A. G. Goodlet in New Orleans, 30 Apr. 1813).
35. *Ibid.*, vol. 1, f. 153 (25 May 1813).
36. *Ibid.*, vol. 1, ff. 158–62, 164, 166, 169, 170.
37. *Ibid.*, vol. 1, f. 172 (26 July 1813).
38. See Lossing, p. 504.
39. See letter, photostatic copy in the Filson Club files from Draper MSS 3N175 (George Croghan to his father William Croghan, Sr., 11 Sept. 1813).
40. Jesup Papers, vol. 15, ff. 4108–10 (To Rep. F. W. Bowdon, 4 Oct. 1848).
41. *Ibid.*, vol. 15, ff. 4108–10 (To F. W. Bowdon, 4 Oct. 1848).
42. (1) WCL, Jesup Papers (Cass to Jesup, 8 Nov. 1813); (A&IG to Jesup, 2 Dec. 1813). (2) Jesup Papers, vol. 1, f. 1821. (3) Francis B. Heitman, *Historical Register and Dictionary of the United States Army* (2 vols., Washington, 1903), I, p. 573. [Hereafter cited as Heitman, *Historical Register.*]
43. Forbes, *Report of the Trial of Brig. Gen. William Hull*, pp. 87–98.
44. Jesup, "Narrative."

Chapter 2
Glory on the Battlefield

1. (1) Jesup Papers, vol. 1, ff. 183–92 ("Memoir of the Campaign on the Niagara"). [Hereafter cited as Jesup, "Memoir."] (2) *Memoirs of Lieut.-General Scott* (2 vols., N.Y., 1864), I, pp. 117–20. [Hereafter cited as Scott, *Memoirs.*] (3) This account of the Niagara campaign is based primarily on Jesup's "Memoir."
2. (1) Jesup, "Memoir." (2) Scott, *Memoirs*, I, pp. 122–23.
3. Lossing, p. 805.
4. Scott, *Memoirs*, I, pp. 127–28.
5. Jesup, "Memoir."
6. Lossing, p. 810.
7. *National Intelligencer*, 27 July 1814 (Scott to C. K. Gardner, AG, 15 July 1814).
8. Henry Adams, *The War of 1812*, Maj. H. A. DeWeerd (ed.), (Washington, 1944), p. 179. [Hereafter cited as Adams, *War of 1812.*]
9. Scott, *Memoirs*, I, p. 134.
10. (1) Lossing, p. 815. (2) Jesup, "Memoir."
11. H. M. Brackenridge, *History of the Late War Between the United States and Great Britain* (Philadelphia, 1836), pp. 229–30.
12. Jesup, "Memoir."
13. (1) *Ibid.* (2) Lossing, pp. 827–28. (3) One of the officers killed was Capt. Abraham F. Hull, the son of Gen. William Hull.
14. Lossing, pp. 824–25.
15. Details are drawn from *Ibid.*, p. 823, and Adams, *War of 1812*, p. 191.
16. Scott, *Memoirs*, I, p. 147.
17. Jesup, "Memoir."
18. *National Intelligencer*, 20 Aug. 1814 (Rpt. Brown to SW Armstrong, 30 July 1814).
19. Jesup Papers, Box 9 (To Capt. W. S. Ketchum, 12 Apr. 1853).
20. Jesup, "Memoir."
21. *Ibid.*
22. Jesup Papers, vol. 1, ff. 220–21 (To an unidentified colonel in Ohio, 8 Sept. 1814).
23. Jesup, "Memoir."

Chapter 3
An Officer of Repute

1. James M. Banner, Jr., *To the Hartford Convention: The Federalists and the Origins of Party Politics in Massachusetts, 1789–1815* (N.Y., 1970), pp. viii–ix, 306 ff. For Madison's proposals, see Marvin A. Kreidberg and

Merton G. Henry, *History of Military Mobilization in the U.S. Army, 1775–1945* (DA Pamphlet No. 20–212, Washington, June 1955), p. 53 ff.

2. Jesup Papers, vol. 1, f. 228 (A&IG to Jesup, 30 Nov. 1814).

3. *Ibid.*, vol. 1, f. 227 (Same to same, 30 Nov. 1814). The enclosure containing the statements of Madison and Monroe was not found with Parker's letter.

4. *Ibid.*, vol. 4, ff. 1012–13 (Monroe to Jesup, 3 Oct. 1827).

5. *Ibid.*, vol. 9, ff. 2474–81 (To Ingersoll, 20 May 1845). Rep. Charles J. Ingersoll was a member of Congress from Pennsylvania. So far as has been determined, this is the only record of Jesup's conversations with Eustis and Monroe on the subject of Jesup's plan. It was included in an answer to a query from Ingersoll, who was planning to write a history of the War of 1812.

6. *Ibid.*

7. *Ibid.*, vol. 1, f. 229 (To Monroe, 10 Dec. 1814).

8. (1) *Ibid.*, vol. 1, f. 232 (To same, 15 Dec. 1814). (2) Jesup was apparently unaware that Captain Howard had already been promoted to major as of 2 October 1814 and transferred to the 1st Infantry. Heitman, *Historical Register*, I, p. 545.

9. Adams, *War of 1812*, p. 279.

10. Jesup Papers, vol. 2, ff. 298–300 (To A&IG, 2 May 1815).

11. *Ibid.*, vol. 1, f. 234 (Lt. Col. Joseph L. Smith to SW, 26 Dec. 1814).

12. *Ibid.*, Box 12 (copy of city ordinance).

13. *Ibid.*, vol. 2, ff. 298–300 (To Monroe, 2 May 1815).

14. *Ibid.*, vol. 2, f. 267 (To Monroe, 20 Jan. 1815).

15. *Ibid.*, vol. 2, f. 279 (Act of 2 Feb. 1815); ff. 298–300 (To Monroe, 2 May 1815).

16. (1) 3 *Stat.*, p. 224 (3 Mar. 1815). (2) Henry P. Beers, *The Western Military Frontier, 1815–1846* (Philadelphia, 1935), p. 28. (3) Risch, *Quartermaster Support of the Army*, pp. 177–78. (4) Heitman, *Historical Register*, I, pp. 17, 252.

17. (1) Jesup Papers, vol. 2, ff. 307, 308 (Parker to Jesup, 31 May 1815; Jesup to Jackson, same date). (2) Heitman, *Historical Register*, I, p. 573.

18. Jesup Papers, vol. 2, f. 313 (A&IG to Jesup, 3 Oct. 1815).

19. LC, Croghan Family Papers, AC. 5276 (Croghan to Jackson, 14 Oct. 1815).

20. Jesup Papers, vol. 2, f. 321 (Butler to Jesup, 18 Feb. 1816); f. 323 (Jackson's GO, 19 Apr. 1816); Box 13 (Jesup Letter Book, 5 June 1816).

21. (1) 3 *Stat.*, 297 (Act of 24 Apr. 1816). (2) Risch, *Quartermaster Support of the Army*, pp. 178–79.

22. Beers, *The Western Military Frontier*, p. 55.

23. Edwin C. McReynolds, *The Seminoles* (University of Oklahoma Press,

1957), pp. 73–76. [Hereafter cited as McReynolds.]

24. (1) LC, Croghan Family Papers (Gaines to Croghan, 4 June 1816). (2) Jesup Papers, vol. 2, f. 330 (To Jackson, 13 June 1816); f. 332 (Patterson to Jesup, 14 June 1816).

25. *Ibid.*, vol. 2, f. 339 (AG, Southern Div., to Jesup, 27 June 1816).

26. *Ibid.*, vol. 2, ff. 347–48 (Jackson to Jesup, 1 Aug. 1816).

27. *Ibid.*, vol. 2, ff. 371–72 (To Patterson, 19 Aug. 1816).

28. *Ibid.*, vol. 2, f. 368 (To Monroe, 21 Aug. 1816).

29. *Ibid.*, vol. 2, f. 353 (To Jackson, 21 Aug. 1816).

30. *Ibid.*, vol. 2, ff. 366–67 (To Jackson, 21 Aug. 1816).

31. *Ibid.*, vol. 2, ff. 370, 380 (To Monroe, 3 and 5 Sept. 1816).

32. *Ibid.*, vol. 2, ff. 382–92 (To Monroe, 8 Sept. 1816). For an earlier expression of these ideas, see *ibid.*, vol. 2, f. 331 (To Jackson, 18 Aug. 1816).

33. *Ibid.*, f. 354.

34. *Ibid.*, vol. 2, f. 438 (Leavenworth to Jesup, Nov. 1816).

35. See *Ibid.*, vol. 2, ff. 429–30 (Lt. George W. Boyd to Jesup, 14 Dec. 1816); Box 13 ("General Orders").

36. *Ibid.*, vol. 2, ff. 431–32 (Ripley to Jesup, 21 Dec. 1816).

37. *Ibid.*, vol. 2, f. 452 (Jackson to Jesup, 6 Feb. 1817).

38. *Ibid.*, vol. 2, f. 441 (Jesup statement of money due him); *ibid.*, Box 13.

39. Jesup Papers, Box 13 (To Graham, 3 June 1817).

40. (1) PHS, Daniel Parker Papers, Box 24 (Jesup to Parker, 20 June 1817). (2) Heitman, *Historical Register*, I, p. 663.

41. Jesup Papers, vol. 2, f. 483 (W. S. Hamilton to Jesup, 13 June 1817). Jesup's letter to Hamilton was not found and presumably was not preserved.

42. *Ibid.*, vol. 2, f. 485 (Gaines to Jesup, 2 July 1817).

43. *Ibid.*, vol. 2, ff. 486–87 (Trimble to Jesup, 5 July 1817). Jesup's letter to Trimble on 20 June was not found. Trimble served under Ripley in the Niagara campaign and was brevetted lieutenant colonel for gallant conduct in Brown's sortie from Fort Erie in 1814. He resigned from the army on 1 March 1819 and died 12 December 1821.

44. Jesup Papers, vol. 2, f. 482. Ripley's eight-year career in the army ended on 1 February 1820 when he resigned from the service.

45. *Ibid.*, vol. 2, ff. 492–93 (Cross to Jesup, 22 Aug. 1817).

46. *Ibid.*, vol. 2, ff. 494–95 (Brown to Jesup, 1 Oct. 1817).

47. *Ibid.*, vol. 2, f. 498 (To Parker, 20 Jan. 1818).

48. (1) 3 *Stat.*, 426 (Act of 14 Apr. 1818). (2) *National Intelligencer*, 19 May 1818.

49. WCL, Jesup Papers (Crittenden to Jesup, 1 Apr. 1818).

50. (1) RG 94, AGO, Letters Received, 1818, No. 2760 (Cumming to Cal-

houn, 27 Apr. 1818). (2) Heitman, *Historical Register*, I, p. 344. (3) *National Intelligencer*, 22 May 1818.

51. RG 107, SW, Rpts. to Cong., I, p. 436 (Calhoun to John Williams, 6 Feb. 1818).

52. 3 *Stat.*, 426 (Act of 14 Apr. 1818).

Chapter 4
Birth of a Supply Bureau

1. Jesup Papers, vol. 2, f. 501.
2. (1) Fred E. Hagen, "Thomas Sidney Jesup," *The Quartermaster Review*, XI, No. 1 (Sept.–Oct. 1931), 45 (Jesup to Joseph N. Crouch, Urbana, O., 27 May 1818). (2) Jesup Papers, vol. 2, f. 510 (Findlay to Jesup, 15 Aug. 1818).
3. RG 107, OSW, Letters Received, J–134 (11) (5 June 1818).
4. RG 92, OQMG Letter Book, vol. 1, pp. 4, 9 (12 and 27 June 1818).
5. RG 92, OQMG Letter Book, vol. 1, pp. 13–16 (Jesup's Project on Regulations, 17 July 1818).
6. Jesup Papers, vol. 12, f. 3309, f. 3324 (Boulvin to Jesup, 15 Jan. 1847 and reply, 16 Jan. 1847).
7. RG 92, OQMG Letter Book, vol. 2, p. 386 (Jesup to G. Bender, 1 Feb. 1821).
8. (1) *Ibid.*, vol. 1, pp. 13–16 (Regulations, 17 July 1818). (2) DAB, X, 63.
9. (1) See, for example, *General Regulations for the Army* (Washington, 1821, 1825, 1855, 1861, 1881, 1901, 1917). (2) RG 92, OQMG Letters Sent, I, 16–17 (Jesup to Calhoun, 20 July 1818).
10. (1) *American State Papers, Military Affairs*, II, pp. 247–52 (Scott to Calhoun, 2 Sept. 1818). (2) RG 107, OSW, Military Book, vol. 2, p. 205 (GO, 18 May 1821).
11. Jesup Papers, vol. 1, ff. 276–77 (Cross to Capt. George Bender, 13 May 1819).
12. *Ibid.*, vol. 1, p. 115 (Jesup to Calhoun, 25 Nov. 1818).
13. RG 107, SW, Rpts. to Cong., II, 27–28 (Jesup to Calhoun, 19 Oct. 1818).
14. RG 107, OSW, Military Book, vol. 10, p. 122 (Calhoun to Jackson, 22 Aug. 1818).
15. (1) *Ibid.*, vol. 10, pp. 33–34 (Calhoun to Gen. Smith, 16 Mar. 1818). (2) Beers, *The Western Military Frontier, 1815–1846*, pp. 39–44.
16. (1) RG 192, CGS, Letters Sent, vol. 1, p. 3 (Gibson to Calhoun, 20 Nov. 1818). (2) House *Doc.* No. 110, 16th Cong., 2d Sess., p. 226.
17. (1) *Ibid.*, pp. 6–7 (contract); pp. 178–79 (R. M. Johnson to Jesup, 17 Nov. 1818). (2) RG 92, OQMG Letter Book, vol. 1, p. 154 (Jesup to McGunnegle, 31 Dec. 1818).
18. RG 107, OSW, Military Book, vol. 10, p. 130 (Calhoun to Gen. J. G. Swift, 1 Sept. 1818).

19. House *Doc.* No. 110, 16th Cong., 2d Sess., pp. 6–7.
20. *Ibid.*, p. 246.
21. RG 107, OSW, Military Book, vol. 10, p. 266 (Calhoun to Jackson, 6 Mar. 1819).
22. RG 92, OQMG Letter Book, vol. 1, p. 154 (31 Dec. 1818); pp. 186–87 (16 Feb. 1819); pp. 198–99 (3 Mar. 1819).
23. (1) RG 107, OSW, Military Book, vol. 10, p. 290 (Calhoun to Jesup, 27 Mar. 1819). (2) RG 92, OQMG Letter Book, vol. 1, p. 237 (Jesup to Calhoun, 8 Apr. 1819).
24. Beers, *The Western Military Frontier*, pp. 42–43.
25. (1) Jesup Papers, vol. 3, ff. 550–51 (To Calhoun, 12 June 1819). (2) RG 107, OSW, Letters Received, J–130 (13) (Jesup Memoranda, Dec. 1819).
26. *Ibid.*, J-220 (12) and encls. (R. M. Johnson to Calhoun, 29, 30 Mar. and 3 Apr. 1819).
27. (1) House *Doc.* No. 110, 16th Cong., 2d Sess., pp. 15–18. (2) RG 107, OSW, Letters Received, C–26 (13) (Col. Chambers to Gen. Bissell, 21 May 1819).
28. Jesup Papers, vol. 3, ff. 556–57 (To Calhoun, 25 June 1819).
29. (1) *Ibid.*, vol. 3, ff. 556–57 (To SW, 25 June 1819). (2) Beers, *The Western Military Frontier*, pp. 42–45.
30. (1) Jesup Papers, vol. 3, ff. 558–59 (To J. Johnson, 4 July 1819). (2) RG 107, OSW, Letters Received, J–36 (13) (Jesup to Calhoun, 8 July 1819).
31. RG 107, OSW, Letters Received, J–12 (13) (R. M. Johnson to Calhoun, 5 and 9 July 1819).
32. (1) RG 107, OSW, Military Book, vol. 10, pp. 317–19 (Calhoun to R. M. Johnson, 20 July 1819). (2) RG 107, OSW, Letters Received, J–222 (13); P–40 (13 Enc) (R. M. Johnson to Calhoun, 9 and 26 July 1819).
33. RG 107, OSW, Military Book, vol. 10, pp. 315–16 (Calhoun to Jesup, 19 July 1819).
34. (1) *Ibid.*, vol. 10, pp. 322–23 (Calhoun to R. M. Johnson, 23 July 1819). (2) RG 107, OSW, Letters Received, J–40 (13) (R. M. Johnson to Calhoun, 3 Aug. 1819).
35. RG 107, OSW, Military Book, vol. 10, pp. 347–49 (Calhoun to R. M. Johnson, 15 Aug. 1819).
36. Jesup Papers, vol. 3, f. 562 (To J. Johnson, 27 Aug. 1819).
37. (1) *Ibid.*, vol. 3, ff. 565–66 (To Calhoun, 30 Aug. 1819). (2) Beers, *The Western Military Frontier*, pp. 43–45. (3) *American State Papers, Military Affairs*, II, p. 32 (Jesup to Calhoun, 28 Dec. 1819).
38. RG 107, OSW, Letters Received, J–63 (13) (Jesup to Calhoun, 31 Aug. 1819).
39. *Ibid.*, J–68 (13); J–67 (13) (Jesup to Calhoun, 9 Sept. 1819).
40. RG 92, OQMG Letter Book, vol. 1, pp. 416–17 (Cross to SW, 1 Oct. 1819).
41. (1) *American State Papers, Military Affairs*, II, p. 69. (2) RG 92, OQMG

Letter Book, vol. 2, pp. 35–36 (Jesup to Calhoun, 31 Jan. 1820).

42. *Ibid.*, vol. 1, pp. 495–96 (Jesup to Calhoun, 16 Dec. 1819).

43. See *American State Papers, Military Affairs*, III, p. 32 (Jesup to Calhoun, 28 Dec. 1819, statement No. 4); II, pp. 68–69 (Calhoun to Clay, 2 Feb. 1820).

44. (1) *Annals of Congress*, 16th Cong., 1st Sess., pp. 548-51. (2) Beers, *The Western Military Frontier*, p. 44.

45. RG 92, OQMG Letter Book, vol. 2, pp. 391–407 (5 Feb. 1820).

46. (1) *American State Papers, Military Affairs*, II, pp. 324–25 (Rpt. to House, 1 Mar. 1821). (2) RG 92, OQMG Letter Book, vol. 2, pp. 167–68 (Cross to 3d Auditor, 12 June 1820); vol. 8, pp. 220–21 (Jesup to Duff Green, 20 Sept. 1825). (3) RG 107, OSW, Military Book, vol. 2, p. 66 (Calhoun to Arbitrators, 30 June 1820).

47. *Annals of Congress*, 16th Cong., 1st Sess., vol. 2, p. 2233 (11 May 1820).

48. RG 92, OQMG Letter Book, vol. 2, pp. 95–105 (Jesup to SW, 31 Mar. 1820).

49. *American State Papers, Military Affairs*, II, pp. 188–93.

50. *Ibid.*, II, pp. 194, 452.

51. (1) *Ibid.*, II, pp. 559–60 (Jesup to SW, 22 Nov. 1823). (2) 3 *Stat.*, 615.

52. *American State Papers, Military Affairs*, II, pp. 559–60 (Jesup to SW, 22 Nov. 1823).

53. Jesup Papers, Box "Photostats of Taylor's Letters," AC 5214 (Taylor to Jesup, 18 June 1821). Had it not been for Jesup, Taylor might never have been president. Taylor's retention in the army made it possible for him to achieve the fame in the Mexican War that led to his election in 1848.

54. *Ibid.* (Taylor to Jesup, 20 Apr. 1820).

55. *Ibid.* (Taylor to Jesup, 15 Dec. 1820).

56. CHS, George P. Torrence Papers, Box 13 "Findlay Papers," (Jesup to James Findlay, 3 Feb. 1822).

Chapter 5
A Bachelor Takes a Wife

1. George Rogers Clark lived at Locust Grove for the last nine years of his life, cared for by his sister Lucy, after he suffered a paralytic stroke. He died there on 13 February 1818. The home became an historical shrine to his memory, restored to its original appearance and opened to the public in 1964. See (1) Dr. Samuel W. Thomas, "A Guide to the Historic House Museum Locust Grove," Jan. 1965 (draft copy). (2) Margaret Bridwell, "A House Full of History," *Louisville Courier–Journal*, 9 Nov. 1958.

2. Eugene II. Conner and Samuel W. Thomas, "John Croghan [1780–1848]: An Enterprising Kentucky Physician," *The Filson Club History Quarterly*, vol. 40, No. 3 (1966), pp. 205–34.

3. (1) The Filson Club, "Rogers Index." (2) Jesup Papers, Box 15 (Croghan memo, 18 May 1822).
4. Jesup Papers, vol. 3, ff. 784–85 (Ann Jesup to Mrs. James Findlay, Sept. 1822).
5. RG 107, OSW, Letters Received, J–52 (16) (Jesup to Calhoun, 20 Oct. 1822).
6. *American State Papers, Military Affairs*, II, pp. 559–60 (Jesup to Calhoun, 22 Nov. 1823).
7. (1) RG 92, OQMG Letter Book, vol. 6, p. 450 (Jesup to SW, 3 Aug. 1824). (2) RG 92, OQMG, Estimate and Rpts. (1822–26).
8. (1) RG 107, OSW, Letters Received, Q–130 (17) (Jesup to SW, 9 Feb. 1824). (2) RG 92, OQMG Letter Book, vol. 10, pp. 96–114 (Jesup to SW, 13 Oct. 1826).
9. 4 *Stat.*, 173 (Act of 18 May 1826).
10. RG 107, OSW, Letters Received, Q–8 (32) (9 Mar. 1833).
11. RG 94, AGO, Letters Received, J–39 (26 Aug. 1835).
12. (1) *Washington Globe*, 2 Nov. 1836. (2) Jesup Papers, vol. 5, f. 1304.
13. 4 *Stat.*, 173 (Act of 18 May 1826).
14. See Jesup Papers, Box 15 (G. Croghan to Jesup, 15 Nov. 1825); (Dr. Croghan to Jesup, 15 May 1826).
15. Compare views expressed in *American State Papers, Military Affairs*, VI, pp. 152–53 (Jesup to Cass, 15 Feb. 1836).
16. RG 92, OQMG Letter Book, vol. 7, p. 367 (Circular, 11 Apr. 1825).
17. 4 *Stat.*, 22–23 (Act of 30 Apr. 1824).
18. See, for example, 4 *Stat.*, 5 (31 Jan. 1824); p. 135 (3 Mar. 1825), pp. 227–28 (2 Mar. 1827).
19. *American State Papers, Military Affairs*, III, p. 117 (Jesup to SW, 26 Nov. 1825); *ibid.*, V, p. 384 (QMG Annual Rpt., 22 Nov. 1834).
20. *Ibid.*, IV, p. 2 (QMG Annual Rpt., 24 Nov. 1828).
21. (1) RG 107, OSW, Military Book. vol. 12, p. 425 (SW to Jesup, 3 Apr. 1829). (2) *American State Papers, Military Affairs*, IV, p. 193. (3) RG 107, OSW, Letters Received, Q–27 (39) (Hunt to SW, 24 May 1836).
22. RG 92, OQMG Letter Book, vol. 6, pp. 55–56 (Jesup to Shriver, 17 Jan. 1824).
23. RG 107, OSW, Military Book, vol. 12, p. 27 (SW to QMG *et al.*, 19 Feb. 1824).
24. *American State Papers, Military Affairs*, II, pp. 640–41 (Rpt., 31 Oct. 1827); IV, pp. 192–95, 747–49 (Rpts., 23 Nov. 1829, 2 Nov. 1831).
25. Jesup Papers, Box 13 (n.d.)
26. *Ibid.*, vol. 4, f. 846.
27. *Ibid.*, Box 15 (Dr. Croghan to Jesup, 20 May 1825).
28. *Ibid.*, vol. 4, ff. 1009–10 (To an unidentified friend, 31 Aug. 1827).
29. *Ibid.*
30. *Ibid.*, vol. 4, ff. 1083–85 (Jesup to Macomb, 16 June 1829).

31. *Ibid.*, Box 15 (Dr. Croghan to Jesup, 25 Feb. 1823); (G. Croghan to Jesup, n.d.); *ibid.*, vol. 4, ff. 867–68 (Dr. Croghan to Jesup, 12 July 1824); ff. 868–69 (G. Croghan to Jesup, 22 Aug. 1824).

32. Jesup Papers, Box 15 (Croghan to Harrison, 1 July 1818, and Harrison reply, 21 July 1818); (Croghan to Harrison, 24 May 1825).

33. *Ibid.*, Box 15 (Croghan to Harrison, 5 Aug. 1825); (Harrison to Croghan, 31 Aug. 1825); (Croghan to Harrison, 22 Sept. 1825); (Harrison to Croghan, 24 Oct. 1825); (Croghan to Harrison, 30 Dec. 1825).

34. *Ibid.*, Box 15 (G. Croghan to Jesup, 6 Feb. 1826). Although Croghan did not authorize their use, all six of his letters to Harrison during their controversy were reproduced in the *Washington Globe*, 17 Aug. 1840, in the unsuccessful attempt to defeat Harrison's bid for the presidency. The newspaper stated that they were submitted by "a gentleman of high standing in Ohio."

35. Jesup Papers, vol. 7, ff. 966–67 (William Croghan to Jesup, 1 Aug. 1826); *ibid.*, Box 15 (W. Croghan to Jesup, 30 Dec. 1826).

36. (1) *Ibid.*, vol. 4, ff. 1054–55 (Col. William Lindsay to Jesup, 9 Aug 1828); Box 15 (Dr. Croghan to Jesup, 26 May 1829); (G. Croghan to Jesup, 19 June and 11 Aug. 1829). (2) Thomas, "George Croghan," *The Filson Club History Quarterly*, vol. 41, No. 4, p. 314.

37. Francis Paul Prucha (ed.), *Army Life on the Western Frontier, Selections from the Official Reports Made between 1826 and 1845 by Colonel George Croghan* (University of Oklahoma Press, 1958).

38. Jesup Papers, vol. 7, f. 1861 (10 Apr. 1839).

39. (1) *Ibid.*, vol. 7, ff. 1815–16 (Ann Jesup to her husband, 7 Feb. 1839). (2) George Croghan died of cholera in New Orleans on 8 January 1849, bringing to a close one of the strangest careers in the history of the United States Army. He is buried at Fremont, Ohio, near the site of old Fort Stephenson where he had achieved fame.

40. Details of the duel are contained in a letter from Jesup to Joseph R. Underwood, 4 March 1853, which includes copies of the complete correspondence between the two principals as well as that exchanged by their seconds, along with other documents pertaining to the episode. See LC, Henry Clay Papers (Box containing data on duel).

41. (1) RG 107, OSW, Letters Received, J–50 (23) (Jesup to Barbour, 28 Feb. 1828). (2) When Brig. Gen. E. W. Ripley retired early in 1820, Jesup had asked to succeed him in the line, but Secretary of War Calhoun instead had promoted Col. Henry Atkinson to that post, promising Jesup that he would be entitled to all the perquisites of other brigadiers. See Jesup Papers, vol. 4, ff. 834–37 (To Paymaster General Nathan Towson, 23 Apr. 1823).

42. *Ibid.*, vol. 4, ff. 1056-57 (Cross to Jesup, 11 Aug. 1828).

43. CHS, Torrence Papers, Box 13, Item 27 (Jesup to Thomas Sloo, 18 Nov. 1826).

44. Jesup Papers, vol. 4, f. 997 (28 May 1827).
45. He was the grandfather of Oscar W. Underwood, senator from Alabama who was candidate for the presidency at the 1924 National Democratic Convention.
46. Jesup Papers, vol. 4, ff. 1064–65 (5 Oct. 1828). Samuel was a highly respected farmer. He was elected to the state legislature, serving first in the Kentucky House and then for eight years in the state Senate.
47. Jesup Papers, Box 11.
48. *Ibid.*, vol. 5, ff. 1148–49 (Jesup to Dr. Croghan, 24 Mar. 1832).
49. Jesup Papers, Box "Photostats of Taylor Letters" (Taylor to Jesup, 4 Dec. 1832).
50. *Ibid.*, Box 12 (Ann Jesup to her husband, 6 Dec. 1832).
51. Jesup Papers, Box 15 (William Croghan to Ann Jesup, 25 Oct. 1835); (Dr. Croghan to Jesup, 9 Apr. 1835); *ibid.*, vol. 5, ff. 1264–68.
52. *Ibid.*, Box 12 (Ann Jesup to her husband, 29 Mar. 1836).

Chapter 6
Commander in the Creek War

1. Treaty of Payne's Landing, 9 May 1832.
2. See Clarence E. Carter, *The Territorial Papers of the United States* (26 vols., Washington, 1934–62), XXV, pp. 182–83, 186–87 (Clinch to AG, 8 and 17 Oct. 1835); p. 188 (SW to Clinch, 22 Oct. 1835). [Hereafter cited as Carter, *Territorial Papers.*]
3. *Ibid.*, XXV, pp. 209–10 (Clinch to AG, 9 Dec. 1835); pp. 216–17 (Richard K. Call to President, 22 Dec. 1835).
4. John T. Sprague, *The Origin, Progress, and Conclusion of the Florida War* (Floridiana Facsimile Reprint Series, University of Florida Press, 1964), pp. 97, 106. [Hereafter cited as Sprague.]
5. *American State Papers, Military Affairs,* VI, pp. 1043–44.
6. RG 92, OQMG Letter Book, vol. 22, p. 400 (Hunt to Clinch, 17 Dec. 1835), pp. 455–56, 458–60 (Hunt to Engle, Dimmock, Shannon, 19 Jan. 1836), pp. 467–69 (Hunt to Scott, 21 Jan. 1836), p. 475 (Jesup to Shannon, 23 Jan. 1836).
7. *Ibid.*, vol. 24, pp. 195–200 (Cross to Recorder of Court of Inquiry, 23 Nov. 1836).
8. *Ibid.*, vol. 22, pp. 476–77 (QMG to Cross, 26 Jan. 1836).
9. *American State Papers, Military Affairs,* VII, pp. 131–32 (Deposition of Dimmock, 5 Dec. 1836).
10. RG 92, OQMG Letter Book, vol. 24, pp. 195–200 (Cross to Recorder of Court of Inquiry, 23 Nov. 1836).
11. John Bemrose, *Reminiscences of the Second Seminole War,* John K. Mahon (ed.) (University of Florida Press, 1966), p. 78. [Hereafter cited as Bemrose.]

12. (1) *Ibid.*, p. 88. (2) Sprague, p. 138 (Scott's testimony at his court-martial).
13. The foregoing account of Gaines's experience in Florida is based on the following sources: (1) Sprague, pp. 107–13, 126–34, 138–39. (2) Mc-Reynolds, pp. 162–63. (3) Mark F. Boyd, "Asi–Yaholo or Osceola," *The Florida Historical Quarterly*, XXXIII, Nos. 3 and 4 (Jan.–Apr. 1955), pp. 282–84. [Hereafter cited as Boyd]. (4) *Washington Globe*, 2 Apr. 1836.
14. *Washington Globe*, 2 Apr. 1836 (Hitchcock to Lyon, 11 Mar. 1836).
15. *Ibid.*, 8 Apr. 1836.
16. Senate *Doc.* 224, 24th Cong., 2d Sess., pp. 368–69. [Hereafter cited as Senate *Doc.* 224.]
17. *Washington Globe*, 1 June 1836.
18. Senate *Doc.* 224, pp. 400–01 (18 May 1836).
19. *American State Papers, Military Affairs*, VI, pp. 622–23.
20. RG 92, OQMG Letter Book, vol. 23, p. 222 (19 May 1836).
21. *Ibid.*, vol. 23, p. 232 (Hunt to Stanton, 22 May 1836).
22. Senate *Doc.* 224, pp. 415–16.
23. *American State Papers, Military Affairs*, VI, p. 631.
24. Jesup Papers, Box 15 (Account Book).
25. Jacob Rhett Motte, *Journey into Wilderness: An Army Surgeon's Account of Life in Camp and Field during the Creek and Seminole Wars, 1836–1838*, James F. Sunderman (ed.) (University of Florida Press, 1963), p. 11. [Hereafter cited as Motte.]
26. Jesup gave twenty dollars to the Indians in his escort. Jesup Papers, Box 13 (Account Book).
27. Senate *Doc.* 224, p. 429.
28. *American State Papers, Military Affairs*, VII, p. 325 (Jesup to SW, 11 June 1836).
29. Senate *Doc.* 224, p. 458.
30. *American State Papers, Military Affairs*, VII, p. 332 (Jesup to Scott, 15–16 June 1836).
31. Senate *Doc.* 224, p. 120 (Scott to AG, 12 June 1836).
32. *American State Papers, Military Affairs*, VII, pp. 330–31 (Scott to Jesup, 16 June 1836).
33. *Ibid.*, VII, p. 334 (Jesup to Scott, 17 June 1836).
34. *Ibid.*, VII, pp. 332–33 (Scott to Jesup, 17 June 1836).
35. Senate *Doc.* 224, pp. 449–50 (Jesup to Scott, 19 June 1836).
36. *Ibid.*, pp. 450–52 (Scott to Jesup, 19 June 1836).
37. *Ibid.*, pp. 456–58 (Jesup to Scott, 20 June 1836).
38. *Ibid.*, pp. 458–59 (Scott to Jesup, 21 June 1836).
39. *Ibid.*, pp. 460–61 (Jesup to Scott, 22 June 1836).
40. *Ibid.*, pp. 459–60 (Scott to Jesup, 23 June 1836).

41. *American State Papers, Military Affairs*, VII, p. 340 (Scott to AG, 23 June 1836).
42. *Ibid.*, VII, pp. 347–48 (Jesup to Cass, 25 June 1836).
43. *Washington Globe*, 23 July 1836 (Copy of Scott's Order No. 27, 7 July 1836).
44. (1) *American State Papers, Military Affairs*, VII, pp. 336–37. (2) Jesup originally intended to send the letter to Colonel Croghan, but thinking the latter might be absent from the city, he sent it instead to Blair. PHS, Daniel Parker Papers, Box 31 (Jesup to Parker, 15 Apr. 1839).
45. *Washington Globe*, 29 July 1836 (quoting a Whig paper).
46. (1) LC, Blair Family Papers, Box 1 (Jackson to Blair, 12 Aug. 1836). (2) *Washington Globe*, 1 June 1836.
47. LC, Blair Family Papers, Box 1 (Blair to Jackson, 10 July 1836).
48. *Washington Globe*, 29 July 1836.
49. *Ibid.*, 19 Aug. 1840 (Rep. William Butler of Kentucky in House, 11 June 1840).
50. *Ibid.*, 4 Aug. 1836.
51. (1) *American State Papers, Military Affairs*, VII, p. 362 (Jesup to Blair, 3 Sept. 1836). (2) *Washington Globe*, 26 Sept. 1836.
52. (1) E. D. Keyes, *Fifty Years' Observation of Men and Events Civil and Military* (New York, 1884), pp. 119–20. (2) *Washington Globe*, 18 Oct. 1836 (AGO Special Order No. 65, 3 Oct. 1836).
53. RG 92, OQMG Letter Book, vol. 23, p. 222.
54. Senate *Doc.* No. 224, pp. 370–71 (White to Macomb, 13 Dec. 1836).
55. The foregoing discussion of the court of inquiry is based on Senate *Doc.* No. 224, pp. 168–90.
56. Copies of both the committee's letter and Jesup's reply were published in the *Washington Globe*, 12 October 1836.
57. House *Doc.* No. 80, 27th Cong., 3d Sess., s.n. 420, pp. 1–3 (Jesup to SW, 17 Jan. 1843).
58. *Ibid.*
59. *Ibid.*, Doc. A appended, pp. 9–10.
60. *American State Papers, Military Affairs*, VI, p. 831 (Annual Rpt. of SW to President, 22 Nov. 1836).
61. Jesup Papers, vol. 8, ff. 2074–80 (Jesup to SW, 28 Dec. 1841).
62. (1) *Ibid.*, vol. 16, ff. 4289 (SW to Jesup, 11 July, Jackson to Jesup, 2 and 3 Aug. 1836). (2) Sprague, p. 162.
63. (1) Jesup Papers, vol. 6, f. 1569. (2) Tragedy overtook Colonel Lane on 19 October, about two weeks after his arrival in Florida. He contracted what was termed "brain fever," and in pain and despondency committed suicide. Motte, p. 259, n. 5. (3) *Washington Globe* (2 and 30 Nov.; 19 Dec. 1836).
64. (1) Jesup Papers, vol. 16, f. 4291 (Jackson to Jesup, 3 Aug. 1836). (2)

Washington Globe, 1 Oct. 1836 (Call to Cass, 18 Sept. 1836).

65. Motte, pp. 34–35.

66. RG 92, OQMG Letter Book, vol. 24, pp. 218–19 (Cross to Jesup, 30 Nov. 1836).

Chapter 7
An Embattled General in the Seminole War

1. Carter, *Territorial Papers*, XXV, pp. 339–41 (Butler to Call, 4 Nov. 1836).

2. *Ibid.*, XXV, pp. 341–43 (Butler to Jesup, 4 Nov. 1836).

3. *Ibid.*, XXV, pp. 344–57 (Call to Butler, 2 Dec. 1836).

4. *American State Papers, Military Affairs*, VII, pp. 820–21 (Jesup to AG, 9 Dec. 1836).

5. McReynolds, pp. 164, 166.

6. *American State Papers, Military Affairs*, VII, pp. 820–21 (Jesup to AG, 8 and 12 Dec. 1836).

7. *Ibid.*, VII, pp. 821–22 (Jesup to Butler, 17 and 18 Dec. 1836).

8. (1) Sprague, p. 216. (2) Carter, *Territorial Papers*, XXV, pp. 189–90, 194.

9. *American State Papers, Military Affairs*, VII, pp. 822–23 (Jesup to Butler, 23 Dec. 1836).

10. RG 92, OQMG Consolidated Correspondence File, Boxes 305–08 (Stanton to Jesup, 20 Jan. 1841, and enclosures).

11. *American State Papers, Military Affairs*, VII, pp. 822–23 (Jesup to Butler, 23 Dec. 1836).

12. RG 92, OQMG Letter Book, vol. 24, p. 263 (Cross to Jesup, 23 Dec. 1836).

13. *American State Papers, Military Affairs*, VII, pp. 824–25 (1 and 12 Jan. 1837).

14. *Ibid.*, VII, pp. 327–29 (Jesup to AG, 7 Feb. 1837).

15. RG 92, OQMG Consolidated Correspondence File, 1795–1915, Box 477 (Jesup to AQMG Cross, 20 Feb. 1837).

16. *American State Papers, Military Affairs*, VII, pp. 827–29 (Jesup to AG, 7 Feb. 1837).

17. Scott, *Memoirs*, I, p. 264.

18. Carter, *Territorial Papers*, XXV, pp. 385–87 (Jesup to SW, 9 Apr. 1837).

19. *American State Papers, Military Affairs*, VII, p. 575 (Annual Rpt. of SW, 2 Dec. 1837).

20. (1) *Ibid.* (2) The appended report by Jesup on his operations in Florida is also to be found in Senate *Doc.* 507, 25th Cong., 2d Sess., s.n. 319 (Jesup to SW, 6 July 1838).

21. Motte, p. 144.

22. (1) Sprague, pp. 168–70. (2) Motte, p. 271, note 1.

23. Jesup Papers, Box 13 (7 Feb. 1837).

24. Boyd, pp. 290–91.
25. (1) *American State Papers, Military Affairs*, VII, p. 834. (2) Sprague, pp. 177–78. (3) Motte, p. 267, note 12.
26. Carter, *Territorial Papers*, XXV, pp. 380–81 (Jesup to AG, 18 Mar. 1837).
27. RG 107, OSW, Military Book, vol. 17, p. 227 (Butler to Jesup, 11 Mar. 1837).
28. Joshua R. Giddings, *The Exiles of Florida* (Columbus, Ohio, 1858), pp. 148–49. [Hereafter cited as Giddings.]
29. Carter, *Territorial Papers*, XXV, pp. 385–87 (Jesup to Poinsett, 9 Apr. 1837).
30. *American State Papers, Military Affairs*, VII, p. 795 (Macomb to Jesup, 7 Apr. 1837); p. 837 (Jesup to AG, 8 May 1837).
31. Jesup Papers, Box 15 (Account Book, 1836–37).
32. Giddings, elected to Congress as an Antislavery Whig from Ohio, resigned in March of 1842 after being censured by the House, but ran for reelection, won back the same seat, and retained it until 1859.
33. House *Doc.* 225, 25th Cong., 3d Sess., p. 2 (Order No. 79, 5 Apr. 1837); pp. 55–56 (G. Humphreys *et al.*, to Poinsett, 18 Mar. 1837).
34. Giddings, p. 152.
35. House *Doc.* 225, 25th Cong., 2d Sess., pp. 13–14 (Jesup to McClintock, 1 May; to Armistead, 2 May 1837).
36. Reprinted in *Washington Globe*, 9 May 1837.
37. OIA, Letters Received, M 234, Roll 290 (Jesup to C. A. Harris, 15 Apr. 1837).
38. Through Jesup's influence, Harney was appointed a lieutenant in 1818 before he was eighteen years of age. Beers, *The Western Military Frontier*, p. 63n.
39. Boyd, p. 292.
40. Carter, *Territorial Papers*, XXV, p. 390 (Jesup to SW, 8 May 1837).
41. Giddings, pp. 150, 153.
42. Carter, *Territorial Papers*, XXV, p. 392.
43. (1) Sprague, p. 178. (2) Motte, pp. 265–66, note 13.
44. McReynolds, p. 178.
45. Carter, *Territorial Papers*, XXV, p. 394.
46. Sprague, p. 180.
47. *American State Papers, Military Affairs*, VII, pp. 871–72 (Jesup to Poinsett, 7 June 1837).
48. (1) Senate *Doc.* 507, 25th Cong., 2d Sess., p. 2 (Jesup to SW, 6 July 1838). (2) *American State Papers, Military Affairs*, VII, p. 796 (Macomb to Jesup, 10 June 1837). [Hereafter cited as Senate *Doc.* 507.]
49. (1) *Ibid.*, VII, pp. 871–72 (Poinsett to Jesup, 22 June 1837); pp. 842–43 (Jesup to AG, 25 July 1837). (2) Senate *Doc.* 507, p. 1.
50. *American State Papers, Military Affairs*, VII, p. 872 (Jesup to SW, 10 June 1837).

51. (1) House *Doc.* 78, 25th Cong., 2d Sess., vol. 3, s.n. 323, pp. 49–50 (Jesup to Butler, 5 Dec. 1836). (2) *American State Papers, Military Affairs,* VII, pp. 820–21 (Jesup to Butler, 9 and 12 Dec. 1836); p. 872 (Jesup to Poinsett, 10 June 1837).
52. "Letters of Lieutenant John Phelps, U.S.A., 1836, 1837," *The Florida Historical Quarterly,* VI, p. 82 (Phelps to his sister Helen).
53. RG 107, OSW, Military Book, vol. 17, pp. 241–45 (SW to Jesup, 25 July 1837).

Chapter 8
Jesup's Second Campaign Against the Seminoles

1. RG 107, OSW, Military Book, vol. 17, pp. 388–89 (SW to Jesup, 25 Aug. 1837).
2. Senate *Doc.* 507, p. 3.
3. (1) *Ibid.,* p. 5. (2) *Washington Globe,* 4 Nov. 1840 (J. R. Underwood speech in House, 13 July 1840).
4. (1) Senate *Doc.* 507, p. 4. (2) *Washington Globe,* 18 June 1838 (Benton speech in Senate, 8 June 1838).
5. (1) Senate *Doc.* 507, p. 3. (2) *Army and Navy Chronicle,* VI, No. 5, 1 Feb. 1838, p. 93; No. 9, 1 Mar. 1838, pp. 137–40.
6. RG 75, OIA, M 234, Roll 290, "Florida Superintendency Emigration, 1828–38" (Jesup to Maj. W. G. Freeman, 9 Sept. 1837).
7. *American State Papers, Military Affairs,* VII, p. 882 (Jesup to SW, 22 Sept. 1837).
8. Jesup Papers, vol. 9, ff. 2443–49 (Jesup to Rep. Howell Cobb, 12 Feb. 1845).
9. *Washington Globe,* 20 Sept. 1837.
10. (1) Jesup Papers, vol. 6, f. 1665 (Underwood to Jesup, 19 Sept. 1837). (2) *Washington Globe,* 19 Sept., 14 Oct. 1837.
11. Motte, p. 116.
12. (1) *Ibid.,* pp. 118–23. (2) Senate *Doc.* 507, pp. 3–4.
13. *Ibid.,* p. 4.
14. *Ibid.*
15. House *Doc.* 327, 25th Cong., 2d Sess., s.n. 329, vol. 9, p. 12 (Jesup to Hernandez, 21 Oct. 1837). [Hereafter cited as House *Doc.* 324.]
16. Boyd, pp. 296–97.
17. House *Doc.* 327, p. 4.
18. *Ibid.,* pp. 5–6 (Hernandez to Jesup, 22 Oct. 1837).
19. (1) Senate *Doc.* 507, p. 5. (2) Boyd, pp. 300–01.
20. Senate *Doc.* 507, pp. 4–5.
21. Boyd, p. 297.
22. Motte, pp. 141–42.

23. (1) Boyd, p. 297. (2) "Letters of Samuel Forry, Surgeon in the U.S. Army," *The Florida Historical Quarterly*, VII, p. 95.
24. *Washington Globe,* 23–24 Jan. 1838.
25. *Ibid.*, 24 Jan. 1838.
26. Richard Biddle was the brother of Nicholas Biddle, president of the Bank of the United States.
27. *Washington Globe*, 24 Jan. 1838.
28. (1) Senate *Doc.* 507, pp. 5–7. (2) Motte, pp. 142–43.
29. LC, Zachary Taylor Papers, vol. 1, series 2, ff. 102–03 (8 Nov. 1837).
30. Senate *Doc.* 507, p. 7 (Jesup to SW, 6 July 1838).
31. (1) McReynolds, pp. 197–98. (2) Boyd, p. 298.
32. Senate *Doc.* 507, p. 7.
33. Jesup Papers, vol. 6, ff. 1688–89 (Statement of Auguste to Lt. W. G. Freeman, 4th Artillery, at camp near Fort Jupiter, 18 Feb. 1838).
34. Senate *Doc.* 507, pp. 7–8.
35. (1) *Ibid.* (2) Boyd, p. 310. (3) McReynolds, pp. 198–99.
36. Senate *Doc.* 507, pp. 7–8.
37. RG 85, OIA, M 234, Roll 800, Seminole Agency (Ross to SW Bell, 12 Apr. 1841).
38. Quoted in *Washington Globe*, 22 Dec. 1837.
39. Boyd, p. 299.
40. (1) *Ibid.*, p. 300. (2) McReynolds, p. 195. (3) Sprague, pp. 219–20.
41. Boyd, p. 303.
42. Senate *Doc.* 507, pp. 5–6.
43. Senate *Doc.* 227 25th Cong., 2d Sess., pp. 1–13 (Taylor to AG, 4 Jan. 1838).
44. Senate *Doc.* 507, p. 8.
45. (1) Motte, p. 170. (2) Senate *Doc.* 507, p. 7.
46. *Ibid.*, pp. 7–8.
47. Sprague, pp. 220–21 (Jesup to Hernandez, 13 Jan. 1838).
48. Motte, pp. 182–83.
49. *Ibid.*, p. 188.
50. *Ibid.*, pp. 186, 192.
51. *Ibid.*, pp. 189, 190.
52. *Ibid.*, p. 194.
53. *Ibid.*, p. 195.
54. RG 94, AG Letters Received, M 567, Roll 167 (Jesup to AG, 26 Jan. 1838).
55. (1) Senate *Doc.* 507, p. 8. (2) Motte, p. 201.
56. *Ibid.*, p. 202.
57. Senate *Doc.* 507, pp. 8–9.
58. RG 92, OQMG Consolidated Correspondence File, 1795–1915, Box 477 (Jesup to Cross, 20 Feb. 1837).

59. Senate *Doc.* 507, pp. 9–10.
60. Motte, p. 199.
61. Senate *Doc.* 507, p. 9.
62. Motte, pp. 207–08.
63. House *Doc.* 219, 25th Cong., 2d Sess., s.n. 823, vol. 8, pp. 5–7 (Jesup to SW, 11 Feb. 1838).
64. Motte, p. 209.
65. (1) Motte, p. 210. (2) Senate *Doc.* 507, p. 10.
66. Motte, pp. 219–20.
67. RG 107, OSW, Military Book, vol. 17, pp. 241–45.
68. Carter, *Territorial Papers*, XXV, pp. 494–95.
69. RG 107, OSW, Military Book, vol. 18, pp. 398–99 (1 Mar. 1838).
70. Senate *Doc.* 507, p. 10.
71. *Washington Globe*, 16 Mar. 1838.
72. *Florida Herald*, 22 Mar., 5 Apr. 1838.
73. *Washington Globe*, 24 and 25 Jan. 1838.
74. Boyd, pp. 298–99.
75. (1) *Ibid.*, p. 304. (2) McReynolds, p. 209. (3) Dr. Weedon's wife, Mary, was the sister of the murdered Indian Agent Wiley Thompson.
76. Clay, governor of Alabama during the Creek Indian uprising and a staunch supporter of Jesup, had been elected to the United States Senate on 19 June 1837.
77. *Washington Globe*, 15 June 1838 (Senate proceedings, 7 June).
78. *Ibid.*, 12 June 1838.
79. Motte, p. 212.
80. Senate *Doc.* 507, p. 11.
81. *Ibid.*, p. 10.
82. (1) Motte, pp. 220, 222, 225, 229–36, 238. (2) Senate *Doc.* 507, p. 11.
83. (1) House *Doc.* 78, 25th Cong., 2d Sess., pp. 88–89 (Jesup to AG, 5 June 1837). (2) Senate *Doc.* 507, p. 2.
84. (1) Jesup Papers, vol. 7, ff. 1702–03. Vinton was a religious man who helped conduct Bible classes for the soldiers in Florida. (2) Motte, p. 273.

Chapter 9
Between Two Wars

1. Jesup Papers, Box 15 (Dr. J. Croghan to Jesup, 28 June 1838).
2. Senate *Doc.* 507, p. 12.
3. RG 107, OSW, Military Book, vol. 19, p. 256 (7 July 1838).
4. Jesup Papers, vol. 9, ff. 2357–66 (Jesup to SW William Wilkins, 22 May 1844).
5. *Ibid.*, vol. 9, ff. 2439–40 (Scott to SW, 6 Feb. 1845).

6. RG 107, OSW, Letters Sent, No. 20, p. 397 (Poinsett to Jesup, 13 Apr. 1839).

7. (1) *Washington Globe*, 12 June 1838 (Senate proceedings of 8 June 1838). (2) Thomas Hart Benton, *Thirty Years View* (2 vols., New York, 1854–56), II, pp. 76–85.

8. *Washington Globe*, 6 Apr. 1839 (House proceedings, 27 Feb. 1839).

9. 5 *Stat.*, 256 (5 July 1838).

10. Heitman, *Historical Register*, I, pp. 341, 557, 916, 1030.

11. Jesup Papers, Box 13 (Account Books, 26 May 1836–9 Dec. 1837); vol. 7, ff. 1760–61 (Hagner to SW, 19 July 1838 and SW notation).

12. *Ibid.*, Box 13 (Account Book, 29 May 1837–29 Apr. 1839).

13. *Ibid.*, vol. 7, ff. 1751–55; ff. 1943–45.

14. (1) For details of his property transactions, see *ibid.*, vol. 7, ff. 1778–79, 1780–81, 1782–83, 1784, 1806, 1843, 1846–47, 1876, 1878, 1881–82, 1887–88. Part of his property was acquired from Col. George Croghan in return for paying the latter's debts. (2) *Ibid.*, vol. 7, ff. 1764–65 (Partnership papers, c. Nov. 1838).

15. *Washington Globe*, 13 Feb. 1839.

16. (1) Carter, *Territorial Papers*, XXV, pp. 563–65 (Jesup to Benton, 19 Jan. 1839). (2) *Washington Globe*, 19 Feb., 4 Mar. 1839). (3) 5 *Stat.* 502 (4 Aug. 1842).

17. Jesup Papers, vol. 7, f. 1795 (Gordon to Jesup, 3 Jan. 1839).

18. *Ibid.*, vol. 7, ff. 1815–16 (7 Feb. 1839).

19. (1) Carter, *Territorial Papers*, XXV, pp. 597–99 (Poinsett to Macomb, 18 Mar. 1839). (2) Sprague, pp. 229–32.

20. (1) Carter, *Territorial Papers*, XXV, pp. 612–13 (Poinsett to Macomb, 25 May 1839). (2) *Washington Globe*, 30 May 1839.

21. (1) Sprague, pp. 232–33. (2) Senate *Doc.* 507, vol. 1, 26th Cong., 1st Sess., s.n. 354, p. 44.

22. (1) Jesup Papers, vol. 7, ff. 1846–47 (Ann to Jesup, 2 Apr. 1839); f. 1861 (Jesup to Dr. Croghan, 10 Apr. 1839); *ibid.*, Box 14 (Account Book, 20 Apr. 1838–19 June 1841). (2) The house was razed about 1914 to make way for the construction of store buildings in the heart of the city's business section. *Washington Post*, 8 June 1914.

23. Jesup Papers, Boxes 10 and 14.

24. Sprague, p. 227.

25. RG 92, OQMG Letter Book, vol. 30, pp. 105–07 (Jesup to Col. S. W. Kearny, 4 June 1840).

26. *Washington Globe*, 10 and 20 Jan. 1840 (Senate proceedings, 7 and 12 Jan. 1840).

27. *Ibid.*, 27 and 30 Mar. 1840 (House proceedings, 26 Mar. 1840).

28. *Ibid.*, 20 Feb. 1840 (House proceedings, 12 Feb. 1840).

29. Butler had been brevetted a major for distinguished service in the Bat-

tle of New Orleans and had later served briefly as Jackson's aide.

30. *Washington Globe,* 19 Aug. 1840 (House proceedings, 11 June 1840).
31. (1) LC, Blair Family Papers, Box 1 (Jackson–Blair Correspondence, 1840–44). (2) Jesup Papers, vol. 7, ff. 1929–32 (Jackson to Blair, 28 July 1840); f. 1936 (Donelson to Blair, 29 July 1840).
32. *Washington Globe,* 4 Nov. 1840 (House proceedings, 13 July 1840).
33. *Ibid.,* 23 Oct. 1840.
34. Jesup Papers, vol. 7, ff. 1943–45 (Jesup to Dr. Croghan, 17 Sept. 1840).
35. Senate *Doc.* 1, vol. 1, s.n. 375, 26th Cong., 2d Sess., p. 22 (SW to President, 5 Dec. 1840).
36. Jesup Papers, vol. 7, f. 1915 (AG to Gen. Macomb, 12 Feb. 1840).
37. *Ibid.,* vol. 7, ff. 1938–39 (To SW, 14 Aug. 1840).
38. RG 92, OQMG Consolidated Corr. File, 1794–1915, Box 477.
39. (1) *Washington Globe,* 6 Mar. 1841. (2) WCL, Jesup Papers (4 Mar. 1841). (3) RG 92, OQMG, Jesup Letters, 1839–46, Unnumbered Box.
40. Jesup Papers, vol. 8, ff. 2043–44 (29 June 1841).
41. *Washington Globe,* 24 Sept. 1841.
42. RG 75, OIA, Seminole–Emigration, 1827–46, M 234, Roll 806 (Ross to Bell, 12 Apr. 1841).
43. *Ibid.,* M 234, Roll 800, Seminole Agency, 1824–45 (Jesup to Bell, 3 May 1841).
44. McReynolds, pp. 206, 229–30.
45. *Ibid.,* p. 230.
46. RG 75, OIA, M 234, Roll 800, Seminole Agency, 1824–45 (Jesup to SW Wilkins, 22 May 1844).
47. Charles J. Kappler, ed., *Indian Affairs, Laws and Treaties* (3 vols., Washington, 1903), II, pp. 550–52.
48. Senate *Doc.* 1, vol. 1, s.n. 395, 27th Cong., 2d Sess., p. 69 (Rpt. of SW to President, 1 Dec. 1841). See also QMG Rpt. appended, p. 113.
49. (1) Senate *Doc.* 1, vol. 1, s.n. 413, 27th Cong., 3d Sess., p. 183 (SW Rpt., 26 Nov. 1842). (2) House *Doc.* 80, 27th Cong., 3d Sess., s.n. 420, pp. 1–3 and annexed documents. (3) Jesup Papers, vol. 9, ff. 2443–49 (Jesup to Rep. Howell Cobb, 12 Feb. 1845).
50. Jesup Papers, vol. 9, ff. 2669–70 (Jesup to SW, 30 May 1844).
51. McReynolds, pp. 258–59.
52. Sprague, p. 275 (Order No. 1, 8 June 1841).
53. *Ibid.,* pp. 441–45 (Worth to Scott, 14 Feb. 1841).
54. House *Doc.* 82, 28th Cong., 1st Sess., s.n. 442, pp. 3–4 (SW to Worth, 10 May 1842).
55. *Ibid.,* pp. 6–7 (Scott to Worth, 11 May 1842); p. 10 (Worth's Order No. 28, 14 Aug. 1842).
56. Sprague, pp. 514–16.
57. *Ibid.*
58. 5 *Stat.,* 512.

59. Jesup Papers, vol. 9, ff. 2342–45 (To SW, 4 Apr. 1844).

60. (1) *Washington Globe*, 3 Sept., 7 June, 23 June 1842. (2) 5 *Stat.*, 512 (23 Aug. 1842). (3) Heitman, *Historical Register*, II, p. 626.

61. Jesup Papers, vol. 8, f. 2176 (Sherburne to Jesup, 16 Aug. 1842).

62. *Ibid.*, vol. 8, ff. 2189–90 (To Sherburne, 24 Sept. 1842).

63. *Ibid.*, vol. 8, f. 2191 (Sherburne to Jesup, 27 Sept. 1842).

64. *Ibid.*, vol. 8, f. 2215 (Cantis to Jesup, 20 Jan. 1843); f. 2227 (Jesup to Cantis, 22 Mar. 1843).

65. Senate *Doc.* 1, vol. 1, 28th Cong., 2d Sess., s.n. 449, p. 126 (SW Rpt. to President, 30 Nov. 1844).

66. Jesup Papers, vol. 9, f. 2461 (To SW, 5 Apr. 1845).

67. Margaret M. Bridwell, *The Story of Mammoth Cave National Park* (3d ed., 1963), p. 25.

68. Jesup Papers, vol. 9, f. 2484 (To Jackson, 30 May 1845).

69. *Ibid.*, vol. 10, f. 2527 (Jackson to Jesup, 3 June 1845).

70. RG 92, OQMG Letter Book, vol. 35, pp. 441–42 (Jesup to Col. William Davenport, Fort Crawford, 21 Mar. 1844).

71. Jesup Papers, vol. 10, ff. 2537–38 (6 Apr. 1846).

72. RG 94, AGO, Letters Received, 120–J (1845).

73. LC, Blair Family Papers, Box 43 (F. P. Blair, Sr. to Mrs. Ann Croghan Jesup, 2 Oct. 1845).

Chapter 10
Support of Taylor in the Mexican War

1. House *Doc.* 60, 30th Cong., 1st Sess., pp. 79–82 (SW to Taylor, 28 May, 15 June 1845).

2. Jesup Papers, vol. 9, ff. 2497–98.

3. House *Doc.* 60, p. 643. See also *ibid.*, pp. 576–77, 578.

4. *Ibid.*, p. 581 (To Cross, 18 Dec. 1845).

5. Jesup Papers, vol. 9, f. 2519 (To Cross, 13 Jan. 1846).

6. House *Doc.* 60, 30th Cong., 1st Sess., pp. 649–50 (Cross to Jesup, 16 Feb. 1846).

7. *Ibid.*, pp. 97–98, 99–100 (Taylor to AG, 28 July, 15 Aug. 1845).

8. (1) *Ibid.*, p. 347 (Cross to Hunt, 6 Mar. 1846). (2) RG 92, OQMG Consolidated Corr. File, Box 660 (Cross to Jesup, 10 and 16 Mar., 4 Apr. 1846).

9. (1) House *Doc.* 60, pp. 138–39, 143 (Taylor to AG, 15 and 23 Apr. 1846). (2) Milo M. Quaife (ed.), *The Diary of James K. Polk During His Presidency, 1845–1849* (4 vols., Chicago, 1910), II, pp. 223–24. [Hereafter cited briefly as Polk, *Diary.*]

10. House *Doc.* 119, 29th Cong., 2d Sess., p. 197 (GO 58, 7 May 1846). [Hereafter cited as House *Doc.* 119.]

11. House *Doc.* 60, p. 288 (Taylor to AG, 26 Apr. 1846).

12. (1) Jesup Papers, vol. 10, f. 2524; ff. 2661–62 (To Jane, 5 Oct. 1846). (2) *Washington Daily Union*, 24 Apr. 1846. (3) *Georgetown Advocate*, 28 Apr. 1846).

13. (1) 9 *Stat.*, 9, 11 (13 May 1846). (2) House *Doc.* 4, 29th Cong., 2d Sess., pp. 47, 54 (SW Rpt., 5 Dec. 1846).

14. (1) 9 *Stat.*, 17, 123 (18 June 1846, 11 Feb. 1847). (2) RG 92, OQMG Consolidated Corr. File, Box 477 (Jesup to SW, 14 Apr. 1846).

15. RG 92, OQMG Letter Book, vol. 37, pp. 160–61 (Stanton to Cross, 17 Oct. 1846).

16. House *Doc.* 60, pp. 153–55 (SW to Kearny, 3 June 1846).

17. (1) *Ibid.*, pp. 299, 306 (Taylor to AG, 20 May and 3 June 1846). (2) *Washington Daily Union*, 10 June 1846 (SW to Gaines, 2 June 1846). (3) House *Doc.* 60, p. 495.

18. House *Doc.* 119, p. 210 (Taylor's Order 108, 28 Aug. 1846); see also, p. 61 (Taylor to Polk, 1 Aug. 1846).

19. Polk, *Diary*, I, p. 485.

20. RG 92, OQMG Letter Book, Clothing, vol. 9, pp. 113, 137 (Jesup to Stanton, 10 and 17 May 1846). Specifically, the orders included the following: 650 wall tents, 3,523 common tents, 800 spades, 1,760 axes, 4,082 hatchets, 3,523 camp kettles, 7,045 mess pans, and 20,000 each of tin canteens, haversacks, and knapsacks.

21. *Washington Daily Union*, 30 Jan. 1846 (Kendall to Thomas Ritchie, 26 Jan. 1846).

22. (1) RG 92, CGP, Letters Sent, No. 402, p. 526 (Stanton to Jesup, 22 Nov. 1848). (2) RG 92, OQMG Letter Book, Clothing, vol. 9, pp. 261–62 (Stanton to Jesup, 15 Jan. 1847).

23. (1) RG 92, OQMG Letter Book, vol. 40, p. 526 (Jesup to Capt. A. C. Myers, 22 Feb. 1848). (2) 9 *Stat.*, 210.

24. (1) RG 92, CGP, Letters Sent, No. 402, p. 522 (Stanton to Jesup, 22 Nov. 1848). (2) RG 92, Rpts. of QMG to SW, I, pp. 468–69 (28 Aug. 1851).

25. (1) House *Doc.* 60, p. 558 (Taylor to SW, 1 Sept. 1846). (2) RG 92, OQMG Letter Book, vol. 38, p. 253 (Jesup to Stanton, 6 Nov. 1846). (3) RG 92, CGP, Letters Sent, No. 402, p. 552 (Stanton to Jesup, 22 Nov. 1848).

26. (1) RG 92, OQMG Letter Book, vol. 37, pp. 428–29 (Jesup to Capt. Edward Harding, 27 May 1846). (2) RG 92, OQMG Letter Book, Clothing, vol. 9, p. 157 (Jesup to Maj. D. D. Tompkins, 9 June 1846).

27. (1) Jesup Papers, vol. 10, f. 2723 (To Stanton, 30 Oct. 1846). (2) RG 92, OQMG Letter Book, vol. 9, p. 158 (Jesup to Stanton, 1 June 1846).

28. House *Doc.* 60, pp. 585–86 (Jesup to Whiting, 3 June 1846).

29. (1) RG 92, OQMG Letter Book, vol. 37, p. 425 (Jesup to D. D. Tompkins, 26 May 1846). (2) House *Doc.* 119, p. 285 (Stanton to Tompkins, 15 May 1846), p. 286 (Jesup to Edward Harding, 2 June 1846).

30. *Ibid.*, pp. 409–10 (Dusenberry to Jesup, 24 July 1846), p. 397 (Hetzel to Jesup, 28 July 1846).
31. House *Doc.* 119, p. 321 (Jesup to Capts. Clark and Thistle, 20 Aug. 1846).
32. (1) *Ibid.*, pp. 557–58 (Taylor to AG, 1 Sept. 1846). (2) House *Doc.* 60, p. 590 (Jesup to Whiting, 17 June 1846).
33. Polk, *Diary*, II, pp. 117–19.
34. (1) *Ibid.* (2) Jesup Papers, Box 15 (Croghan to Jesup, 1 July 1846). (3) LC, Zachary Taylor Papers, vol. 2, ff. 252–54 (Taylor to Gen. N. Young, 18 July 1846).
35. (1) House *Doc.* 60, p. 564 (Jesup to SW, 7 Nov. 1847). (2) RG 92, OQMG Letter Book, vol. 38, pp. 450–51 (Stanton to Jesup, 20 Feb. 1847). (3) Risch, *Quartermaster Support of the Army*, pp. 259–62.
36. (1) RG 92, OQMG Letter Book, vol. 37, p. 400 (Jesup to Whiting, 11 May 1846), p. 434 (Jesup to Stanton, 30 May 1846), p. 454 (Same to D. H. Vinton, 6 June 1846), p. 477 (Same to Hunt, 17 June 1846). (2) House *Doc.* 119, pp. 287–88 (Same to same, 9 June 1846).
37. (1) *Ibid.*, pp. 28, 381 (Taylor to AG, 21 May and 17 June 1846). (2) House *Doc.* 60, p. 547 (Taylor to AG, 10 June 1846).
38. Justin Smith, *The War with Mexico* (2 vols., New York, 1919), I, p. 491, n. 5.
39. (1) House *Doc.* 119, p. 388 (Thomas to Jesup, 15 May 1846), p. 348 (Thomas to Hunt, 18 May 1846), pp. 349–50 (W. W. S. Bliss to Thomas, 24 May 1846), p. 350 (Thomas to Hunt, 31 May 1846), p. 351 (Bliss to Sanders, 28 May 1846), p. 352 (Hunt to Sanders, 5 June 1846). (2) House *Doc.* 60, pp. 559–61 (Jesup to SW, 5 Dec. 1846).
40. House *Doc.* 60, pp. 590–91 (Jesup to Col. Taylor, 17 June 1846).
41. *Ibid.*, p. 553 (Jesup to Sanders, 24 June 1846).
42. *Ibid.*, pp. 553–54 (Sanders to Jesup, 2 July 1846).
43. (1) Jesup Papers, Box 15 (Croghan to Jesup, 20 Oct. 1846). (2) House *Doc.* 119, pp. 366–67 (Whiting to Jesup, 23 July 1846).
44. House *Doc.* 60, p. 554 (Jesup to Sanders, 5 July 1846).
45. *Ibid.*, pp. 555–56 (SW to Jesup, 10 Feb. 1847, and enclosures).
46. *Ibid.*, pp. 556–57 (Jesup to SW, 18 Feb. 1847).
47. *Ibid.*, p. 676 (Whiting to Jesup, 3 Aug. 1846).
48. *Ibid.*, pp. 557–58 (Taylor to AG, 1 Sept. 1846).
49. *Ibid.*, pp. 679–81 (Whiting to Jesup, 28 Aug. and 3 Sept. 1846).
50. *Ibid.*, p. 559 (Marcy to Jesup, 21 Sept. 1846).
51. *Ibid.*, p. 562 (Jesup to SW, 26 Sept. 1846).

Chapter 11
Quartermaster General at the War Front

1. (1) RG 107, OSW, Military Book, vol. 26, p. 504 (SW to Jesup, 1 Oct.

1846). (2) Jesup Papers, vol. 10, f. 2619 (29 Sept. 1846).

2. *Ibid.*, vol. 13, ff. 3346–47 (Jesup to daughter Jane, 20 Jan. 1847).

3. (1) House *Doc.* 60, p. 746 (Jesup memo, 5 Oct. 1846); pp. 746–47 (Jesup to Long, 12 Oct. 1846). (2) Jesup Papers, vol. 10, f. 2626, 2689–90 (To Stanton, 4 and 20 Oct. 1846).

4. House *Doc.* 8, 30th Cong., 1st Sess., p. 545 (QMG Annual Rpt., 24 Nov. 1847). [Hereafter cited as House *Doc.* 8.]

5. House *Doc.* 119, 29th Cong., 2d Sess., s.n. 499, pp. 19–20 (Kearny to AG, 24 Aug. 1846).

6. House *Doc.* 8, p. 545 (QMG Annual Rpt., 24 Nov. 1847).

7. House *Doc.* 60, pp. 752–53 (Jesup to Whiting, 4 Nov. 1846); p. 751 (Jesup to Stanton, 2 Nov. 1846).

8. *Ibid.*, pp. 685–87 (Whiting to Jesup, 30 Nov. 1846).

9. (1) House *Doc.* 60, p. 566 (Jesup to SW, 28 Nov. 1846). (2) House *Doc.* 119, pp. 273–74 (Jesup to SW, 2 Jan. 1847).

10. Jesup Papers, vol. 13, f. 3307 (Abert to Jesup, 15 Jan. 1847); ff. 3422–23 (Jesup to Abert, 25 Jan. 1847).

11. *Ibid.*, vol. 13, f. 3500 (Abert to Jesup, 4 Feb. 1847).

12. (1) House *Doc.* 60, p. 564 (Jesup to SW, 6 Nov. 1846). (2) House *Doc.* 8, p. 546 (QMG Annual Rpt., 24 Nov. 1847). (3) Jesup Papers, vol. 11, f. 2812 (To Stanton, 16 Nov. 1846); vol. 14, ff. 3637–38 (To Stanton, 20 Feb. 1847).

13. House *Doc.* 60, pp. 569–70 (Jesup to SW, 1 Jan. 1847).

14. (1) RG 107, OSW, Military Book, vol. 27, pp. 195–96 (SW to Jesup, 8 Feb. 1847). (2) Jesup Papers, vol. 11, f. 2903 (To Stanton, 27 Nov. 1846); vol. 13, ff. 3599–3600 (To SW, 16 Feb. 1847).

15. (1) 9 *Stat.*, 123. (2) RG 107, OSW, Rpts. to Congress, vol. 6, p. 26 (SW to Benton, 29 Jan. 1847).

16. (1) House *Doc.* 8, p. 548 (QMG Annual Rpt., 24 Nov. 1847). (2) 37 *Stat.*, 591.

17. (1) House *Doc.* 60, p. 567 (Jesup to SW, 3 Dec. 1846). (2) House *Doc.* 119, p. 441 (Jesup to Capt. J. R. Irwin, 16 Nov. 1846).

18. House *Doc.* 1, 30th Cong., 2d Sess., s.n. 537 (QMG Rpt., 18 Nov. 1848, and appended Babbitt Rpt.).

19. (1) Polk, *Diary*, II, pp. 198–99 (22 Oct. 1846); pp. 242–43 (18 Nov. 1846). (2) LC, Zachary Taylor Papers, vol. 2, ff. 271–73 (Taylor to brother Joseph, 14 Jan. 1847).

20. House *Doc.* 60, pp. 559–61 (Jesup to SW, 5 Dec. 1846).

21. (1) LC, Zachary Taylor Papers, vol. 2, ff. 280–82 (Taylor to brother, 27 Mar. 1847). (2) For example, see Jesup Papers, Box of photostats of Taylor's letters (Taylor to Jesup, Oct. 1839).

22. LC, Zachary Taylor Papers, vol. 2, ff. 298–300 (Taylor to brother, 9 May 1847).

23. *Ibid.*, vol. 2, ff. 290–91 (25 April 1847), ff. 298–300 (2 May 1847), ff. 304–06 (29 May 1847).

24. (1) *Washington Daily Union,* 1 Feb. 1847. (2) Polk, *Diary,* II, pp. 354–56.

25. (1) RG 92, OQMG Letter Book, vol. 38, p. 284 (Stanton to Jesup, 20 Nov. 1846). (2) House *Doc.* 8, pp. 546–47 (QMG Annual Rpt., 24 Nov. 1847).

26. House *Doc.* 60, pp. 566–67 (Jesup to SW, 3 Dec. 1846).

27. Jesup Papers, vol. 12, f. 3003 (Jesup to Irwin, 10 Dec. 1846).

28. *Ibid.*, vol. 12, f. 3156 (Jesup to Hunt, 17 Dec. 1846).

29. *Ibid.*, vol. 12, f. 3124 (Jesup to James Blair, 29 Dec. 1846), ff. 3168–69 (Jesup to Hunt, 23 Dec. 1846).

30. (1) *Ibid.*, vol. 12, f. 3218 (Jesup to Capt. E. A. Ogden, 31 Dec. 1846). (2) House *Doc.* 60, p. 760 (Jesup to Stanton, 26 Dec. 1846).

31. *Ibid.*, pp. 568–69 (Scott endorsement on Jesup letter to SW, 27–28 Dec. 1847).

32. (1) RG 107, OSW, Military Book, vol. 27, pp. 95–96 (SW to Jesup, 11 Dec. 1846). (2) House *Doc.* 60, pp. 568–69 (Jesup to SW, 27 Dec. 1846).

33. RG 107, OSW, Military Book, vol. 27, pp. 117–18 (SW to Jesup, 15 Dec. 1846).

34. House *Doc.* 60, pp. 1218–27 (Scott to Marcy, 24 Feb. 1848), pp. 1253–55 (Jesup to SW, 17 Apr. 1848).

35. *Ibid.*, pp. 844–46, 865–66 (Scott to SW, 12 and 26 Jan. 1847).

36. Jesup Papers, vol. 13, ff. 3515–16, 3573 (To Hunt, 31 Jan. and 3 Feb. 1847), ff. 3599–3600 (To SW, 16 Feb. 1847).

37. *Ibid.*, vol. 13, ff. 3527–29 (Jesup to Stanton, 6 Feb. 1847).

38. *Ibid.*, vol. 13, f. 3480 (Hunt to Jesup, 31 Jan. 1847).

39. *Ibid.*, vol. 13, ff. 3516–17 (31 Jan. 1847).

40. *Ibid.*, vol. 14, ff. 3645–46 (Jesup to Mary, 21 Feb. 1847).

41. House *Doc.* 60, pp. 891–92, 897–98 (Scott to SW, 12 and 28 Feb. 1847).

42. House *Doc.* 8, p. 547 (QMG Annual Rpt., 24 Nov. 1847).

43. (1) Jesup Papers, vol. 14, ff. 3747–48 (To Scott, 25 Feb. 1847), ff. 3752–53 (To Hunt, 28 Feb. 1847). (2) RG 92, OQMG Letter Book, vol. 38, pp. 384–85, 450–51 (Stanton to Jesup, 14 Jan. and 20 Feb. 1847).

44. *Ibid.*, vol. 41, p. 256 (Jesup to C. M. Bagbee, 20 Oct. 1848).

45. (1) House *Doc.* 8, pp. 216–17 (Scott to SW, 12 Mar. 1847). (2) William G. Temple, *Memoir of the Landing of the United States Troops at Vera Cruz in 1847* (Philadelphia, 1896), pp. 63–66. (3) George C. Furber, *The Twelve Months Volunteer* (Cincinnati, 1850), pp. 510–13.

46. (1) *Ibid.* (2) House *Doc.* 8, pp. 220–21 (Scott to SW, 17 Mar. 1847).

47. (1) Jesup Papers, vol. 14, f. 3821 (To Stanton, 28 Mar. 1847); vol. 15,

ff. 4052–53 (To SW, 22 Apr. 1848). (2) House *Doc.* 8, p. 547 (QMG Annual Rpt., 24 Nov. 1847).

48. RG 92, OQMG Letter Book, vol. 41, p. 256 (Jesup to C. M. Bagbee, 20 Oct. 1848).

49. (1) House *Doc.* 60, pp. 908–12 (Scott to SW, 5 Apr. 1847), p. 913 (Scott to Jesup, 19 Mar. 1847). (2) Jesup Papers, vol. 14, ff. 3792–93 (To Stanton, 20 Mar. 1847).

50. (1) House *Doc.* 60, pp. 917–18 (Quitman to H. L. Scott, 7 Apr. 1847). (2) House *Doc.* 8, p. 547 (QMG Annual Rpt., 24 Nov. 1847).

51. (1) Polk, *Diary*, II, pp. 429–31 (20 Mar. 1847). (2) (RG 92, OQMG Letter Book, vol. 38, p. 518 (Stanton to Jesup, 22 Mar. 1847).

52. House *Doc.* 60, p. 915 (GO 91, 3 Apr. 1847), pp. 928–29 (Scott to SW, 11 Apr. 1847).

53. (1) House *Doc.* 1, vol. 1, 30th Cong., 2d Sess., s.n. 537 (Annexed report of Babbitt to QMG Annual Rpt., 18 Nov. 1848). (2) RG 92, OQMG Consolidated Corr. File, Box 660 (Hunt Rpt., 2 May 1846–6 July 1847).

54. Jesup Papers, vol. 15, f. 3909 (Jesup to Hunt, 15 Apr. 1847).

55. House *Doc.* 60, pp. 946–47 (Scott to Col. Henry Wilson, 23 Apr.); pp. 963–66 (Scott to SW, 20 May); pp. 993–94 (Scott to SW, 4 June 1847).

56. RG 92, OQMG Letter Book, vol. 39, pp. 158, 165–66 (Jesup to Hunt, 24 and 25 May 1847).

57. Jesup Papers, vol. 15, ff. 3959–61 (Sherburne to Jesup, 18 June 1847), ff. 3962–63 (Jesup to Sherburne, 21 June 1847).

58. Polk, *Diary*, III, pp. 79–82 (10 July 1847).

59. Jesup Papers, vol. 15, ff. 3942–43 (Irwin to Jesup, 30 Apr. 1847).

60. RG 92, OQMG Letter Book, vol. 39, p. 375 (Jesup to Hunt, 4 Aug. 1847).

61. Polk, *Diary*, III, pp. 125–29 (18 Aug. 1847).

62. *Ibid.*, III, pp. 131–34 (21 Aug. 1847); IV, pp. 130–31 (23 Sept. 1848).

63. *Ibid.*, III, pp. 136–39 (24 Aug. 1847).

64. *Ibid.*, III, pp. 140–46, 150–51.

65. House *Doc.* 60, p. 1210 (6 Nov. 1847).

66. *Washington Daily Union*, 3 Jan. 1848.

67. House *Doc.* 60, pp. 1218–27 (Scott to SW, 24 Feb. 1848), pp. 1240–41 (SW to Scott, 21 Apr. 1848).

68. *Ibid.*, p. 1255 (Jesup to SW, 17 Apr. 1848).

69. Jesup Papers, vol. 15, ff. 4041–42 (Office Order, 10 Apr. 1848), f. 4043 (Jesup to SW, 14 Apr. 1848).

70. *Ibid.*, vol. 15, f. 4043 (Jesup to SW, 14 Apr. 1848).

71. (1) RG 92, OQMG Letter Book, vol. 40, p. 470 (Jesup to Osborn Cross, 30 May 1848), p. 497 (Jesup to D. H. Vinton, 9 June 1848). (2) House *Doc.* 1, s.n. 537 (Cross Rpt., 7 Sept. 1848 appended to QMG Annual Rpt., 18 Nov. 1848).

72. *Ibid.*, pp. 189, 194 (QMG Annual Rpt., 18 Nov. 1848).
73. House *Doc.* 8, p. 549 (QMG Annual Rpt., 24 Nov. 1847).

Chapter 12
Last Years of a Long Career

1. House *Doc.* 1, 31st Cong., 2d Sess., Pt. 2, s.n. 587, pp. 121–22 (QMG Annual Rpt., 20 Nov. 1850).
2. (1) *Ibid.*, pp. 245–46. (2) House *Doc.* 2, 35th Cong., 2d Sess., s.n. 999, pp. 795–96 (QMG Annual Rpt., 13 Nov. 1858). (3) Senate *Doc.* 1, 36th Cong., 2d Sess., p. 189 ff., s.n. 1079 (AG Rpt., 20 Nov. 1860).
3. House *Doc.* 1, 31st Cong., 2d Sess., Pt. 2, s.n. 587, pp. 120–26 (QMG Annual Rpt., 20 Nov. 1850).
4. (1) RG 92, OQMG Letter Book, vol. 42, p. 578 (Jesup to Lt. Col. Braxton Bragg, 3 Apr. 1850). (2) RG 92, Rpts. of QMG to SW and Dept. Heads, vol. 1, pp. 237–39 (3 May 1850).
5. Senate *Doc.* 1, 32d Cong., 1st Sess., s.n. 611, p. 218 (QMG Annual Rpt., 6 Nov. 1851).
6. RG 107, OSW, Letters Sent, M 6, Roll 31 (Conrad to QMG, CG of Subsistence, and Chief of Ord., 29 Jan. 1851), (Conrad to Maj. Gen. P. F. Smith, Pacific Div., 24 Feb. 1851), (Conrad to AG, 25 Feb. 1851).
7. (1) RG 107, Letters Received, SW, Q–90 (73) (DQMG Thomas to SW, 25 July 1851). (2) RG 92, OQMG, Clothing Letter Book 12, p. 268 (Jesup to Maj. George H. Crosman). (3) *Washington Daily Union*, 3 Dec. 1850.
8. Risch, *Quartermaster Support of the Army*, pp. 308–17.
9. RG 107, SW, Letters Received, Q–90 (73) (DQMG Thomas to SW, 25 July 1851).
10. (1) Senate *Doc.* 1, 32d Cong., 1st Sess., s.n. 611, p. 218 (QMG Annual Rpt., 6 Nov. 1851). (2) RG 92, QMG Rpts. to SW and Heads of Depts., vol. 1, p. 298 (4 Nov. 1850).
11. (1) House *Doc.* 1, 33d Cong., 1st Sess., s.n. 711, pp. 134–35 (QMG Annual Rpt., 22 Nov. 1853). (2) House *Doc.* 1, 34th Cong., 3d Sess., s.n. 894, p. 257 (QMG Annual Rpt., 26 Nov. 1856).
12. Senate *Doc.* 1, 32d Cong., 2d Sess., Pt. 2, s.n. 612, p. 74 (QMG Annual Rpt., 20 Nov. 1852).
13. (1) 10 *Stat.*, 214. (2) RG 92, OQMG Letter Book, vol. 45, pp. 508, 510, 577–78 (Jesup to D. H. Vinton, 21 Apr.; to Osborn Cross, 13 Apr.; to G. H. Crosman, 24 May 1853).
14. House *Doc.* 1, vol. 1, 30th Cong., 2d Sess. (Swords Rpt., 8 Oct. 1847, appended to QMG Annual Rpt., 18 Nov. 1848).
15. (1) House *Doc.* 1, 31st Cong., 2d Sess., Pt. 2, pp. 121–22, s.n. 587

(QMG Annual Rpt., 20 Nov. 1850). (2) Jesup Papers, vol. 16, f. 4201 (To Gen. Mathew Arbuckle, 27 June 1849).

16. (1) RG 92, OQMG Letters Sent, M 745, Roll 26 (13 Sept. 1830). (2) RG 107, SW Letters Sent, M 745, Roll 30 (8 Nov. 1850).

17. (1) Jesup Papers, vol. 16, ff. 4331–32, 4353 (Stanton to Jesup, 27 Sept. 1850 and 26 Feb. 1851). (2) RG 92, OQMG Letters Sent, M 745, Roll 26 (Jesup to Stanton, 6 Oct. 1850); (Jesup to Whiting, 8 Oct. 1850).

18. (1) RG 92, OQMG Letter Book, vol. 50, p. 591 (Jesup to Thomas, 5 June 1857). (2) House *Doc.* 71, 35th Cong., 1st Sess., pp. 30–32, s.n. 956 (Col. E. B. Alexander to AG, 9 Oct. 1858), p. 63 (List of stores burned).

19. (1) *Ibid.*, p. 99 (Lt. Col. Philip Cooke to AAG, 21 Nov. 1857). (2) House *Doc.* 2, 35th Cong., 2d Sess., s.n. 998, pp. 7–8 (SW Annual Rpt., 6 Dec. 1858); s.n. 999, p. 979 (QMG Annual Rpt., 13 Nov. 1858). (3) RG 92, OQMG Letter Book, vol. 52, p. 77 (Jesup to Gen. P. F. Smith, 17 Apr. 1858).

20. Jesup Papers, vol. 16, ff. 4341–42 (To Mary Blair, 10 Nov. 1850).

21. *Ibid.*, vol. 16, ff. 4414–15 (To daughter Jane, 9 June 1851).

22. Unaware that his brother was already dead, Dr. John Croghan had left Locust Grove to Colonel Croghan, but under a provision of the will the property descended to the colonel's son.

23. (1) Will Book 4, p. 121, Jefferson County, Ky., Court Records. (2) Two of Jesup's grandchildren—Mrs. Violet Blair Janin and Miss Mary J. Sitgreaves—sold their two-thirds interest in Mammoth Cave on 1 January 1929 to the Mammoth Cave National Park Association for $446,400. At least three formations in the cave had been named by Dr. Croghan for Jesup's daughters—Julia's Dome, Lucy's Dome, and Mary's Vineyard. Margaret M. Bridwell, *The Story of Mammoth Cave National Park*, p. 49.

24. The Filson Club, Jesup MSS file (Contract between T. S. Jesup and James Jesup, 30 Aug. 1851).

25. Jesup Papers, vol. 16, f. 4370 (Division of land, 27 June 1851); Box 14 (Jesup's Diary, 18 May–15 Sept. 1851).

26. *Ibid.*, Box 14 (Jesup's Diary, 18 May–15 Sept. 1851) (14 Sept. 1851).

27. *Washington Daily Union*, 10 July 1852, from the *New York Evening Post*.

28. Scott, *Memoirs*, II, pp. 594–95.

29. See Senate *Doc.* 62, 34th Cong., 3d Sess., s.n. 881, "Purchase, Importation, and Use of Camels and Dromedaries to be Employed for Military Purposes, 1857."

30. H. G. Jesup, *Edward Jessup and His Descendants* (Cambridge, 1887), pp. 154–55 (Wayne to Sitgreaves, 21 Dec. 1872).

31. Jesup Papers, Box 9 (To daughter Jane Nicholson, 26 July 1857).

32. RG 92, OQMG Letter Book, vol. 54, p. 153 (Jesup to Senator W. K. Sebastian, 13 Mar. 1860).

33. Jesup Papers, vol. 16, ff. 4343–44 (Gilpin to Jesup, 10 Nov. 1850).

34. *Washington Daily Union*, 25 Oct. 1856 (Jesup to Yulee, 15 Aug. 1856).

35. (1) Jesup Papers, Box 9 (To Chase, 18 Dec. 1856). (2) Chase was a graduate of West Point who resigned from the army in October of 1856 in the unfulfilled hope of being elected as a senator from Florida.

36. Jesup Papers, vol. 2, f. 331 (To Jackson, 18 Aug. 1816); *ibid.*, Gen. Corr., 1853 (Patterson to Jesup, 5 Feb. 1853).

37. *Ibid.*, vol. 8, f. 2227 (To James L. Cantis, 22 March 1843).

38. *Ibid.*, Box 9 (To Chase, 18 Dec. 1856); *ibid.*, vol. 16, ff. 4205–06 (To Dr. Adam G. Goodlet, 19 July 1849).

39. *Ibid.* (Chase to Jesup, 5 Feb. 1857).

40. *Ibid.* (To Gilpin, 22 Dec. 1856), (To Jane, 21 June, 1858); *ibid.*, Box 13 (To Henry B. Dawson, 21 May 1860).

41. *Ibid.*, vol. 16, ff. 4123–27 (To William, 16 Aug. 1849).

42. *Ibid.*, Box 9 (Secy. H. G. Jones, Historical Society of Pennsylvania to Jesup, 9 Apr. 1855).

43. *Ibid.*, vol. 16, f. 4312 (To Charles, 28 June 1850).

44. *Ibid.*, Box 9 (To Charles, 25 July 1858).

45. His other son, William, died at the age of twenty-six, five months after the general's death.

46. (1) RG 92, OQMG Letter Book, vol. 54, p. 71 (Jesup to Governor-Elect M. S. Latham of California, 7 Jan. 1860). (2) Jesup Papers, Box 9 (Daniel Stinson to Jesup, 17 Feb. 1860); Box 13 (Jesup's Account Book, 1857–60).

47. *Ibid.*, Box 9 (AGO, GO, 11 June 1860).

48. (1) 11 June 1860. (2) Following a military funeral attended by President Buchanan and other dignitaries, Jesup's body was placed in a vault at the Congressional Cemetery. Later, 1 April 1862, it was removed to the Oak Hill Cemetery in Georgetown where it is today with the remains of his wife and children.

Bibliography

National Archives

In recent years, much of the archival material pertinent to this biography has been microfilmed. Since most of the research at the archives was completed before microfilming was accomplished, the reader will find citations made to documents in the various record groups used, with no effort made to convert to microfilmed record and roll numbers. Where microfilmed material has been used, it has been so identified. The most valuable archival records for this biography are the following:

Record Group No. 75. Records of the Office of Indian Affairs (OIA).
> Pertinent to this biography are the letters received by this office, which have been microfilmed under M 234, the series being arranged alphabetically by name of the superintendency or agency. Of particular interest are Rolls 290 and 291, "Florida Superintendency Emigration, 1828–38 and 1839–53"; Roll 800, "Seminole Agency"; and Roll 806, "Seminole Agency Emigration."

Record Group No. 92. Records of the Office of the Quartermaster General (OQMG).
> This record group number is given to all quartermaster documents. It includes hundreds of bound volumes and boxes of documents, many of which are pertinent to quartermaster supply operations under the direction of Maj. Gen. Thomas S. Jesup. Of particular importance are the following collections:

> Letter Books. During Jesup's administration, all outgoing correspondence was copied in letter books.
> Letters Received. Incoming correspondence was filed in boxes and indexed in registers.
> Clothing Book, Letters Sent. The outgoing correspondence relative to clothing was entered in these books.
> OQMG Consolidated Correspondence File. To be found filed in boxes

are letters received relating to a common subject, which clerks consolidated for convenience in use and filed under subject heads.
Letters from Maj. Gen. Thomas S. Jesup. Covering the period 1828–1846, these are letters filed in one box.
OQMG Estimates and Reports.
Reports of QMG to SW and Heads of Departments. 8 vols.
Records of the Office of the Commissary General of Purchases (CGP), Letters Sent. Because the functions of this office were later absorbed by the OQMG, its records are included in Record Group 92.

Record Group No. 94. Records of the Adjutant General's Office (AGO). Letters Received.

Record Group No. 107. Records of the Office of the Secretary of War (OSW).

OSW, Military Book. There are Letters Sent, which in Jesup's time were called Military Books.
OSW, Letters Received.
OSW, Reports to Congress.

Manuscript Collections

Blair, Francis P. Francis P. Blair Family Papers. Manuscript Division, Library of Congress (LC).
Brown, Jacob. Official Letter Books. Manuscript Division, LC.
Clay, Henry. Papers of Henry Clay. 34 vols., Manuscript Division, LC.
Clay, Thomas J. Papers of Thomas J. Clay, 1837–1927. 33 vols., Manuscript Division, LC.
Croghan. Croghan Family Papers. Manuscript Division, LC.
Croghan. Croghan Papers. The Filson Club, Louisville, Ky.
Findlay, James. Gen. James Findlay Papers, Box 13 of the George P. Torrence Papers. Cincinnati Historical Society (CHS).
Harrison, William Henry. 16 vols., 3 boxes. Manuscript Division, LC.
Janin. Janin Collection. Family Papers of the Blairs and Janins. Henry E. Huntington Library. San Marino, Calif.
Jesup, Thomas S. Jesup Papers. Assembled in boxes and volumes. Manuscript Division, LC.
Jesup, Thomas S. Jesup Papers. William L. Clements Library (WLC). Ann Arbor, Mich.
Parker, Daniel. Daniel Parker Papers. The Historical Society of Pennsylvania (PHS). Philadelphia, Pa.
Polk, James K. Polk Papers. Manuscript Division, LC.
Taylor, Zachary. Zachary Taylor Papers. Manuscript Division, LC.
Towsend-LeMaistre Collection. The Historical Society of Pennsylvania (PHS).

Printed Primary Sources

American State Papers. 38 vols. Washington, 1832–61. Class V, *Military Affairs*. 7 vols.

Benton, Thomas Hart. *Thirty Years' View*. 2 vols., New York, 1854–56.

Carter, Clarence E. (ed.). *The Territorial Papers of the United States*, XXV, *The Territory of Florida, 1834–39*. Washington, 1960.

Casselman, Alexander C. (ed.). *Richardson's War of 1812*. Toronto, 1902.

Cohen, Myer M. *Notices of Florida – The Campaigns*. New York, 1836.

Forbes, Lt. Col. James G. *Report of the Trial of Brig. Gen. William Hull*. New York, 1814.

Forry, Samuel. "Letters of Samuel Forry, Surgeon in the U.S. Army," *The Florida Historical Quarterly*, vols. VI (Jan.-Apr. 1928), and VII (July 1928).

French, Samuel G. *Two Wars: An Autobiography*. Nashville, 1901.

Furber, George C. *The Twelve Months Volunteer*. Cincinnati, 1850.

Kappler, Charles J. (ed.). *Indian Affairs, Laws, and Treaties*. 3 vols., Washington, 1903.

Keyes, Bvt. Brig. Gen. E. D. *Fifty Years' Observation of Men and Events, Civil and Military*. New York, 1884.

Mahon, John K. (ed.). *Reminiscences of the Second Seminole War* by John Bemrose. University of Florida Press, 1966.

Phelps, John. "Letters of Lieutenant John Phelps, U.S.A., 1836, 1837," *The Florida Historical Quarterly*, VI.

Prucha, Francis Paul (ed.). *Army Life on the Western Frontier, Selections from the Official Reports Made between 1826 and 1845 by Colonel George Croghan*. University of Oklahoma Press, 1958.

Quaife, Milo M. (ed.). *The Diary of James K. Polk During his Presidency, 1845 to 1849*. 4 vols., Chicago, 1910.

Scott, Winfield. *Memoirs of Lieut.-General Scott*. 2 vols., New York, 1864.

Smith, Margaret Bayard. *The First Forty Years of Washington Society*. New York, 1906.

Sunderman, James F. (ed.). *Journey into Wilderness: An Army Surgeon's Account of Life in Camp and Field During the Creek and Seminole Wars, 1836–1838* by Jacob Rhett Motte. University of Florida Press, 1963.

Temple, William G. *Memoir of the Landing of the United States Troops at Vera Cruz in 1847*. Philadelphia, 1896.

Thian, Ralph P. *Legislative History of the General Staff of the Army of the United States*. Washington, 1901.

Printed Military Sources

Annual Reports. The Annual Reports of the Secretary of War and the Quartermaster General are located as follows:

American State Papers, Class V, *Military Affairs.* The annual reports for 1822 to 1838 are printed in these volumes.

Senate and House *Executive Documents,* 25th–36th Congress. The annual reports for the years 1839–1860 are printed either in the Senate or House *Executive Documents* for those years.

Registers. The following provide the military service record of officers:

Hamersly, Thomas H. D. *Complete Regular Army Register of the United States for One Hundred Years, 1779–1879.* Washington, 1880.
Heitman, Francis B. *Historical Register and Dictionary of the United States Army, 1789–1903.* 2 vols., Washington, 1903.

Legislative Sources

Annals of Congress, 1789–1824. 42 vols., Washington, 1825–37.

House *Executive Documents:*

No. 60, 30th Cong., 1st Sess. "Correspondence . . . on the Subject of the Mexican War." Washington, 1848.
No. 78, 25th Cong., 2d Sess., s.n. 323, "Scott Court of Inquiry."
No. 80, 27th Cong., 3d Sess., s.n. 420.
No. 82, 28th Cong., 1st Sess., s.n. 442.
No. 110, 16th Cong., 2d Sess., s.n. 55, "In relation to the claim of James Johnson for transportation on the Missouri and Mississippi Rivers." Washington, 1821.
No. 119, 29th Cong., 2d Sess., s.n. 499, "Correspondence with General Taylor."
No. 219, 25th Cong., 2d Sess., vol. 8, s.n. 323.
No. 225, 25th Cong., 3d Sess.
No. 227, 25th Cong., 2d Sess., s.n. 316.
No. 272, 25th Cong., 2d Sess., s.n. 323.
No. 327, 25th Cong., 2d Sess., vol. 9, s.n. 329.
No. 783, 69th Cong., 2d Sess. "Biographical Directory of the American Congress, 1774–1927." Washington, 1928.

Senate *Executive Documents:*

No. 62, 34th Cong., 3d Sess., s.n. 881. "Purchase, Importation and Use of Camels and Dromedaries to be Employed for Military Purposes, 1857."
No. 224, 24th Cong., 2d Sess. "Proceedings of the Military Court of Inquiry in the Case of Major General Scott and Major General Gaines."
No. 507, 25th Cong., 2d Sess., s.n. 319. "A report from Major General

Jesup of his operations whilst commanding the army in Florida, in compliance with a resolution of the Senate of the 6th instant."

U.S. Statutes at Large

Secondary Works

Banner, James M., Jr. *To the Hartford Convention: The Federalists and the Origins of Party Politics in Massachusetts, 1789–1815.* New York, 1970.

Beers, Henry P. *The Western Military Frontier, 1815–1846.* Philadelphia, 1935.

Beirne, Francis F. *The War of 1812.* New York, 1949.

Brackenridge, H. M. *History of the Late War between the United States and Great Britain.* Philadelphia, 1836.

Bridwell, Margaret M. *The Story of Mammoth Cave National Park.* 3d ed., n.p.

Campbell, Maria. *Revolutionary Services and Civil Life of General William Hull.* New York, 1848.

Collins, Lewis. *History of Kentucky.* Revised ed., 2 vols. in one. Covington, Ky., 1874.

DeWeerd, Maj. H. A. (ed.). *The War of 1812 by Henry Adams.* Washington Infantry Journal, 1944.

Dunbar, Seymour. *A History of Travel in America.* New York, 1937.

Giddings, Joshua R. *The Exiles of Florida.* Columbus, Ohio, 1858.

Hamilton, Homan. *Zachary Taylor — Soldier in the White House.* New York, 1951.

Jacobs, James R. *The Beginning of the U.S. Army, 1783–1812.* Princeton, 1947.

James, Marquis. *The Life of Andrew Jackson.* New York, 1940.

Jesup, H. G. *Edward Jessup and His Descendants.* Cambridge, 1887.

Kreidberg, Marvin A., and Henry, Merton G. *History of Military Mobilization in the U.S. Army, 1775–1945.* (DA Pamphlet No. 20–212). Washington, June 1955.

Lossing, Benson J. *The Pictorial Field-Book of the War of 1812.* New York, 1869.

McAfee, Robert B. *History of the Late War in the Western Country.* Lexington, Ky., 1816.

McReynolds, Edwin C. *The Seminoles.* Norman: University of Oklahoma Press, 1957.

Pratt, Fletcher. *Eleven Generals, Studies in American Command.* New York, 1949.

Risch, Erna. *Quartermaster Support of the Army: A History of the Corps, 1775–1939.* Washington, 1962.

Searight, Thomas B. *The Old Pike, A History of the National Road.* Union-town, Pa., 1894.

Smith, Justin H. *The War with Mexico.* 2 vols., New York, 1919.

Smith, William E. *The Francis Preston Blair Family in Politics.* 2 vols., New York, 1933.

Sprague, John T. *The Origin, Progress, and Conclusion of the Florida War.* Floridiana Facsimile Reprint Series, University of Florida Press, 1964.

Westrate, Edison V. *Those Fatal Generals.* New York, 1936.

Wiltse, Charles M. *John C. Calhoun, Nationalist, 1782–1828.* New York, 1944.

Magazine Articles

Army and Navy Chronicle, VI, new series (Jan.-June, 1838).

Boyd, Mark F. "Asi—Yaholo or Osceola," *The Florida Historical Quarterly,* XXXIII, Nos. 3 and 4 (Jan.-Apr., 1955).

Clark, Allen C. "The Mayors of the Corporation of Washington: Thomas Carbery," *Records* of the Columbia Historical Society, vol. 19.

Conner, Eugene H., and Samuel W. Thomas. "John Croghan (1790–1849): An Enterprising Kentucky Physician," *The Filson Club Historical Quarterly,* vol. 40, No. 3 (1966).

Hagen, Fred E. "Thomas Sidney Jesup," *Quartermaster Review,* XI, No. 1 (Sept.-Oct., 1931).

Thomas, Samuel W. "George Croghan (1791–1849): A Study of the Non-Political Life of the Inspector General of the United States Army," *The Filson Club Historical Quarterly,* vol. 41, No. 4, (1967).

Williams, Samuel. "Two Western Campaigns in the War of 1812," Ohio Valley Historical Series, *Miscellanies,* VII, No. 2 (1871).

"The White Flag," *The Florida Historical Quarterly,* XXXIII, Nos. 3 and 4 (Jan.-Apr., 1955).

Newspapers

Boston Sentinel
Florida Herald
Georgetown Advocate
Louisville Courier-Journal
Louisville Daily Focus
National Intelligencer
New York Evening Post
Washington Daily Union

Washington Globe
Western Spy and Literary Cadet

Unpublished Material

Rogers, Hopewell L. "Hopewell L. Rogers' Index." The Filson Club, Louisville, Ky.
Thomas, Samuel W. "A Guide to the Historic House Museum Locust Grove," Jan. 1963.
———. "The Croghan Papers," Mar. 1967.

Index